Collins

Cambridge IGCSE™

Chemistry

TEACHER'S GUIDE

Chris Sunley, Sam Goodman

William Collins' dream of knowledge for all began with the publication of his first book in 1819. A self-educated mill worker, he not only enriched millions of lives, but also founded a flourishing publishing house. Today, staying true to this spirit, Collins books are packed with inspiration, innovation and practical expertise. They place you at the centre of a world of possibility and give you exactly what you need to explore it.

Collins. Freedom to teach.

Published by Collins
An imprint of HarperCollins*Publishers*
The News Building
1 London Bridge Street
London
SE1 9GF

HarperCollins*Publishers*
1st Floor
Watermarque Building
Ringsend Road
Dublin 4
Ireland

Browse the complete Collins catalogue at
www.collins.co.uk

© HarperCollins*Publishers* Limited 2021

10 9 8 7 6 5 4 3 2

ISBN 978-0-00-843089-4

All rights reserved. No part of this publication may be reproduced, stored in a retrieval system, or transmitted in any form by any means, electronic, mechanical, photocopying, recording or otherwise, without the prior written permission of the Publisher or a licence permitting restricted copying in the United Kingdom issued by the Copyright Licensing Agency Ltd, 5th Floor, Shackleton House, 4 Battle Bridge Lane, London SE1 2HX.

British Library Cataloguing-in-Publication Data. A catalogue record for this publication is available from the British Library.

Updating author: **Chris Sunley**
Authors of previous edition: **Chris Sunley, Sam Goodman**
In-house editor: **Letitia Luff**
Project manager: **Nivedhitha Souriyan**
Copyeditor: **Jessica Ashdale**
Proofreader: **Jan Schubert, Sarah Binns**
Safety checker: **Joe Jefferies**
Internal designer, typesetter and illustrator:
  Jouve India Private Limited
Cover designer: **Gordon MacGilp**
Cover artwork: **Drawlab19/Shutterstock**
Production controller: **Lyndsey Rogers**
Printed and Bound in the UK using 100% Renewable Electricity at **CPI Group (UK) Ltd**

The publishers gratefully acknowledge the permission granted to reproduce the copyright material in this book. Every effort has been made to trace copyright holders and to obtain their permission for the use of copyright material. The publishers will gladly receive any information enabling them to rectify any error or omission at the first opportunity.

Cambridge International copyright material in this publication is reproduced under licence and remains the intellectual property of Cambridge Assessment International Education.

Exam-style questions and sample answers have been written by the authors. In examinations, the way marks are awarded may be different. References to assessment and/or assessment preparation are the publisher's interpretation of the syllabus requirements and may not fully reflect the approach of Cambridge Assessment International Education.

Third-party websites and resources referred to in this publication have not been endorsed by Cambridge Assessment International Education

MIX
Paper from
responsible sources
FSC™ C007454

This book is produced from independently certified FSC paper to ensure responsible forest management.

For more information visit: **www.harpercollins.co.uk/green**

Contents

⑤ indicates activities that cover the extended syllabus only and so may be omitted if students are not studying the extended syllabus. The core syllabus only includes core content. The extended syllabus includes both core and supplement content.

Introduction	**5**
Teaching sequence	**7**
Content overview	**9**
Section 1: States of matter	**37**
C1.1 States of matter	**38**
C1.1a Orientation	39
C1.1b Solids, liquids and gases	40
C1.1c Diffusion	43
C1.1d Consolidation and summary	45
Section 2: Atoms, elements and compounds	**47**
C2.1 Atoms, elements and compounds	**48**
C2.1a Orientation	50
C2.1b Subatomic particles	52
C2.1c The arrangement of electrons in atoms	54
C2.1d Consolidation and summary	58
C2.2 Ions and ionic bonds	**60**
C2.2a Orientation	62
C2.2b The formation of ions	63
C2.2c Properties of ionic compounds	66
C2.2d Consolidation and summary	68
C2.3 Molecules and covalent bonds	**71**
C2.3a Orientation	73
C2.3b The formation of covalent molecules	74
C2.3c Properties of simple covalent compounds	77
C2.3d Giant covalent structures	78
C2.3e Consolidation and summary	80
⑤ **C2.4 Metallic bonding**	**83**
⑤ C2.4a Orientation	84
⑤ C2.4b Metallic bonding	85
⑤ C2.4c Consolidation and summary	86
Section 3: Stoichiometry	**88**
C3.1 Stoichiometry	**89**
C3.1a Orientation	91
C3.1b Writing chemical equations	92
C3.1c Relative masses	95
C3.1d Reacting quantities and the mole concept	96
⑤ C3.1e Percentage yield	112
C3.1f Consolidation and summary	115
Sections 1, 2 and 3: Exam-style questions mark scheme	**118**
Section 4: Electrochemistry	**120**
C4.1 Electrochemistry	**121**
C4.1a Orientation	123
C4.1b Electrolysis of molten electrolytes	125
C4.1c Electrolysis of aqueous electrolytes	127
C4.1d The production of electrical energy from simple cells	133
C4.1e Consolidation and summary	134
Section 5: Chemical energetics	**136**
C5.1 Chemical energetics	**137**
C5.1a Orientation	139
C5.1b Measuring energy transfers (1)	143
C5.1c Measuring energy transfers (2)	146
C5.1d Reaction pathway diagrams, bond breaking and bond forming	151
C5.1e Consolidation and summary	152
Section 6: Chemical reactions	**154**
C6.1 Rate of reaction	**155**
C6.1a Orientation	157
C6.1b Monitoring the rate of reaction	161
C6.1c Concentration of solutions	164
C6.1d Temperature	166
C6.1e Surface area of solids	169
C6.1f Use of a catalyst	172
C6.1g Consolidation and summary	**175**
C6.2 Reversible reactions and equilibrium	**178**
C6.2a Orientation	180
⑤ C6.2b Changing the position of equilibrium	183
⑤ C6.2c The Haber and Contact industrial processes	184
C6.2d Consolidation and summary	186
C6.3 Redox reactions	**188**
C6.3a Orientation	190
⑤ C6.3b Electron transfer	192
C6.3c Consolidation and summary	195
Section 7: Acids, bases and salts	**197**
C7.1 Acids, bases and salts	**198**
C7.1a Orientation	200
C7.1b Acids, bases, alkalis and salts	204
C7.1c Making soluble salts	208
⑤ C7.1d Making insoluble salts	215
C7.1e Consolidation and summary	217
Sections 4, 5, 6 and 7: Exam-style questions mark scheme	**220**

Section 8: The Periodic Table	**222**
C8.1 The Periodic Table	**223**
C8.1a Orientation	224
C8.1b Arrangement of the elements	225
C8.1c Consolidation and summary	226
C8.2 Group I elements	**228**
C8.2a Orientation	229
C8.2b Reactions of the Group I elements	230
C8.2c Consolidation and summary	232
C8.3 Group VII elements	**234**
C8.3a Orientation	235
C8.3b Displacement reactions of the halogens	236
C8.3c Consolidation and summary	241
C8.4 Transition elements and noble gases	**243**
C8.4a Orientation	245
C8.4b The transition elements	246
C8.4c The noble gases	250
C8.4d Consolidation and summary	251
Section 9: Metals	**253**
C9.1 Metals	**254**
C9.1a Orientation	256
C9.1b Properties of metals	258
C9.1c Reactivity series	262
C9.1d Extraction of metals	271
C9.1e Uses of metals	275
C9.1f Consolidation and summary	278
Section 10: Chemistry of the environment	**281**
C10.1 Chemistry of the environment	**282**
C10.1a Orientation	284
C10.1b Water	285
C10.1c The composition of the air	288
C10.1d Air quality and climate	290
C10.1e Consolidation and summary	294
Sections 8, 9 and 10: Exam-style questions mark scheme	**296**
Section 11: Organic chemistry	**299**
C11.1 General introduction to organic chemistry	**300**
C11.1a Orientation	301
C11.2 Fuels	**302**
C11.2a Orientation	303
C11.2b The fractional distillation of petroleum	304
C11.2c Consolidation and summary	308
C11.3 Alkanes	**310**
C11.3a Orientation	312
C11.3b The chemical properties of alkanes	315
S C11.3c The structure of alkanes	316
C11.3d Consolidation and summary	317
C11.4 Alkenes	**319**
C11.4a Orientation	321
C11.4b Cracking crude oil fractions	322
C11.4c The chemical properties of alkenes	326
C11.4d Consolidation and summary	329
C11.5 Alcohols	**331**
C11.5a Orientation	333
C11.5b The manufacture of ethanol	334
C11.5c Reactions of ethanol	336
C11.5d Consolidation and summary	338
C11.6 Carboxylic acids	**340**
C11.6a Orientation	342
S C11.6b The formation of ethanoic acid	343
C11.6c The properties of ethanoic acid	344
C11.6d Consolidation and summary	346
C11.7 Polymers	**348**
C11.7a Orientation	350
C11.7b Synthetic polymers	351
S C11.7c Proteins	356
C11.7d Consolidation and summary	357
Section 11: Exam-style questions mark scheme	**359**
Section 12: Experimental techniques	**361**
C12.1 Experimental techniques	**362**
C12.1a Orientation	363
C12.1b Criteria for purity	364
C12.1c Methods of purification	367
C12.1d Consolidation and summary	370
C12.2 Identification of ions and gases	**372**
C12.2a Orientation	374
C12.2b Identifying cations	375
C12.2c Identifying anions	381
C12.2d Identifying gases	386
C12.2e Consolidation and summary	389
Section 12: Exam-style questions mark scheme	**391**

Introduction

Welcome to the Collins Cambridge IGCSE™ Chemistry Teacher's Guide, which has been written by experienced authors and teachers to help you deliver an effective and successful Cambridge IGCSE Chemistry course.

Overview

This **printed book** follows the Student Book topics and includes:

- **learning episode plans** with resource lists, learning objectives, and detailed guidance
- **practical activities** including teacher demonstrations and student experiments
- **worksheets** for students with instructions to follow and questions to answer
- **technician's notes** so **practicals and demonstrations** can be safely planned and executed
- **answers** to all the questions in the Student Book
- **a content overview** that maps all practical activities and shows at a glance all the topics linked with the syllabus learning objectives.

Downloadable files

Everything in the printed book is available in PDF and in editable format so that you can tailor lessons and activities. It also includes:

- **technician's notes** with lists of equipment, resources and set-up information for each section collated in one document that you can hand to your technician
- printable **end of topic checklists** that students can use to map their own progress
- one document with all the **Student Book answers** to in-text, end of topic and exam-style questions.

Learning episode plans

The Teacher's Guide has been matched topic by topic to the Student Book to allow easy cross-referencing between the books. Each topic is introduced with a brief introduction, links to other topics and an overview of the learning episodes in an easy-to-navigate table. Learning episode plans give guidance on delivering learning episodes that can be combined for longer lessons to give you complete flexibility and control. For further safety information on demonstrations and practical activities, please refer to the CLEAPSS website: www.cleapss.org.uk

Teachers should make sure that they do not contravene any school, education authority or government regulations. Responsibility for safety matters rests with centres. In addition, the following general advice should be given to students:

'Be careful with chemicals. Never ingest them and always wash your hands after handling them.'

Learning episode plans cover the following:

- **learning objectives** from the syllabus linked to the activities and the Student Book
- **learning aims** which reflect the intended outcomes of the consolidation and summary sessions.
- **common misconceptions** held by students, which may need addressing
- **resources** you will need for activities
- a detailed pick-up-and-teach approach for **differentiated**, varied tasks
- **demonstration** and **practical activity** technician's notes so you can easily check that you have everything you need
- **answers** to worksheets and all the questions in the Student Book.
- **career links** are included and can be used to enrich teaching by providing context and links to careers in different fields of chemistry.

Worksheets

Worksheets provide engaging activities for students. Those that deal with practical work give step-by-step guidance for students to ensure that they carry out their investigations safely and successfully.

All worksheets are available in editable format as well as in one printable document containing all the worksheets in each section.

Technician's notes

Detailed **technician's notes** are provided for every learning episode, with lists of resources needed for practical activities and/or demonstrations, set-up instructions and safety notes.

For up-to-date safety information, which you will need to check before you set up any practical activity or demonstration, please refer to your employer's guidelines or visit: www.cleapss.org.uk

Technician's notes appear within the learning episode plans for your reference, and as separate printable files to download.

Answers

Every learning episode plan in this book includes the **answers** to the associated questions in the Student Book and any worksheets. Answers to the **end of topic** and **exam-style questions** are provided. A document with all the answers collated for easy printing is available to download.

Exam-style questions and sample answers have been written by the authors. In examinations, the way marks are awarded may be different. References to assessment and/or assessment preparation are the publisher's interpretation of the syllabus requirements and may not fully reflect the approach of Cambridge Assessment International Education.

Checklists

Editable checklists that students can use to record their progress are provided to download. These have the same content as those at the end of each topic in the Student Book.

Content overview

The detailed **content overview** at the back of this book provides a comprehensive overview of our Cambridge IGCSE course, matching each learning episode to the learning objectives in the syllabus. It also shows at a glance where the practical activities and demonstrations occur so that you can plan ahead. An editable version of the content overview is available to download.

Teachers should always refer back to the current syllabus when devising a scheme of work for students.

Science in context boxes

Please note that the **science in context** boxes in the Student Book put the ideas that students are learning into real-life context. It is not necessary for students to learn the content of these boxes as it is beyond the requirements of the syllabus. However, they do provide interesting examples of scientific applications that are designed to enhance their understanding. Some science in context boxes contain one or more questions which provide the opportunity to explore the content more deeply.

Teaching sequence

The course can be taught in syllabus order and it will work well to do so. If you want to change the teaching sequence for the course, you should keep in mind the considerations below. An example alternative teaching sequence has been provided.

- There should be a logical progression in the development of concepts and knowledge in order to aid students' understanding.
- The course should have a 'storyline' so that wherever possible the sequence can be easily explained to students.
- Consider carefully how to introduce the more difficult concepts. For example, ensure that they are not introduced too early in the course, which may demotivate students, or put in a sequence where they all come one after another.
- Maintain the emphasis on practical and investigative work throughout the course.
- You will need to allocate different amounts of teaching time to different topics, depending on levels of difficulty or extent of the content.
- It is important to retain some flexibility so that you can revisit difficult ideas or apply new ideas in different contexts.
- You will need time for revision at the end of the course. It is also recommended that you encourage students to revisit material for revision throughout the course. This could be done using the flashcards that they create at the end of each topic.

Alternative teaching sequence

This example alternative teaching sequence is based on a two-year course taught in six terms. It is mapped over five terms on the assumption that much of the sixth term is spent on revision. For different numbers of terms or semesters, where the course is started early, or where the time allocated each week is either generous or limited, you will need to adjust this sequence.

First year, 1st term

C1.1 States of matter
C12.1 Experimental techniques
C2.1 Atoms, elements and compounds
C2.2 Ions and ionic bonds
C2.3 Molecules and covalent bonds
C7.1 Acids, bases and salts
C10.1 Chemistry of the environment

First year, 2nd term

C3.1 Stoichiometry
C8.1 The Periodic Table
C8.2 Group I elements
C8.3 Group VII elements
C8.4 Transition elements and noble gases
C6.1 Rate of reaction

First year, 3rd term

C3.1 Stoichiometry
C2.4 Metallic bonding
C9.1 Metals
C4.1 Electrochemistry
C12.2 Identification of ions and gases

Second year, 1st term

C5.1 Chemical energetics
C6.2 Reversible reactions and equilibrium
C11.1 General introduction to organic chemistry
C11.2 Fuels
C11.3 Alkanes
C11.4 Alkenes

Second year, 2nd term

C6.3 Redox reactions
C11.5 Alcohols
C11.6 Carboxylic acids
C11.7 Polymers

Content overview

The information in this section is taken from the Cambridge IGCSE Chemistry syllabus (0620/0971) for examination from 2023. You should always refer to the appropriate syllabus document for the year of your examination to confirm the details and for more information. The syllabus document is available on the Cambridge International website at www.cambridgeinternational.org.

Learning episode	Learning objectives and learning aims	Syllabus reference	Student Book pages	Practical activity
	Learning objectives are given which link to the syllabus. Learning aims reflect the intended outcomes of the consolidation and summary sessions.			
C1.1a Orientation	Learning objective: • 1.1.1 State the distinguishing properties of solids, liquids and gases.	1. States of matter	11	Demonstration: Solids, liquids and gases
C1.1b The kinetic particle theory	Learning objectives: • 1.1.2 Describe the structure of solids, liquids and gases in terms of particle separation, arrangement and motion. • 1.1.3 Describe changes of state in terms of melting, boiling, evaporating, freezing and condensing. • 1.1.4 Describe the effects of temperature and pressure on the volume of a gas. • Supplement 1.1.5 Explain changes of state in terms of kinetic particle theory, including the interpretation of heating and cooling curves. • Supplement 1.1.6 Explain changes of state in terms of kinetic particle theory, the effects of temperature and pressure on the volume of a gas.	1. States of matter	11–15	
C1.1c Diffusion	Learning objectives: • 1.2.1 Describe and explain diffusion in terms of kinetic particle theory. • Supplement 1.2.2 Describe and explain the effect of relative molecular mass on the rate of diffusion of gases.	1. States of matter	16–18	Class practical: Diffusion activities Demonstration: Diffusion of hydrogen chloride and ammonia
C1.1d Consolidation and summary	Learning aims: • Review the learning points of the topic summarised in the end of topic checklist. • Test understanding of the topic content by answering the end of topic questions.	1. States of matter	19–21	
C2.1a Orientation	Learning objective: • To describe the differences between elements, compounds and mixtures.	2. Atoms, elements and compounds	22–24	

Content overview

C2.1b Subatomic particles	Learning objectives: • **2.2.1** Describe the structure of the atom as a central nucleus containing neutrons and protons surrounded by electrons in shells. • **2.2.2** State the relative charges and relative masses of a proton, a neutron and an electron. • **2.2.3** Define proton number / atomic number as the number of protons in the nucleus of an atom. • **2.2.4** Define mass number / nucleon number as the total number of protons and neutrons in the nucleus of an atom. • **2.3.1** Define isotopes as different atoms of the same element that have the same number of protons but different numbers of neutrons. • **2.3.2** Interpret and use symbols for atoms, e.g. $^{12}_{6}C$, and ions, e.g. $^{35}_{17}Cl^{-}$. • Supplement **2.3.3** State that isotopes of the same element have the same chemical properties because they have the same number of electrons and therefore the same electronic configuration. • Supplement **2.3.4** Calculate the relative atomic mass of an element from the relative masses and abundances of its isotopes.	2. Atoms, elements and compounds	25–29
C2.1c The arrangement of electrons in atoms	Learning objectives: • **2.2.5** Determine the electronic configuration of elements and their ions with proton number 1 to 20 e.g. 2,8,3. • **2.2.6** State that: (a) Group VIII noble gases have a full outer shell (b) the number of outer shell electrons is equal to the group number in Groups I to VII (c) the number of occupied electron shells is equal to the period number.	2. Atoms, elements and compounds	30–33
C2.1d Consolidation and summary	Learning aims: • Review the learning points of the topic summarised in the end of topic checklist. • Test understanding of the topic content by answering the end of topic questions.	2. Atoms, elements and compounds	34–37
C2.2a Orientation	Learning aims: • To revise ideas on atomic structure. • To map out the main purposes of the topic. • To know the structure of an atom by interpreting proton and nucleon numbers. • To know the arrangement of electrons in shells for the first 20 elements.	2. Atoms, elements and compounds	26
C2.2b The formation of ions	Learning objectives: • **2.4.1** Describe the formation of positive ions, known as cations, and negative ions, known as anions. • **2.4.2** State that an ionic bond is a strong electrostatic attraction between oppositely charged ions. • **2.4.3** Describe the formation of ionic bonds between elements from Group I and Group VII, including the use of dot-and-cross diagrams. • Supplement **2.4.6** Describe the formation of ionic bonds between ions of metallic and non-metallic elements, including the use of dot-and-cross diagrams.	2. Atoms, elements and compounds	38–40

Content overview

C2.2c Properties of ionic compounds	Learning objectives:
	• **2.4.4** Describe the properties of ionic compounds:
	  (a) high melting points and boiling points
	  (b) good electrical conductivity when aqueous or molten and poor when solid
	• Supplement **2.4.5** Describe the giant lattice structure of ionic compounds as a regular arrangement of alternating positive and negative ions.
	• Supplement **2.4.7** Explain in terms of structure and bonding the properties of ionic compounds:
	  (a) high melting points and boiling points
	  (b) good electrical conductivity when aqueous or molten and poor when solid
		2. Atoms, elements and compounds	41–44

C2.2d Consolidation and summary	Learning aims: • Review the learning points of the topic summarised in the end of topic checklist. • Test understanding of the topic content by answering the end of topic questions.	2. Atoms, elements and compounds	45–46
C2.3a Orientation	Learning aims: • To revise ideas on atomic structure and ionic bonding. • To map out the main purposes of the topic. • To know the structure of an atom by interpreting proton and nucleon numbers. • To know the arrangement of electrons in shells for the first 20 elements.	2. Atoms, elements and compounds	
C2.3b The formation of covalent molecules	Learning objectives: • **2.5.1** State that a covalent bond is formed when a pair of electrons is shared between two atoms leading to noble gas electronic configurations. • **2.5.2** Describe the formation of covalent bonds in simple molecules, including H_2, Cl_2, H_2O, CH_4, NH_3 and HCl. Use dot-and-cross diagrams to show the electronic configurations in these and similar molecules. • Supplement **2.5.4** Describe the formation of covalent bonds in simple molecules, including CH_3OH, C_2H_4, O_2, CO_2 and N_2. Use dot-and-cross diagrams to show the electronic configurations in these and similar molecules.	2. Atoms, elements and compounds	47–51

C2.3c Properties of simple molecular covalent compounds	Learning objectives:
	• **2.5.3** Describe in terms of structure and bonding the properties of simple molecular compounds:
	  (a) low melting points and boiling points
	  (b) poor electrical conductivity
	• Supplement **2.5.5** Explain in terms of structure and bonding the properties of simple molecular compounds:
	  (a) low melting points and boiling points in terms of weak intermolecular forces (specific types of intermolecular forces are **not** required)
	  (b) poor electrical conductivity
		2. Atoms, elements and compounds	51–52

Content overview

C2.3d Giant covalent structures	Learning objectives:
	• **2.6.1** Describe the giant covalent structures of graphite and diamond.
	• **2.6.2** Relate the structures and bonding of graphite and diamond to their uses, limited to:
	  (a) graphite as a lubricant and as an electrode
	  (b) diamond in cutting tools
	• Supplement **2.6.3** Describe the giant covalent structure of silicon(IV) oxide, SiO_2
	• Supplement **2.6.4** Describe the similarity in properties between diamond and silicon(IV) oxide, related to their structures
		2. Atoms, elements and compounds	52–55

C2.3e Consolidation and summary	Learning aims: • Review the learning points of the topic summarised in the end of topic checklist. • Test understanding of the topic content by answering the end of topic questions.	2. Atoms, elements and compounds	56–57
C2.4a Supplement Orientation	Learning aims: • To revise ideas on atomic structure and ionic bonding. • To map out the main purposes of the topic. • To know that an atom is made up of a positively charged nucleus containing protons and neutrons(except hydrogen) with electrons in shells around the nucleus. • To know that metal atoms lose electrons when they form ionic compounds.	2. Atoms, elements and compounds	

C2.4b Supplement Metallic bonding	Learning objectives:
	• Supplement **2.7.1** Describe metallic bonding as the electrostatic attraction between the positive ions in a giant metallic lattice and a 'sea' of delocalised electrons.
	• Supplement **2.7.2** Explain in terms of structure and bonding the properties of metals:
	  (a) good electrical conductivity
	  (b) malleability and ductility
		2. Atoms, elements and compounds	58–60

C2.4c Supplement Consolidation and summary	Learning aims: • Review the learning points of the topic summarised in the end of topic checklist. • Test understanding of the topic content by answering the end of topic questions.	2. Atoms, elements and compounds	59–63
C3.1a Orientation	Learning objectives: • **3.1.1** State the formulae of the elements and compounds named in the subject content. • **3.1.2** Define the molecular formula of a compound as the number and type of different atoms in one molecule. • **3.1.3** Deduce the formula of a simple compound from the relative numbers of atoms present in a model or a diagrammatic representation. • Supplement **3.1.6** Deduce the formula of an ionic compound from the relative numbers of the ions present in a model or a diagrammatic representation or from the charges on the ions.	3. Stoichiometry	66–70

Content overview

	Learning objectives / aims	Topic	Pages	Practicals
C3.1b Writing chemical equations	Learning objectives: • **3.1.4** Construct word equations and symbol equations to show how reactants form products, including state symbols. • Supplement **3.1.7** Construct symbol equations with state symbols, including ionic equations. • Supplement **3.1.8** Deduce the symbol equation with state symbols for a chemical reaction, given relevant information.	3. Stoichiometry	71–75	
C3.1c Relative masses	Learning objectives: • **3.2.1** Describe relative atomic mass, A_r, as the average mass of the isotopes of an element compared to 1/12th of the mass of an atom of ^{12}C. • **3.2.2** Define relative molecular mass, M_r, as the sum of the relative atomic masses. Relative formula mass, M_r, will be used for ionic compounds.	3. Stoichiometry	76–78	
C3.1d Reacting quantities and the mole concept	Learning objectives: • **3.2.3** Calculate reacting masses in simple proportions. Calculations will **not** involve the mole concept. • **3.3.1** State that concentration can be measured in g / dm³ or mol / dm³. • Supplement **3.3.2** State that the mole, mol, is the unit of amount of substance and that one mole contains 6.02×10^{23} particles, e.g. atoms, ions, molecules; this number is the Avogadro constant. • Supplement **3.3.3** Use the relationship $$\text{amount of substance (mol)} = \frac{\text{mass (g)}}{\text{molar mass}\left(\frac{g}{mol}\right)}$$ to calculate: (a) amount of substance (b) mass (c) molar mass (d) relative atomic mass or relative molecular/formula mass (e) number of particles, using the value of the Avogadro constant • Supplement **3.3.4** Use the molar gas volume, taken as 24 dm³ at room temperature and pressure, r.t.p. in calculations involving gases. • Supplement **3.3.5** Calculate stoichiometric reacting masses, limiting reactants, volumes of gases at r.t.p., volumes of solutions and concentrations of solutions expressed in g / dm³ and mol / dm³, including conversion between cm³ and dm³. • Supplement **3.3.6** Use experimental data from a titration to calculate the moles of solute, or the concentration or volume of a solution. • Supplement **3.3.7** Calculate empirical formulae and molecular formulae, given appropriate data.	3. Stoichiometry	78–91	Demonstration - burning magnesium ribbon in a Bunsen flame. Class practical – burning magnesium ribbon in a crucible to form magnesium oxide. (Worksheet C3.1d(2)) Class practical – reduction of copper(II) oxide. (Worksheet C3.1d(3)) Class practical – thermal decomposition of zinc carbonate. (Worksheet C3.1d(4)) Class practical – thermal decomposition of copper(II) carbonate. (Worksheet C3.1d(6))
C3.1e Supplement Percentage yield	Learning objective: • Supplement **3.3.8** Calculate percentage yield, percentage composition by mass and percentage purity, given appropriate data.	3. Stoichiometry	92	
C3.1f Consolidation and summary	Learning aims: • Review the learning points of the topic summarised in the end of topic checklist. • Test understanding of the topic content by answering the end of topic questions.	3. Stoichiometry	93–98	

Content overview

	Learning objectives		Pages	Activities

C4.1a Orientation	Learning objectives:
	• **4.11** Define electrolysis as the decomposition of an ionic compound, when molten or in aqueous solution, by the passage of an electric current.
	• **4.1.2** Identify in simple electrolytic cells:
	  (a) the anode as the positive electrode
	  (b) the cathode as the negative electrode
	  (c) the electrolyte as the molten or aqueous substance that undergoes electrolysis
	• Supplement **4.1.8** Describe the transfer of charge during electrolysis to include:
	  (a) the movement of electrons in the external circuit
	  (b) the loss or gain of electrons at the electrodes
	  (c) the movement of ions in the electrolyte
		4. Electrochemistry	108–110	Demonstration – use of copper to conduct electricity.

C4.1b Electrolysis of molten electrolytes	Learning objectives: • **4.1.3** Identify the products formed at the electrodes and describe the observations made during the electrolysis of molten lead(II) bromide using inert electrodes made of platinum or carbon / graphite. • **4.1.4** State that metals or hydrogen are formed at the cathode and that non-metals (other than hydrogen) are formed at the anode. • **4.1.5** Predict the identity of the products at each electrode for the electrolysis of a binary compound in the molten state. • Supplement **4.1.11** Construct ionic half-equations for reactions at the anode (to show oxidation) and at the cathode (to show reduction).	4. Electrochemistry	110–112	Demonstration – electrolysis of a molten electrolyte (anhydrous zinc chloride or equivalent).

C4.1c Electrolysis of aqueous electrolytes	Learning objectives:
	• **4.1.3** Identify the products formed at the electrodes and describe the observations made during the electrolysis of:
	  (a) concentrated aqueous sodium chloride
	  (b) dilute sulfuric acid
	using inert electrodes made of platinum or carbon / graphite.
	• **4.1.4** State that metals or hydrogen are formed at the cathode and that non-metals (other than hydrogen) are formed at the anode.
	• **4.1.6** State that metal objects are electroplated to improve their appearance and resistance to corrosion.
	• **4.1.7** Describe how metals are electroplated.
	• Supplement **4.1.9** Identify the products formed at the electrodes and describe the observations made during the electrolysis of aqueous copper(II) sulfate using inert carbon / graphite electrodes and when using copper electrodes.
	• Supplement **4.1.10** Predict the identity of the products at each electrode for the electrolysis of a halide compound in dilute or concentrated aqueous solution.
	• Supplement **4.1.11** Construct ionic half-equations for reactions at the anode (to show oxidation) and at the cathode (to show reduction).
		4. Electrochemistry	112–119	Class practical – testing a range of liquids and solutions to identify electrolytes (Worksheet C4.1c(1)).
				Class practical – electrolysis of sodium chloride solution (Worksheet C4.1c(2)).

Content overview

C4.1d The production of electrical energy from simple cells	Learning objectives: • 4.2.1 State that a hydrogen–oxygen fuel cell uses hydrogen and oxygen to produce electricity with water as the only chemical product. • Supplement 4.2.2 Describe the advantages and disadvantages of using hydrogen–oxygen fuel cells in comparison with gasoline/petrol engines in vehicles.	119–120	4. Electrochemistry	
C4.1e Consolidation and summary	Learning aims: • Review the learning points of the topic summarised in the end of topic checklist. • Test understanding of the topic content by answering the end of topic questions.	121–125	4. Electrochemistry	
C5.1a Orientation	Learning objectives: • 5.1.1 State that an exothermic reaction transfers thermal energy to the surroundings leading to an increase in the temperature of the surroundings. • 5.1.2 State that an endothermic reaction takes in thermal energy from the surroundings leading to a decrease in the temperature of the surroundings.	128–130	5. Chemical energetics	Demonstration – burning magnesium ribbon in a Bunsen flame. Class practical – measuring the temperature changes in five different reactions to identify them as endothermic or exothermic (Worksheet C5.1a).
C5.1b Measuring energy transfers (1)	Learning aims: • To investigate 'cold packs'. • To measure temperature changes in a reaction using a polystyrene cup as a simple calorimeter. • To describe how a polystyrene cup can be used to carry out simple calorimetric experiments to determine thermal energy changes (such as dissolving solids or displacement or neutralisation reactions).		5. Chemical energetics	Class practical – Investigating the quantities of KCl and H$_2$O needed in combination to produce a temperature drop of 10°C (Worksheet C5.1b)

C5.1c Measuring energy transfers (2)	Learning objectives:
	• 5.1.3 Interpret reaction pathway diagrams showing exothermic and endothermic reactions.
	• Supplement 5.1.4 State that the transfer of thermal energy during a reaction is called the enthalpy change, ΔH, of the reaction. ΔH is negative for exothermic reactions and positive for endothermic reactions.
	• Supplement 5.1.5 Define activation energy, E_a, as the minimum energy that colliding particles must have to react.
	• Supplement 5.1.6 Draw and label reaction pathway diagrams for exothermic and endothermic reactions using information provided, to include:
	  (a) reactants
	  (b) products
	  (c) enthalpy change of reaction, ΔH
	  (d) activation energy, E_a
		130–131	5. Chemical energetics	Class practical – use of spirit burners to measure the energy released when a fuel is burned (Worksheet C5.1c).

Content overview

	Learning objectives		Pages	

C5.1d Reaction pathway diagrams and bond breaking and bond forming	Learning objectives:
	• **5.1.3** Interpret reaction pathway diagrams showing exothermic and endothermic reactions.
	• Supplement **5.1.6** Draw and label reaction pathway diagrams for exothermic and endothermic reactions using information provided, to include:
	  (a) reactants
	  (b) products
	  (c) enthalpy change of reaction, ΔH
	  (d) activation energy, E_a
	• Supplement **5.1.7** State that bond breaking is an endothermic process and bond making is an exothermic process and explain the enthalpy change of a reaction in terms of bond breaking and bond making.
	• Supplement **5.1.8** Calculate the enthalpy change of a reaction using bond energies.
		5. Chemical energetics	131–137	

C5.1e Consolidation and summary	Learning aims: • Review the learning points of the topic summarised in the end of topic checklist. • Test understanding of the topic content by answering the end of topic questions.	5. Chemical energetics	138–141	
C6.1a Orientation	Learning objective: • **6.1.1** Identify physical and chemical changes, and describe the differences between them.	6. Chemical reactions	144–145	Demonstration – various reactions that occur at different speeds.

C6.1b Monitoring the rate of a reaction	Learning objectives:
	• **6.2.3** Describe practical methods for investigating the rate of a reaction including change in mass of a reactant or a product and the formation of a gas.
	• **6.2.4** Interpret data, including graphs, from rate of reaction experiments.
	• Supplement **6.2.5** Describe collision theory in terms of:
	  (a) number of particles per unit volume
	  (b) frequency of collisions between particles
	  (c) kinetic energy of particles
	  (d) activation energy, E_a
	• Supplement **6.2.8** Evaluate practical methods for investigating the rate of a reaction including change in mass of a reactant or a product and the formation of a gas.
		6. Chemical reactions	145–149	Demonstration – measuring the volume of carbon dioxide produced by the reaction between HCl and marble chips.
				Class practical – measuring the volume of hydrogen gas produced by the reaction between HCl and Mg ribbon (Worksheet C6.1b)

C6.1c Concentration of solutions	Learning objectives: • **6.2.1a** Describe the effect on the rate of reaction of changing the concentration of solutions. • Supplement **6.2.6a** Describe and explain the effect on the rate of reaction of changing the concentration of solutions using collision theory.	6. Chemical reactions	150–152	Class practical – investigating the effect of changing the concentration of HCl on the rate of reaction between HCl and marble chips (Developing Practical Skills activity from pages 144-146 of the Student Book).

Content overview

C6.1d Temperature	Learning objectives: • **6.2.1d** Describe the effect on the rate of reaction of changing the temperature. • **6.2.3** Describe practical methods for investigating the rate of a reaction including change in mass of a reactant or a product and the formation of a gas. • **6.2.4** Interpret data, including graphs, from rate of reaction experiments. • Supplement **6.2.6d** Describe and explain the effect on the rate of reaction of changing the temperature using collision theory. • Supplement **6.2.8** Evaluate practical methods for investigating the rate of a reaction including change in mass of a reactant or a product and the formation of a gas.	6. Chemical reactions	152–154	Class practical - investigating the effect of changing the temperature of HCl on the rate of reaction between HCl and marble chips (Worksheet C6.1d)
C6.1e Particle size of solids	Learning objectives: • **6.2.1c** Describe the effect on the rate of reaction of changing the surface area of solids. • **6.2.3** Describe practical methods for investigating the rate of a reaction including change in mass of a reactant or a product and the formation of a gas. • **6.2.4** Interpret data, including graphs, from rate of reaction experiments. • Supplement **6.2.6c** Describe and explain the effect on the rate of reaction of changing the surface area of solids using collision theory.	6. Chemical reactions	154–155	Demonstration – 'loss of mass' method to find the rate of reaction for HCl and marble chips. Class practical - investigating the effect of changing the surface area/particle size of marble chips on the rate of reaction between HCl and marble chips (Worksheet C6.1e).
C6.1f Use of a catalyst	Learning objectives: • **6.2.1e** Describe the effect on the rate of reaction of adding or removing a catalyst, including enzymes. • **6.2.2** State that a catalyst increases the rate of a reaction and is unchanged at the end of a reaction • **6.2.3** Describe practical methods for investigating the rate of a reaction including change in mass of a reactant or a product and the formation of a gas. • **6.2.4** Interpret data, including graphs, from rate of reaction experiments. • Supplement **6.2.6e** Describe and explain the effect on the rate of reaction of adding or removing a catalyst, including enzymes, using collision theory. • Supplement **6.2.7** State that a catalyst decreases the activation energy, E_a, of a reaction.	6. Chemical reactions	155–156	Class practical – investigation of possible catalysts for the decomposition of hydrogen peroxide (Worksheet C6.1f). Demonstration – use of manganese(IV) oxide as a catalyst in the decomposition of hydrogen peroxide.
C6.1g Consolidation and summary	Learning objectives: • **6.2.1b** Describe the effect on the rate of reaction of changing the pressure of gases. • Supplement **6.2.6b** Describe and explain the effect on the rate of reaction of changing the pressure of gases, using collision theory. Learning aims: • Review the learning points of the topic summarised in the end of topic checklist. • Test understanding of the topic content by answering the end of topic questions.	6. Chemical reactions	156–160	
C6.2a Orientation	Learning objectives: • **6.3.1** State that some chemical reactions are reversible as shown by the symbol $\rightleftharpoons$. • **6.3.2** Describe how changing the conditions can change the direction of a reversible reaction for: (a) the effect of heat on hydrated compounds (b) the addition of water to anhydrous compounds limited to copper (II) sulfate and cobalt (II) chloride.	6. Chemical reactions	161–163	Class practical – reversible reactions of copper(II) sulfate and cobalt(II) chloride with heat and water (Worksheet C6.2a).

Content overview

C6.2b **Supplement** Changing the position of equilibrium	Learning objectives: • **Supplement** **6.3.3** State that a reversible reaction in a closed system is at equilibrium when: (a) the rate of the forward reaction is equal to the rate of the reverse reaction (b) the concentrations of reactants and products are no longer changing • **Supplement** **6.3.4** Predict and explain for any reversible reaction, how the position of equilibrium is affected by: (a) changing temperature (b) changing pressure (c) changing concentration (d) using a catalyst using information provided.	6. Chemical reactions	163–166	
C6.2c **Supplement** The Haber and Contact industrial processes	Learning objectives: • **Supplement** **6.3.5** State the symbol equation for the production of ammonia in the Haber process, $N_2(g) + 3H_2(g) \rightleftharpoons 2NH_3(g)$. • **Supplement** **6.3.6** State the sources of the hydrogen (methane) and nitrogen (air) in the Haber process. • **Supplement** **6.3.7** State the typical conditions in the Haber process as 450 °C, 20 000 kPa/200atm and an iron catalyst. • **Supplement** **6.3.8** State the symbol equation for the conversion of sulfur dioxide to sulfur trioxide in the Contact process, $2SO_2(g) + O_2(g) \rightleftharpoons 2SO_3(g)$. • **Supplement** **6.3.9** State the sources of the sulfur dioxide (burning sulfur or roasting sulfide ores) and oxygen (air) in the Contact process. • **Supplement** **6.3.10** State the typical conditions for the conversion of sulfur dioxide to sulfur trioxide in the Contact process as 450 °C, 200 kPa / 2 atm and a vanadium(V) oxide catalyst. • **Supplement** **6.3.11** Explain, in terms of rate of reaction and position of equilibrium, why the typical conditions stated are used in the Haber process and in the Contact process, including safety considerations and economics.	6. Chemical reactions	165–168	Demonstration – production of ammonia by warming ammonium chloride with sodium hydroxide.
C6.2d Consolidation and summary	Learning aims: • Review the learning points of the topic summarised in the end of topic checklist. • Test understanding of the topic content by answering the end of topic questions.	6. Chemical reactions	169–171	
C6.3a Orientation	Learning objectives: • **6.4.1** Use a Roman numeral to indicate the oxidation number of an element in a compound. • **6.4.2** Define redox reactions as involving simultaneous oxidation and reduction. • **6.4.3** Define oxidation as gain of oxygen and reduction as loss of oxygen. • **6.4.4** Identify redox reactions as reactions involving gain and loss of oxygen. • **6.4.5** Identify oxidation and reduction in redox reactions.	6. Chemical reactions	172–174	

Content overview

	Learning objectives			

C6.3b Supplement Electron transfer	Learning objectives:
	• **Supplement 6.4.6** Define oxidation in terms of:
	  (a) loss of electrons
	  (b) an increase in oxidation number
	• **Supplement 6.4.7** Define reduction in terms of:
	  (a) gain of electrons
	  (b) a decrease in oxidation number
	• **Supplement 6.4.8** Identify redox reactions as reactions involving gain and loss of electrons.
	• **Supplement 6.4.9** Identify redox reactions by changes in oxidation number using:
	  (a) the oxidation number of elements in their uncombined state is zero
	  (b) the oxidation number of a monatomic ion is the same as the charge on the ion
	  (c) the sum of the oxidation numbers in a compound is zero
	  (d) the sum of the oxidation numbers in an ion is equal to the charge on the ion
	• **Supplement 6.4.10** Identify redox reactions by the colour changes involved when using acidified aqueous potassium manganate (VII) or aqueous potassium iodide.
	• **Supplement 6.4.11** Define an oxidising agent as a substance that oxidises another substance and is itself reduced.
	• **Supplement 6.4.12** Define a reducing agent as a substance that reduces another substance and is itself oxidised.
	• **Supplement 6.4.13** Identify oxidising agents and reducing agents in redox reactions.
		6. Chemical reactions	172–176	Demonstration – use of acidified potassium manganate(VII) solution as an oxidising agent and potassium iodide as a reducing agent.

C6.3c Consolidation and summary	Learning aims: • Review the learning points of the topic summarised in the end of topic checklist. • Test understanding of the topic content by answering the end of topic questions.	6. Chemical reactions	177–179	

C7.1a Orientation	Learning objectives:
	• **7.1.2** Describe acids in terms of their effect on:
	  (a) litmus
	  (b) thymolphthalein
	  (c) methyl orange
	• **7.1.5** Describe alkalis in terms of their effect on:
	  (a) litmus
	  (b) thymolphthalein
	  (c) methyl orange
		7. Acids, bases and salts	182–184	Class practical – use of indicators to measure the pH of a range of solutions (Worksheet C7.1a).

Content overview

| C7.1b Acids, bases, alkalis and salts | Learning objectives:
• **7.1.1** Describe the characteristic properties of acids in terms of their reactions with:
  (a) metals
  (b) bases
  (c) carbonates
• **7.1.4** Describe the characteristic properties of bases in terms of their reactions with:
  (a) acids
  (b) ammonium salts
• **7.1.3** State that bases are oxides or hydroxides of metals and that alkalis are soluble bases.
• **7.1.6** State that aqueous solutions of acids contain H$^+$ ions and aqueous solutions of alkalis contain OH$^-$ ions.
• **7.1.7** Describe how to compare hydrogen ion concentration, neutrality, relative acidity and relative alkalinity in terms of colour and pH using universal indicator paper.
• **7.1.8** Describe the neutralisation reaction between an acid and an alkali to produce water, H$^+$(aq) + OH$^-$(aq) $\rightarrow$ H$_2$O(l)
• **7.2.1** Classify oxides as acidic, including SO$_2$ and CO$_2$, or basic, including CuO and CaO, related to metallic and non-metallic character.
• **7.3.3** Define a hydrated substance as a substance that is chemically combined with water and an anhydrous substance as a substance containing no water.
• Supplement **7.1.9** Define acids as proton donors and bases as proton acceptors.
• Supplement **7.1.10** Define a strong acid as an acid that is completely dissociated in aqueous solution and a weak acid as an acid that is partially dissociated in aqueous solution.
• Supplement **7.1.11** State that hydrochloric acid is a strong acid, as shown by the symbol equation, HCl(aq) $\rightarrow$ H$^+$(aq) + Cl$^-$(aq)
• Supplement **7.1.12** State that ethanoic acid is a weak acid, as shown by the symbol equation, CH$_3$COOH(aq) $\rightleftharpoons$ H$^+$(aq) + CH$_3$COO$^-$(aq)
• Supplement **7.2.2** Describe amphoteric oxides as oxides that react with acids and with bases to produce a salt and water.
• Supplement **7.2.3** Classify Al$_2$O$_3$ and ZnO as amphoteric oxides.
• Supplement **7.3.5** Define the term water of crystallisation as the water molecules present in hydrated crystals, including CuSO$_4$•5H$_2$O and CoCl$_2$•6H$_2$O. | 7. Acids, bases and salts | 184–189 | Class practical – testing the pH of a range of metal and non-metal oxides (Worksheet C7.1b). |

Content overview

	Learning objectives / aims	Topic	Pages	Notes

C7.1c Making soluble salts	Learning objectives:
	• **7.3.1** Describe the preparation, separation and purification of soluble salts by reaction of an acid with:
	  (a) an alkali by titration
	  (b) excess metal
	  (c) excess insoluble base
	  (d) excess insoluble carbonate
	• **7.3.2** Describe the general solubility rules for salts:
	  (a) sodium, potassium and ammonium salts are soluble
	  (b) nitrates are soluble
	  (c) chlorides are soluble, except lead and silver
	  (d) sulfates are soluble, except barium, calcium and lead
	  (e) carbonates are insoluble, except sodium, potassium and ammonium
	  (f) hydroxides are insoluble, except sodium, potassium, ammonium and calcium (partially)
		7. Acids, bases and salts	189–192	Class practical – Making a soluble salt using titration (Worksheet C7.1c(1)).
				Class practical – Making a soluble salt without titration (Worksheet C7.1c(2)).

C7.1d Making insoluble salts	Learning objective: • **Supplement 7.3.4** Describe the preparation of insoluble salts by precipitation.	7. Acids, bases and salts	193–194	Class practical – making an insoluble salt (Worksheet C7.1d).
C7.1e Consolidation and summary	Learning aims: • Review the learning points of the topic summarised in the end of topic checklist. • Test understanding of the topic content by answering the end of topic questions.	7. Acids, bases and salts	195–199	
C8.1a Orientation	Learning objectives: • **2.1.1** Describe the differences between elements, compounds and mixtures. • **2.2.1** Describe the structure of the atom as a central nucleus containing neutrons and protons surrounded by electrons in shells. • **2.2.5** Determine the electronic configuration of elements and their ions with proton number 1 to 20 e.g. 2,8,3.	8. The Periodic Table		Demonstration – samples showing the nature of Na, Cu and Cl_2 as elements.
C8.1b The arrangement of the elements	Learning objectives: • **8.1.1** Describe the Periodic Table as an arrangement of elements in periods and groups and in order of increasing proton number / atomic number. • **8.1.2** Describe the change from metallic to non-metallic character across a period. • **8.1.3** Describe the relationship between group number and the charge of the ions formed from elements in that group. • **8.1.4** Explain similarities in the chemical properties of elements in the same group of the Periodic Table in terms of their electronic configuration. • **8.1.5** Explain how the position of an element in the Periodic Table can be used to predict its properties. • **Supplement 8.1.6** Identify trends in groups, given information about the elements.	8. The Periodic Table	210–214	
C8.1c Consolidation and summary	Learning aims: • Review the learning points of the topic summarised in the end of topic checklist. • Test understanding of the topic content by answering the end of topic questions.	8. The Periodic Table	215–217	

Content overview

C8.2a Orientation	Learning objective: • **8.2.1** Describe the Group I alkali metals, lithium, sodium and potassium, as relatively soft metals with general trends down the group, limited to: (a) decreasing melting point (b) increasing density (c) increasing reactivity	8. The Periodic Table	218–219	Demonstration – Showing the appearance of samples of Li, Na and K in sample bottles and being cut.
C8.2b Reactions of the Group 1 elements	Learning objective: • **8.2.2** Predict the properties of other elements in Group I, given information about the elements	8. The Periodic Table	220–222	Demonstration – addition of Li, Na and K to water.
C8.2c Consolidation and summary	Learning aims: • Review the learning points of the topic summarised in the end of topic checklist. • Test understanding of the topic content by answering the end of topic questions.	8. The Periodic Table	223–224	
C8.3a Orientation	Learning objectives: • **8.3.1** Describe the Group VII halogens, chlorine, bromine and iodine, as diatomic non-metals with general trends down the group, limited to: (a) increase in density (b) decrease in reactivity • **8.3.2** State the appearance of the halogens at r.t.p. as: (a) chlorine, a pale yellow-green gas (b) bromine, a red-brown liquid (c) iodine, a grey-black solid • **8.3.4** Predict the properties of other elements in Group VII, given information about the elements.	8. The Periodic Table	225–226	Demonstration – Showing samples of Cl_2, Br_2 and I_2.
C8.3b Displacement reactions of the halogens	Learning objectives: • **8.3.3** Describe and explain the displacement reactions of halogens with other halide ions. • **8.3.4** Predict the properties of other elements in Group VII, given information about the elements	8. The Periodic Table	227–228	Demonstration – displacement reactions of the halogens using chlorine solution, bromine solution and iodine solution with sodium chloride, sodium bromide and sodium iodide solutions (Worksheet C8.3b).
C8.3c Consolidation and summary	Learning aims: • Review the learning points of the topic summarised in the end of topic checklist. • Test understanding of the topic content by answering the end of topic questions.	8. The Periodic Table	232–233	
C8.4a Orientation	Learning aims: • To review the significance of the positioning of the transition metals in the Periodic Table. • To review the significance of the positioning of the noble gases in the Periodic Table. • To know the positions of the transition metals and noble gases in the Periodic Table. • To know some of the key differences between the transition metals and the Group 1 metals. • To know some of the key differences between the noble gases and the Group VII elements.	8. The Periodic Table		Demonstration – samples of a range of transition metals compared to a sample of sodium.

Content overview

C8.4b The transition elements	Learning objectives:
	• 8.4.1 Describe the transition elements as metals that:
	  (a) have high densities
	  (b) have high melting points
	  (c) form coloured compounds
	  (d) often act as catalysts as elements and as compounds
	• Supplement 8.4.2 Describe transition elements as having ions with variable oxidation numbers, including iron(II) and iron(III)
		8. The Periodic Table	234–236	Class practical – investigating the colour changes of transition metals when sodium hydroxide and ammonia are added (Worksheet C8.4b).

C8.4c The noble gases	Learning objective: • 8.5.1 Describe the Group VIII noble gases as unreactive, monatomic gases and explain this in terms of electronic configuration	8.The Periodic Table	236	
C8.4d Consolidation and summary	Learning aims: • Review the learning points of the topic summarised in the end of topic checklist. • Test understanding of the topic content by answering the end of topic questions.	8.The Periodic Table	237–239	
C9.1a Orientation	Learning objective: • 8.1.5 Explain how the position of an element in the Periodic Table can be used to predict its properties.	9. Metals	243	Demonstration – addition of sodium and copper to water.

C9.1b Properties of metals	Learning objectives:
	• 9.1.1 Compare the general physical properties of metals and non-metals, including:
	  (a) thermal conductivity
	  (b) electrical conductivity
	  (c) malleability and ductility
	  (d) melting and boiling points
	• 9.1.2 Describe the general chemical properties of metals, limited to their reactions with:
	  (a) dilute acids
	  (b) cold water and steam
	  (c) oxygen
	• 9.3.1 Describe an alloy as a mixture of a metal with other elements, including:
	  (a) brass as a mixture of copper and zinc
	  (b) stainless steel as a mixture of iron and other elements such as chromium, nickel and carbon
	• 9.3.2 State that alloys can be harder or stronger than the pure metals and are more useful.
	• 9.3.3 Describe the uses of alloys in terms of their physical properties, including stainless steel in cutlery because of its hardness and resistance to rusting.
	• 9.3.4 Identify representations of alloys from diagrams of structure.
	• Supplement 9.3.5 Explain in terms of structure how alloys can be harder or stronger than the pure metals because the different sized atoms in alloys mean the layers can no longer slide over each other.
		9. Metals	242–246	Class practical – investigating the physical properties of metals and non-metals (Worksheet C9.1b).

Content overview

	Learning objectives		Pages	

C9.1c Reactivity series	Learning objectives:
	• **9.4.1** State the order of the reactivity series as: potassium, sodium, calcium, magnesium, aluminium, carbon, zinc, iron, hydrogen, copper, silver, gold.
	• **9.4.2** Describe the reactions, if any, of:
	  (a) potassium, sodium and calcium with cold water
	  (b) magnesium with steam
	  (c) magnesium, zinc, iron, copper, silver and gold with dilute hydrochloric acid
	and explain these reactions in terms of the position of the metals and hydrogen in the reactivity series.
	• **9.4.3** Deduce an order of reactivity from a given set of experimental results.
	• Supplement **9.4.4** Describe the relative reactivities of metals in terms of their tendency to form positive ions, by displacement reactions, if any, with the aqueous ions of magnesium, zinc, iron, copper and silver.
	• Supplement **9.4.5** Explain the apparent unreactivity of aluminium in terms of its oxide layer.
		9. Metals	247–250	Demonstration – reaction between magnesium and steam.
				
				Class practical – comparing reactivities of different metals with HCl and H_2SO_4 (Worksheet C9.1c(1)).
				Class practical – obtaining metals from metal oxides using carbon (Worksheet C9.1c(2)).
				Class practical – metal displacement reactions (Worksheet C9.1c(3)).

C9.1d Extraction of metals	Learning objectives:
	• **9.6.1** Describe the ease in obtaining metals from their ores, related to the position of the metal in the reactivity series
	• **9.6.2** Describe the extraction of iron from hematite in the blast furnace, limited to:
	  (a) the burning of carbon (coke) to provide heat and produce carbon dioxide
	  (b) the reduction of carbon dioxide to carbon monoxide
	  (c) the reduction of iron(III) oxide by carbon monoxide
	  (d) the thermal decomposition of calcium carbonate / limestone to produce calcium oxide
	  (e) the formation of slag
	Symbol equations are **not** required
	• **9.6.3** State that the main ore of aluminium is bauxite and that aluminium is extracted by electrolysis
	• Supplement **9.6.4** State the symbol equations for the extraction of iron from hematite
	  (a) $C + O_2 \rightarrow CO_2$
	  (b) $C + CO_2 \rightarrow 2CO$
	  (c) $Fe_2O_3 + 3CO \rightarrow 2Fe + 3CO_2$
	  (d) $CaCO_3 \rightarrow CaO + CO_2$
	  (e) $CaO + SiO_2 \rightarrow CaSiO_3$
	• Supplement **9.6.5** Describe the extraction of aluminium from purified bauxite / aluminium oxide, including:
	  (a) the role of cryolite
	  (b) why the carbon anode needs to be regularly replaced
	  (c) the reactions at the electrodes, including ionic half-equations
	Details of the purification of bauxite are **not** required.
		9. Metals	252–258	

Content overview

	Learning objectives:			

C9.1e Uses of metals	Learning objectives:
	• **9.2.1** Describe the uses of metals in terms of their physical properties, including:
	  (a) aluminium in the manufacture of aircraft because of its low density
	  (b) aluminium in the manufacture of overhead electrical cables because of its low density and good electrical conductivity
	  (c) aluminium in food containers because of its resistance to corrosion
	  (d) copper in electrical wiring because of its good electrical conductivity and ductility
	• **9.5.1** State the conditions required for the rusting of iron and steel to form hydrated iron(III) oxide.
	• **9.5.2** State some common barrier methods, including painting, greasing and coating with plastic.
	• **9.5.3** Describe how barrier methods prevent rusting by excluding oxygen or water.
	• Supplement **9.5.4** Describe the use of zinc in galvanising as an example of a barrier method and sacrificial protection.
	• Supplement **9.5.5** Explain sacrificial protection in terms of the reactivity series and in terms of electron loss.
		9. Metals	244–252	Class practical – investigating methods of corrosion prevention (Worksheet C9.1e).

C9.1f Consolidation and summary	Learning aims: • Review the learning points of the topic summarised in the end of topic checklist. • Test understanding of the topic content by answering the end of topic questions.	9. Metals	259–263	
C10.1a Orientation	Learning aims: • To review knowledge on the composition of the air. • To revise understanding of hydrated salts. • To highlight the content areas in the topic. • To know that oxygen is a key component of air and reacts with elements and compounds to form oxides. • Supplement To know that hydrated salts contain water of crystallisation.	10. Chemistry of the environment		

Content overview

C10.1b Water	Learning objectives:
	• **10.1.1** Describe chemical tests for the presence of water using anhydrous cobalt(II) chloride and anhydrous copper(II) sulfate.
	• **10.1.2** Describe how to test for the purity of water using melting point and boiling point.
	• **10.1.3** Explain that distilled water is used in practical chemistry rather than tap water because it contains fewer chemical impurities.
	• **10.1.4** State that water from natural sources contains substances, including:
	  (a) dissolved oxygen
	  (b) metal compounds
	  (c) plastics
	  (d) sewage
	  (e) harmful microbes
	  (f) nitrates from fertilisers
	  (g) phosphates from fertilisers and detergents
	• **10.1.5** State that some of these substances are beneficial, including:
	  (a) dissolved oxygen for aquatic life
	  (b) some metal compounds provide essential minerals for life
	• **10.1.6** State that some of these substances are potentially harmful, including:
	  (a) some metal compounds are toxic
	  (b) some plastics harm aquatic life
	  (c) sewage contains harmful microbes which cause disease
	  (d) nitrates and phosphates lead to deoxygenation of water and damage to aquatic life
	Details of the eutrophication process are **not** required.
	• **10.1.7** Describe the treatment of the domestic water supply in terms of:
	  (a) sedimentation and filtration to remove solids
	  (b) use of carbon to remove tastes and odours
	  (c) chlorination to kill microbes
	• **10.2.1** State that ammonium salts and nitrates are used as fertilisers.
	• **10.2.2** Describe the use of NPK fertilisers to provide the elements nitrogen, phosphorus and potassium for improved plant growth.
		10. Chemistry of the environment	267–270	Demonstration – addition of water to anhydrous copper(II) sulfate and anhydrous cobalt(II) chloride.

C10.1c The composition of the air	Learning objectives: • **10.3.1** State the composition of clean, dry air as approximately 78% nitrogen, N_2, 21% oxygen, O_2 and the remainder as a mixture of noble gases and carbon dioxide, CO_2. • **10.3.5** Describe photosynthesis as the reaction between carbon dioxide and water to produce glucose and oxygen in the presence of chlorophyll and using energy from light. • **10.3.6** State the word equation for photosynthesis, carbon dioxide + water $\rightarrow$ glucose + oxygen • Supplement **10.3.9** State the symbol equation for photosynthesis, $6CO_2 + 6H_2O \rightarrow C_6H_{12}O_6 + 6O_2$	10. Chemistry of the environment	267–273	

Content overview

C10.1d
Air quality and climate
	Learning objectives:
	• **10.3.2** State the source of each of these air pollutants, limited to:
	  (a) carbon dioxide from the complete combustion of carbon-containing fuels
	  (b) carbon monoxide and particulates from the incomplete combustion of carbon-containing fuels
	  (c) methane from the decomposition of vegetation and waste gases from digestion in animals
	  (d) oxides of nitrogen from car engines
	  (e) sulfur dioxide from the combustion of fossil fuels which contain sulfur compounds
	• **10.3.3** State the adverse effects of these air pollutants, limited to:
	  (a) carbon dioxide: higher levels of carbon dioxide leading to increased global warming, which leads to climate change
	  (b) carbon monoxide: toxic gas
	  (c) particulates: increased risk of respiratory problems and cancer
	  (d) methane: higher levels of methane leading to increased global warming, which leads to climate change
	  (e) oxides of nitrogen: acid rain, photochemical smog and respiratory problems
	  (f) sulfur dioxide: acid rain
	• **10.3.4** State and explain strategies to reduce the effects of these environmental issues, limited to:
	  (a) climate change: planting trees, reduction in livestock farming, decreasing use of fossil fuels, increasing use of hydrogen and renewable energy e.g. wind, solar
	  (b) acid rain: use of catalytic converters in vehicles, reducing emissions of sulfur dioxide by using low-sulfur fuels and flue gas desulfurisation with calcium oxide
	• Supplement **10.3.7** Describe how the greenhouse gases carbon dioxide and methane cause global warming, limited to:
	  (a) the absorption, reflection and emission of thermal energy
	  (b) reducing thermal energy loss to space
	• Supplement **10.3.8** Explain how oxides of nitrogen form in car engines and describe their removal by catalytic converters, e.g. $2CO + 2NO \rightarrow 2CO_2 + N_2$
		10. Chemistry of the environment	274–279

C10.1e Consolidation and summary	Learning aims: • Review the learning points of the topic summarised in the end of topic checklist. • Test understanding of the topic content by answering the end of topic questions.	10. Chemistry of the environment	280–283

Content overview

C11.1a Orientation	Learning objectives:
	• 11.1.1 Draw and interpret the displayed formula of a molecule to show all the atoms and all the bonds.
	• 11.1.2 Write and interpret general formulae of compounds in the same homologous series, limited to:
	  (a) alkanes, C_nH_{2n+2}
	  (b) alkenes, C_nH_{2n}
	  (c) alcohols, $C_nH_{2n+1}OH$
	  (d) carboxylic acids, $C_nH_{2n+1}COOH$
	• 11.1.3 Identify a functional group as an atom or group of atoms that determine the chemical properties of a homologous series
	• 11.1.4 State that a homologous series is a family of similar compounds with similar chemical properties due to the presence of the same functional group
	• 11.1.5 State that a saturated compound has molecules in which all carbon–carbon bonds are single bonds.
	• 11.1.6 State that an unsaturated compound has molecules in which one or more carbon–carbon bonds are not single bonds.
	• Supplement 11.1.7 State that a structural formula is an unambiguous description of the way the atoms in a molecule are arranged, including $CH_2=CH_2$, CH_3CH_2OH, CH_3COOCH_3.
	• Supplement 11.1.9 Describe the general characteristics of a homologous series as:
	  (a) having the same functional group
	  (b) having the same general formula
	  (c) differing from one member to the next by a –CH_2– unit
	  (d) displaying a trend in physical properties
	  (e) sharing similar chemical properties
		11. Organic Chemistry	292–293

C11.2a Orientation	Learning objectives: • 11.3.1 Name the fossil fuels: coal, natural gas and petroleum. • 11.3.2 Name methane as the main constituent of natural gas. • 11.3.3 State that hydrocarbons are compounds that contain hydrogen and carbon only. • 11.3.4 State that petroleum is a mixture of hydrocarbons.	11. Organic Chemistry	294

Content overview

C11.2b The fractional distillation of crude oil	Learning objectives:
	• **11.3.5** Describe the separation of petroleum into useful fractions by fractional distillation.
	• **11.3.6** Describe how the properties of fractions obtained from petroleum change from the bottom to the top of the fractionating column, limited to:
	  (a) decreasing chain length
	  (b) higher volatility
	  (c) lower boiling points
	  (d) lower viscosity
	• **11.3.7** Name the uses of the fractions as:
	  (a) refinery gas fraction for gas used in heating and cooking
	  (b) gasoline/petrol fraction for fuel used in cars
	  (c) naphtha fraction as a chemical feedstock
	  (d) kerosene/paraffin fraction for jet fuel
	  (e) diesel oil/gas oil fraction for fuel used in diesel engines
	  (f) fuel oil fraction for fuel used in ships and home heating systems
	  (g) lubricating oil fraction for lubricants, waxes and polishes
	  (h) bitumen fraction for making roads
		11. Organic Chemistry	295–297	Demonstration – fractional distillation of a crude oil substitute (Worksheet C11.2b).

C11.2c Consolidation and summary	Learning aims: • Review the learning points of the topic summarised in the end of topic checklist. • Test understanding of the topic content by answering the end of topic questions.	11. Organic Chemistry	295–301	
C11.3a Orientation	Learning objectives: • **11.4.1** State that the bonding in alkanes is single covalent and that alkanes are saturated hydrocarbons. • **11.1.2a** Write and interpret the general formula of alkanes as C_nH_{2n+2}. • **11.2.1a** Name and draw the displayed formulae of methane and ethane. • **11.2.2** State the type of compound present, given a chemical name ending in -ane, or from a molecular formula or displayed formula. • Supplement **11.2.3a** Name and draw the structural and displayed formulae of unbranched alkanes containing up to four carbon atoms per molecule. • Supplement **11.1.8** Define structural isomers as compounds with the same molecular formula, but different structural formulae, including C_4H_{10} as $CH_3CH_2CH_2CH_3$ and $CH_3CH(CH_3)CH_3$.	11. Organic Chemistry	302–306	Demonstration – show samples of alkanes (photos could be used instead).
C11.3b The chemical properties of alkanes	Learning objectives: • **11.4.2** Describe the properties of alkanes as being generally unreactive, except in terms of combustion and substitution by chlorine. • Supplement **11.4.3** State that in a substitution reaction one atom or group of atoms is replaced by another atom or group of atoms. • Supplement **11.4.4** Describe the substitution reaction of alkanes with chlorine as a photochemical reaction, with ultraviolet light providing the activation energy, E_a, and draw the structural or displayed formulae of the products, limited to monosubstitution.	11. Organic Chemistry	305–307	

Content overview

C11.3c Supplement The structure of alkanes	Learning objective: • **Supplement** **11.1.8** Define structural isomers as compounds with the same molecular formula, but different structural formulae, including C_4H_{10} as $CH_3CH_2CH_2CH_3$ and $CH_3CH(CH_3)CH_3$.	11. Organic Chemistry	306–307	
C11.4d Consolidation and summary	Learning aims: • Review the learning points of the topic summarised in the end of topic checklist. • Test understanding of the topic content by answering the end of topic questions.	11. Organic Chemistry	308–310	
C11.4a Orientation	Learning objectives: • **11.1.2b** Write and interpret the general formula of alkenes as C_nH_{2n}. • **11.2.1b** Name and draw the displayed formula of ethene. • **11.2.2** State the type of compound present, given a chemical name ending in -ene, or from a molecular formula or displayed formula. • **11.5.1** State that the bonding in alkenes includes a carbon-carbon double covalent bond and that alkenes are unsaturated hydrocarbons. • **Supplement** **11.1.8** Define structural isomers as compounds with the same molecular formula, but different structural formulae, including C_4H_8 as $CH_3CH_2CH=CH_2$ and $CH_3CH=CHCH_3$. • **Supplement** **11.2.3b** Name and draw the structural and displayed formulae of unbranched alkenes containing up to four carbon atoms per molecule, including but-1-ene and but-2-ene.	11. Organic Chemistry	311–312	
C11.4b Cracking crude oil fractions	Learning objectives: • **11.5.2** Describe the manufacture of alkenes and hydrogen by the cracking of larger alkane molecules using a high temperature and a catalyst. • **11.5.3** Describe the reasons for the cracking of larger alkane molecules.	11. Organic Chemistry	313–314	Class practical – cracking of liquid paraffin (Worksheet C11.4b)

C11.4c The chemical properties of alkenes	Learning objectives:
	• **11.5.4** Describe the test to distinguish between saturated and unsaturated hydrocarbons by their reaction with aqueous bromine.
	• **Supplement** **11.5.5** State that in an addition reaction only one product is formed.
	• **Supplement** **11.5.6** Describe the properties of alkenes in terms of addition reactions with:
	  (a) bromine or aqueous bromine
	  (b) hydrogen in the presence of a nickel catalyst
	  (c) steam in the presence of an acid catalyst.
	  (d) and draw the structural or displayed formulae of the products.
		11. Organic Chemistry	315–318	Demonstration – Addition of bromine solution to an alkene.

C11.4d Consolidation and summary	Learning aims: • Review the learning points of the topic summarised in the end of topic checklist. • Test understanding of the topic content by answering the end of topic questions.	11. Organic Chemistry	317–321	

Content overview

C11.5a Orientation	Learning objectives:
	• **11.1.2c** Write and interpret the general formulae of alcohols, $C_nH_{2n+1}OH$.
	• **11.2.1c** Name and draw the displayed formula of ethanol.
	• **11.2.2** State the type of compound present, given a chemical name ending in -ol, or from a molecular formula or displayed formula.
	• **11.6.3** State the uses of ethanol as:
	  (a) a solvent
	  (b) a fuel
	• Supplement **11.2.3c** Name and draw the structural and displayed formulae of unbranched alcohols containing up to four carbon atoms per molecule, including propan-1-ol, propan-2-ol, butan-1-ol and butan-2-ol.
		11. Organic Chemistry	322–324	

C11.5b The manufacture of ethanol	Learning objectives:
	• **11.6.1** Describe the manufacture of ethanol by:
	  (a) fermentation of glucose solution at 25–35 °C in the presence of yeast and in the absence of oxygen
	  (b) catalytic addition of steam to ethene at 300 °C and 6000 kPa/ 60 atm in the presence of an acid catalyst.
	• Supplement **11.6.4** Describe the advantages and disadvantages of the manufacture of ethanol by:
	  • fermentation
	  • catalytic addition of steam to ethene
		11. Organic Chemistry	324–327	Demonstration – Fermentation method for making ethanol from sugar.
				Demonstration – fractional distillation to separate ethanol from water after fermentation.
				Demonstration – burning a small amount of ethanol.

C11.5c Reactions of ethanol	Learning objectives:
	• **11.6.2** Describe the combustion of ethanol.
	• **11.6.3** State the uses of ethanol as:
	  (a) a solvent
	  (b) a fuel
	• Supplement **11.6.4** Describe the advantages and disadvantages of the manufacture of ethanol by:
	  (a) fermentation
	  (b) catalytic addition of steam to ethene
		11. Organic Chemistry	325–327	Demonstration – burning of ethanol in a spirit burner.

C11.5d Consolidation and summary	Learning aims: • Review the learning points of the topic summarised in the end of topic checklist. • Test understanding of the topic content by answering the end of topic questions.	11. Organic Chemistry	329–331	
C11.6a Orientation	Learning objectives: • **11.1.2d** Write and interpret the general formula of carboxylic acids, $C_nH_{2n+1}COOH$. • **11.2.1d** Name and draw the displayed formula for ethanoic acid. • **11.2.2** State the type of compound present, given a chemical name ending in -oic acid, or from a molecular formula or displayed formula. • Supplement **11.2.3d** Name and draw the structural and displayed formulae of unbranched carboxylic acids containing up to four carbon atoms per molecule.	11. Organic Chemistry	332–333	

Content overview

C11.6b **Supplement** The formation of ethanoic acid	Learning objective:
	• **Supplement** **11.7.2** Describe the formation of ethanoic acid by the oxidation of ethanol:
	  (a) with acidified aqueous potassium manganate (VII)
	  (b) by bacterial oxidation during vinegar production
		11. Organic Chemistry	333	

C11.6c The properties of ethanoic acid	Learning objectives:
	• **11.7.1** Describe the reaction of ethanoic acid with:
	  (a) metals
	  (b) bases
	  (c) carbonates
	including names and formulae of the salts produced.
	• **Supplement** **11.7.3** Describe the reaction of a carboxylic acid with an alcohol using an acid catalyst to form an ester.
	• **Supplement** **11.2.4** Name and draw the displayed formulae of the unbranched esters which can be made from unbranched alcohols and carboxylic acids, each containing up to four carbon atoms.
		11. Organic Chemistry	333–334	Demonstration – producing an ester from alcohol and carboxylic acid with a sulfuric acid catalyst.

C11.6d Consolidation and summary	Learning aims: • Review the learning points of the topic summarised in the end of topic checklist. • Test understanding of the topic content by answering the end of topic questions.	11. Organic Chemistry	335–336	
C11.7a Orientation	Learning objective: • **11.8.1** Define polymers as large molecules built up from many smaller molecules called monomers.	11. Organic Chemistry	337–338	

Content overview

	Learning objectives:			

C11.7b Synthetic polymers	Learning objectives:
	• **11.8.2** Describe the formation of poly(ethene) as an example of addition polymerisation using ethene monomers.
	• **11.8.3** State that plastics are made from polymers.
	• **11.8.4** Describe how the properties of plastics have implications for their disposal.
	• **11.8.5** Describe the environmental challenges caused by plastics, limited to:
	  (a) disposal in land fill sites
	  (b) accumulation in oceans
	  (c) formation of toxic gases from burning
	• Supplement **11.8.6** Identify the repeat units and/or linkages in addition polymers and in condensation polymers.
	• Supplement **11.8.7** Deduce the structure or repeat unit of an addition polymer from a given alkene and vice versa.
	• Supplement **11.8.8** Deduce the structure or repeat unit of a condensation polymer from given monomers and vice versa, limited to:
	  (a) polyamides from a dicarboxylic acid and a diamine
	  (b) polyesters from a dicarboxylic acid and a diol
	• Supplement **11.8.9** Describe the differences between addition and condensation polymerisation
	• Supplement **11.8.10** Describe and draw the structure of:
	  (a) nylon, a polyamide
	  (b) PET, a polyester
	The full name for PET, polyethylene terephthalate is **not** required.
	• Supplement **11.8.11** State that PET can be converted back into monomers and re-polymerised
		11. Organic Chemistry	338–342	Class practical – identification of addition polymers (Worksheet C11.7b).
				Demonstration – making nylon.

C11.7c Supplement Proteins	Learning objectives: • Supplement **11.8.12** Describe proteins as natural polyamides and that they are formed from amino acid monomers with the general structure: where R represents different types of side chain. • Supplement **11.8.13** Describe and draw the structure of proteins as:	11. Organic Chemistry	343–344	
C11.7d Consolidation and summary	Learning aims: • Review the learning points of the topic summarised in the end of topic checklist. • Test understanding of the topic content by answering the end of topic questions.	11. Organic chemistry	345–347	

Content overview

C12.1a Orientation	Learning objectives:
	• **12.1.1** Name appropriate apparatus for the measurement of time, temperature, mass and volume, including:
	  (a) stop-watches
	  (b) thermometers
	  (c) balances
	  (d) burettes
	  (e) volumetric pipettes
	  (f) measuring cylinders
	  (g) gas syringes
	• **12.1.2** Suggest advantages and disadvantages of experimental methods and apparatus.
	• **12.1.3** Describe a:
	  (a) solvent as a substance that dissolves a solute
	  (b) solute as a substance that is dissolved in a solvent
	  (c) solution as a mixture of one or more solutes dissolved in a solvent
	  (d) saturated solution as a solution containing the maximum concentration of a solute dissolved in the solvent at a specified temperature
	  (e) residue as a substance that remains after evaporation, distillation, filtration or any similar process
	  (f) filtrate as a liquid or solution that has passed through a filter.
		12. Experimental techniques	356–363	Demonstration – showing the methods of distillation, fractional distillation, filtration, crystallisation and chromatography.

C12.1b Criteria for purity	Learning objectives:
	• **12.3.1** Describe how paper chromatography is used to separate mixtures of soluble coloured substances, using a suitable solvent.
	• **12.3.2** Interpret simple chromatograms to identify:
	  unknown substances by comparison with known substances
	  pure and impure substances.
	• **Supplement 12.3.3** Describe how paper chromatography is used to separate mixtures of soluble colourless substances, using a suitable solvent and a locating agent.
	Knowledge of specific locating agents is **not** required.
	• **Supplement 12.3.4** State and use the equation for R_f:
	$$R_f = \frac{\text{distance travelled by substance}}{\text{distance travelled by solvent}}$$
		12. Experimental techniques	358–360	Class practical – paper chromatography of different inks (Worksheet C12.1b).

C12.1c Methods of purification	Learning objectives:
	• **12.4.1** Describe and explain methods of separation and purification using:
	  (a) a suitable solvent
	  (b) filtration
	  (c) crystallisation
	  (d) simple distillation
	  (e) fractional distillation
	• **12.4.2** Suggest suitable separation and purification techniques, given information about the substances involved.
	• **12.4.1** Identify substances and assess their purity using melting and boiling point information.
		12. Experimental techniques	361–364	Class practical – simple distillation of ink (Worksheet C12.1c).

Content overview

		Learning aims / objectives	Pages		

C12.1d Consolidation and summary	12. Experimental techniques	Learning aims:
		• Review the learning points of the topic summarised in the end of topic checklist.
		• Test understanding of the topic content by answering the end of topic questions.
		Learning objectives:
		• 12.2.1 Describe an acid-base titration to include the use of:
		  (a) burette
		  (b) volumetric pipette
		  (c) suitable indicator.
		• 12.2.2 Describe how to identify the end-point of a titration using an indicator.
			365–367		

C12.2a Orientation	12. Experimental techniques	Learning aims: • To recap on existing knowledge of ions and identification tests for gases. • To know that metals form positive ions which are called cations. • To know that non-metals form negative ions which are called anions. • To know the identification tests for hydrogen, oxygen and carbon dioxide.	365–367		

C12.2b Identifying cations	12. Experimental techniques	Learning objectives:
		• 12.5.2 Describe tests using aqueous sodium hydroxide and aqueous ammonia to identify the aqueous cations:
		  (a) aluminium, Al^{3+}
		  (b) ammonium, NH_4^+
		  (c) calcium, Ca^{2+}
		  (d) chromium(III), Cr^{3+}
		  (e) copper(II), Cu^{2+}
		  (f) iron(II), Fe^{2+}
		  (g) iron(III), Fe^{3+}
		  (h) zinc, Zn^{2+}
		• 12.5.4 Describe the use of a flame test to identify the cations:
		  (a) lithium, Li^+
		  (b) sodium, Na^+
		  (c) potassium, K^+
		  (d) copper(II), Cu^{2+}
		  (e) calcium, Ca^{2+}
		  (f) barium, Ba^{2+}
			368–371	Demonstration and class practical – flame tests to identify cations (Worksheet C12.2b(1)
				Class practical – identifying metal ions in solution (Worksheet C12.2b(2)).
				Demonstration – identifying ammonium ions.	

C12.2c Identifying anions	12. Experimental techniques	Learning objectives:
		• 12.5.1 Describe tests to identify the anions:
		  (a) carbonate, CO_3^{2-}, by reaction with dilute acid and then testing for carbon dioxide gas
		  (b) chloride, Cl^-, bromide, Br^-, and iodide I^-, by acidifying with dilute nitric acid then adding aqueous silver nitrate
		  (c) nitrate, NO_3^-, by reduction with aluminium foil and aqueous sodium hydroxide and then testing for ammonia gas
		  (d) sulfate, SO_4^{2-}, by acidifying with dilute nitric acid then adding aqueous barium nitrate
		  (e) sulfite, SO_3^{2-}, by reaction with acidified aqueous potassium manganate(VII).
			372–374	Demonstration – identification of carbonate ions, nitrate ions and sulfite ions.
				Class practical – identification of halide ions and sulfate ions (Worksheet C12.2c).	

Content overview

C12.2d Identifying gases	Learning objective:
	• **12.5.3** Describe tests to identify the gases:
	  (a) ammonia, NH_3, using damp red litmus paper
	  (b) carbon dioxide, CO_2, using limewater
	  (c) chlorine, Cl_2, using damp litmus paper
	  (d) hydrogen, H_2, using a lighted splint
	  (e) oxygen, O_2, using a glowing splint
	  (f) sulfur dioxide, SO_2, using acidified aqueous potassium manganate(VII)
		12. Experimental techniques	375	Class practical – testing samples of hydrogen, oxygen, carbon dioxide, ammonia, chloride and sulfur dioxide (Worksheet C12.2d).

C12.2e Consolidation and summary	Learning aims: • Review the learning points of the topic summarised in the end of topic checklist. • Test understanding of the topic content by answering the end of topic questions.	12. Experimental techniques	376–377	

Section 1: States of matter

Contents
C1.1 States of matter

Overview of the section
This section may go back over ideas that students have already met, so it does not need to take up much teaching time. Nevertheless, it is worth making sure there are no misconceptions and it is important for your students to understand the kinetic particle theory and the concept of diffusion.

Starting points
The Student Book section opener (pages 8–9) puts the ideas in the section into context and sets the scene. It also allows students to acknowledge and value their prior learning, and provides a benchmark against which future learning can be compared.

The questions provide a structure for introducing the section and can be used in a number of different ways:
- You could ask students to consider the questions as an introductory homework task.
- You could put students into groups to share their own ideas and understanding and then to report back to the whole class.
- Students could be given access to the Internet, preferably with a tight timescale, to find out the information required.

You could then use a spider chart or other form of wall chart to summarise everybody's ideas.

Recording these initial ideas allows you to retain them for reference as the individual topics are developed. In this way, your students' progress in learning can be readily acknowledged.

C1.1 States of matter

Introduction
The kinetic particle theory links to work on a simple collision theory in Topic 6.1 Rate of reaction, and to an explanation of fractional distillation in Topic 11.2 *Fuels*.

Links to other topics

Section	Essential background knowledge	Useful links
2 Atoms, elements and compounds		2.1 Atoms, elements and compounds
6 Chemical reactions		6.1 Rate of reaction
11 Organic chemistry		11.2 Fuels

Topic overview

C1.1a	**Orientation**
	The purpose of this learning episode is to recap students' current knowledge and understanding of the three states of matter and the names of the processes involved when substances change states.
C1.1b	**Solids, liquids and gases**
	This learning episode introduces the particulate models of solids, liquids and gases. The focus is on the different arrangements and movements of the particles in the three states. The names of the processes that bring about a change in state are emphasised and it relates these changes to the energy involved.
	Supplement An explanation of the changes of state using the kinetic particle theory is then considered.
	Supplement An explanation of the effects of temperature and pressure on the volume of a gas using the kinetic particle theory.
C1.1c	**Diffusion**
	This learning episode involves a series of simple diffusion experiments that involve dissolving crystals and mixing gases. Some of the experiments can be demonstrated and some are undertaken by the students themselves.
	Supplement The Developing Practical Skills feature in the Student Book (the diffusion of ammonia and hydrogen chloride in a sealed tube) is used to describe the dependency of rate of diffusion on relative molecular mass.
C1.1d	**Consolidation and summary**
	This learning episode allows for a quick recap of the key ideas of the topic and provides a link to subsequent work on atoms, elements and compounds.

Career links
These are some scientific careers that focus on this area of chemistry but careers in many other fields use the knowledge and skills gained studying science.

Many roles in chemistry rely on an understanding of the behaviour of different states of matter. For example, some paleoclimatologists study the interaction between ice and water in ice sheets or look at the composition of bubbles of air found in ice cores.

Topic 1.1: States of matter

Learning episode C1.1a Orientation

Learning objective

- State the distinguishing properties of solids, liquids and gases.

Resources

Student Book page 11

Resources for demonstration (see Technician's notes, below)

Approach

Students should be familiar with classifying solids, liquids and gases. They may also know the names of the processes that cause changes of state. So this learning episode can be relatively short.

Ask students to list four solids, four liquids and four gases they are familiar with. Emphasise that substances with the same classification can have quite different properties. For example: a candle and a metal rod (hardness), water and liquid honey (viscosity), air and bromine gas (colour). Use page 11 of the Student Book to summarise the different properties of solids, liquids and gases. Explain that these distinguishing properties are generally true, but that students need to be careful. For example, sand is obviously a solid, but it takes the shape of any container it is put in.

Finally, ask students to name some of the processes involved in changing states, such as melting, boiling (evaporation) and freezing.

SAFETY INFORMATION
Wear eye protection - splash proof goggles when using bromine.
Wear chemical resistant gloves.
Keep bromine in fume cupboard.

Technician's notes

Be sure to check the latest safety notes on these resources before proceeding.

The following resources are needed for the demonstration on solids, liquids and gases:

a candle, a metal rod (similar diameter to a candle), a jar of liquid honey
a gas jar of bromine gas (in fume cupboard), eye protection (splash-proof goggles), chemical resistant gloves

Answers

Page 11

1. (l).
2. Only the solid state has a fixed shape.
3. Fine sand will pour or flow like a liquid; it takes the shape of the container it is poured into (although under a microscope you would see gaps at the sides of the container).

Topic 1.1: States of matter

Learning episode C1.1b Solids, liquids and gases

Learning objectives

- Describe the structures of solids, liquids and gases in terms of particle separation, arrangement and motion.
- Describe changes of state in terms of melting, boiling, evaporating, freezing and condensing.
- Describe the effects of temperature and pressure on the volume of a gas.
- Supplement Explain changes of state in terms of kinetic particle theory, including the interpretation of heating and cooling curves.
- Supplement Explain, in terms of kinetic particle theory, the effects of temperature and pressure on the volume of a gas.

Common misconceptions

Some students think that the particles in a liquid are not touching, that is, that the arrangement of particles in a liquid is closer to that of a gas than to that of a solid.

Resources

Student Book pages 11–15

Worksheet C1.1b The particulate nature of matter

Approach

Refer to the particle arrangements in solids, liquids and gases. Emphasise the arrangements and movements of the particles in each model.

Ask students to speculate on the strength of the forces between the particles in the three models. Then ask them to use their ideas to explain why gases expand on heating more than solids and liquids. Refer to the changes in the arrangement of particles as a solid changes into a liquid and then into a gas.

Emphasise the names of the key processes: melting/freezing, evaporating/boiling/condensing. Ensure that students understand the different types of movement of the particles. They should also understand the average energy of the particles in each of the three states of matter – solid (vibration – relatively low energy), liquid (moving around – translation – more energy than in a solid hence the possibility of evaporation) and gas (rapid movement – translation – relatively high energy). Ask the students to use the kinetic model to predict the relationship between pressure and volume, and temperature and pressure, of a gas.

Supplement Use the flowchart on page 12 of the Student Book to emphasise the nature of the changes in particles as one state changes into another.

Finally, use Worksheet C1.1b to check that students understand the key differences between the three states.

Answers

Science in Context, page 14

The particles of fine sand are able to flow like the particles in a liquid.

Page 15

1. The particles in a solid state vibrate about a fixed point.
2. Water particles are held together more strongly in solid water.
3. Evaporation is the process in which faster-moving particles escape from the surface of the liquid.
4. A solid changes to a liquid at its melting point.
5. Supplement Increasing pressure will force the particles of the gas to move closer together, restricting their movement. As the particles will be closer together the volume, the space they occupy, will be less.

Worksheet C1.1b

1. False;   2. True;   3. True;   4. True;   5. True;   6. True;   7. True;
8. False;   9. True;   10. True;   11. False;   12. False.

Note: 11 – at the melting point, generally, the volume of solid and volume of liquid will be the same.

Topic 1.1: States of matter

Worksheet C1.1b The particulate nature of matter

Cut out the cards and then sort them into piles of 'True', 'False' or 'Not sure'.

1	2	3
In a solid the particles are not moving.	The particles in a gas are very far apart.	In a liquid the particles will be constantly bumping into each other.

4	5	6
The particles in a gas are moving at high speed.	The particles in a solid are held together by various types of forces.	Solid A has a higher melting point than solid B so the forces holding the particles together in A are stronger than those in B.

7	8	9
As a liquid is heated the particles move faster.	As a solid is heated the particles stay still.	The forces between gas particles are very small.

10	11	12
When a liquid evaporates particles escape from the surface of the liquid.	When a solid melts and forms a liquid the particles usually move further apart.	When gas particles mix together, this is known as dispersion.

Topic 1.1: States of matter

Learning episode C1.1c Diffusion

Learning objectives

- Describe and explain diffusion in terms of kinetic particle theory.
- **Supplement** Describe and explain the effect of relative molecular mass on the rate of diffusion of gases.

Common misconceptions

Some students think that gas particles move relatively slowly because the diffusion of gases is relatively slow.

Resources

Student Book pages 16–18

Resources for demonstration and class practical (see Technician's notes, below)

Approach

Arrange a mixture of student practical activities and demonstrations. For example:

Student practical activities – diffusion

1. Add a crystal of potassium manganate(VII) to still water in a Petri dish. Leave the Petri dish unmoved for at least 20 minutes. Compare observations with those on page 16 of the Student Book.

2. Mix carbon dioxide and air in test-tubes and test with limewater (a safer alternative to the hydrogen and air equivalent – see Student Book page 17). You may have to introduce the test for carbon dioxide if students have not seen it before.

A simple carbon dioxide generator (marble chips and dilute hydrochloric acid) can be used to provide a source of the gas. One test-tube is filled with carbon dioxide and then connected vertically to a test-tube containing air. The tubes are held together for a few minutes and then each tube is tested with limewater to identify carbon dioxide.

The experiment can be performed twice: once with the carbon dioxide test-tube on the bottom; once with the carbon dioxide test-tube on the top. You should be able to observe diffusion in both cases, even though carbon dioxide is heavier than air.

SAFETY INFORMATION
Wear eye protection (splash-proof goggles).
Potassium manganate(VII) oxidising, moderate hazard and hazardous to the aquatic environment. Do not pour potassium manganate(VII) down the sink.
Limewater moderate hazard.

Supplement Demonstration: diffusion of hydrogen chloride and ammonia (see tech notes)

Hydrogen chloride and ammonia – see Student Book page 17. Pay attention to safety – this demonstration needs to be set up very carefully. The concentrated hydrochloric acid and concentrated ammonia solution must be in separate small beakers and kept a good distance apart (or kept in stoppered reagent bottles), in a fume cupboard. Soak one cotton wool ball in each solution and squeeze to remove excess liquid. Use tongs or tweezers to carefully place the cotton wool in the ends of the long tube. Replace the rubber bungs. While you are waiting you can demonstrate what happens when the two gases come into contact with each other.

Supplement Students can then tackle the Developing Practical Skills section on page 17 of the Student Book.

Topic 1.1: States of matter

> **SAFETY INFORMATION**
>
> *Wear eye protection (splash-proof goggles).*
>
> *Keep hydrogen chloride and ammonia solutions in separate beakers and a suitable distance apart, or in stoppered reagent bottles, in a fume cupboard. Avoid inhaling vapour and wear chemical resistant gloves. Use tongs or tweezers to handle cotton wool soaked with hydrogen chloride and ammonia solutions.*

Technician's notes

Be sure to check the latest safety notes on these resources before proceeding.

The following resources are needed for the demonstration and class practical on diffusion, per group:

potassium manganate(VII) crystals and Petri dishes
carbon dioxide generator (marble chips and dilute hydrochloric acid), test-tubes
limewater and droppers

The following resources are needed for the demonstration of diffusion of hydrogen chloride and ammonia:

long glass tube, cotton wool balls, rubber bungs, stands and clamps (Student book page 17)
concentrated ammonia solution, beaker and tongs
concentrated hydrochloric acid solution, beaker and tongs

Answers

Developing Practical Skills, page 18

1. Using tongs and with the students wearing eye protection and rubber gloves.
2. Avoiding breathing the fumes or use a fume cupboard.
3. The ammonia.
4. It travelled approximately twice as far as the hydrogen chloride.
5. The hydrogen chloride has approximately double the relative molecular mass of the ammonia

Page 18

1. Diffusion is the mixing and moving of particles in liquids and gases.
2. The particles in the potassium manganate(VII) dissolve in the water and diffuse throughout the solution.
3. The particles of perfume vapour/gas diffuse in the air and spread throughout the whole room.
4. **Supplement** Hydrogen has a much lower relative molecular mass than oxygen (M_r H_2 = 2; M_r O_2 = 32), so the particles of hydrogen will move more rapidly at a particular temperature than those of oxygen. As a result the hydrogen will diffuse more rapidly than oxygen

Topic 1.1: States of matter

Learning episode C1.1d Consolidation and summary

Learning aims

- Review the learning points of the topic summarised in the end of topic checklist.
- Test understanding of the topic content by answering the end of topic questions.

Resources

Student Book pages 19–21

Approach

Explain that for the rest of the course the term 'particle' will not be precise enough. Students will need to use terms like 'atoms' and 'molecules' (and 'ions') correctly to identify the type of particle. Emphasise that students will be learning more about these types of particles in the topics that follow.

Use the science in context feature on *The States of Matter* (Student Book page 14) to discuss plasma as a potential fourth state of matter. This content is beyond the syllabus but provides the opportunity to explore the content more deeply.

Ask students to work with a partner to make a list of key words from this topic. They could then work together to produce a spider diagram showing how the different concepts are linked. They could compare their list with the list of key terms given in the Student Book. Discuss the checklist and ask questions to see how much of the content students are comfortable with.

Students could make flashcards of the key content and then use the flashcards to quiz each other on the information.

Ask students to work individually through the end of topic questions in the Student Book without looking at the text. As they work, walk around the classroom observing their answers and questioning them as necessary to find out which questions are causing difficulties.

After a set period, ask students to stop working. Discuss any areas of difficulty you observed as you walked round the class.

Students should complete any unanswered questions for homework, but you should stress that they should answer the questions without looking at the text, so that they can see how much they have remembered.

Topic 1.1: States of matter

End of topic questions mark scheme

The marks available for a question can indicate the level of detail you need to provide in your answer.

Question	Correct answer	Marks
1	Gas.	1 mark
2	The particles in a liquid are close together, often touching.	1 mark
	The particles can move around and are not in a fixed position.	1 mark
3	Solid.	1 mark
4	The forces between the particles (atoms) in aluminium are greater than those between the particles (atoms) in sodium.	1 mark
5	B	1 mark
6	The boiling point.	1 mark
7	The particles in a liquid are constantly moving even at low temperatures in the polar regions.	1 mark
	Water particles can break away from the surface (evaporate) and form water vapour.	1 mark
8	The student's statement is correct. In both solids and liquids the particles are quite close together – in a gas the particles are much further apart.	1 mark
	The speeds at which the particles in solids and liquids are moving are more similar – in a gas the particles are moving at very high speeds.	1 mark
9	Diffusion.	1 mark
10	There is no physical barrier between the particles of bromine and air. The particles in these gases are moving at high speed and colliding with each other.	1 mark
	Over time the mixing will be complete and so there will be air and bromine particles in both gas jars.	1 mark
Supplement 11 a)	As the temperature increases the particles move more rapidly and move further apart. As a result the volume increases.	1 mark
Supplement 11 b)	As pressure increases the particles of the gas will move closer together and so the volume will decrease.	1 mark
Supplement 12	Nitrogen will diffuse at the greatest rate.	1 mark
	Nitrogen has the lowest (relative) molecular mass.	1 mark
	Total:	18 marks

Section 2: Atoms, elements and compounds

Contents

C2.1 Atoms, elements and compounds

C2.2 Ions and ionic bonds

C2.3 Molecules and covalent bonds

C2.4 Metallic bonding

Overview of the section

As the list of contents suggests, this section is focused on chemical bonding. Fundamental to the study of chemical bonding are the substances in which bonding is critical, i.e. compounds and not mixtures. This leads on to the different types of bonding in elements, including giant covalent structures such as diamond and graphite, and then on to metals. The nature of atomic structure underpins the study with the importance of electronic structure a key feature. Nuclear structure is also considered through the study of isotopes.

Detailed study starts with ionic bonding and then, in the next subsection, covalent bonding. The differences in these types of bonding lead to the typical properties of ionic and covalent compounds.

The section as a whole is an essential starting point for much of the remaining content of the course. For example, ionic bonding is crucial in the study of electrochemistry, and covalent bonding in the study of organic compounds.

Starting points

The Student Book section opener (pages 22–23) puts the ideas in the section into context and sets the scene. It also allows students to acknowledge and value their prior learning, and provides a benchmark against which future learning can be compared.

The questions provide a structure for introducing the section and can be used in a number of different ways:

- You could ask students to consider the questions as an introductory homework task.
- You could put students into groups to share their own ideas and understanding and then to report back to the whole class.
- Students could be given access to the Internet, preferably with a tight timescale, to find out the information required.

You could then use a spider chart or other form of wall chart to summarise everybody's ideas.

Recording these initial ideas allows you to retain them for reference as the individual topics are developed. In this way, your students' progress in learning can be readily acknowledged.

C2.1 Atoms, elements and compounds

Introduction

This topic is the basis for future work on chemical bonding and more detailed work on the Periodic Table. It has strong links to Topic 2.2 *Ions and ionic bonds*, Topic 2.3 M*olecules and covalent bonds,* Topic 2.4 *Metallic bonding* and Section 8 *The Periodic Table*.

The work on atomic structure introduces the subatomic particles. This leads students to drawing and interpreting diagrams showing the numbers of protons and neutrons, and the arrangement of electrons in shells. There is reference to isotopes and the important uses of radioactive isotopes. There are no opportunities for practical work but plenty of opportunities for individual and group work.

Links to other topics

Section	Essential background knowledge	Useful links
1 States of matter	1.1 States of matter	
2 Atoms, elements and compounds		2.2 Ions and ionic bonds
		2.3 Molecules and covalent bonds
		2.4 Metallic bonding
8 The Periodic Table		8.1 The Periodic Table

Topic overview

C2.1a	**Orientation**
	Students should be aware about the differences between elements, compounds and mixtures so this would be a good starting point. Students may have some knowledge of atomic structure and of particles called protons, neutrons and electrons. They may know something about how elements are arranged in the Periodic Table. The purpose of this learning episode is to find their level of understanding and to decide how much teaching time to spend on the topic.
C2.1b	**Subatomic particles**
	This learning episode starts with a brief consideration of Dalton's atomic theory. The learning episode then focuses on the protons, neutrons and electrons in an atom and how the standard representation of proton number and nucleon number gives information about the number of these particles in an atom.
	Consideration is also given to isotopes. A Science in Context section includes the nature and the uses of some radioactive isotopes.
	The arrangement of electrons is covered in the next learning episode.
C2.1c	**The arrangement of electrons in atoms**
	This learning episode introduces the arrangement of electrons in shells around the nucleus and the use of atom diagrams to represent the structure of an atom. The significance of the number of electrons in the outer electron shell is emphasised, along with the relationship between the number of electrons in the outer electron shell and the position of an element in the Periodic Table.
	This provides a very useful introduction to Section 8 *The Periodic Table*.
C2.1d	**Consolidation and summary**
	This learning episode provides a quick recap of the key ideas of the topic.

Career links

These are some scientific careers that focus on this area of chemistry but careers in many other fields use the knowledge and skills gained studying science.

Radiographers are trained medical professionals who use radioactive isotopes to diagnose and treat diseases.

Researchers, engineers and nuclear physicists at the CERN institute conduct experiments to study the fundamental particles making up all matter.

Topic 2.1: Atoms, elements and compounds

Learning episode C2.1a Orientation

Learning objective

- Describe the differences between elements, compounds and mixtures.

Common misconceptions

Some students think that all atoms of the same element are the same (that is, they ignore the existence of isotopes).

Resources

Student Book pages 22–24

Worksheet C2.1a What do you know about atomic structure?

Approach

The orientation exercise can be based around the True/False quiz on Worksheet C2.1a. The 'not sure' column is meant to stop students from guessing. Collect students' responses and explore any areas of misunderstanding and lack of knowledge. You should then be able to determine how much time to devote to each of the activities that follow. You can then share the overall objectives of the topic.

Answers

Worksheet C2.1a

1. True
2. True
3. True
4. False (the hydrogen atom has an isotope with no neutrons).
5. False (the electron is the smallest).
6. False (only protons and neutrons are found in the nucleus).
7. False (a proton has a positive charge).
8. True
9. True
10. False (not all isotopes are radioactive).
11. True
12. True

Topic 2.1: Atoms, elements and compounds

Worksheet C2.1a What do you know about atomic structure?

This quiz is intended to find out what you already know about atoms and their structure. For each statement, choose one option from TRUE, FALSE, NOT SURE.

STATEMENT	TRUE	FALSE	NOT SURE
1. All substances are made up of atoms.			
2. An atom is the smallest particle of an element that can exist on its own.			
3. Hydrogen is the smallest/lightest atom.			
4. Atoms are always made up of three subatomic particles called protons, neutrons and electrons.			
5. Protons are the smallest of these subatomic particles.			
6. The subatomic particles are found in the nucleus of the atom.			
7. A proton is a particle with a negative charge.			
8. A neutron is a particle with no charge.			
9. Isotopes are atoms of the same element with different numbers of neutrons.			
10. Isotopes are radioactive.			
11. Elements are arranged in the Periodic Table in order of the number of protons they have.			
12. Elements are arranged in the Periodic Table in order of the number of electrons they have.			

Topic 2.1: Atoms, elements and compounds

Learning episode C2.1b Subatomic particles

Learning objectives

- Describe the structure of the atom as a central nucleus containing neutrons and protons surrounded by electrons in shells.
- State the relative charges and relative masses of a proton, a neutron and an electron.
- Define proton number / atomic number as the number of protons in the nucleus of an atom.
- Define mass number / nucleon number as the total number of protons and neutrons in the nucleus of an atom.
- Define isotopes as different atoms of the same element that have the same number of protons but different numbers of neutrons.
- Interpret and use symbols for atoms, e.g. $^{12}_{6}C$, and ions, e.g. $^{35}_{17}Cl^-$.
- Supplement State that isotopes of the same element have the same chemical properties because they have the same number of electrons and therefore the same electronic configuration.
- Supplement Calculate the relative atomic mass of an element from the relative masses and abundances of its isotopes.

Common misconceptions

Some students think that all isotopes are radioactive.

Resources

Student Book pages 25–29

Approach

This is a relatively brief learning episode starting with consideration of Dalton's atomic theory. All the key learning points are covered in the Student Book pages. Electron arrangements and atom diagrams are covered in learning episode C2.1c.

Once you have introduced the relative masses and charges of the proton, neutron and electron and the proton number/nucleon number notation (atomic number/mass number notation), ask students to use this notation to work out the structures of a number of atoms. Some possible examples include:

$^{56}_{26}Fe$ $^{127}_{53}I$ $^{108}_{47}Ag$ $^{197}_{79}Au$ $^{80}_{35}Br$ $^{35}_{17}Cl$ $^{37}_{17}Cl$

Chlorine is included to introduce the idea of isotopes. Looking at the Periodic Table shows that the proton number is used but the relative atomic mass is used in preference to the nucleon number. For a number of elements, the relative atomic mass is not a whole number (for example, Cl 35.5) – this clearly shows that the atom must have a number of different isotopes.

Refer to the uses of some radioactive isotopes (Science in Context page 29) and emphasise that not all isotopes are radioactive. Refer to the Science in Context feature on subatomic particles (Student Book page 29).The content of these Science in Context features is beyond the syllabus but provides the opportunity to explore the content more deeply.

Supplement Explain that isotopes of the same element have the same chemical properties as they have the same number of electrons in their outer electron shells (electron arrangements are covered later).

Topic 2.1: Atoms, elements and compounds

Answers

Page 27

1. The electron has the smallest relative mass.

2. Atoms are neutral. The number of positive charges (protons) must equal the number of negative charges (electrons).

3. a) The nucleon number is 27.

   b) 14 neutrons.

Science in Context, page 29

Add a liquid containing a radioactive tracer to the sewage system. After a reasonable time period use a radioactive counter to take readings above ground on the route of the sewage pipe. A higher reading would indicate where the tracer is leaking out of the pipe into the ground.

Science in Context, page 30

The Big Bang theory is the most common theory for explaining how the current stars and galaxies were formed. The theory suggests that the starting point was a very hot, small and dense 'point' which expanded very rapidly. The universe is still expanding today.

Page 30

1. Isotopes are atoms of the same element with different numbers of neutrons.
2. Supplement Different isotopes of the same element have the same number of electrons. Chemical properties are determined by the number and arrangement of electrons.
3. Supplement The relative atomic mass of copper = 63.6. (The abundances were rounded up; copper is usually quoted with a relative atomic mass of 63.5.)

Topic 2.1: Atoms, elements and compounds

Learning episode C2.1c The arrangement of electrons in atoms

Learning objectives

- Determine the electronic configuration of elements, and their ions with proton number 1 to 20, e.g. 2,8,3.
- State that:
(a) Group VIII noble gases have a full outer shell
(b) The number of outer shell electrons is equal to the group number in Groups I to VII
(c) The number of occupied electron shells is equal to the period number.

Resources

Student Book pages 30–33

Worksheet C2.1c Atomic structures

Approach

This learning episode follows closely from the previous. Introduce the idea that electron shells can hold a maximum number of electrons, and that these numbers differ depending on which shell is being occupied by electrons.

Use the Student Book to illustrate the nature of atom diagrams and then the detailed electronic structure of the first 20 elements. You can then make the link between the number of outer electrons and the position of the element in the Periodic Table. This idea will be revised at the start of Section 8 *The Periodic Table*.

Use Worksheet C2.1c to reinforce the ideas introduced in this learning episode.

Answers

Page 33

1. a) 2 electrons.

   b) Magnesium is in Group II.

2. a) Aluminium   b) Calcium

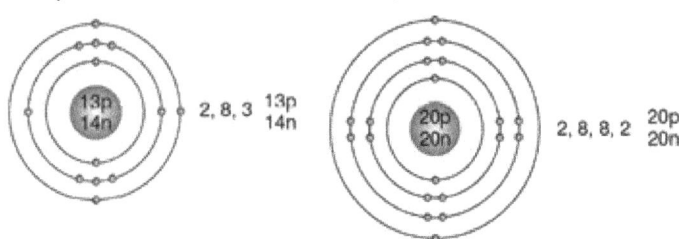

3. The noble gases have a full outer shell of electrons or have 8 electrons in their outer shell and so do not lose or gain their electrons easily.

Topic 2.1: Atoms, elements and compounds

Worksheet C2.1c

1.

Atom	Proton number	Nucleon number	No. of protons	No. of neutrons	No. of electrons
Carbon, C	6	12	6	6	6
Nitrogen, N	7	**14**	7	7	7
Chlorine, Cl	**17**	35	17	**18**	17
Sodium, Na	11	23	11	12	11
Argon, Ar	**18**	40	**18**	**22**	18
Uranium, U	92	238	92	146	92

2. First shell: 2; second shell: 8; third shell: 8

3. Students' diagrams show:

	Li	C	N	O	Ne	Na	Cl	Ar
Protons	3	6	7	8	10	11	17	18
Neutrons	4	6	7	8	10	12	18	22
Electron arrangement	2,1	2,4	2,5	2,6	2,8	2,8,1	2,8,7	2,8,8

4.

Element	Electronic configuration	Element	Electronic configuration	Element	Electronic configuration
Hydrogen	1				
Helium	2				
Lithium	2,1	Sodium	**2,8,1**	Potassium	**2,8,8,1**
Beryllium	**2,2**	Magnesium	**2,8,2**	Calcium	2,8,8,2
Boron	**2,3**	Aluminium	**2,8,3**		
Carbon	2,4	Silicon	**2,8,4**		
Nitrogen	2,5	Phosphorus	**2,8,5**		
Oxygen	2.6	Sulfur	**2,8,6**		
Fluorine	2,7	Chlorine	**2,8,7**		
Neon	**2,8**	Argon	2,8,8		

Topic 2.1: Atoms, elements and compounds

Worksheet C2.1c Atomic structures

1. Complete this table for proton number and nucleon number.

Atom	Proton number	Nucleon number	No. of protons	No. of neutrons	No. of electrons
Carbon, C	6	12			
Nitrogen, N	7			7	
Chlorine, Cl		35	17		
Sodium, Na		23		12	
Argon, Ar		40			18
Uranium, U	92	238			

2. Electrons moving around the nucleus are arranged in shells. How many electrons can each shell hold? Complete this diagram and explain what is meant by an atom's **electronic configuration**.

The third shell can hold up to _____

The second shell can hold up to _____ electrons

The first shell can hold up to _____

Topic 2.1: Atoms, elements and compounds

3. Complete these atom diagrams to show
   a) the composition of the nucleus
   b) the electronic configuration, by drawing crosses to represent electrons.

lithium, Li proton number 3 nucleon number 7	carbon, C proton number 6 nucleon number 12	nitrogen, N proton number 7 nucleon number 14	oxygen, O proton number 8 nucleon number 16
neon, Ne proton number 10 nucleon number 20	sodium, Na proton number 11 nucleon number 23	chlorine, Cl proton number 17 nucleon number 35	argon, Ar proton number 18 nucleon number 40

4. a) Complete the missing electronic configurations for the first 20 elements:

Element	electronic configuration	Element	Electronic configuration	Element	Electronic configuration
Hydrogen	1				
Helium	2				
Lithium	2,1	Sodium		Potassium	
Beryllium		Magnesium		Calcium	2,8,8,2
Boron		Aluminium			
Carbon	2,4	Silicon			
Nitrogen		Phosphorus			
Oxygen		Sulfur			
Fluorine	2,7	Chlorine			
Neon		Argon	2,8,8		

b) In your own words, explain why the electronic configurations of atoms are important.

Topic 2.1: Atoms, elements and compounds

Learning episode C2.1d Consolidation and summary

Learning aims

- Review the learning points of the topic summarised in the end of topic checklist.
- Test understanding of the topic content by answering the end of topic questions.

Resources

Student Book pages 34–37

Approach

Ask students to work with a partner to make a list of key words from this topic. They could then work together to produce a spider diagram showing how the different concepts are linked. They could compare their list with the list of key terms given in the Student Book. Discuss the checklist and ask questions to see how much of the content students are comfortable with.

Students could make flashcards of the key content and then use the flashcards to quiz each other on the information.

Ask students to work individually through the end of topic questions in the Student Book without looking at the text. As they work, walk around the classroom observing their answers and questioning them as necessary to find out which questions are causing difficulties.

After a set period, ask students to stop working. Discuss any areas of difficulty you observed as you walked round the class.

Students should complete any unanswered questions for homework, but you should stress that they should answer the questions without looking at the text, so that they can see how much they have remembered. Focus on the end of topic checklist and questions. Aim for a mix of individual and group work and provide plenty of opportunities for the students to articulate their ideas and understanding.

End of topic questions mark scheme

The marks available for a question can indicate the level of detail you need to provide in your answer.

Question	Correct answer	Marks
1	C	1 mark
2 a)	The proton number is the number of protons (= number of electrons) in an atom.	1 mark
2 b)	The nucleon number is the number of protons + neutrons in an atom.	1 mark
3 a)	Isotopes are atoms of the same element with different numbers of neutrons.	1 mark
3 b)	chlorine-35: 17 protons; 18 neutrons; 17 electrons.	1 mark
	chlorine-37: 17 protons; 20 neutrons; 17 electrons.	1 mark
4 a)	Treating cancerous tumours OR sterilising medical equipment.	1 mark
4 b)	As a tracer for detecting leaks in pipes.	1 mark

Topic 2.1: Atoms, elements and compounds

Question	Correct answer	Marks
5	Completed table as shown below:	4 marks

Atom	Number of protons	Number of neutrons	Number of electrons	Electron arrangement
Si	14	14	14	2,8,4
Mg	12	12	12	2,8,2
S	16	16	16	2,8,6
Ar	18	22	18	2,8,8

Question	Correct answer	Marks
6 a)	i) C	1 mark
	ii) B	1 mark
	iii) C or E or F	1 mark
	iv) B	1 mark
	v) C	1 mark
6 b)	Diagram should have 6 protons and 8 neutrons in the nucleus.	1 mark
	There should be 2 electron shells with 2 electrons in the inner shell, and 4 in the outer shell.	1 mark
7 a)	Diagram should have 8 protons and 8 neutrons in the nucleus. There should be two electron shells with 2 electrons in the inner shell and 6 electrons in the outer shell.	2 marks
7 b)	Diagram should have 19 protons and 20 neutrons in the nucleus. There should be 4 electrons shells with electrons arranged as 2,8,8,1.	2 marks
8 a)	False	1 mark
8 b)	False	1 mark
8 c)	False	1 mark
8 d)	True. The number of electrons in the outer shell is the same as the group number.	1 mark
9 Supplement	Chemical properties depend on the number of electrons.	1 mark
	Both isotopes have the same number of electrons (17).	1 mark
10 Supplement	$\dfrac{(24 \times 79) + (25 \times 10) + (26 \times 11)}{100}$	1 mark
	= 24.32	1 mark
	Total:	31 marks

C2.2 Ions and ionic bonds

Introduction

This topic builds on previous ideas about atomic structure from Topic 2.1 *Atoms, elements and compounds*. It links to covalent bonding in Topic 2.3 *Molecules and covalent bonds*. There are also a number of other topics where knowledge of ions and ionic bonding is fundamental to understanding the content. These include Topic 4.1 *Electrochemistry*; Topic 7.1 *Acids, bases and salts*; Topic 8.2 *Group I elements*; Topic 8.3 *Group VII elements*; Topic 12.2 *Identification of ions and gases*. For the supplementary syllabus there are also links to Topic 6.3 *Redox reactions*.

This topic has two main aspects: the nature of ionic bonding and, for following the supplementary syllabus, the lattice structure and associated properties of ionic compounds.

Links to other topics

Section	Essential background knowledge	Useful links
2 Atoms, elements and compounds	2.1 Atoms, elements and compounds	2.3 Molecules and covalent bonds
4 Electrochemistry		4.1 Electrochemistry
6 Chemical reactions		6.3 Redox reactions
8 The Periodic Table		8.2 Group I elements
		8.3 Group VII elements
12 Experimental techniques		12.2 Identification of ions and gases

Topic overview

C2.2a	**Orientation**
	This learning episode recaps previous work on atomic structure, with emphasis on electron arrangements.
	Considering the properties of ionic compounds provides an insight into the nature of the bonding in these compounds.
C2.2b	**The formation of ions**
	This learning episode involves modelling the process of ionic bonding and then provides plenty of practice for producing dot-and-cross diagrams. Reference to the relationship between ion charges and the Periodic Table will provide a link to future work in that area.
	Supplement Consideration is given to compounds formed by elements other than those in Group I and Group VII.
C2.2c	**Properties of ionic compounds**
	This learning episode focuses on the description of the characteristic properties of ionic compounds and contrasts them with other compounds (essentially covalent compounds).
	Supplement An explanation of the properties of ionic compounds in terms of structure and bonding provides greater depth. The idea of a giant ionic lattice structure as a representation of how ions are arranged in an ionic compound is also covered.
C2.2d	**Consolidation and summary**
	This learning episode provides a quick recap of the ideas encountered and an opportunity to answer the end of topic questions in the Student Book.

Topic 2.2: Ions and ionic bonds

Career links

These are some scientific careers that focus on this area of chemistry but careers in many other fields use the knowledge and skills gained studying science.

Geochemists study the composition of ionic compounds in the form of minerals in the Earth's mantle and crust to find resources such as metals and help with the understanding of environmental issues such as soil depletion.

Oceanographers study the presence of ions dissolved in seawater to measure changes in salinity which are influenced by climate change.

Topic 2.2: Ions and ionic bonds

Learning episode C2.2a Orientation

Learning aims

- To revise ideas on atomic structure.
- To map out the main purposes of the topic.
- Know the structure of an atom by interpreting proton and nucleon numbers.
- Know the arrangement of electrons in shells for the first 20 elements.

Common misconceptions

Some students think that all compounds are made up of molecules.

Resources

Student Book page 26

Approach

Start by revising the ideas on atomic structure, emphasising the electronic structures of atoms and the arrangement of electrons in shells around the nucleus.

Ask students to research the melting points of some common substances, including a range of ionic compounds and covalent compounds. Ask them to see if there is a pattern in the compounds that have melting points in the higher ranges. The students should identify the inclusion of a metal as a common feature.

Supplement Explain that these properties must be a result of how metals and non-metals combine together – a process that produces particles known as ions.

Topic 2.2: Ions and ionic bonds

Learning episode C2.2b The formation of ions

Learning objectives

- Describe the formation of positive ions, known as cations, and negative ions, known as anions.
- State that an ionic bond is a strong electrostatic attraction between oppositely charged ions.
- Describe the formation of ionic bonds between elements from Group I and Group VII, including the use of dot-and-cross diagrams.
- Supplement Describe the formation of ionic bonds between ions of metallic and non-metallic elements, including the use of dot-and-cross diagrams.

Common misconceptions

Some students think that all compounds are made up of molecules.

Resources

Student Book pages 38–40

Worksheet C2.2b Ionic bonding: dot-and-cross diagrams

Approach

Revise the idea of atom diagrams. Use the examples on page 39 of the Student Book to introduce dot-and-cross diagrams.

Emphasise the importance of electron transfer from metal to non-metal. In the examples that students are likely to meet, both the metal and non-metal acquire a full outer shell of electrons (that is, 2 or 8). Take time to explain that the resulting particles are no longer atoms (no longer neutral) and are known as ions.

Emphasise that the ion charges in the chemical formula of an ionic compound cancel each other out. Use the questions on page 41 of the Student Book to allow for practice producing simple dot-and-cross diagrams.

Ask students if they can see a pattern between the charge on the resulting ions and their position in the Periodic Table.

Supplement Students consider the formation of ionic bonds where more than one electron is transferred (that is, compounds other than those formed from Group I and Group VII elements). Worksheet C2b.2 gives some examples of the transfer of more than one electron.

Answers

Page 41

1.

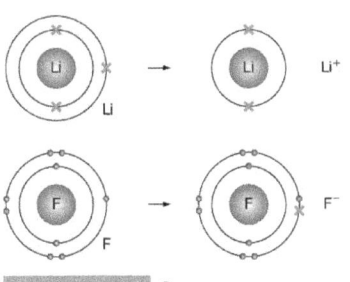

Supplement 2.

Topic 2.2: Ions and ionic bonds

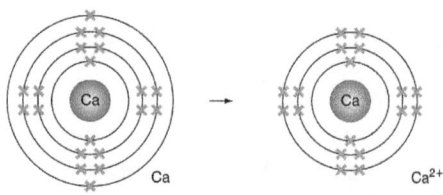

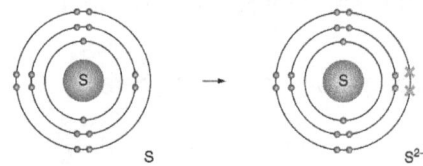

Supplement 3. Both phosphorus and oxygen are non-metals. (A metal is needed to form an ionic bond.)

Supplement Worksheet C2.2b

Potassium oxide

2K (2,8,8,1) → 2K⁺ (2,8,8)   O (2,6) → O²⁻ (2,8)

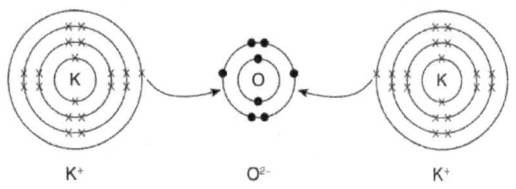

Calcium chloride

Ca (2,8,8,2) → Ca²⁺ (2,8,8)   2Cl (2,8,7) → 2Cl⁻ (2,8,8)

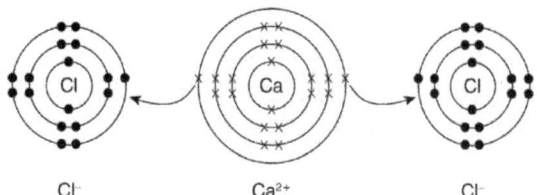

Lithium sulfide

2Li (2,1) → 2Li⁺ (2)   S (2,8,6) → S²⁻ (2,8,8)

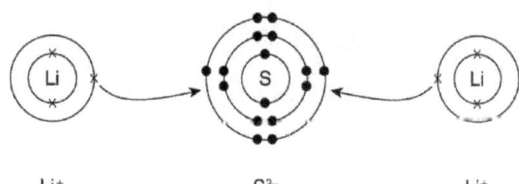

Aluminium oxide

2Al (2,8,3) → 2Al³⁺ (2,8)   3O (2,6) → 3O²⁻ (2,8)

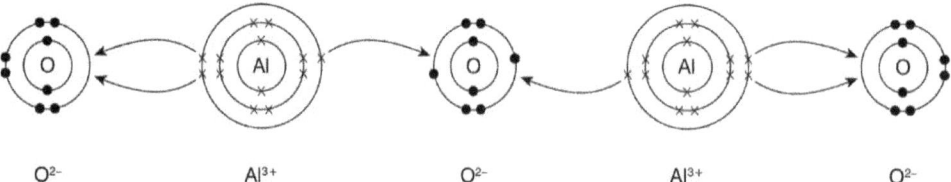

Topic 2.2: Ions and ionic bonds

Supplement Worksheet C2.2b Ionic bonding: dot-and-cross diagrams

Ionic bonding is the type of bonding that occurs between metals and non-metals. Metal atoms lose electrons from their outer electron shells and form positive ions; non-metal atoms gain electrons to fill their outer electron shells and form negative ions.

Remember: The number of positive and negative charges must balance.

Draw dot-and-cross diagrams to show the ionic bonding in the following compounds. Write the formulae of the ions formed in each case.

Potassium oxide   (Proton numbers O = 8; K = 19)
Calcium chloride   (Proton numbers Cl = 17; Ca = 20)
Lithium sulfide   (Proton numbers Li = 3; S = 16)
Aluminium oxide   (Proton numbers O = 8; Al = 13)

Topic 2.2: Ions and ionic bonds

Learning episode C2.2c Properties of ionic compounds

Learning objectives

- Describe the properties of ionic compounds:
(a) high melting points and boiling points
(b) good electrical conductivity when aqueous or molten and poor when solid.
- Supplement Describe the giant lattice structure of ionic compounds as a regular arrangement of alternating positive and negative ions.
    - Supplement Explain in terms of structure and bonding the properties of ionic compounds:
    (a) high melting points and boiling points
    (b) good electrical conductivity when aqueous or molten and poor when solid.

Resources

Student Book pages 41–44

Resources for a demonstration (see Technician's notes, below)

Approach

Use Table 2.7 on page 42 of the Student Book to summarise the properties of sodium chloride. Mention that these properties apply to all ionic compounds. Refer to the Science in Context feature on ionic crystals (Student Book page 43). The content of these Science in Context features is beyond the syllabus but provides the opportunity to explore the content more deeply.

Supplement If possible, use models to illustrate the 3D structure of ionic compounds such as sodium chloride. Explain that the attractions between positive and negative ions are called electrostatic attractions and that multiple attractions in all directions produce a very strong structure that is not easily broken down; for example, the melting point of sodium chloride is 801 °C. Use this structure to support the explanations in Table 2.7.

Supplement Ask students how the properties of magnesium oxide would compare with those of sodium chloride. Explain the higher melting point of magnesium oxide in terms of a stronger electrostatic attraction between doubly charged ions. You may refer to aluminium oxide as a further example of the concept.

Technician's notes

Be sure to check the latest safety notes on these resources before proceeding.

The following resources are needed for the demonstration of models of ionic structure:

molecular model, made up to show two or three ionic compounds such as sodium chloride

Topic 2.2: Ions and ionic bonds

Answers

Science in Context, page 43

Aluminium oxide is an ionic compound containing Al^{3+} ions and O^{2-} ions. As a result of the high charges on these ions, they form a lattice with very strong electrostatic forces.

Science in Context, page 44

As calcium is below magnesium in Group II the calcium ion will be larger than the magnesium ion. As a result the packing arrangements in the two oxides will be different, as will the attractive force between the ions in the structure.

Page 44

1. High melting point, high boiling point, good conductor of electricity when aqueous or molten.
2. Supplement The ions are held together strongly in a giant lattice structure. The ions can vibrate but cannot move around.
3. Supplement Sodium chloride is made up of singly charged ions, Na^+ and Cl^-, whereas the magnesium ion in magnesium oxide has a double charge, Mg^{2+}. The higher the charge on the positive ion the stronger the attractive forces between the positive ion and the negative ion.

Topic 2.2: Ions and ionic bonds

Learning episode C2.2d Consolidation and summary

Learning aims

- Review the learning points of the topic summarised in the end of topic checklist.
  - Test understanding of the topic content by answering the end of topic questions.

Resources

Student Book pages 45–46

Approach

Ask students to work with a partner to make a list of key words from this topic. They could then work together to produce a spider diagram showing how the different concepts are linked. They could compare their list with the list of key terms given in the Student Book. Discuss the checklist and ask questions to see how much of the content students are comfortable with.

Students could make flashcards of the key content and then use the flashcards to quiz each other on the information.

Ask students to work individually through the end of topic questions in the Student Book without looking at the text. As they work, walk around the classroom observing their answers and questioning them as necessary to find out which questions are causing difficulties.

After a set period, ask students to stop working. Discuss any areas of difficulty you observed as you walked round the class.

Students should complete any unanswered questions for homework, but you should stress that they should answer the questions without looking at the text, so that they can see how much they have remembered.

If you have chosen to teach Topic 2.3 M*olecules and covalent bonds* as the next topic, then the link can be emphasised.

Topic 2.2: Ions and ionic bonds

End of topic questions mark scheme

The marks available for a question can indicate the level of detail you need to provide in your answer.

Question	Correct answer	Marks
1	C	1 mark
2 a)	K^+ OR $[K]^+$	1 mark
2 b)	Al^{3+} OR $[Al]^{3+}$	1 mark
2 c)	S^{2-} OR $[S]^{2-}$	1 mark
2 d)	F^- OR $[F]^-$	1 mark
3	Completed table as shown below: <table><tr><th>Atom</th><th>Electronic arrangement of the atom</th><th>Electronic arrangement of the ion</th><th>Charge on the ion</th></tr><tr><td>X</td><td>2,6</td><td>2,8</td><td>2–</td></tr><tr><td>Y</td><td>2,8,8,2</td><td>2,8,8</td><td>2+</td></tr><tr><td>Z</td><td>2,1</td><td>2</td><td>1+ (or +)</td></tr></table>	3 marks
4	Diagram of potassium atom transferring an electron to a fluorine atom, forming K^+ and F^- (KF).	2 marks
Supplement 5 a)	Diagram showing 2 potassium atoms each transferring one electron to an oxygen atom, forming $2K^+$ and O^{2-} (K_2O).	2 marks
Supplement 5 b)	magnesium chlorine	2 marks

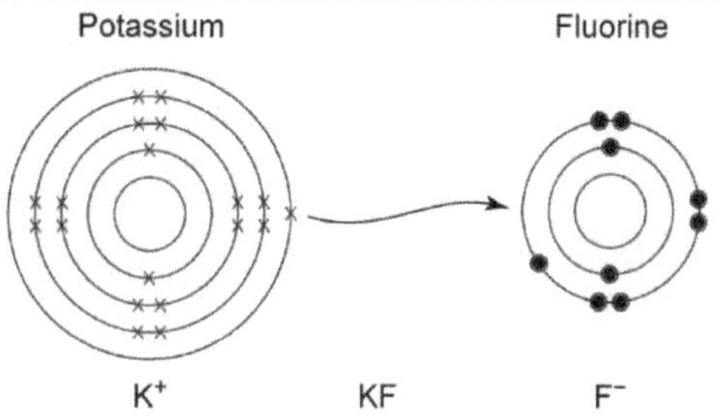

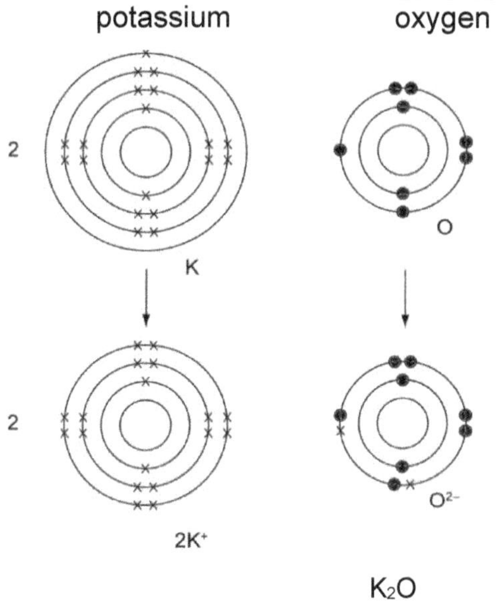

Topic 2.2: Ions and ionic bonds

Question	Correct answer	Marks
	(Diagrams showing Mg and Cl atoms with electron shells, arrows to Mg²⁺ and Cl⁻ ions)	
Supplement 6 a)	There are strong electrostatic attractive forces between the ions.	1 mark
	A lot of energy needs to be applied to break these attractions to form a liquid.	1 mark
Supplement 6 b)	The ions are able to carry the electric current.	1 mark
	The ions need to be free to move; therefore the potassium chloride needs either to be in a molten state or in solution.	1 mark
Supplement 7	Magnesium forms a 2+ ion, oxygen a 2– ion, sodium a 1+ ion and chlorine a 1– ion.	1 mark
	The electrostatic attraction between 2+ and 2– ions is greater than between 1+ and 1– ions, resulting in a higher melting point and boiling point.	1 mark
	Total:	20 marks

Topic 2.3: Molecules and covalent bonds

C2.3 Molecules and covalent bonds

Introduction

This topic builds on previous work on atomic structure. Students must understand the nature of covalent bonding and the properties of covalent compounds in order to study a number of topics later in the course.

Topic 2.1 *Atoms, elements and compounds* gave important information about electronic structures. Covalent bonding features in all the topics in Section 11 *Organic chemistry*. For the supplementary syllabus, bond breaking and forming is an aspect of Topic 5.1 *Chemical energetics*.

This topic has three main aspects: the nature of covalent bonding; the typical properties of covalent compounds and how they compare with the properties of ionic compounds; and the covalent bonding in the giant covalent structures of diamond, graphite and silicon(IV) oxide.

Links to other topics

Section	Essential background knowledge	Useful links
2 Atoms, elements and compounds	2.1 Atoms, elements and compounds	2.2 Ions and ionic bonds
5 Chemical energetics		5.1 Chemical energetics
11 Organic chemistry		11.2 Fuels
		11.3 Alkanes
		11.4 Alkenes
		11.5 Alcohols
		11.6 Carboxylic acids
		11.7 Polymers

Topic overview

C2.3a	Orientation
	This learning episode builds on earlier work on atomic structure and ionic bonding. Covalent bonding is contrasted with that of ionic bonding and the differences in typical properties of covalent and ionic compounds are highlighted.
C2.3b	**The formation of covalent molecules**
	This learning episode involves modelling the process of covalent bonding and then providing plenty of practice producing dot-and-cross diagrams. Reference to the relationship between the number of covalent bonds an atom can form and the Periodic Table will provide a link to future work in that area.
	Supplement The formation of multiple covalent bonds is considered through examples such as ethene, oxygen, carbon dioxide and nitrogen.
C2.3c	**Properties of simple covalent molecules**
	This learning episode focuses on the characteristic properties of simple covalent molecules and contrasts them with other compounds (essentially ionic compounds). It also introduces the idea of a relatively weak force existing between molecules in simple molecular substances.
	Supplement The differences in the melting and boiling points of simple covalent and ionic compounds are explained in terms of differences in the strength of the intermolecular

		forces.
C2.3d	**Giant covalent structures**	
	This learning episode looks at the nature of the covalent bonding and giant covalent structures in diamond and graphite. Differences in physical properties are explained in terms of their differing structures.	
	Supplement The giant covalent structure of silicon(IV) oxide is considered and similarities in the properties of diamond and silicon(IV) oxide are related to their structures.	
C2.3e	**Consolidation and summary**	
	This learning episode provides an opportunity for a quick recap of the ideas encountered in the topic as well as time for students to answer the end of topic questions in the Student Book.	

Career links

These are some scientific careers that focus on this area of chemistry but careers in many other fields use the knowledge and skills gained studying science.

A team of professors and academics at the University of Manchester, from backgrounds in material science, engineering, chemistry and physics, work together to research the properties and uses of graphite and graphene.

Cryogenicists use liquid nitrogen to study the effects of very cold temperatures on materials.

Topic 2.3: Molecules and covalent bonds

Learning episode C2.3a Orientation

Learning aims

- To revise ideas on atomic structure and ionic bonding.
- To map out the main purposes of the topic.
- Know the structure of an atom from its proton and nucleon numbers.
- Know the arrangement of electrons in shells for the first 20 elements.

Approach

If you choose to teach this topic soon after Topic 2.2 *Ions and ionic bonds*, you will be able to revise atomic structure very quickly. Refer to the exercise on melting points from C2.2a Orientation, and the differences between compounds made from only non-metals and those that contain a metal.

Explain that these differences can be explained in terms of the relative strengths of the attractive forces between the ions (in ionic compounds) and between the molecules in covalent compounds. Tell students that it is important to distinguish between the attractive forces **within** molecules (covalent bonds) and the attractive forces **between** molecules.

Explain that the topic will explore another way that atoms/elements can combine to form compounds. It will then look in more detail at the properties of compounds with covalent bonds (made up of molecules) compared with those with ionic bonds (made up of ions). Finally, the topic will focus on some giant covalent structures, looking at the structures and properties of diamond, graphite and silicon(IV) oxide (sand).

Topic 2.3: Molecules and covalent bonds

Learning episode C2.3b The formation of covalent molecules

Learning objectives

- State that a covalent bond is formed when a pair of electrons is shared between two atoms leading to noble gas electronic configurations.
- Describe the formation of covalent bonds in simple molecules, including H_2, Cl_2, H_2O, CH_4, NH_3 and HCl. Use dot-and-cross diagrams to show the electronic configurations in these and similar molecules.
- Supplement Describe the formation of covalent bonds in simple molecules, including CH_3OH, C_2H_4, O_2, CO_2 and N_2. Use dot-and-cross diagrams to show the electronic configurations in these and similar molecules.

Resources

Student Book pages 47–51

Worksheet C2.3b Covalent bonding: dot-and-cross diagrams

Approach

Use examples from the Student Book to illustrate how non-metals (which do not like to give up electrons) share electrons to achieve the electronic configuration of the nearest noble gas (full outer electron shells). Emphasise the importance of showing shared electrons in shared pairs in single (and multiple) covalent bonds.

It is also a good idea to show non-bonding electrons as electron pairs. This will help students to avoid mistakes in showing the correct number.

Introduce the structure of covalent molecules represented by a displayed formula. At this level it is acceptable to draw methane with a square planar displayed formula, as opposed to a pyramidal one.

Use the questions on page 50 of the Student Book and Worksheet C2.3b to give students practice at producing dot-and-cross diagrams.

Ask students if they notice a relationship between the number of covalent bonds an atom can form and its position in the Periodic Table.

Supplement Use the Student Book to look at the formation of molecules with more than two different types of atoms (methanol) and then with double covalent bonds (ethene, oxygen, carbon dioxide) and triple covalent bonds (nitrogen).

Topic 2.3: Molecules and covalent bonds

Answers

Page 50

1.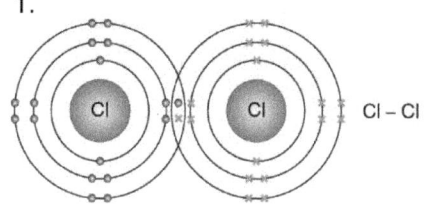

2.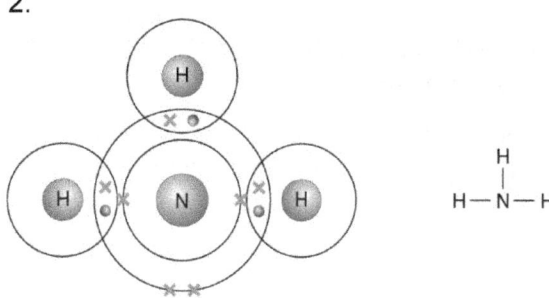

3. Supplement
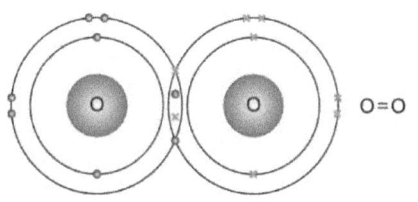

4. Supplement
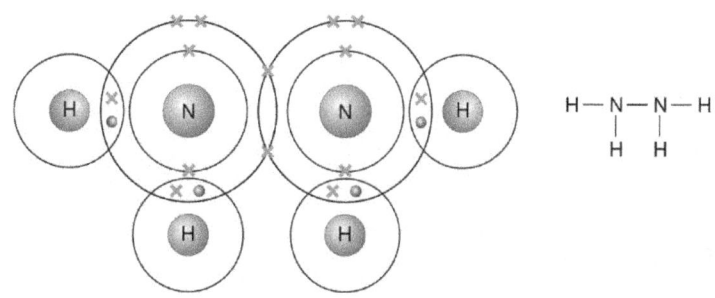

Worksheet C2.3b

Hydrogen sulfide
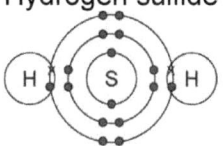

Chlorine oxide
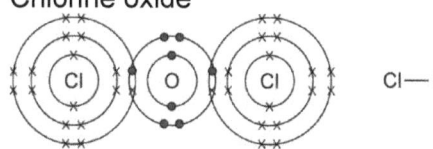

Phosphorus chloride
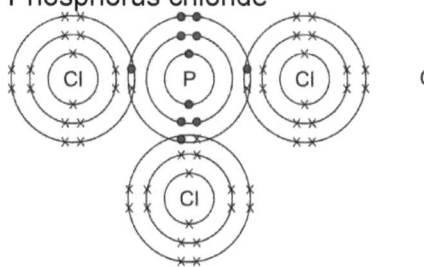

Propane Supplement
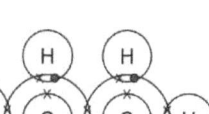 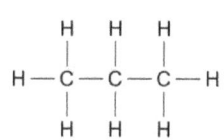

Topic 2.3: Molecules and covalent bonds

Worksheet C2.3b Covalent bonding: dot-and-cross diagrams

Covalent bonding is the type of bonding that occurs between non-metals. The atoms share electrons from their outer electron shells and form molecules. In most cases you will encounter, the atoms achieve the electron configuration of the nearest noble gas (a full outer shell of electrons) by sharing electrons with one or more other atoms.

Draw dot-and-cross diagrams to show the covalent bonding in the following compounds. Write the displayed formula of the molecule formed in each case. (You will need to consider how many atoms of each element will be in the compound.)

Hydrogen sulfide

(Proton numbers H = 1; S = 16)

Chlorine oxide

(Proton numbers O = 8; Cl = 17)

Phosphorus chloride

(Proton numbers P = 15; Cl = 17)

Supplement Propane

(Proton numbers H = 1; C = 6; propane contains hydrogen atoms and three carbon atoms)

Topic 2.3: Molecules and covalent bonds

Learning episode C2.3c Properties of simple covalent compounds

Learning objectives

- Describe in terms of structure and bonding the properties of simple molecular compounds:
  (a) low melting points and boiling points
  (b) poor electrical conductivity.
- Supplement Explain in terms of structure and bonding the properties of simple molecular compounds:
  (a) low melting points and boiling points in terms of weak intermolecular forces (specific types of intermolecular forces are **not** required)
  (b) poor electrical conductivity.

Common misconceptions

Some students think that a covalent bond is weaker than an ionic bond and that covalent bonds are weak bonds.

Resources

Student Book pages 51–52

Approach

Decide whether to introduce the terms 'intramolecular' and 'intermolecular' (these terms are not specifically required in the syllabus). Alternatively, you could use the terms 'within molecules' and 'between molecules'. Many students are confused by the difference, so it is worth spending a little time explaining this.

Use the table on page 52 of the Student Book to identify the characteristic properties of simple covalent compounds. Emphasise the lack of electrical conductivity due to the absence of ions.

Contrast the properties of these simple molecular structures with those that are characteristic of ionic compounds.

Supplement Ask the students to explain the differences in melting and boiling points of covalent and ionic compounds, in terms of the intermolecular forces.

Answers

Page 52

1. No. There are no ions or delocalised electrons present.
2. Supplement The intermolecular forces of attraction between the molecules are weak.

Topic 2.3: Molecules and covalent bonds

Learning episode C2.3d Giant covalent structures

Learning objectives

- Describe the giant covalent structures of graphite and diamond.
- Relate their structures and bonding to their uses, limited to:
  (a) graphite as a lubricant and as an electrode
  (b) diamond in cutting tools.
- **Supplement** Describe the giant covalent structure of silicon(IV) oxide, SiO_2.
- **Supplement** Describe the similarity in properties between diamond and silicon(IV) oxide, related to their structures.

Common misconceptions

Some students think that graphite is soft.

Resources

Student Book pages 52–55

Resources for a demonstration (see Technician's notes, below)

Approach

The structures and properties (such as melting point) of diamond and graphite illustrate very convincingly that covalent bonds are strong bonds. Use the term 'giant covalent structures'.

If possible, use models of the two structures to identify similarities and differences. Refer to the diagrams and explanations in the Student Book on page 53 and the Science in Context box on diamonds (page 54). The content of these Science in Context features is beyond the syllabus but provides the opportunity to explore the content more deeply.

Supplement Use the Student Book to look at the structure of silicon(IV) oxide (page 55). Emphasise that the tetrahedral arrangement is similar to the arrangement of carbon atoms in diamond. Refer to the comparison of properties of diamond and silicon(IV) oxide on page 55 of the Student Book.

Technician's notes

Be sure to check the latest safety notes on these resources before proceeding.

The following resources are needed for the demonstration of the structure of macromolecules:

molecular models showing the structure of diamond and graphite

Topic 2.3: Molecules and covalent bonds

Answers

Science in Context, page 54

In diamond each carbon atom is joined to four other carbon atoms in the giant covalent structure. In graphite each carbon atom is only joined to three others and the unbonded electron forms, with other unbonded electrons, a delocalised electron cloud that covers the whole structure. This difference in structure, for example, explains the electrical conductivity of graphite.

Page 55

1. Each carbon atom is strongly covalently bonded to 4 other atoms, forming a very strong giant lattice structure. A very high temperature is required to break the bonds between the carbon atoms.
2. Each carbon atom in graphite is strongly covalently bonded to 3 other carbon atoms. The remaining outer shell carbon electron is delocalised and so can move along the layers formed by the covalently bonded carbon atoms.

Topic 2.3: Molecules and covalent bonds

Learning episode C2.3e Consolidation and summary

Learning aims

- Review the learning points of the topic summarised in the end of topic checklist.
  - Test understanding of the topic content by answering the end of topic questions.

Resources

Student Book pages 56–57

Approach

Ask students to work with a partner to make a list of key words from this topic. They could then work together to produce a spider diagram showing how the different concepts are linked. They could compare their list with the list of key terms given in the Student Book. Discuss the checklist and ask questions to see how much of the content students are comfortable with.

Students could make flashcards of the key content and then use the flashcards to quiz each other on the information.

Ask students to work individually through the end of topic questions in the Student Book without looking at the text. As they work, walk around the classroom observing their answers and questioning them as necessary to find out which questions are causing difficulties.

After a set period, ask students to stop working. Discuss any areas of difficulty you observed as you walked round the class.

Students should complete any unanswered questions for homework, but you should stress that they should answer the questions without looking at the text, so that they can see how much they have remembered.

Ask students to produce a table summarising the differences between the bonding and properties of ionic and covalent compounds.

Topic 2.3: Molecules and covalent bonds

End of topic questions mark scheme

The marks available for a question can indicate the level of detail you need to provide in your answer.

Question	Correct answer	Marks
1	D	1 mark
2 a)	Dot-and-cross diagram of hydrogen fluoride showing: H–F (1 mark for the correct electron arrangements, 1 mark for correct sharing of electrons)	2 marks
2 b)	Dot-and-cross diagram of carbon disulfide showing: S = C = S (1 mark for the correct electron arrangements, 1 mark for correct sharing of electrons)	2 marks
2 c)	Dot-and-cross diagram of ethanol: H–C(H)(H)–C(H)(H)–O–H (1 mark for the correct electron arrangements, 1 mark for correct sharing of electrons)	2 marks
3	The forces of attraction between the candle wax molecules are (relatively) weak. The energy needed to break these forces is (relatively) low.	1 mark 1 mark
4	The attractive forces between the particles (atoms or molecules) in a gas are (relatively) weak. In an ionic compound the attractive forces between the particles (ions) are (relatively) strong.	1 mark 1 mark
Supplement 5	The attractive forces between the methane molecules are (relatively) weak. A (relatively) small amount of energy at the melting point is needed to break these attractive forces in solid methane.	1 mark 1 mark
Supplement 6 a)	X is likely to be a liquid or a gas. In a simple molecular structure the attractive forces between the particles (atoms or molecules) are (relatively) weak, as in a liquid or gas.	1 mark 1 mark
Supplement 6 b)	X is likely to have a much lower boiling point than sodium chloride. The attractive forces between the particles in liquid X are (relatively)	1 mark 1 mark

Cambridge IGCSE Chemistry Teacher's Guide

Topic 2.3: Molecules and covalent bonds

Question	Correct answer	Marks
	weak and so not much energy is needed at the boiling point to break them. In sodium chloride the attractive forces between the ions are very strong.	
7 a)	The layers of carbon atoms in graphite are held together by strong covalent bonds. As the covalent bonds in the layers are not easily broken, they will add strength to the tennis racquet.	1 mark 1 mark
7 b)	Between the covalently bonded layers in the graphite are delocalised electrons. These are able to move and carry an electric current.	1 mark 1 mark
8 a)	Diamond is a giant covalent structure with each carbon atom covalently bonded to 4 other carbon atoms. The lattice of strong covalent bonds gives diamond its hardness.	1 mark 1 mark
8 b)	Diamond is used in drills/cutting tools.	1 mark
	Total:	24 marks

Topic 2.4: Metallic bonding

Supplement C2.4 Metallic bonding

Introduction

This is a very short topic and is intended for the supplementary syllabus. There are strong links to Topic 2.1 *Atoms, elements and compounds* (the characteristic physical properties of metals were introduced here) and to Topic 2.4 *Ions and ionic bonds*. In addition, there are links to Topic 8.1 *The Periodic Table*, and to several inorganic chemistry topics dealing with metals: Topic 8.2 *Group I elements*, Topic 8.4 *Transition elements* and Topic 9.1 *Metals*.

In the teaching sequence the topic is likely to follow on from work on ionic and covalent bonding, completing the work on structure and bonding. Later in the course you can reinforce students' understanding of metallic bonding.

Some, if not all, of the activities could be combined into a single lesson. The main focus of the topic is the model illustrating the structure of metals.

Links to other sections

Section	Essential background knowledge	Useful links
2 Atoms, elements and compounds	2.1 Atoms, elements and compounds 2.2 Ions and ionic bonds	
8 The Periodic Table		8.1 The Periodic Table 8.2 Group I elements 8.4 Transition elements and noble gases
9 Metals		9.1 Metals

Topic overview

C2.4a	**Supplement Orientation**
	This learning episode builds on the work done on atomic structure and ionic bonding, and reviews the properties of metals and the features that can explain these properties.
C2.4b	**Supplement Metallic bonding**
	This is the main learning episode of the topic. The model for the structure of a metal is introduced and then used to explain the characteristic properties of metals. Alloys are also included as a means of optimising the properties of a metal.
C2.4c	**Supplement Consolidation and summary**
	This learning episode allows for a very quick recap on the ideas encountered and gives time for the students to answer the end of topic questions in the Student Book.

Career links

These are some scientific careers that focus on this area of chemistry but careers in many other fields use the knowledge and skills gained studying science.

Engineering metallurgists analyse the physical and electrical properties of alloys and how these are linked to the bonding and structure of the elements in the metal.

Topic 2.4: Metallic bonding

Supplement Learning Episode C2.4a Orientation

Learning aims

- To summarise knowledge and understanding of atomic structure and ionic bonding.
- To map out the main purposes of the topic.
- Know that an atom is made up of a positively charged nucleus containing protons and neutrons (except hydrogen) with electrons in shells around the nucleus.
- Know that metal atoms lose electrons when they form ionic compounds.

Approach

If you taught Topic 2.2 *Ions and ionic bonds* much earlier in the course, this topic provides a good opportunity to revise the key features of ionic bonding.

Ask students to work in small groups. Ask them to write down quickly five things that they know about ionic bonding and ionic compounds.

Collect together their responses and focus on what they have said about the role of metal atoms in ionic bonding, such as: they lose electrons and form positive ions. Explain that this easy release of electrons is the key to the properties of metals.

Ask students what the characteristic physical properties of metals are (covered in Topic 2.1 *Atoms, elements and compounds*). If necessary, remind them of the high electrical conductivity of metals and their malleability. The model for the structure of a metal provides an explanation of these properties.

Ask students if alloys are metals. Are they elements? Are they compounds? Are they mixtures?

Topic 2.4: Metallic bonding

Supplement Learning Episode C2.4b Metallic bonding

Learning objectives

- **Supplement** Describe metallic bonding as the electrostatic attraction between the positive ions in a giant metallic lattice and a 'sea' of delocalised electrons.
- **Supplement** Explain in terms of structure and bonding the properties of metals:
(a) good electrical conductivity
(b) malleability and ductility.

Resources

Student Book page 58–60

Approach

Using page 59 of the Student Book, introduce the model that describes the structure of a metal. Emphasise that the individual atoms release their outermost electrons to form a 'sea' of electrons. Introduce the term 'delocalised' to describe the process.

Electrostatic attraction between the nuclei and the sea of electrons is relative strong, and this explains the relatively high melting points of most metals. You may wish to refer to the Group I metals as an exception to this general rule.

Make sure that students understand the terms 'malleable' and 'ductile' and explain these properties in terms of the model.

Answers

Supplement Page 59

1. A cation is a positive ion.

2. Metals contain delocalised electrons that are not fixed to a particular atom. They can move throughout the structure.

3. The structure is not rigid, so the ions can move into different positions when the metal is bent.

Supplement Science in Context, page 60

Two properties of copper are particularly important: it is ductile and so can be drawn into wires and it is a very good conductor of electricity.

Topic 2.4: Metallic bonding

Supplement Learning Episode C2.4c Consolidation and summary

Learning aims

- Review the learning points of the topic summarised in the end of topic checklist.
- Test understanding of the topic content by answering the end of topic questions.

Resources

Student Book pages 59–63

Approach

Ask students to work with a partner to make a list of key words from this topic. They could then work together to produce a spider diagram showing how the different concepts are linked. They could compare their list with the list of key terms given in the Student Book. Discuss the checklist and ask questions to see how much of the content students are comfortable with.

Students could make flashcards of the key content and then use the flashcards to quiz each other on the information.

Also refer to the Science in Context feature on page 59 of the Student Book, which provides a number of links to other topics, as well as some information on alloys. The content of these Science in Context features is beyond the syllabus but provides the opportunity to explore the content more deeply.

Ask students to work individually through the end of topic questions in the Student Book without looking at the text. As they work, walk around the classroom observing their answers and questioning them as necessary to find out which questions are causing difficulties.

After a set period, ask students to stop working. Discuss any areas of difficulty you observed as you walked round the class.

Students should complete any unanswered questions for homework, but you should stress that they should answer the questions without looking at the text, so that they can see how much they have remembered.

Topic 2.4: Metallic bonding

Supplement End of topic questions mark scheme

The marks available for a question can indicate the level of detail you need to provide in your answer.

Question	Correct answer	Marks
1	A	1 mark
2 a)	Metals contain a 'sea' or 'cloud' of delocalised electrons.	1 mark
	The electrons are able to move and carry the electric current.	1 mark
2 b)	The structure is held together by the attractive forces between the ions and the electrons. Beating the metal disrupts the arrangement of the ions but does not break the attractive forces between the ions and the electrons.	1 mark 1 mark
3	In the graphite structure the delocalised electrons are between the layers of covalently bonded carbon atoms. The electrons are not delocalised over the whole structure and so can only conduct electricity in one plane. In a metal the electrons are delocalised over the whole metal structure and so can conduct in all planes.	1 mark 1 mark 1 mark
4 a)	C	1 mark
4 b)	A	1 mark
4 c)	D	1 mark
4 d)	B	1 mark
5 a)	An alloy is a mixture of a metal and one or more other elements.	1 mark
5 b)	They modify the property of the pure metal making it more useful.	1 mark
	Alloys (e.g. steel) can be stronger/more hardwearing than the pure metal.	1 mark
	Total:	15 marks

Section 3: Stoichiometry

Contents
C3.1 Stoichiometry

Overview of the section
This is a pivotal section in the course. The mole concept is only required for the supplementary syllabus.

The work on chemical formulae is a necessary part of generating chemical equations. Previously students may have only been introduced to word equations. If so, mastering the process will be essential if progress is to be made. It introduces chemical equations as the chemist's 'shorthand' for both describing reactions and, when relative atomic and molecular (formula) masses have been introduced, to provide quantitative details.

The quantitative demands should not be underestimated and so a lot of practice will prove beneficial.

Starting points
The Student Book section opener (pages 64–65) puts the ideas in the section into context and sets the scene. It also allows students to acknowledge and value their prior learning, and provides a benchmark against which future learning can be compared.

The questions provide a structure for introducing the section and can be used in a number of different ways:
- You could ask students to consider the questions as an introductory homework task.
- You could put students into groups to share their own ideas and understanding and then to report back to the whole class.
- Students could be given access to the Internet, preferably with a tight timescale, to find out the information required.

You could then use a spider chart or other form of wall chart to summarise everybody's ideas.

Recording these initial ideas allows you to retain them for reference as the individual topics are developed. In this way, your students' progress in learning can be readily acknowledged.

C3.1 Stoichiometry

Introduction

The work on formulae and equations builds on the ideas encountered in Topic 2.1 *Atoms, elements and compounds*, Topic 2.2 *Ions and ionic bonds* and Topic 2.3 *Molecules and covalent bonds*.

Supplement Ionic equations are only required for students following the supplementary syllabus.

This work links to Topic 7.1 *Acids, bases and salts*, Topic 6.2 *Reversible reactions and equilibrium* and Topic 12.2 *Identification of ions and gases*.

The first three learning episodes focus on writing chemical formulae and balanced chemical equations. It also introduces quantitative aspects through a study of relative atomic and molecular masses.

Supplement Empirical formulae and ionic equations are only required for the supplementary syllabus.

The next two learning episodes focus on reacting quantities and the mole concept.

Supplement The mole concept is applied to solids, gases and solutions and is only required for the supplementary syllabus.

Supplement Percentage yield is introduced from the supplementary syllabus to reflect the inevitable differences between the theoretical amounts indicated by a balanced chemical equation for a reaction and the practical yields actually obtained.

There are opportunities for practical work, particularly quantitative practicals. These provide practice of the full range of practical skills.

Links to other sections

Section	Essential background knowledge	Useful links
2 Atoms, elements and compounds	2.1 Atoms, elements and compounds	
	2.2 Ions and ionic bonds	
	2.3 Molecules and covalent bonds	
6 Chemical reactions		6.2 Reversible reactions and equilibrium
7 Acids, bases and salts		7.1 Acids, bases and salts
12 Experimental techniques		12.2 Identification of ions and gases

Note: All topics after this one will make use of chemical formulae and chemical equations. The topics listed are the strongest links.

Topic 3.1: Stoichiometry

Topic overview

C3.1a	**Orientation**
	The purpose of this learning episode is to revise and reinforce students' abilities to write chemical formulae.
	Supplement The focus here is on the use of ion charges to write chemical formulae.
C3.1b	**Writing chemical equations**
	Students should be familiar with word equations and this learning episode is intended to help students to become more familiar with symbol equations and how they can be balanced.
	Supplement Emphasis is placed on the use of state symbols. Ionic equations are introduced as a way of generalising reactions by removing spectator ions.
C3.1c	**Relative masses**
	This learning episode introduces the idea of using a relative mass scale to show the different masses of atoms (relative atomic masses). The concept is extended to include the calculation of relative molecular masses and relative formula masses (for ionic compounds).
C3.1d	**Reacting quantities and the mole concept**
	This long learning episode has several parts.
	Supplement **Part 1** Introduction to the mole and the Avogadro constant.
	Supplement **Part 2** Students use experimental results and the mole concept to work out the formulae of simple compounds. Practical activities relating to calculating the empirical formulae of magnesium oxide and copper(II) oxide are included.
	Part 3 Students use equations to calculate the amount of products generated in reactions.
	Calculations involving reacting masses are introduced and undertaken using relative atomic masses, molecular masses, formula masses and simple proportion, that is, without reference to the mole.
	Supplement Calculations involving reacting quantities are introduced, including molar volumes of gases and molarity of solutions, using the mole concept. Situations are also considered where there are limiting reactants with consequently one of the reactants in excess. Practical activities relating to the action of heat on zinc carbonate and copper(II) carbonate are included.
C3.1e	**Supplement** **Percentage yield**
	This short learning episode highlights how actual amounts of substances produced in reactions can be compared with the theoretical amounts.
C3.1f	**Consolidation and summary**
	This learning episode provides a quick recap of the key ideas encountered in the topic.

Career links

These are some scientific careers that focus on this area of chemistry but careers in many other fields use the knowledge and skills gained studying science.

Synthetic chemists and process chemists work with **process engineers** to develop the equipment and manufacturing plants that take reactions developed in a research lab and scale them up so that they can be used commercially.

Topic 3.1: Stoichiometry

Learning episode C3.1a Orientation

Learning objectives

- State the formulae of the elements and compounds named in the subject content.
- Define the molecular formula of a compound as the number and type of different atoms in one molecule.
- Deduce the formula of a simple compound from the relative numbers of atoms present in a model or diagrammatic representation.
- Supplement Determine the formula of an ionic compound from the relative numbers of the ions present in a model or a diagrammatic representation or from the charges on the ions.

Resources

Student Book pages 66–70

Approach

Part 1

Students may already be familiar with rules on combining powers (and ion charges – see below) and/or the use of the Periodic Table to write chemical formulae. However, if they are not, then this learning episode will provide the practice needed.

The Student Book sets out how combining powers can be derived from the position of the element in the Periodic Table and then presents a systematic approach to writing chemical formulae. Radicals are introduced and the use of brackets in formulae is explained.

Supplement The use of ion charges to write chemical formulae links to the work covered in Topic 2.2 *Ions and ionic bonds*. A short section in the Student Book (page 70) highlights this approach to writing formulae. Emphasise that this approach only applies to ionic compounds, that is, compounds formed between a metal and a non-metal.

Part 2

Explain that the rest of the topic concentrates on writing chemical equations and on how quantitative aspects of chemistry are linked to chemical formulae and equations. Stress that knowing whether a reaction takes place is one aspect, but that knowing the quantities of reactants needed to produce a certain amount of product is of fundamental importance in the industrial manufacture of chemicals.

Answers

Page 70

1. a) KBr b) CaO c) $AlCl_3$ d) CH_4
2. a) $Cu(NO_3)_2$ b) $Al(OH)_3$ c) $(NH_4)_2SO_4$ d) $Fe_2(CO_3)_3$

Supplement 3. a) $ZnCl_2$ b) Cr_2O_3 c) $Fe(OH)_2$

Topic 3.1: Stoichiometry

Learning episode C3.1b Writing chemical equations

Learning objectives

- Construct word equations and symbol equations to show how reactants form products, including state symbols.
- Supplement Construct symbol equations with state symbols, including ionic equations.
- Supplement Deduce the symbol equation with state symbols for a chemical reaction, given relevant information.

Resources

Student Book pages 71–75

Worksheet C3.1b Balancing equations

Approach

You will need to decide just how much time you want to devote to this activity. Clearly there will be opportunities throughout the rest of the course to practise writing chemical equations, but establishing the basic principles and methodology is equally important.

The Student Book gives examples of how word equations can be translated into chemical equations. The process of balancing equations is then developed through the use of worked examples. Worksheet C3.1b provides examples for the students to try. Students will need to know the non-metallic elements that exist as diatomic molecules and not as single atoms.

The use of state symbols is introduced. Time will need to be devoted to consideration of the section on balancing more complex equations that contain radicals.

The questions on page 75 of the Student Book include some more difficult examples for extra challenge.

Supplement Use the Student Book to focus on balancing ionic equations. The supplementary questions on Worksheet C3.1b (9 and 10) require the balancing of ionic equations.

Answers

Page 74

1. a) $2Ca(s) + O_2(g) \rightarrow 2CaO(s)$

   b) $2H_2S(g) + 3O_2(g) \rightarrow 2SO_2(g) + 2H_2O(l)$

   c) $2Pb(NO_3)_2(s) \rightarrow 2PbO(s) + 4NO_2(g) + O_2(g)$

2. a) $S(s) + O_2(g) \rightarrow SO_2(g)$

   b) $2Mg(s) + O_2(g) \rightarrow 2MgO(s)$

   c) $CuO(s) + H_2(g) \rightarrow Cu(s) + H_2O(l)$

Page 75

1. a) $2C_5H_{10}(g) + 15O_2(g) \rightarrow 10CO_2(g) + 10H_2O(l)$

   b) $Fe_2O_3(s) + 3CO(g) \rightarrow 2Fe(s) + 3CO_2(g)$

   c) $2KMnO_4(s) + 16HCl(aq) \rightarrow 2KCl(aq) + 2MnCl_2(aq) + 8H_2O(l) + 5Cl_2(g)$

Topic 3.1: Stoichiometry

Worksheet C3.1b

1. $2CO(g) + O_2(g) \rightarrow 2CO_2(g)$
2. $H_2(g) + Cl_2(g) \rightarrow 2HCl(g)$
3. $2Ca(s) + O_2(g) \rightarrow 2CaO(s)$
4. $2P(s) + 3Cl_2(g) \rightarrow 2PCl_3(l)$
5. $2Fe(OH)_3(s) \rightarrow Fe_2O_3(s) + 3H_2O(l)$
6. $N_2(g) + 3H_2(g) \rightarrow 2NH_3(g)$
7. $Mg(s) + 2HCl(aq) \rightarrow MgCl_2(aq) + H_2(g)$
8. $2Pb(NO_3)_2(s) \rightarrow 2PbO(s) + 4NO_2(g) + O_2(g)$

Supplement 9. $Fe^{2+}(aq) + 2OH^-(aq) \rightarrow Fe(OH)_2(s)$

Supplement 10. $Al^{3+}(aq) + 3OH^-(aq) \rightarrow Al(OH)_3(s)$

Topic 3.1: Stoichiometry

Worksheet C3.1b Balancing equations

Balance the following equations. Remember:
- You must not change any chemical formulae.
- You can only put numbers in front of the formulae.

1. $CO(g)$ + $O_2(g)$ → $CO_2(g)$

2. $H_2(g)$ + $Cl_2(g)$ → $HCl(g)$

3. $Ca(s)$ + $O_2(g)$ → $CaO(s)$

4. $P(s)$ + $Cl_2(g)$ → $PCl_3(l)$

5. $Fe(OH)_3$ → $Fe_2O_3(s)$ + $H_2O(l)$

6. $N_2(g)$ + $H_2(g)$ → $NH_3(g)$

7. $Mg(s)$ + $HCl(aq)$ → $MgCl_2(aq)$ + $H_2(g)$

8. $Pb(NO_3)_2(s)$ → $PbO(s)$ + $NO_2(g)$ + $O_2(g)$

Supplement 9. $Fe^{2+}(aq)$ + $OH^-(aq)$ → $Fe(OH)_2(s)$

Supplement 10. $Al^{3+}(aq)$ + $OH^-(aq)$ → $Al(OH)_3(s)$

Topic 3.1: Stoichiometry

Learning episode C3.1c Relative masses

Learning objectives

- Describe relative atomic mass, A_r, as the average mass of the isotopes of an element compared to 1/12th of the mass of an atom of ^{12}C.
- Define relative molecular mass, M_r, as the sum of the relative atomic masses. Relative formula mass, M_r, will be used for ionic compounds.

Common misconceptions

Some students think that the relative mass scale is based on a comparison of atom masses with the mass of the hydrogen atom (that is, as it used to be).

Resources

Student Book pages 76–78

Approach

Explain the need for a relative atomic mass scale because atoms are too small to weigh. Next, explain that the original standard was hydrogen but it is now the carbon-12 isotope. Use page 77 of the Student Book to illustrate this relative mass scale.

Explain how relative atomic masses are used to calculate relative molecular masses. Explain that for ionic compounds (that is, compounds that do not contain molecules) the correct terminology is relative formula mass.

The next learning episode introduces the mole concept and reacting quantities. You may decide to finish the topic at this point and return to it later in the course.

Answers

Page 78

1. 16
2. 46
3. 48

Topic 3.1: Stoichiometry

Learning episode C3.1d Reacting quantities and the mole concept

Learning objectives

- Calculate reacting masses in simple proportions. Calculations will **not** involve the mole concept.
- State that concentration can be measured in g / dm^3 or mol / dm^3
- Supplement Define the empirical formula of a compound as the simplest whole number ratio of the different atoms or ions in a compound.
- Supplement State that the mole, mol, is the unit of amount of substance and that one mole contains 6.02 × 10^{23} particles, e.g. atoms, ions, molecules; this number is the Avogadro constant.
- Supplement Use the relationship: amount of substance (mol) = $\frac{\text{mass (g)}}{\text{molar mass (g / mol)}}$ to calculate:
    a) amount of substance
    b) mass
    c) molar mass
    d) relative atomic mass or relative molecular / formula mass
    e) number of particles, using the value of the Avogadro constant
- Supplement Use the molar gas volume, taken as 24 dm^3 at room temperature and pressure, r.t.p., in calculations involving gases.
- Supplement Calculate stoichiometric reacting masses, limiting reactants, volumes of gases at r.t.p., volumes of solutions and concentrations of solutions expressed in g / dm^3 and mol / dm^3, including conversion between cm^3 and dm^3.
- Supplement Use experimental data from a titration to calculate the moles of solute, or the concentration or volume of a solution.
- Supplement Calculate empirical formulae and molecular formulae, given appropriate data.

Resources

Student Book pages 78–91

Supplement Worksheet C3.1d(1) Moles of atoms

Supplement Worksheet C3.1d(2) Working out the formula of magnesium oxide

Supplement Worksheet C3.1d(3) Working out the formula of copper(II) oxide

Worksheet C3.1d(4) Obtaining zinc oxide from zinc carbonate

Supplement Worksheet C3.1d(5) Relative formula masses and molar volumes

Supplement Worksheet C3.1d(6) Calculating the molar volume of carbon dioxide

Resources for class practicals (see Technician's notes, following)

Approach

This is a long learning episode supported by a series of worksheets. There are opportunities for a number of different practical/investigative activities and a decision will need to be taken as to how many of these will be used. Many of the activities are intended for those students following the supplementary syllabus.

Supplement Part 1

Introduce the mole as an amount of substance that contains approximately 6.02 × 10^{23} particles (atoms, molecules, formula units, ions). Explain that this number is known as the Avogadro constant or number.

Illustrate the use of the relative atomic mass to express the mass of 1 mole of atoms (for example, A_r of C = 12; 1 mole of carbon atoms is 12 g); similarly, illustrate the use of the relative molecular mass or

Topic 3.1: Stoichiometry

formula mass to express the mass of 1 mole of molecules or formula units (for example, M_r of CO_2 = 44; 1 mole of CO_2 = 44 g).

The mole concept is then used in Part 2 to calculate the formula of a compound from experimental results.

Supplement Part 2

i) Students will be familiar with the reaction of magnesium and oxygen but demonstrate it again **(see tech notes)** and ask students to focus on what happens to the magnesium oxide. Explain that if the masses of magnesium and oxygen are measured then they can be used to work out the formula of magnesium oxide.

Explain to students that they must undertake this reaction very carefully. They need accurate results if they are going to work out the correct formula.

The experiment is described on Worksheet C3.1d(2). It is also on page 78 of the Student Book. The Student Book section could be used as an introduction to the experiment or as consolidation after the practical work is completed.

The crucial part of the experiment is to minimise the loss of the magnesium oxide produced. Use the Student Book to explore how similar calculations can be used to find the formulae of copper(II) oxide, water and salts such as hydrated copper(II) sulfate.

Consider the examples on pages 78–79 of the Student Book illustrating how formulae can be worked out from experimental quantities.

SAFETY INFORMATION

Wear eye protection (splash-proof goggles).

*For longer lengths of magnesium ribbon burnt by the teacher or burning in oxygen, do **not** look directly at the flame. A welding filter or even viewing it through a 1 mm gap between the fingers of one hand will offer protection. Magnesium burns with such brightness that viewing it directly may cause retinal damage.*

Raising and lowering the crucible lid should not allow a direct view of the burning magnesium.

---

ii) Students should already have been introduced to the formula of copper(II) oxide in the Student Book. The purpose of this experiment is to try to get accurate results to verify that the formula of copper(II) oxide is CuO.

Details of the reduction of copper(II) oxide are included on Worksheet C3.1d(3). In addition, the Developing Practical Skills feature on pages 80-81 of the Student Book relates to the experiment. You will need to decide at what stage to use Developing Practical Skills, as the questions in the Student Book overlap at some points with the worksheet.

Supplement Introduce the concept of an empirical formula as the simplest formula that shows the whole number ratio of atoms in the compound. Link it to the molecular formula, which shows the actual whole number of atoms in a compound. Refer to the examples in the Student Book. Ask students to explain whether the formulae they deduced in worksheets C3.1d(2) and C3.1d(3) are the molecular formula, empirical formula or both.

SAFETY INFORMATION

Wear eye protection (splash-proof goggles) and use safety screens.

Copper(II) oxide is a moderate hazard and hazardous to the aquatic environment.

Dispose of copper(II) oxide safely. Do not dispose of copper(II) oxide down the sink.

Ensure that the laboratory is well ventilated.

Teacher should supervise lighting the flame from the combustion tube.

Part 3

This part of the learning episode focuses on reacting quantities. The Student Book provides a series of worked examples as well as questions to answer. Illustrate how some of the reacting mass calculations can be worked out from simple proportions without direct use of the mole concept.

Topic 3.1: Stoichiometry

Supplement Use pages 89–90 of the Student Book to introduce the idea of molar volumes as a convenient way of measuring the quantities of gases. Worksheet C3.1d(5) provides some examples of calculations involving relative formula masses, the mole and molar volumes. Additionally, consider how the mole concept can be applied to solutions. Devote some time to this, as it is often an aspect that students find difficult. Use the examples in the Student Book to clarify understanding. The first part of Worksheet C3.1d(6) can be used to provide additional practice.

The Developing Practical Skills feature on pages 88–89 of the Student Book looks at the titration technique and the calculation to work out the molarity of a solution.

The work on reacting quantities can then be extended with two practical activities.

i) The first practical activity involves the decomposition of zinc carbonate. It reinforces the idea that you can compare experimental results with theoretical results derived from the chemical equation.

Make this into a competition by dividing students into groups for a class practical. Assign to each group a different starting mass of zinc carbonate by using different numbers of spatula measures. Worksheet C3.1d(4) gives details of the experiment.

> **SAFETY INFORMATION**
>
> *Wear eye protection (splash-proof goggles).*
>
> *If the mineral wool (ceramic fibre) is classified as non-hazardous it may be handled with care, if not wear disposable gloves.*
>
> *Ensure that the laboratory is well ventilated.*

The number of spatula measures covered by the groups should range from 1 to 4. Two groups might have the same starting quantity. The worksheet gives a context for introducing percentage yield, so providing a link to learning episode C3.1e.

ii) The second practical activity involves the decomposition of copper(II) carbonate. As well as giving practice in calculating molar volumes, the practical requires careful and accurate quantitative work in order to achieve results of acceptable accuracy. Full details are provided on Worksheet C3.1d(6).

Supplement Finally, explain how in most reactions there a limited amount of one reactant, and the other reactant(s) will therefore be in excess.

> **SAFETY INFORMATION**
>
> *Wear eye protection (splash-proof goggles).*
>
> *Copper(II) carbonate is harmful. Avoid direct contact with the powder or causing it to become dust in the air.*
>
> *If the mineral wool (ceramic fibre) is classified as non-hazardous it may be handled with care, if not wear disposable gloves.*
>
> *Ensure that the laboratory is well ventilated.*

Technician's notes

Be sure to check the latest safety notes on these resources before proceeding.

The following resources are needed for the demonstration of burning magnesium:

magnesium ribbon
metal tongs
Bunsen burner and heatproof mat
Eye protection (splash-proof goggles) and a welding filter lens (shade 9)

Topic 3.1: Stoichiometry

The following resources are needed for the class practical C3.1d(2), per group:

crucible and lid
pipeclay triangle
tripod
Bunsen burner and heatproof mat
metal tongs
2 cm length of magnesium ribbon
abrasive paper such as emery cloth
eye protection (splash-proof goggles)
access to a balance accurate in grams to 2 decimal places

The following resources are needed for the class practical C3.1d(3), per group:

rubber tubing
connecting tube and bung
combustion tube (oven dry)
Bunsen burner and heatproof mat
stand and clamp
spatula
copper(II) oxide – about 1 g
eye protection (splash-proof goggles) and safety screens

The following resources are needed for the class practical C3.1d(4), per group:

dry test-tube
test-tube holder
mineral wool (Superwool 607®, for example, is classified as low hazard, and should be used in preference to other types)
access to a balance accurate in grams to 2 decimal places
spatula
zinc carbonate – about 2 g
eye protection (splash-proof goggles)
gloves or tweezers – thin protective gloves are fine but should not be too large for students' hands

The following resources are needed for the class practical C3.1d(6), per group:

oven-dried test-tube, test-tube rack
mineral wool (Superwool 607®, for example, is classified as low hazard)
access to a balance accurate in grams to 2 decimal places
copper(II) carbonate – about 4 g
spatula
tweezers or gloves (thin protective gloves are fine but should not be too large for students' hands)
eye protection (splash-proof goggles)

Topic 3.1: Stoichiometry

Answers

Supplement Worksheet C3.1d(1)

1. a) 12 g   b) 69 g   c) 2.4 g   d) 64 g   e) 20 g   f) 0.28 g
2. a) 2 moles   b) 0.1 mole   c) 4 moles   d) 2 moles   e) 0.01 mole
3. a) 1, hydrogen   b) 80, bromine   c) 32, sulfur   d) 40, calcium   e) 56, iron

Supplement Worksheet C3.1d(5)

1. a) calcium oxide: 56; propane: 44; carbon dioxide: 44; magnesium sulfate: 120; copper(II) carbonate: 124; nitric acid: 63; aluminium hydroxide: 78; copper(II) nitrate: 188

   b) 88 g, 22 g, 6.3 g, 560 g

2. 4 g, 22 g, 11 g, 0.0083 g, 0.73 g, 0.053 g

Supplement Developing Practical Skills, page 80

1. It will not be possible to heat any copper(II) oxide near the mouth of the tube without melting the rubber bung.
2. To prevent the gas pressure from blowing the copper(II) oxide through the jet.
3. To prevent the hot copper from reacting with oxygen in the air.
4. Black (copper(II) oxide) to pink (copper).
5. Mass of copper(II) oxide = 1.00 g; mass of copper = 0.77 g; mass of oxygen = 0.23 g
6. Number moles of copper = $\frac{77}{64}$ = 0.012, number moles of oxygen = $\frac{0.23}{16}$ = 0.014
7. Ratio Cu:O is 1:1.17
8. CuO
9. Loss of copper(II) oxide during weighing or through the jet during heating; not all copper(II) oxide converted into copper; some copper(II) oxide reformed from hot copper if the cooling was not complete when the gas flow stopped.

Supplement Page 81

1. a) To allow oxygen from the air into the crucible.
   b) To prevent the loss of the magnesium oxide.
   c) White.

Supplement Page 83

1. Fe_2O_3
2. ZnO
3. C_4H_{10}
4. H_2O_2

Supplement Developing Practical Skills, page 88

5. a) The pipette should have been washed first with distilled water and then with a small amount of the potassium hydroxide solution (discarding the solution used for washing).
   b) The burette should have been washed with distilled water first and then with a small amount of the sulfuric acid solution (discarding the solution used for washing).

Topic 3.1: Stoichiometry

6. A pipette bulb (suction bulb) could be used to suck the potassium hydroxide solution into the pipette.
7. Using a funnel (and pouring below eye level by lifting the stand off the bench and down onto a stool).
8. Use a white tile or white card/paper under the conical flask. The methyl orange changes from yellow (in the potassium hydroxide solution) to pink (when too much sulfuric acid solution has been added).
9. The student could have washed the conical flask with distilled water and discarded the washings.
10. In the first experiment the student had no real idea how much acid would be needed. After the first experiment she knew approximately how much acid was needed and would be much more likely to get the colour change on adding just one drop.
11. 17.0 cm^3. The result from the first experiment is very different and likely to be the most inaccurate (as just explained).
12. Moles of H_2SO_4 added = $\frac{17.0}{1000}$ × 0.1 = 0.0017 moles

    From the equation the ratio of H_2SO_4:KOH is 1:2

    Moles of KOH = 0.0034 moles

    Concentration of KOH = 1000/25 × 0.0034 = 0.136 mol/dm^3

Page 89

1. 28 g
2. 10 g

Supplement 3. a) 2 moles b) 0.01 mole c) 0.25 mole

Supplement Page 90

1. a) 2 moles b) 0.5 mole c) 0.1 mole
2. a) 0.5 mole b) 0.1 mole c) 2 moles

Supplement Science in Context, page 91

A well-known situation is that involving Rosalind Franklin who played a key role in the discovery of the structure of DNA. Initially all the credit was given to two other scientists, Watson and Crick. It was only after Rosalind Franklin's death that her role was fully acknowledged. There will be other examples the students may refer to.

Topic 3.1: Stoichiometry

Supplement Worksheet C3.1d(1) Moles of atoms

Use the following formula to answer the questions:

$$\text{moles} = \frac{\text{mass}}{\text{relative atomic mass}}$$

The A_r values are given in brackets.

1. What is the mass of the following?
   a) 1 mole of carbon atoms (C = 12)
   b) 3 moles of sodium atoms (Na = 23)
   c) 0.1 mole of magnesium atoms (Mg = 24)
   d) 2 moles of sulfur atoms (S = 32)
   e) 0.5 mole of calcium atoms (Ca = 40)
   f) 0.01 mole of silicon atoms (Si = 28)

2. How many moles of atoms are there in the following?
   a) 54 g of aluminium (Al = 27)
   b) 4 g of argon atoms (Ar = 40)
   c) 36 g of beryllium atoms (Be = 9)
   d) 71 g of chlorine atoms (Cl = 35.5)
   e) 0.635 g of copper atoms (Cu = 63.5)

3. What are the relative atomic masses of the following? Which element is each one?
   a) 3 moles of atoms has a mass of 3 g
   b) 0.5 moles of atoms has a mass of 40 g
   c) 0.1 mole of atoms has a mass of 3.2 g
   d) 0.25 mole of atoms has a mass of 10 g
   e) 0.01 mole of atoms has a mass of 0.56 g

Topic 3.1: Stoichiometry

Supplement Worksheet C3.1d(2) Working out the formula of magnesium oxide

Magnesium burns in air to form magnesium oxide. The formula of magnesium oxide can be calculated if the exact masses of magnesium and oxygen that react together can be worked out.

Apparatus

crucible and lid (dry)

abrasive paper such as emery cloth

pipeclay triangle

metal tongs

tripod

Bunsen burner and heatproof mat

magnesium ribbon

access to a balance, accurate in grams to 2 decimal places

eye protection (splash-proof goggles) and blue glass, if available

SAFETY INFORMATION
Wear eye protection (splash-proof goggles).
*For longer lengths of magnesium ribbon burnt by the teacher or burning in oxygen, do **not** look directly at the flame. A welding filter or even viewing it through a 1 mm gap between the fingers of one hand will offer protection. Magnesium burns with such brightness that viewing it directly may cause retinal damage.*
Raising and lowering the crucible lid should not allow a direct view of the burning magnesium.

Method

1. Put on eye protection.

2. Weigh a clean, dry crucible and lid (A).

3. Clean a 10 cm strip of magnesium ribbon with abrasive paper such as emery cloth. Make the magnesium into a loose coil and place it in the crucible. Weigh the crucible, lid and magnesium (B).

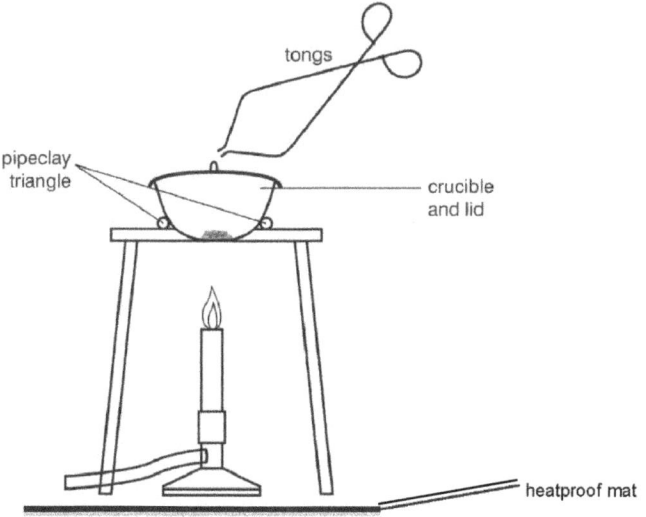

Page 1 of 2

Topic 3.1: Stoichiometry

4. Set up the apparatus as shown and heat the crucible strongly, if possible with the lid slightly off centre. From time to time carefully use tongs to lift the crucible lid a very small distance and then replace it. TRY TO AVOID ANY LOSS OF WHITE SMOKE.
5. When there is no further sign of a reaction allow the crucible and lid to cool. Then weigh the crucible, lid and magnesium oxide (C).

Observing, measuring and recording

Record your results below:

Mass of crucible + lid (A) = _____ g

Mass of crucible + lid + magnesium (B) = _____ g

Mass of crucible + lid + magnesium oxide (C) = _____ g

Mass of magnesium (B − A) = _____ g

Mass of oxygen (C − B) = _____ g

Handling experimental observations and data

A_r: O = 16; Mg = 24

Number of moles of magnesium = $\dfrac{\text{mass of magnesium}}{24}$ = _____

Number of moles of oxygen = $\dfrac{\text{mass of oxygen}}{16}$ = _____

Ratio (n) = $\dfrac{\text{number of moles of oxygen}}{\text{number of moles of magnesium}}$ = _____

Formula of magnesium oxide = MgO_n

Evaluating methods

6. Why was it important to avoid losing the white smoke?
7. Why was it necessary to clean the magnesium ribbon with abrasive paper?
8. Magnesium oxide has the formula MgO. What was the percentage error in your experiment?
9. What were the sources of error in the experiment?

Supplement Worksheet C3.1d(3) Working out the formula of copper(II) oxide

To work out the formula of copper(II) oxide you must find out the exact masses of copper and oxygen that combine together. In this experiment you start with copper(II) oxide and remove the oxygen to form copper. The removal of oxygen (reduction) is accomplished by heating the copper(II) oxide in a stream of natural gas, which contains a small amount of hydrogen.

Apparatus

rubber tubing, spatula

connecting tube and bung

combustion tube (oven dry)

Bunsen burner, heatproof mat, stand and clamp

copper(II) oxide and spatula

access to a balance, accurate in grams to 2 decimal places

eye protection (splash-proof goggles) and safety screens for each student

SAFETY INFORMATION
Wear eye protection (splash-proof goggles) and use safety screens. Copper(II) oxide is a moderate hazard and hazardous to the aquatic environment. Dispose of copper(II) oxide safely. Do not dispose of copper(II) oxide down the sink.
Ensure that the laboratory is well ventilated.
Teacher should supervise lighting the flame from the combustion tube.

Method

1. Put on eye protection.

2. Weigh a dry combustion tube (A).

3. Carefully put a spatula measure of copper(II) oxide two-thirds of the way along the tube. Remove any copper(II) oxide that has been spilt near the mouth of the tube. Reweigh the tube and copper(II) oxide (B).

4. Set up the apparatus as shown below.

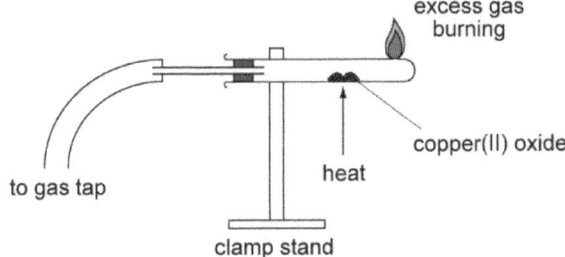

   Ask your teacher to check and to tell you when to turn on the gas supply. Turn the gas on very slowly and after 10 s light the gas at the end of the test-tube. Adjust the flame until it is about 5 cm high. Heat the copper(II) oxide strongly until it has all turned into pink copper. If the flame at the end of the combustion tube goes out, relight it.

5. Stop heating but leave the gas passing through the tube until the tube has cooled down.

6. When the combustion tube is cool, turn off the gas supply and weigh the tube and the copper (C).

Topic 3.1: Stoichiometry

Observing, measuring and recording

Record your results below.

Mass of combustion tube (A) = _____ g

Mass of combustion tube + copper(II) oxide (B) = _____ g

Mass of combustion tube + copper (C) = _____ g

Mass of copper (C − A) = _____ g

Mass of oxygen (B − C) = _____ g

Handling experimental observations and data

A_r: O = 16; Cu = 64

Number of moles of copper = $\dfrac{\text{mass of copper}}{64}$ = _____

Number of moles of oxygen = $\dfrac{\text{mass of oxygen}}{16}$ = _____

Ratio (n) = $\dfrac{\text{number of moles of oxygen}}{\text{number of moles of copper}}$ = _____

Formula of copper(II) oxide = CuO_n

Evaluating methods

7. Why was it important not to have too great a flow of gas through the tube?
8. Why was it necessary to leave the natural gas flowing over the copper whilst the combustion tube was cooling?
9. Copper(II) oxide has the formula CuO. What was the percentage error in your experiment?
10. What were the sources of error in the experiment?

Topic 3.1: Stoichiometry

Worksheet C3.1d(4) Obtaining zinc oxide from zinc carbonate

When zinc carbonate is heated, zinc oxide and carbon dioxide are produced. Your task is to find out the relationship between the mass of zinc carbonate and the mass of zinc oxide that can be obtained from it.

zinc carbonate → zinc oxide + carbon dioxide

$ZnCO_3(s)$ → $ZnO(s)$ + $CO_2(g)$

(A_r: C = 12; O = 16; Zn = 65)

Apparatus

dry test-tube, spatula

test-tube holder

mineral wool

access to a balance accurate in grams to 2 decimal places

zinc carbonate

eye protection (splash-proof goggles)

Bunsen burner, heatproof mat, gloves or tweezers

SAFETY INFORMATION
Wear eye protection (splash-proof goggles).
If the mineral wool (ceramic fibre) is classified as non-hazardous it may be handled with care, if not wear disposable gloves.
Ensure that the laboratory is well ventilated.

Method

1. Put on eye protection. Put on gloves when handling the mineral wool or have tweezers to hand.

2. Weigh a clean, dry test-tube and a plug of mineral wool (A). Use tongs or gloves to handle the mineral wool.

3. Add a number of spatula measures of zinc carbonate to the tube (your teacher will tell you how many). Reweigh the tube containing the zinc carbonate and the mineral wool (B). If using gloves, take them off carefully.

4. Heat the zinc carbonate gently at first and then more strongly until it has all turned yellow. Then allow the tube to cool before reweighing the tube, zinc oxide and mineral wool (C).

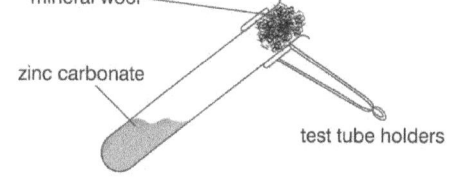

Observing, measuring and recording

Record your results below.

Mass of test-tube + mineral wool + zinc carbonate (B) = _____ g

Mass of test-tube + mineral wool + zinc oxide (C) = _____ g

Mass of test-tube + mineral wool (A) = _____ g

Mass of zinc carbonate (B − A) = _____ g

Mass of zinc oxide (C − A) = _____ g

Page 1 of 2

Topic 3.1: Stoichiometry

Class results

Group	Mass of zinc carbonate / g	Mass of zinc oxide / g
1		
2		
3		
4		
5		
6		
7		
8		

Handling experimental observations and data

5. Draw a graph of mass of zinc carbonate (*y*-axis) against mass of zinc oxide (*x*-axis). Include the origin (0, 0) on the graph. Add all the class results and draw a line of best fit through the origin and the class results.

6. Use the equation to calculate the mass of zinc oxide that should be produced from 2.5 g of zinc carbonate (the theoretical yield). Add your result to the graph and draw another line from the origin to this point.

Evaluating methods

7. Why was the mineral wool used?
8. How do the class results compare to the line showing the theoretical yield?
9. Suggest reasons for any differences between the line of best fit for the class results and the theoretical yield line.

Topic 3.1: Stoichiometry

Supplement Worksheet C3.1d(5) Relative formula masses and molar volumes

1. Answering these questions will help you to become familiar with working out relative formula masses and molar masses.

   a) Calculate the formula masses of the following compounds:

   A_r: H = 1; C = 12; N = 14; O = 16; Mg = 24; Al = 27; S = 32; Ca = 40; Cu = 64

   calcium oxide: CaO

   propane: C_3H_8

   carbon dioxide: CO_2

   magnesium sulfate: $MgSO_4$

   copper(II) carbonate: $CuCO_3$

   nitric acid: HNO_3

   aluminium hydroxide: $Al(OH)_3$

   copper(II) nitrate: $Cu(NO_3)_2$

   b) Calculate the mass of the following:

   2 moles of propane

   0.5 mole of carbon dioxide

   0.1 mole of nitric acid

   10 moles of calcium oxide

2. Answering these questions will help you to become familiar with working with molar volumes of gases.

   1 mole of any gas occupies 24 000 cm^3 at room temperature and pressure (r.t.p.)

   Calculate the mass of the following:

   48 000 cm^3 of hydrogen: H_2

   12 000 cm^3 of carbon dioxide: CO_2

   6000 cm^3 of propane: C_3H_8

   100 cm^3 of hydrogen: H_2

   400 cm^3 of carbon dioxide: CO_2

   40 cm^3 of oxygen: O_2

Topic 3.1: Stoichiometry

Supplement Worksheet C3.1d(6) Calculating the molar volume of carbon dioxide

When heated strongly, copper(II) carbonate breaks down into copper(II) oxide and carbon dioxide. Although the carbon dioxide gas will escape during the reaction, the mass of the gas can be calculated from the loss in total mass during the reaction. This loss in mass can then be converted into a corresponding volume.

copper(II) carbonate $\rightarrow$ copper(II) oxide + carbon dioxide

$CuCO_3(s) \rightarrow CuO(s) + CO_2(g)$

Apparatus

dry test-tube and test-tube holder

mineral wool and gloves or tweezers

copper(II) carbonate

spatula

access to a balance accurate in grams to 2 decimal places

eye protection (splash-proof goggles)

Bunsen burner and heatproof mat

SAFETY INFORMATION
Wear eye protection (splash-proof goggles).
Copper(II) carbonate is harmful. Avoid direct contact with the powder or causing it to become dust in the air.
If the mineral wool (ceramic fibre) is classified as non-hazardous it may be handled with care, if not wear disposable gloves.
Ensure that the laboratory is well ventilated.

Method

1. Put on eye protection.
2. Weigh a clean, dry test-tube with a small plug of mineral wool near the top of the tube. Record your result in a table.
3. Remove the mineral wool and carefully add about 2 spatula measures of the copper(II) carbonate powder to the tube. Replace the plug of mineral wool and reweigh the tube. Record your result.
4. Heat the tube, slowly at first to prevent the copper(II) carbonate powder from escaping from the tube, and then more strongly until all the green powder has changed to a black powder.
5. Allow the tube to cool in a test-tube rack.
6. Once cool, reweigh the tube and contents. Record your result.

Using and organising techniques, apparatus and materials

7. Why was the mineral wool used?

Topic 3.1: Stoichiometry

Observing, measuring and recording

Record your results in a suitable table.

Use your results to calculate the mass of carbon dioxide produced in the reaction.

Handling experimental observations and data

8. Calculate the number of moles of carbon dioxide produced in the reaction (A_r: C = 12; O = 16).

9. Calculate the volume that this number of moles would occupy at r.t.p. (1 mole of gas occupies 24 000 cm^3 at r.t.p.).

10. Calculate the number of moles of copper(II) carbonate used (A_r: C = 12; O = 16; Cu = 64).

11. Use your answer from Question 3, and the equation, to calculate what volume of carbon dioxide should have been produced in the reaction (the theoretical volume according to the equation).

Evaluating methods

12. The result you calculated from your experiment and the theoretical result are likely to be different. Suggest why.

Topic 3.1: Stoichiometry

Supplement Learning episode C3.1e Percentage yield

Learning objective

- Supplement Calculate percentage yield, percentage composition by mass and percentage purity, given appropriate data.

Resources

Student Book page 92

Supplement Worksheet C3.1e(1) Chemical calculations

Supplement Worksheet C3.1e(2) Working out % yield

Approach

This short learning episode introduces calculations of percentage yield and percentage purity, supported by the Student Book (page 92). It also provides an opportunity to calculate percentage yields and to recap on some of the ideas encountered in the previous learning episode (molarity and reacting quantities) through the use of Worksheet C3.1e(5).

The concept of a yield in a reaction is central to Topic 6.2 *Reversible reactions and equilibrium*.

Answers

Supplement Worksheet C3.1e(1)

1. a) 1 mol / dm^3
   b) 0.5 mol / dm^3
   c) 0.1 mol / dm^3
   d) 0.2 mol / dm^3
   e) 2 mol / dm^3
2. a) 2 moles
   b) 1.5 moles
   c) 1 mole
   d) 0.4 mole
   e) 0.25 mole
3. a) 75%
   b) 41%
   c) 80%
   d) 80%
4. 4.4 g

Topic 3.1: Stoichiometry

Supplement Worksheet C3.1e(1) Chemical calculations

1. What is the concentration of the following solutions?
   a) A solution containing 2 moles of solute in 2 dm^3 of solution
   b) A solution containing 2 moles of solute in 4 dm^3 of solution
   c) A solution containing 1 mole of solute in 10 dm^3 of solution
   d) A solution containing 0.1 mole of solute in 500 cm^3 of solution
   e) A solution containing 0.5 mole of solute in 250 cm^3 of solution

2. How many moles of solute are there in the following solutions?
   a) 1 dm^3 of 2 mol / dm^3 solution
   b) 3 dm^3 of 0.5 mol / dm^3 solution
   c) 0.5 dm^3 of 2 mol / dm^3 solution
   d) 100 cm^3 of 4 mol / dm^3 solution
   e) 250 cm^3 of 1 mol / dm^3 solution

3. What is the percentage yield obtained in the following experiments?
   a) 1.5 g of calcium carbonate was obtained when the theoretical amount was 2.0 g.
   b) 14 tonnes of ammonia was obtained when the theoretical amount was 34 tonnes.
   c) 1.2 tonnes of sodium hydroxide was obtained when the theoretical amount was 1.5 tonnes.
   d) 2 moles of carbon dioxide was obtained when the theoretical amount was 2.5 moles.

4. Calcium carbonate reacts with dilute hydrochloric acid to produce carbon dioxide.

   $CaCO_3(s) + 2HCl(aq) \rightarrow CaCl_2(aq) + CO_2(g) + H_2O(l)$

   What is the maximum theoretical mass of carbon dioxide that could be made from 10 g of calcium carbonate? Assume that the hydrochloric acid is in excess so that all the calcium carbonate will react. (Relative atomic masses: H = 1; C = 12; O = 16; Ca = 40)

Topic 3.1: Stoichiometry

Supplement Worksheet C3.1e(2) Working out % yield

When calcium carbonate is heated strongly it decomposes to form calcium oxide and carbon dioxide. Your task is to design an experiment which will enable you to calculate the percentage yield of calcium oxide when 2 g of calcium carbonate are heated. (C = 12, O = 16, Ca = 40)

Your plan should:

a) Show how to safely use techniques, apparatus and materials.
b) Show in detail the procedure you would use to obtain an accurate result.
c) Show how you would record your observations and measurements.
d) Show how you would use your results to calculate the percentage yield.
e) List the possible sources of errors in your method.

Topic 3.1: Stoichiometry

Learning episode C3.1f Consolidation and summary

Learning aims

- Review the learning points of the topic summarised in the end of topic checklist.
- Test understanding of the topic content by answering the end of topic questions.

Resources

Student Book pages 93–98

Approach

Ask students to work with a partner to make a list of key words from this topic. They could then work together to produce a spider diagram showing how the different concepts are linked. They could compare their list with the list of key terms given in the Student Book. Discuss the checklist and ask questions to see how much of the content students are comfortable with.

Students could make flashcards of the key content and then use the flashcards to quiz each other on the information.

Ask students to work individually through the end of topic questions in the Student Book without looking at the text. As they work, walk around the classroom observing their answers and questioning them as necessary to find out which questions are causing difficulties.

After a set period, ask students to stop working. Discuss any areas of difficulty you observed as you walked round the class.

Students should complete any unanswered questions for homework, but you should stress that they should answer the questions without looking at the text, so that they can see how much they have remembered.

End of topic questions mark scheme

The marks available for a question can indicate the level of detail you need to provide in your answer.

Question	Correct answer	Marks
1 a)	NaCl	1 mark
1 b)	MgF_2	1 mark
1 c)	AlN	1 mark
1 d)	Li_2O	1 mark
1 e)	CO_2	1 mark
2 a)	Fe_2O_3	1 mark
2 b)	PCl_5	1 mark
2 c)	$CrBr_3$	1 mark
2 d)	SO_3	1 mark
2 e)	SO_2	1 mark
3 a)	K_2CO_3	1 mark
3 b)	NH_4Cl	1 mark
3 c)	H_2SO_4	1 mark
3 d)	$Mg(OH)_2$	1 mark
3 e)	$(NH_4)_2SO_4$	1 mark
4 a)	$C(s) + O_2(g) \rightarrow CO_2(g)$	1 mark

Topic 3.1: Stoichiometry

4 b)	$4Fe(s) + 3O_2(g) \rightarrow 2Fe_2O_3(s)$	1 mark
4 c)	$2Fe_2O_3(s) + 3C(s) \rightarrow 4Fe(s) + 3CO_2(g)$	1 mark
4 d)	$CaCO_3(s) + 2HCl(aq) \rightarrow CaCl_2(aq) + CO_2(g) + H_2O(l)$	1 mark
5 a)	28	1 mark
5 b)	64	1 mark
5 c)	32	1 mark
6 a)	2 moles Mg → 2 moles MgO	1 mark
	48 g Mg → 80 g MgO	1 mark
	4.8 g Mg → 8 g MgO	1 mark
6 b)	3.2 g oxygen	1 mark
7	2 moles of Na → 2 moles NaOH	1 mark
	46 g Na → 80 g NaOH	1 mark
	2.3 g Na → 4 g NaOH	1 mark
Supplement 8 a)	0.25 mole	1 mark
Supplement 8 b)	0.1 mole	1 mark
Supplement 8 c)	3 moles	1 mark
Supplement 9 a)	220 g	1 mark
Supplement 9 b)	10 g	1 mark
Supplement 9 c)	10.9 g	1 mark
Supplement 10 a)	1 mole	1 mark
Supplement 10 b)	0.05 mole	1 mark
Supplement 11	0.64 g Cu reacts with 0.16 g oxygen.	1 mark
	0.01 mole Cu reacts with 0.01 mole oxygen; formula is therefore CuO.	1 mark
Supplement 12 a)	2.3 g Na reacts with 8.0 g Br.	
	0.1 mole Na reacts with 0.1 mole Br.	1 mark
	Formula is NaBr.	1 mark
Supplement 12 b)	0.6 g C reacts with 1.6 g O.	1 mark
	0.05 mole C reacts with 0.1 mole O; formula is therefore CO_2.	1 mark
Supplement 12 c)	11.12 g Fe reacts with 21.08 g Cl.	1 mark
	0.2 mole Fe reacts with 0.6 mole Cl; formula is therefore $FeCl_3$.	1 mark
Supplement 13		

	Ti	Cl	
Mass/RAM	$\frac{25}{48}$	$\frac{75}{35.5}$	1 mark
			1 mark
Moles	0.52	2.1	
Ratio	$\frac{0.52}{0.52} = 1$	$\frac{2.1}{0.52} = 4.04$	1 mark
Formula is $TiCl_4$			

Topic 3.1: Stoichiometry

Supplement 14	Empirical formula mass = 14	1 mark
	Molecular formula is therefore 2 × empirical formula	1 mark
	and so molecular formula is C_2H_4.	1 mark
Supplement 15 a)	$\quad\quad\quad\quad\quad\quad\quad\quad\quad$ C $\quad\quad\quad\quad$ H $\quad\quad\quad\quad\quad\quad\quad\quad$ Mass/RAM $\quad\quad\quad\quad \frac{92.3}{12} \quad\quad\quad \frac{7.7}{1}$	1 mark
	Moles $\quad\quad\quad\quad\quad\quad\quad\quad$ 7.7 $\quad\quad\quad\quad$ 7.7	
	Ratio $\quad\quad\quad\quad\quad\quad\quad\quad \frac{7.7}{7.7} = 1 \quad\quad \frac{7.7}{7.7} = 1$	
	Empirical formula is CH	1 mark
Supplement 15 b)	Empirical formula mass = 13	1 mark
	Molecular mass = 2 × empirical formula mass so formula is C_2H_2.	1 mark
Supplement 16	Moles barium chloride = $\frac{50}{1000} \times 0.2 = 0.01$	1 mark
	Moles barium sulfate = 0.01	
	1 mole of $BaSO_4$ = 137 + 32 + 16 + 16 + 16 + 16 = 233 g	1 mark
	Mass = 0.01 × 233 = 2.33 g	1 mark
Supplement 17 a)	1 mole iron(III) oxide → 2 moles iron	1 mark
	160 g → 112 g	1 mark
	800 tonnes → 560 tonnes	1 mark
Supplement 17 b)	1 mole iron(III) oxide → 3 moles carbon dioxide	1 mark
	160 g → 72 dm^3	1 mark
	320 g → 144 dm^3	1 mark
Supplement 18	Percentage yield = $\frac{2.1}{2.8} \times 100$	1 mark
	= 75%	1 mark
Supplement 19	Percentage purity = $\frac{0.8}{1.2}$	1 mark
	= 67%	1 mark
Supplement 20 a)	$Ca^{2+}(aq) + CO_3^{2-}(aq) \rightarrow CaCO_3(s)$	1 mark
	(1 mark for correct ions; 1 mark for balancing)	1 mark
Supplement 20 b)	$Fe^{2+}(aq) + 2OH^-(aq) \rightarrow Fe(OH)_2(s)$	1 mark
	(1 mark for correct ions; 1 mark for balancing)	1 mark
Supplement 20 c)	$Ag^+(aq) + Br^-(aq) \rightarrow AgBr(s)$	1 mark
	(1 mark for correct ions; 1 mark for balancing)	1 mark
	Total:	74 marks

Sections 1, 2 and 3: Exam-style questions mark scheme

Exam-style questions and sample answers have been written by the authors. In examinations, the way marks are awarded may be different. References to assessment and/or assessment preparation are the publisher's interpretation of the syllabus requirements and may not fully reflect the approach of Cambridge Assessment International Education.

The marks available for a question can often indicate the level of detail you need to provide in your answer.

Question	Correct answer	Marks
2.	D	1 mark
3 a)	i) From top to bottom:	
	Proton	1 mark
	Electron	1 mark
	Neutron.	1 mark
	ii) 6	1 mark
	iii) 12	1 mark
3 b)	The same: the number of protons and electrons.	1 mark
	Different: the numbers of neutrons.	1 mark
4a)	Metals and non-metals (or non-metals and metals).	2 marks
	Gained and lost (or lost and gained).	2 marks
	High and high.	2 marks
4 b)	i) Mg 2,8,2	1 mark
	Cl 2,8,7	1 mark
	ii) Mg 2,8	1 mark
	Cl 2,8,8	1 mark
Supplement 5.	D	1 mark
	$CaCO_3(s)$ $CO_2(g)$	
	100 g 24 dm^3	
	5 g 1.2 dm^3	
Supplement 6.	2 moles $FeSO_4$ produces 1 mole Fe_2O_3	1 mark
	304 g $FeSO_4$ produces 160 g Fe_2O_3	1 mark
	9.12 g $FeSO_4$ produces 4.8 g Fe_2O_3	1 mark
	So, mass of iron(III) oxide = 4.8 g	
	2 moles of $FeSO_4$ produces 1 mole of SO_3	
	304 g $FeSO_4$ produces 24 000 cm^3 SO_3	1 mark
	9.12 g $FeSO_4$ produces 720 cm^3 SO_3	1 mark
	So, volume of SO_3 = 720 cm^3	1 mark
Supplement 7 a)	Pipette used for potassium hydroxide solution.	1 mark
	Burette for dilute sulfuric acid.	1 mark
	Methyl orange indicator used.	1 mark

Sections 1, 2 and 3: Exam-style questions mark scheme

Question	Correct answer	Marks
	Colour change at end point yellow to pink (Phenolphthalein: colour change at end point pink to colourless).	1 mark
Supplement 7b)	Number of moles KOH = 0.00375	1 mark
	Number of moles of H_2SO_4 = 0.00188	1 mark
	Concentration of H_2SO_4 = 0.125	1 mark
	M or moles / dm^3	1 mark
8 a)	i) A is methane.	1 mark
	ii) B and E are giant structures.	1 mark
	iii) A and C are hydrocarbons.	1 mark
	iv) B.	1 mark
	v) B and E have very high melting points.	1 mark
8 b)	i) Graphite	1 mark
	ii) Diamond or buckminsterfullerene are other forms of carbon.	1 mark
8 c)	NaI	1 mark
8 d)	Substance D is a compound, because two different atoms are bonded together.	1 mark
Supplement 9 a)	They both have a valency of 2 because Group II metals will lose 2 electrons.	1 mark
	Group VI elements will gain 2 electrons.	1 mark
Supplement 9 b)	SCl_2	1 mark
	There should be 8 electrons around both chlorine atoms.	1 mark
	8 electrons around sulfur with 2o and 2x.	1 mark
Supplement 9 c)	i) Liquid strontium chloride does demonstrate electrical conductivity, whereas solid strontium chloride does not. Ions cannot move in the solid state but can in the liquid state.	1 mark
	ii) Liquid strontium chloride does demonstrate electrical conductivity, whereas liquid sulfur chloride does not. There are no ions in sulfur chloride as it is covalent, but strontium chloride is ionic.	1 mark
	Total:	49 marks

Section 4: Electrochemistry

Contents
C4.1 Electrochemistry

Overview of the section
Electrochemistry is a key element of physical chemistry and its applications are continually growing. The use of electricity to generate chemical reactions is of significant industrial importance, whether to produce metals such as aluminium or non-metals such as chlorine. More recently fuel cells are being seen as an effective way of generating electricity and reducing the production of greenhouse gases.

The section starts with the characteristics of electrolytes and electrolysis and introduces the electrolysis of a range of electrolytes. Supplementary material focuses on the fundamentals of charge transfer that underpin electrolysis.

Starting points
The Student Book section opener (pages 106–108) puts the ideas in the section into context and sets the scene. It also allows students to acknowledge and value their prior learning, and provides a benchmark against which future learning can be compared.

The questions provide a structure for introducing the section and can be used in a number of different ways:
- You could ask students to consider the questions as an introductory homework task.
- You could put students into groups to share their own ideas and understanding and then to report back to the whole class.
- Students could be given access to the Internet, preferably with a tight timescale, to find out the information required.

You could then use a spider chart or other form of wall chart to summarise everybody's ideas.

Recording these initial ideas allows you to retain them for reference as the individual topics are developed. In this way, your students' progress in learning can be readily acknowledged.

Topic 4.1: Electrochemistry

C4.1 Electrochemistry

Introduction

This topic builds on the understanding of chemical bonding from Topics 2.2 *Ions and ionic bonds* and Topic 2.3 *Molecules and covalent bonds*. It is also an opportunity to revise the structure of metals (Topic 2.4 *Metallic bonding*) and their property as conductors of electricity. There are clear links to Topic 9.1 *Metals*, because the reactivity series can be used to predict the preferential discharge of ions.

Supplement It can be explained to supplementary students, that the loss or gain of electrons when ions are discharged can be linked to Topic 6.3 *Redox reactions*.

The topic starts with an introduction to electrolytes and electrolysis. You will then consider the electrolysis of molten compounds and aqueous solutions. Electroplating is introduced as a useful application, followed by a short section on conductors and insulators.

Supplement For the supplementary syllabus ionic equations are introduced and the topic ends with hydrogen–oxygen fuel cells.

The concepts of electrolysis can be reinforced by practical demonstrations. This also gives students a good opportunity to develop their practical investigative skills, particularly *Observing, measuring and recording* and *Handling experimental observations and data*.

Links to other topics

Section	Essential background knowledge	Useful links
2 Atoms, elements and compounds	2.2 Ions and ionic bonds 2.3 Molecules and covalent bonds 2.4 Metallic bonding	
6 Chemical reactions		6.3 Redox reactions
9 Metals		9.1 Metals

Topic overview

C4.1a	Orientation
	This learning episode revises ideas on chemical bonding, especially ionic bonding, and then introduces some of the terms associated with electrolysis. Demonstrations highlight the aspects to be covered in the topic.
C4.1b	**Electrolysis of molten electrolytes**
	This learning episode introduces the electrolysis of molten electrolytes using anhydrous zinc chloride as an example. The need for the ions in an electrolyte to be able to move is emphasised. **Supplement** Ionic half-equations are introduced.
C4.1c	**Electrolysis of aqueous electrolytes**
	This is a relatively long learning episode (with five parts) and offers the opportunity for two practical activities for students. Consideration is given to the conditions required for electroplating. **Supplement** The dissociation of water into ions is introduced and is used to explain the products formed from the electrolysis of aqueous solutions. Further emphasis is placed on the use of half-equations to summarise the changes that occur at the electrodes. The reactivity series is introduced to explain the preferential discharge of ions at the cathode.

Topic 4.1: Electrochemistry

C4.1d	**The production of electrical energy from simple cells**
	This learning episode considers the reverse of electrolysis by focusing on how a chemical reaction can generate electricity. It looks at how energy is obtained from hydrogen–oxygen fuel cells.
	Supplement Students are asked to describe the advantages and disadvantages of using fuel cells compared to petrol engines in cars.
C4.1e	**Consolidation and summary**
	This learning episode provides an opportunity for a quick recap of the ideas encountered in the topic.

Career links

These are some scientific careers that focus on this area of chemistry but careers in many other fields use the knowledge and skills gained studying science.

Some electrochemists are involved in the development of medical diagnostic devices which use electrochemistry techniques. Fuel cell material scientists develop new materials that can be used in fuel cell manufacture.

Topic 4.1: Electrochemistry

Learning episode C4.1a Orientation

Learning objectives

- Define electrolysis as the decomposition of an ionic compound, when molten or in aqueous solution, by the passage of an electric current.
- Identify in simple electrolytic cells
    (a) the anode as the positive electrode
    (b) the cathode as the negative electrode
    (c) the electrolyte as the molten or aqueous substance that undergoes electrolysis.
- **Supplement** Describe the transfer of charge during electrolysis to include:
    (a) the movement of electrons in the external circuit
    (b) the loss or gain of electrons at the electrodes
    (c) the movement of ions in the electrolyte.

Common misconceptions

Some students think that electrons (as opposed to ions) move within the electrolyte.

Resources

Student Book pages 108–110

Resources for demonstration (see Technician's notes, following)

Approach

Demonstrate the passage of electricity through a solid conductor such as a strip of copper **(see tech notes)**. Contrast it with the fact that a strip of plastic acts as an insulator.

Ask why a metal conducts electricity but plastic does not. Check that students remember that in metals there are delocalised electrons that allow electrons to flow through the solid when a potential difference (voltage) is applied.

Then demonstrate the passage of electricity through a solution (such as aqueous sodium chloride) and compare it with the lack of conductivity of solid sodium chloride. Ask students what they can remember about the bonding in sodium chloride. Elicit the idea that the mobility of the ions in sodium chloride might have something to do with whether an electric current can pass through it.

Ask what the difference between the ions in solid sodium chloride will be and in sodium chloride solution. Use this demonstration to introduce some terms and definitions for electrode, anode, cathode, electrolyte and electrolysis.

Tell students that the topic will explore further the involvement of ions in electrolysis and why the ions must be able to move. They should have observed gases being produced in the electrolysis of sodium chloride solution.

SAFETY INFORMATION
Wear eye protection (splash-proof goggles).
Turn off the electricity when the teacher smells chlorine.
Chlorine is oxidising, toxic and hazardous to the environment.
Small amounts of Cl_2, which can cause respiratory distress in some people, may be produced. **The laboratory must be well ventilated.**

Finally, for those students following the supplementary syllabus explain how the charge is transferred in electrolysis – in the electrodes (electrons added or removed), wires (electrons) and electrolyte (ions).

Topic 4.1: Electrochemistry

Technician's notes

Be sure to check the latest safety notes on these resources before proceeding.

The following resources are needed for the demonstration of conduction:

copper foil, about 5 cm long, cleaned with abrasive paper such as emery cloth; avoid sharp edges
strip of plastic, about 5 cm long
solid sodium chloride, about 10 g
0.5 mol / dm^3 sodium chloride solution, 50 cm^3
100 cm^3 beaker
6–8 V power supply, bulb, leads, crocodile clips, carbon electrodes

Answers

Page 110

1. The breaking down (decomposition) of a chemical compound by the use of electricity.
2. The positive electrode is the anode.
3. The substance must contain ions and they must be free to move (in molten/liquid state or dissolved in water).

Topic 4.1: Electrochemistry

Learning episode C4.1b Electrolysis of molten electrolytes

Learning objectives

- Identify the products formed at the electrodes and describe the observations made during the electrolysis of molten lead(II) bromide using inert electrodes made of platinum or carbon / graphite.
- State that metals or hydrogen are formed at the cathode and that non-metals (other than hydrogen) are formed at the anode.
- Predict the identity of the products at each electrode for the electrolysis of a binary compound in the molten state.
- **Supplement** Construct ionic half-equations for reactions at the anode (to show oxidation) and at the cathode (to show reduction).

Resources

Student Book pages 110–112

Resources for demonstration (see Technician's notes, following)

Approach

Although lead(II) bromide is in the syllabus, the demonstration should be of anhydrous zinc chloride **(see tech notes)**. This is due to the specific hazards of demonstrating lead(II) bromide in the laboratory. Revise the conditions for electrolysis discussed in the previous learning episode. The section on page 109 of the Student Book should help. Then introduce the electrolysis of molten anhydrous zinc chloride. You must set this up in a working fume cupboard with apparatus similar to that shown in the Student Book (page 111). If possible, have a lamp in the circuit.

Demonstrate that an electric current cannot pass through the anhydrous zinc chloride as a solid, but once it is molten, an electric current does flow. It may be possible to see effervescence at the anode as the chlorine is formed and, after cooling, it might be possible to see the zinc at the bottom of the crucible.

If you need to reinforce the fact that not all molten substances conduct electricity, you could repeat the experiment using candle wax (a covalently bonded compound). Ask students to predict the products of the electrolysis of other molten binary ionic compounds, for example sodium chloride, lead(II) bromide, magnesium chloride and aluminium oxide.

Supplement Introduce the half-equations for the reactions that have occurred at the electrodes in the electrolysis of the molten anhydrous zinc chloride.

Supplement Ask students to write half-equations to represent the changes that occur when some other ionic compounds are electrolysed, for example sodium chloride, lead(II) bromide, magnesium chloride and aluminium oxide.

> **SAFETY INFORMATION**
>
> *Wear eye protection (splash-proof goggles) and use safety screens.*
>
> *Use a fume cupboard for the electrolysis of molten salts, e.g. zinc chloride. Ensure that the fume cupboard door is closed so that air is gently drawn in. These salts are appreciably volatile at melting temperatures.*
>
> *Impure lead bromide may give off bromine on melting and during electrolysis; bromine is very toxic and corrosive and must not be inhaled. Pure lead iodide starts to decompose at just above melting point. Use anhydrous zinc chloride as a safer alternative.*
>
> *Chlorine is oxidising, toxic and hazardous to the environment.*
>
> *Small amounts of Cl_2, which can cause respiratory distress in some people, may be produced.*
> **The laboratory must be well ventilated.**

Topic 4.1: Electrochemistry

Technician's notes

Be sure to check the latest safety notes on these resources before proceeding.

The following resources are needed for the demonstration of electrolysis of anhydrous zinc chloride:

The apparatus should be set up in a fume cupboard.

carbon electrodes in a holder (pencil 'lead' can be used to allow smaller quantities to be used)
leads, crocodile clips, lamp, 6–8 V power pack
tripod, pipeclay triangle, stand and clamp, crucible, heatproof mat
solid anhydrous zinc chloride
possibly also candle wax
eye protection (splash-proof goggles)

Topic 4.1: Electrochemistry

Learning episode C4.1c Electrolysis of aqueous electrolytes

Learning objectives

- Identify the products formed at the electrodes and describe the observations made during the electrolysis of:
    (b) concentrated aqueous sodium chloride
    (c) dilute sulfuric acid.
  using inert electrodes made of platinum or carbon / graphite.
- State that metals or hydrogen are formed at the cathode and that non-metals (other than hydrogen) are formed at the anode.
- State that metal objects are electroplated to improve their appearance and resistance to corrosion.
- Describe how metals are electroplated.
- **Supplement** Identify the products formed at the electrodes and describe the observations made during the electrolysis of aqueous copper(II) sulfate using inert carbon / graphite electrodes and when using copper electrodes.
- **Supplement** Predict the identity of the products at each electrode for the electrolysis of a halide compound in dilute or concentrated aqueous solution.
- **Supplement** Construct ionic half-equations for reactions at the anode (to show oxidation) and at the cathode (to show reduction).

Common misconceptions

Some students think that water is an electrolyte (perhaps arising from knowledge of the dangers associated with electrical appliances in the bathroom).

Resources

Student Book pages 112–119

Worksheet C4.1c(1) Identifying and investigating electrolytes

Worksheet C4.1c(2) The electrolysis of sodium chloride solution

Resources for class practical (see Technician's notes, following)

Approach

1. Investigating electrolytes

Students test a range of liquids and solutions as indicated in Worksheet C4.1c(1), using their knowledge gained from the first two activities. They make predictions before they undertake each test.

They will become aware that effervescence occurs at one electrode at least with all four electrolytes. They should also be able to identify copper as a pink deposit on the cathode when aqueous copper(II) sulfate is electrolysed.

SAFETY INFORMATION
Wear eye protection (splash-proof goggles).
Ethanol is highly flammable.
Chlorine is oxidising, toxic and hazardous to the environment.
Small amounts of Cl_2, which can cause respiratory distress in some people, may be produced. **The laboratory must be well ventilated.**

2. Role of water in electrolysis

Now focus on the role of water in the electrolysis of these solutions – for example, why wasn't sodium formed when sodium chloride was electrolysed? The dissociation of water into ions is essentially only necessary for the supplementary syllabus, but students do need to know that the hydrogen often formed in the electrolysis of aqueous solutions comes from the water.

Supplement The slight dissociation of water into ions is covered in the Student Book on page 113. This may be the first time that students have come across the reversible sign and the idea of an equilibrium reaction.

Supplement Emphasise that there are too few ions present in water for it to behave as an electrolyte, but that more water molecules dissociate as ions are discharged at electrodes. Take some time to explain the half-equations for the formation of hydrogen, oxygen and chlorine.

3. Electrolysis of sodium chloride solution

Students can now use Worksheet C4.1c(2) to look in more detail at the electrolysis of sodium chloride solution. This learning episode introduces the tests for hydrogen and chlorine. If these gases have not been covered previously, you will need to provide some guidance.

SAFETY INFORMATION
Wear eye protection (splash-proof goggles).
Chlorine is oxidising, toxic and hazardous to the environment.
Small amounts of Cl_2, which can cause respiratory distress in some people, may be produced. ***The laboratory must be well ventilated.***

4. Electrolysis of dilute sulfuric acid

The Developing Practical Skills feature on page 118 of the Student Book can be used instead of further practical activity.

Supplement 5. Electrolysis of copper(II) sulfate solution

Pages 114–115 of the Student Book can be used to support the study of the electrolysis of copper(II) sulfate solution with both carbon/graphite and copper electrodes.

Refer back to the observations that the students made for this reaction in Worksheet C4.1c(1). This learning episode can be completed by focusing on the reactivity series as a means of identifying which of the competing ions will be preferentially discharged.

6. Electroplating

From the practical completed with Worksheet C4.1c(1), the students will have seen copper being deposited on the cathode. Use this as an introduction to the important process of electroplating. Details on the process and some of the uses of electroplating are provided on page 117 of the Student Book.

Technician's notes

Be sure to check the latest safety notes on these resources before proceeding.

The following resources are needed for the class practical C4.1c(1), per group:

6–8 V power pack, leads, crocodile clips, lamp, carbon electrodes
100 cm^3 beaker
50 cm^3 ethanol (industrial denatured ethanol) + container for collection of used ethanol
50 cm^3 dilute hydrochloric acid (0.5 mol/dm^3)
50 cm^3 dilute sulfuric acid (0.4 mol/dm^3)
50 cm^3 copper(II) sulfate solution (0.4 mol/dm^3)
50 cm^3 sodium chloride solution (0.4 mol/dm^3)
eye protection (splash-proof goggles)

Topic 4.1: Electrochemistry

The following resources are needed for the class practical 4.1c(2), per group:

electrolysis cell with carbon electrodes
6–8 V power supply, leads, crocodile clips
ignition tubes
sodium chloride solution (0.4 M) to fill electrolysis cell
eye protection (splash-proof goggles)

Answers

Page 117

1. a) An inert electrode is an unreactive electrode. It will not be changed during electrolysis.

    b) Carbon is commonly used as an inert electrode. (Platinum is another inert electrode.)

2. a) Lead and chlorine.   b) Magnesium and oxygen.   c) Aluminium and oxygen.
3. Supplement a) Cathode: Hydrogen (sodium is above hydrogen in the reactivity series).

    Anode: oxygen and bromine (more bromine at higher concentrations)

    b) Cathode: Hydrogen (zinc is above hydrogen in the reactivity series).

    Anode: oxygen and chlorine (more chlorine at higher concentrations)

    c) Cathode: Silver (silver is below hydrogen in the reactivity series).

    Anode: oxygen.

4. Supplement a) $2O^{2-}(aq) \rightarrow O_2(g) + 4e^-$

    b) The change takes place at the anode.

Supplement Developing Practical Skills, page 118

1. Platinum is commonly used as a material for inert electrodes.
2. Hydrogen was formed at the cathode.
3. Solutions that allow an electric current to flow through them are known as electrolytes.
4. The volume of oxygen will be half that of the hydrogen.
5. The ions in dilute sulfuric acid are H^+, SO_4^{2-} and OH^-.
6. $2H^+(aq) + 2e^- \rightarrow H_2(g)$

Supplement Page 119

1. a) Diagram as in Fig 4.11.

    b) At the cathode: $Cu^{2+}(aq) + 2e^- \rightarrow Cu(s)$

    At the anode: $Cu(s) \rightarrow Cu^{2+}(aq) + 2e^-$

Topic 4.1: Electrochemistry

Worksheet C4.1c(1) Identifying and investigating electrolytes

An electrolyte is a substance that allows an electric current to pass through it when it is molten or dissolved in water. In addition, the current breaks down the electrolyte, producing other chemicals. In this experiment you will test some liquids and solutions to see if they are electrolytes.

Your knowledge of chemical bonding should help you to make predictions before you test each liquid or solution. For each electrolyte you will need to write down what you observe at each electrode as the current is flowing through it.

Apparatus

power pack or 6 V battery

bulb and holder

leads

crocodile clips

carbon electrodes

100 cm^3 beaker

substances to test: dilute hydrochloric acid, dilute sulfuric acid, dilute copper(II) sulfate solution, dilute sodium chloride solution, ethanol

eye protection (splash-proof goggles)

SAFETY INFORMATION

Wear eye protection (splash-proof goggles).

Ethanol is highly flammable.

Chlorine is oxidising, toxic and hazardous to the environment.

Small amounts of Cl$_2$, which can cause respiratory distress in some people, may be produced.
The laboratory must be well ventilated.

Method

1. Put on your eye protection.
2. Set up the apparatus as shown in the diagram. A 6 volt DC supply of electricity is suitable.
   The bulb will indicate if the test liquid or solution is an electrolyte or not.
3. Wipe the electrodes between tests.
4. Rinse and dry the beaker between tests but do NOT tip ethanol into the sink, pour it into the container provided by the teacher.

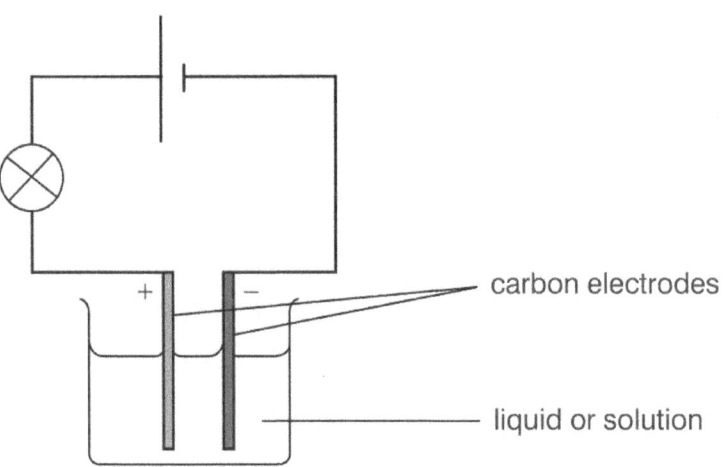

Page 1 of 2

Topic 4.1: Electrochemistry

Observing, measuring and recording

5. Record your results in the table provided.

Liquid/solution	Prediction Electrolyte (Y/N)	Electrolyte observations	
		At the anode	At the cathode
Water			
Dilute hydrochloric acid			
Dilute sulfuric acid			
Copper(II) sulfate solution			
Ethanol			
Sodium chloride solution			

Handling experimental observations and data

6. Which liquids or solutions were NOT electrolytes?
7. Which electrolyte produced a solid coating on one of the electrodes? At which electrode did this coating form?
8. Explain why some of the liquids or solutions did not act as electrolytes whereas others did.

Topic 4.1: Electrochemistry

Worksheet C4.1c(2) The electrolysis of sodium chloride solution

Sodium chloride is an electrolyte and so it will allow an electric current to pass through it when in solution. It will also be broken down by this electric current. In this experiment you will be able to predict the products of the electrolysis and then test your predictions.

Apparatus

electrolysis cell with carbon electrodes

ignition tubes

6 V DC power supply

leads, crocodile clips

sodium chloride solution

eye protection (splash-proof goggles)

SAFETY INFORMATION
Wear eye protection (splash-proof goggles).
Chlorine is oxidising, toxic and hazardous to the environment.
Small amounts of Cl_2, which can cause respiratory distress in some people, may be produced. ***The laboratory must be well ventilated.***

Method

1. Put on your eye protection.
2. Using the apparatus shown, carefully fill the electrolysis cell about two-thirds full of sodium chloride solution.
3. Fill the ignition tubes with sodium chloride solution and carefully invert them over the carbon electrodes.
4. Connect the circuit and record your observations.
5. Turn off the power supply as soon as you finish.

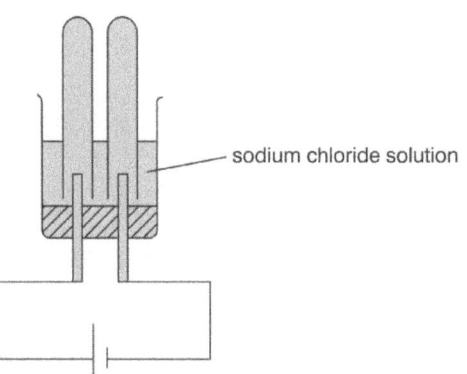

Observing, measuring and recording

6. Record your observations in the table below:

Observations at the anode	Observations at the cathode

Handling experimental observations and data

7. The ion that is discharged at the cathode will have what charge? What do you think this ion is?
8. What do you think is the gas produced at the cathode? What test could you do on the gas to check your prediction? What result would confirm your prediction?
9. The ion that is discharged at the anode will have what charge? What do you think the ion is?
10. What do you think is the gas produced at the anode? What test could you do on the gas to check your prediction? What result would confirm your prediction?
11. Why do you think so little gas collects at the anode?

Topic 4.1: Electrochemistry

Learning episode C4.1d The production of electrical energy from simple cells

Learning objectives

- State that a hydrogen–oxygen fuel cell uses hydrogen and oxygen to produce electricity with water as the only chemical product.
- Supplement Describe the advantages and disadvantages of using hydrogen–oxygen fuel cells in comparison with gasoline / petrol engines in vehicles.

Resources

Student Book pages 119–120

Approach

This is a very short learning episode. The Student Book provides the essential information and this is extended by the Science in Context section on page 120. The content of these Science in Context features is beyond the syllabus but provides the opportunity to explore the content more deeply.

Supplement The discussion of the advantages and disadvantages of hydrogen–oxygen fuel cells could be organised as a class discussion or debate or the feature of a homework question.

Answers

Science in Context, page 120

a) $H_2 (g) \rightarrow 2H^+ (aq) + 2e^-$

b) $2H_2 (g) + O_2(g) \rightarrow 2H_2O(l)$

Topic 4.1: Electrochemistry

Learning episode C4.1e Consolidation and summary

Learning aims

- Review the learning points of the topic summarised in the end of topic checklist.
- Test understanding of the topic content by answering the end of topic questions.

Resources

Student Book pages 121–124

Approach

Approach

Ask students to work with a partner to make a list of key words from this topic. They could then work together to produce a spider diagram showing how the different concepts are linked. They could compare their list with the list of key terms given in the Student Book. Discuss the checklist and ask questions to see how much of the content students are comfortable with.

It is worth stressing the importance of electrolysis in the manufacture of some important chemicals – aluminium, sodium hydroxide and chlorine.

Students could make flashcards of the key content and then use the flashcards to quiz each other on the information.

Ask students to work individually through the end of topic questions in the Student Book without looking at the text. As they work, walk around the classroom observing their answers and questioning them as necessary to find out which questions are causing difficulties.

After a set period, ask students to stop working. Discuss any areas of difficulty you observed as you walked round the class.

Students should complete any unanswered questions for homework, but you should stress that they should answer the questions without looking at the text, so that they can see how much they have remembered.

End of topic questions mark scheme

The marks available for a question can indicate the level of detail you need to provide in your answer.

Question	Correct answer	Marks
1 a)	Electrolysis is the breaking down of a (ionic) compound by a flow of electricity.	1 mark
1 b)	An electrolyte is a substance that when molten or dissolved in water allows an electric current to pass through it.	1 mark
1 c)	An electrode is the substance that is used to pass the electric current into and out of the electrolyte during electrolysis.	1 mark
1 d)	The anode is the positively charged electrode.	1 mark
1 e)	The cathode is the negatively charged electrode.	1 mark
2	B	1 mark
3	The zinc bromide contains ions that are held in a lattice by strong electrostatic attractive forces.	1 mark
	In the solid these ions are not free to move and carry the current.	1 mark

Topic 4.1: Electrochemistry

Question	Correct answer	Marks
4	Completed table as shown: 	Electrolyte	Product at the anode	Product at the cathode	 |---|---|---| 	Silver bromide	*Bromine*	*Silver*	 	Lead(II) chloride	*Chlorine*	*Lead*	 	Aluminium oxide	*Oxygen*	*Aluminium*	 	*Magnesium iodide*	Iodine	Magnesium		4 marks
5 a)	Anode: chlorine.	1 mark
	Cathode: sodium.	1 mark
5 b)	Anode: chlorine and oxygen.	1 mark
	Cathode: hydrogen.	1 mark
6 a)	Cathode.	1 mark
6 b)	Silver.	1 mark
Supplement 7 a)	$Al^{3+}(l) + 3e^- \rightarrow Al(l)$ (1 mark for correct charges; 1 mark for balanced equation)	2 marks
Supplement 7 b)	$Na^+(l) + e^- \rightarrow Na(l)$ (1 mark for correct charges; 1 mark for balanced equation)	2 marks
Supplement 7 c)	$2O^{2-}(l) \rightarrow O_2(g) + 4e^-$ (1 mark for correct charges; 1 mark for balanced equation)	2 marks
Supplement 7 d)	$2Br^-(aq) \rightarrow Br_2(l) + 2e^-$ (1 mark for correct charges; 1 mark for balanced equation)	2 marks
Supplement 7 e)	$4OH^-(aq) \rightarrow 2H_2O(l) + O_2(g) + 4e^-$ (1 mark for correct charges; 1 mark for balanced equation)	2 marks
Supplement 8 a) i)	Chlorine is formed at the anode.	1 mark
Supplement 8 a) ii)	$2Cl^-(aq) \rightarrow Cl_2(g) + 2e^-$ Oxidation (1 mark for oxidation; 1 mark for balancing)	2 marks
Supplement 8 b) i)	Hydrogen is formed.	1 mark
Supplement 8 b) ii)	$2H^+(aq) + 2e^- \rightarrow H_2(g)$ (1 mark for formulae and state symbols; 1 mark for balancing)	2 marks
Supplement 8 c)	The sodium hydroxide forms in the cell.	1 mark
	From the Na^+ and OH^- ions that are not discharged.	1 mark
Supplement 9	Hydrogen–oxygen fuel cells generate electricity without the production of carbon dioxide (a greenhouse gas).	1 mark
	However, in the production of hydrogen significant amounts of carbon dioxide are produced.	1 mark
	Total:	38 marks

Section 5: Chemical energetics

Contents
C5.1 Chemical energetics

Overview of the section
This section is an important element of physical chemistry. Students will be very familiar with exothermic reactions, such as burning fuels, although they may not be familiar with the term 'exothermic'. Endothermic reactions, as they are far less common, may not be at all familiar. Understanding chemical energetics will provide links to a number of important concepts and, particularly, identifying the appropriate conditions for manufacturing important chemicals formed by reversible reactions.

Supplement For supplementary study, energy profile diagrams are introduced as a way of summarising in diagrammatic form the key energy components in a chemical reaction. The energy associated with making and breaking of bonds provides a useful mechanism for calculating energy changes involving covalent bonded elements and compounds.

Starting points
The Student Book section opener (pages 126–127) puts the ideas in the section into context and sets the scene. It also allows students to acknowledge and value their prior learning, and provides a benchmark against which future learning can be compared.

The questions provide a structure for introducing the section and can be used in a number of different ways:
- You could ask students to consider the questions as an introductory homework task.
- You could put students into groups to share their own ideas and understanding and then to report back to the whole class.
- Students could be given access to the Internet, preferably with a tight timescale, to find out the information required.

You could then use a spider chart or other form of wall chart to summarise everybody's ideas.

Recording these initial ideas allows you to retain them for reference as the individual topics are developed. In this way, your students' progress in learning can be readily acknowledged.

Topic 5.1: Chemical energetics

C5.1 Chemical energetics

Introduction

This topic does not need much prior knowledge, although students must understand covalent bonding before they study bond breaking and bond forming in reactions.

There are many links to other topics; for example, energy change in displacement reactions links to Topic 9.1 *Metals*; energy change in neutralisation reactions links to Topic 7.1 *Acids, bases and salts*; and the energy of combustion links to Topic 11.2 *Fuels*, Topic 11.3 *Alkanes*, Topic 11.4 *Alkenes* and Topic 11.5 *Alcohols*. There are also links to Topic 6.1 *Rate of Reaction* (the activation energy of reactions) and Topic 6.2 *Reversible reactions and equilibrium* (temperature affects the equilibrium of exothermic and endothermic reactions).

This topic starts with classifying reactions as exothermic and endothermic and then focuses on two types of calorimetric techniques – first using an insulated cup (for reactions such as displacement and neutralisation), and then a metal container (for combustion reactions). Reaction pathway diagrams (energy level diagrams) are introduced and the origin of these energy transfers is explained in terms of bond breaking and bond forming.

Students have good opportunities to develop their practical/investigative skills, including performing accurate quantitative work.

Links to other topics

Section	Essential background knowledge	Useful links
2 Atoms, elements and compounds	2.3 Molecules and covalent bonds	
3 Stoichiometry	3.1 Stoichiometry	
6 Chemical reactions		6.1 Rate of reaction
		6.2 Reversible reactions and equilibrium
		6.3 Redox reactions
7 Acids, bases and salts		7.1 Acids, bases and salts
9 Metals		9.1 Metals
11 Organic chemistry		11.2 Fuels
		11.3 Alkanes
		11.4 Alkenes
		11.5 Alcohols

Topic overview

C5.1a	Orientation
	Limited background knowledge is required for this topic, other than an understanding of covalent bonding. This learning episode introduces the definitions of exothermic and endothermic reactions and then provides students with a number of practical examples of each type of reaction. Reactions include acid/alkali neutralisation reactions and displacement reactions.
	The physical change of dissolving potassium chloride in water is also introduced as work on 'cold packs' is developed in the next learning episode.

Topic 5.1: Chemical energetics

C5.1b	**Measuring energy transfers (1)**
	This learning episode introduces the calorimetric method for measuring energy changes.
	Students learn that heat transfer to and from a reaction has to be controlled if accurate measurements have to be made. The choice of the reaction vessel is therefore crucial. Refer briefly to the Student Book pages 128–129.
	There is an investigation into 'cold packs'. Students design their own investigation to find out what quantities of potassium chloride and water must be mixed to provide a temperature change of –10 °C. This learning episode provides a good opportunity for students to learn about this simple calorimetric technique.
C5.1c	**Measuring energy transfers (2)**
	This learning episode is in two parts. The first part involves using the calorimetric method to compare the energy produced on burning different fuels. The second part introduces the terminology of enthalpy change, its representation by the symbol ΔH and the use of reaction pathway diagrams to distinguish between exothermic and endothermic reactions. Students use a calorimetric technique to find out the energy transferred when a fuel burns.
	Reaction pathway diagrams are also introduced to contrast exothermic and endothermic reactions.
	The Developing Practical Skills feature on page 133 of the Student Book can be used to reinforce the ideas encountered or could be used later in the consolidation and summary learning episode.
C5.1d	**Reaction pathway diagrams and bond breaking and bond forming**
	This learning episode uses the concept of a reaction pathway diagram or energy level diagram to explain the differences between exothermic and endothermic reactions. The use of the term activation energy is reinforced and a reaction pathway diagram is explained in terms of how it illustrates the difference in the energy required to break bonds and the energy released when bonds are formed.
	Average bond energies are used to calculate the energy of a reaction.
C5.1e	**Consolidation and summary**
	This learning episode recaps on the ideas encountered in the topic. The Developing Practical Skills feature on page 133 of the Student Book could be used as a revision activity if it has not already been used as part of Learning episode 5a.3. Students can also do the end of topic questions.

Career links

These are some scientific careers that focus on this area of chemistry but careers in many other fields use the knowledge and skills gained studying science.

Pyrotechnic engineers design and test fireworks for firework displays. Combustion chemists can be involved in the development of new fuels. Health and safety officers and firefighters looks at which to limit risks from fires and how to deal with fires safely and efficiently.

Topic 5.1: Chemical energetics

Learning episode C5.1a Orientation

Learning objectives

- State that an exothermic reaction transfers thermal energy to the surroundings leading to an increase in the temperature of the surroundings.
- State than an endothermic reaction takes in thermal energy from the surroundings leading to a decrease in the temperature of the surroundings.

Common misconceptions

Students may think that dissolving is a chemical reaction – dissolving potassium chloride in water is a physical change, not a chemical change.

Resources

Student Book pages 128–130

Worksheet C5.1a Exothermic and endothermic reactions

Resources for demonstration and class practical (see Technician's notes, following)

Approach

Demonstrate the burning of magnesium ribbon in a Bunsen flame **(see tech notes)**. Warn students not to look at the flame directly. If possible provide sunglasses/blue glass. Explain that the reaction generates a lot of thermal/ heat energy – energy is transferred from the reaction to the surroundings. Such reactions are known as exothermic reactions.

> **SAFETY INFORMATION**
>
> *Wear eye protection (splash-proof goggles).*
>
> *For longer lengths of magnesium ribbon burnt by the teacher or burning in oxygen, do not look directly at the flame. A welding filter or even viewing it through a 1mm gap between the fingers of one hand will offer protection. Magnesium burns with such brightness that viewing it directly may cause retinal damage.*
>
> Raising and lowering the crucible lid should not allow a direct view of the burning magnesium.

Introduce the practical activity (Worksheet C5.1a). This includes one reaction that results in a fall in the temperature of the surroundings (citric acid and sodium hydrogen carbonate) and a physical change (potassium chloride and water) which also absorbs energy from the surroundings. The other reactions (metal + acid; displacement of a metal ion; neutralisation) are exothermic.

Students may be familiar with metal + acid, displacement and neutralisation reactions. This is an opportunity to recap or to probe their knowledge. Explain that later in the topic they will study techniques for comparing the amount of thermal energy released in exothermic and endothermic reactions, and as an extension, the reasons behind these energy changes.

After completing the practical activity ask the question 'Do all chemical reactions generate thermal energy – are they all exothermic?' In fact, this is not the case. Introduce the terminology of an endothermic reaction – a reaction that absorbs thermal energy from the surroundings.

> **SAFETY INFORMATION**
>
> *Wear eye protection (splash-proof goggles).*
>
> *Sodium hydroxide is corrosive.*
>
> *Copper(II) sulfate is corrosive, hazardous to the aqueous environment and a moderate hazard.*
>
> *Sulfuric acid and citric acid are irritants.*
>
> *Wear disposable gloves.*

Topic 5.1: Chemical energetics

Technician's notes

Be sure to check the latest safety notes on these resources before proceeding.

The following resources are needed for the demonstration of an exothermic reaction:

magnesium ribbon – about 5 cm (supply students with pre-cut lengths)
tongs, Bunsen burner, heatproof mat
eye protection (splash-proof goggles)

The following resources are needed for the class practical 5a.1a, per group:

boiling tubes, boiling tube rack, thermometer, spatula, droppers, stirring rods
potassium chloride
magnesium ribbon (1 cm per group)
1 mol/dm^3 sulfuric acid, 1 mol/dm^3 citric acid, 1 mol/dm^3 sodium hydroxide – about 8 cm^3 of each
1 mol/dm^3 hydrochloric acid, 1 mol/dm^3 copper(II) sulfate – about 8 cm^3 of each
sodium hydrogen carbonate, iron filings
eye protection (splash-proof goggles)

SAFETY INFORMATION
Only the quantities required should be dispensed.

Topic 5.1: Chemical energetics

Worksheet C5.1a Exothermic and endothermic reactions

Almost all chemical reactions involve a transfer of thermal energy. In most reactions thermal energy is transferred to the surroundings and the temperature of the surroundings increases – these reactions are EXOTHERMIC.

In a few reactions thermal energy is absorbed from the surroundings and the temperature of the surroundings decreases – these reactions are ENDOTHERMIC.

Your task is to measure the temperature changes in a series of reactions to classify the reactions as exothermic or endothermic.

Apparatus

boiling tubes and boiling tube rack

thermometer

spatula

droppers and stirring rods

hydrochloric acid, copper(II) sulfate solution, citric acid solution, sulfuric acid, magnesium ribbon, iron filings, sodium hydrogen carbonate, sodium hydroxide solution, potassium chloride

eye protection (splash-proof goggles)

SAFETY INFORMATION
Wear eye protection (splash-proof goggles).
Sulfuric acid and citric acid are irritants. Sodium hydroxide is corrosive.
Copper(II) sulfate is corrosive, a moderate hazard and hazardous to the aquatic environment.
Iron filings are flammable.

Method

1. Put on your eye protection.
2. Put about a 2 cm depth of substance 1 (see the table below) into a boiling tube. Record the temperature of the liquid or solution.
3. Add either 1 heaped spatula measure or, if a solution, about a 2 cm depth of substance 2.
4. Stir the reaction mixture and take the highest or lowest temperature reached.

Topic 5.1: Chemical energetics

Observing, measuring and recording

5. Record your results in the table.

Substance 1	Substance 2	Initial temperature / °C	Final temperature / °C	Temperature change / °C	Exothermic or endothermic
Hydrochloric acid	Magnesium ribbon				
Copper(II) sulfate solution	Iron filings				
Citric acid solution	Sodium hydrogen carbonate				
Sulfuric acid	Sodium hydroxide solution				
Water	Potassium chloride				

Handling experimental observations and data

6. In one of the combinations of substances the temperature change is not the result of a chemical change or chemical reaction. Which one? Explain why this combination of substances could not be described as a chemical reaction.

7. Add 'exothermic' or 'endothermic', as appropriate to the last column in the table.

Topic 5.1: Chemical energetics

Learning episode C5.1b Measuring energy transfers (1)

Learning aims

- To investigate 'cold packs'.
- To measure temperature changes in a reaction using an insulated cup as a simple calorimeter.
- Describe how an insulated cup can be used to carry out simple calorimetric experiments to determine thermal energy changes (such as in dissolving solids or displacement or neutralisation reactions).

Resources

Worksheet C5.1b Designing a 'cold pack'

Resources for class practical (see Technician's notes, below)

Approach

This learning episode introduces the calorimetric technique for measuring energy changes using an insulated beaker.

Designing a 'cold pack' is intended to provide some open-ended practical/investigational work, with the students being required to plan and design their own approach to identifying the quantities of potassium chloride and water in a 'cold pack' that will produce a drop in temperature of 10 °C.

Explain that cold packs can be used to limit the impact of sports injuries. Some manufacturers use potassium chloride and water in these products. (See also the Science in Context section on page 137 of the Student Book, which provides some more information on cold packs. The content of these Science in Context features is beyond the syllabus but provides the opportunity to explore the content more deeply.)

Worksheet C5.1b provides some structure for the practical/ investigation work.

Encourage students to consider what a systematic approach might require – not just to use trial and error. One approach is to repeat the experiment three or four times using different quantities of potassium chloride with a fixed volume of water, then plot results on a graph and extrapolate to identify the quantities required for the target temperature drop.

Students are required to evaluate the procedure they used and to suggest how it could be improved.

SAFETY INFORMATION
Wear eye protection (splash-proof goggles).

Technician's notes

Be sure to check the latest safety notes on these resources before proceeding.

The following resources are needed for the class practical C5.1b per group:

insulated cup
thermometer accurate to 0.1 °C
measuring cylinder
spatula
glass rod
access to electronic balance
potassium chloride, water
eye protection (splash-proof goggles)

Answers

Page 129

1. A reaction that releases thermal energy to the surroundings.

2. A reaction that absorbs thermal energy from the surroundings.

3. Using an insulated calorimeter ensures that very little energy is transferred to the surroundings.

Topic 5.1: Chemical energetics

Worksheet C5.1b Designing a 'cold pack'

Commercially produced 'cold packs' are designed to produce a cooling effect, which can be useful for treating sports injuries. It is likely that cold packs contain two substances that are held in separate compartments.

When you bend the pack the barrier between the two substances breaks and they mix or react together. Whether the cooling effect is a consequence of a chemical reaction, or simply a physical process such as dissolving, may depend on the brand of the cold pack. In this investigation you will investigate the cooling effect produced when potassium chloride is added to water.

Devise and plan an investigation

Your task is to find out:

What quantities of potassium chloride and water are needed to produce a drop in temperature of 10 °C. (The cold pack must hold between 50 cm^3 and 100 cm^3 of liquid.)

Some things to think about:

- Which method or technique will I use?
- What equipment is suitable and will give the accuracy I need?
- What quantities of potassium chloride and water should I use?
- What risk assessments should I make? What are my safety precautions?
- What will I actually do (my method)?

SAFETY INFORMATION
Wear eye protection (splash-proof goggles).

Method

1. Write your method.

Observing, measuring and recording

2. Draw a table to record your results.

Handling experimental observations and data

3. Show how you used your results to decide on the quantities of potassium chloride and water to use in the cold pack.

   Quantities to use in cold pack: potassium chloride _____ g   water _____ cm^3

Evaluating methods

4. Overall, did the method chosen give accurate results?
5. If you were to do the investigation again, what aspects would you change? Give reasons for changes that you would make.

Topic 5.1: Chemical energetics

Learning episode C5.1c Measuring energy transfers (2)

Learning objectives

- Interpret reaction pathway diagrams showing exothermic and endothermic reactions.
- Supplement State that the transfer of thermal energy during a reaction is called the enthalpy change, ΔH, of the reaction. ΔH is negative for exothermic reactions and positive for endothermic reactions.
- Supplement Define activation energy, E_a, as the minimum energy that colliding particles must have in order to react.
- Supplement Draw and label reaction pathway diagrams for exothermic and endothermic reactions using information provided, to include:
   (a) reactants
   (b) products
   (c) enthalpy change of reaction, ΔH
   (d) activation energy, E_a.

Resources

Student Book pages 130–131

Worksheet C5.1c Measuring energy transfers

Resources for class practical (see Technician's notes, below)

Approach

Part 1

This learning episode uses a different calorimetric technique – one that will provide a comparison of the energy released when a series of fuels burn. This provides a link to the topics in the Organic Chemistry section.

A metal container is used as the calorimeter because the metal is a good conductor of heat and will transfer the energy from the flame to the water. The technique involves considerable energy loss but can provide comparative results for a number of different fuels.

The technique is explained on Worksheet C5.1c.

Warn students to be extremely careful when handling the spirit burners. Often the tops of the burners are loose fitting and the fuel can readily escape. Make sure that the wick fits tightly in the holder and that the holder fits tightly in the container. If a spirit burner is knocked over when burning, it could cause a substantial fire. Tell students that if this happens, you will extinguish the flames with a fire blanket.

In the *Handling experimental observations and data* section of the worksheet, students will compare the temperature rise per g of fuel burned, and then in *Planning and evaluating investigations* they will consider why their results are likely to be very different from those quoted in a data book.

SAFETY INFORMATION
Wear eye protection (splash-proof goggles).
Ethanol, propanol and pentanol are highly flammable.
Ensure that the laboratory is well ventilated.

Part 2

Supplement Introduce the convention of using ΔH to represent the enthalpy change of a reaction by referring to the diagrams and explanations on page 131 of the Student Book.

Topic 5.1: Chemical energetics

Introduce the use of a reaction pathway diagram or energy level diagram to illustrate the differences between exothermic and endothermic reactions. The students will come across the use of ΔH when considering the effect of temperature on the equilibrium position in reversible reactions.

Finally, the Developing Practical Skills feature on page 133 of the Student Book could be used to reinforce learning on calorimetric techniques. Alternatively, it could be used later in the Consolidation and Summary learning episode.

Technician's notes

Be sure to check the latest safety notes on these resources before proceeding.

The following resources are needed for class practical C5.1c, per group:

tin or copper can with a capacity of 100–200 cm^3
thermometer
heat resistant boards to use as bench protection and draught screens
50–100 cm^3 measuring cylinder
access to electronic balance accurate in grams to 2 decimal places
boss, clamp and stand
small ($\leq$ 100 cm^3) spirit burners and lids containing ethanol, propanol and pentanol
eye protection (splash-proof goggles)

Check that the lids on the spirit burners are secured and that the wicks are not loose.

Fill the spirit burners or fill the extra space with cotton wool.

Spirit burners should be dedicated to use with a specific alcohol.

Answers

Page 130

1. A high proportion of the energy released transfers to the surrounding air.

2. a) Weighing the spirit burner before and after burning the fuel.

    b) Ethanol – 29; Paraffin – 33; Pentane – 25; Octane – 40.

    c) i) Octane.

      ii) A 10 °C rise would be expected. This time the same energy is transferred to double the volume of water.

3. The group of students using the metal should get more accurate results. The metal conducts the heat from the fuel to the water better than glass does.

Page 132

1. Endothermic reaction. Δ*H is positive,* thermal energy has been absorbed from the surroundings.
2. Supplement The reaction is endothermic.
3. Supplement The activation energy.
4. Supplement
5. Supplement

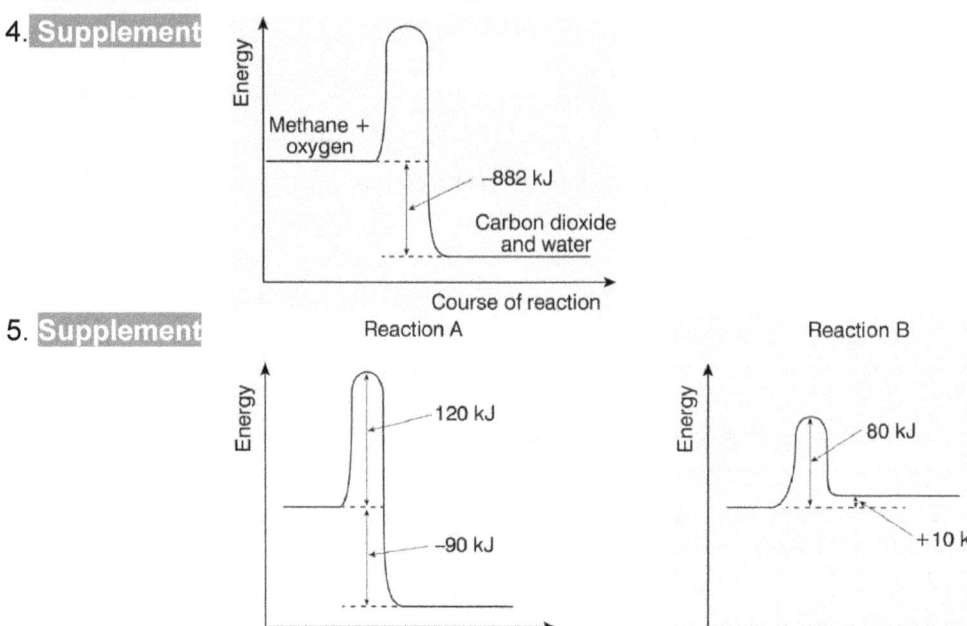

Developing Practical Skills, page 133

1. Measuring cylinder (0–100 cm^3).
2. To ensure that the energy of the reaction was spread equally throughout the whole solution, giving a uniform temperature throughout.
3. Effervescence (a colourless gas produced), the magnesium ribbon slowly disappearing.
4. Reaction A: +7 °C; Reaction B: –5 °C.
5. Reaction A: +70 °C g^{-1}; Reaction B: –2 °C g^{-1}.
6. Reaction A: exothermic; Reaction B: endothermic.
7.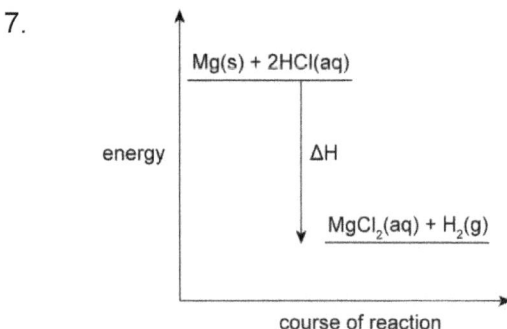
8. Putting a lid on the insulated cup will reduce energy loss.

Topic 5.1: Chemical energetics

Worksheet C5.1c Measuring energy transfers

A calorimetric technique can be used to find out the energy transferred when a fuel burns. The apparatus is shown in the diagram below. A calorimeter is a tin or copper can.

In this activity you will compare how much energy is transferred when three fuels burn.

Apparatus

tin can, thermometer, draught screens, clamp and stand access
to an electronic balance, measuring cylinder spirit burners
containing ethanol, propanol and pentanol eye protection

SAFETY INFORMATION
Wear eye protection.
Ethanol, propanol and pentanol are highly flammable. Ensure that the laboratory is well ventilated.
Students must not be allowed to fill or refill their spirit burners.

Method

1. Put on your eye protection.
2. Put 100 cm^3 (100 g) of water into the calorimeter.
3. Assemble the apparatus as shown in the diagram and take the temperature of the water. Take care to ensure that the arrangement is stable.
4. Measure the mass of the spirit burner and ethanol.
5. Light the spirit burner and heat the water in the calorimeter, stirring all the time with the thermometer, until the temperature has risen by about 20 °C.
6. Take the exact final temperature of the water and immediately reweigh the spirit burner.
7. Repeat the process with propanol and then pentanol.

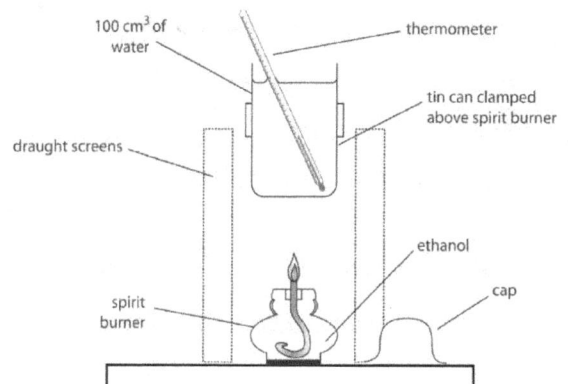

Observing, measuring and recording

Record your results in the tables.

Ethanol

8.	Mass of water being heated	100 g
	Initial temperature of the water	°C
	Final temperature of the water	°C
	Rise in temperature of the water	°C
	Mass of burner + ethanol at the start of the experiment	g
	Mass of burner + ethanol at the end of the experiment	g
	Mass of ethanol burned	g

Page 1 of 2

Topic 5.1: Chemical energetics

Propanol

Mass of water being heated	100 g
Initial temperature of the water	°C
Final temperature of the water	°C
Rise in temperature of the water	°C
Mass of burner + propanol at the start of the experiment	g
Mass of burner + propanol at the end of the experiment	g
Mass of propanol burned	g

Pentanol

Mass of water being heated	100 g
Initial temperature of the water	°C
Final temperature of the water	°C
Rise in temperature of the water	°C
Mass of burner + pentanol at the start of the experiment	g
Mass of burner + pentanol at the end of the experiment	g
Mass of pentanol burned	g

Interpreting experimental observations and data

9. Use your results to complete the following table:

Fuel	Mass of fuel burned / g	Temperature rise / °C	Temperature rise per g of fuel burned / °C / g

10. Put the fuels in order of temperature rise per g of fuel (start with the highest temperature rise per g)

Evaluating methods

11. Why was a tin can used in this experiment rather than a glass beaker?

12. Your temperature rises are likely to be different to those found in a data book. List the sources of errors in your experiment.

Topic 5.1: Chemical energetics

Learning episode C5.1d Reaction pathway diagrams, bond breaking and bond forming

Learning objectives

- Interpret reaction pathway diagrams showing exothermic and endothermic reactions.
    a) Supplement Draw and label reaction pathway diagrams for exothermic and endothermic reactions using information provided, to include: reactants, products, enthalpy change of reaction, ΔH, activation energy, E_a.
- Supplement State that bond breaking is an endothermic process and bond making is an exothermic process and explain the enthalpy change of a reaction in terms of bond breaking and bond making.
- Supplement Calculate the enthalpy change of a reaction using bond energies.

Resources

Student Book pages 131–137

Approach

Reaction pathway diagrams were introduced in the previous learning episode. Explain the origin of the enthalpy changes in exothermic and endothermic reactions in terms of the energy needed to break bonds (an endothermic process) and the energy released on forming bonds (an exothermic process). Supplement Using page 135 of the Student Book, illustrate this in terms of the alkane, propane. Refer to the trend in the molar enthalpy of combustion in the alkane series (page 135).

Supplement Ask students why the molar enthalpy of combustion increases as the alkane molecule becomes bigger. This part of the learning episode also provides an opportunity to review knowledge of the alkane homologous series if Topic 11.3 *Alkanes* has been studied.

Answers

Page 136

1. Supplement The sign indicates whether the reaction is exothermic (negative sign) or endothermic (positive sign).

2. Supplement Energy is needed to break bonds.

3. Supplement In an endothermic reaction more energy is needed to break bonds than is recovered on forming bonds.

4. Supplement The units are kJ mol^{-1}.

5. Supplement Energy needed to break bonds (endothermic) = (2 × 436) + 498 = 1370 kJ

    Energy released on forming bonds (exothermic) = –(4 × 464) = –1856 kJ

    Total energy change = (+1370) – 1856 = –486 kJ

Science in Context, page 138

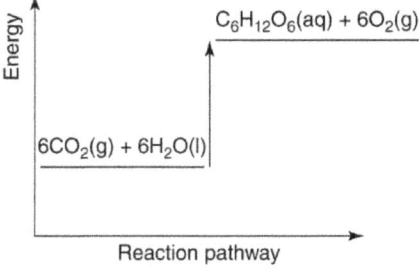

Topic 5.1: Chemical energetics

Learning episode C5.1e Consolidation and summary

Learning aims

- Review the learning points of the topic summarised in the end of topic checklist.
- Test understanding of the topic content by answering the end of topic questions.

Resources

Student Book pages 138–140

Approach

It is worth spending some time to consolidate the learning in this topic, particularly the concept of reaction pathway diagrams.

Supplement You may need to revise bond breaking and bond forming with students studying the supplementary syllabus.

If you have not used it earlier, the Developing Practical Skills feature on page 133 of the Student Book could be used here. The Science in Context feature on endothermic reactions (on page 137 of the Student Book) may also be used as a basis for emphasising certain aspects of the topic. The content of these Science in Context features is beyond the syllabus but provides the opportunity to explore the content more deeply

Ask students to work with a partner to make a list of key words from this topic. They could then work together to produce a spider diagram showing how the different concepts are linked. They could compare their list with the list of key terms given in the Student Book. Discuss the checklist and ask questions to see how much of the content students are comfortable with.

Students could make flashcards of the key content and then use the flashcards to quiz each other on the information.

Ask students to work individually through the end of topic questions in the Student Book without looking at the text. As they work, walk around the classroom observing their answers and questioning them as necessary to find out which questions are causing difficulties.

After a set period, ask students to stop working. Discuss any areas of difficulty you observed as you walked round the class.

Students should complete any unanswered questions for homework, but you should stress that they should answer the questions without looking at the text, so that they can see how much they have remembered. Consider the end of topic checklist as a basis for revising ideas. Give students opportunities to answer the end of topic questions.

Topic 5.1: Chemical energetics

End of topic questions mark scheme

The marks available for a question can indicate the level of detail you need to provide in your answer.

Question	Correct answer	Marks
1	B	1 mark
2 a)	An insulated cup will reduce	1 mark
	energy transfer to the surroundings.	1 mark
2 b)	The reaction is endothermic.	1 mark
3 a)	A metal container.	1 mark
	Metal is a good conductor of heat.	1 mark
3 b)	A considerable amount of energy is lost to the environment.	1 mark
	Not all the energy is transferred to the water.	1 mark
3 c)	Surround the fuel and container with heat resistant mats	1 mark
	to exclude drafts.	1 mark
4 a)	The reaction is exothermic.	1 mark
Supplement 4 b)	The energy released on forming new bonds is greater than the energy used to break the bonds.	1 mark
		1 mark
Supplement 5	Correct activation energy	1 mark
	Correct enthalpy change	1 mark
Supplement 6	The energy needed to break the H–H and Cl–Cl bonds	1 mark
	is less than the energy released on forming H–Cl bonds.	1 mark
Supplement 7 a)	Energy needed to break bonds = 4E(C-H) + 2E(O=O)	
	= (4 × 413) + (2 × 498) = 2648 kJ	1 mark
	Energy released on forming bonds = 2E(C=O) + 4E(O-H)	
	= (2 × 745) + (4 × 464) = 3346 kJ	1 mark
	Energy change = 2648 − 3346 = −698 kJ / mole	1 mark
Supplement 7 b)	The reaction is exothermic.	1 mark
	Total:	20 marks

Section 6: Chemical reactions

Contents
C6.1 Chemical reactions
C6.2 Reversible reactions and equilibrium
C6.3 Redox reactions

Overview of the section
This section does not feature all chemical reactions as key chemical reactions feature in many other sections, such as the reactions of acids and the many reactions covered in the organic chemistry section. Students should be familiar with the differences between physical and chemical changes and so only a brief revision is included. Investigating the factors that govern the rate of a reaction has great industrial importance and have widescale applicability across very many reactions. The focus then shifts to particular types of reaction. The concept of reversible and equilibrium reactions will be new to many students and the study illustrates how important it is to control the reaction conditions under which these reactions occur. The topic on redox reactions emphasises the importance of the inseparable nature of the processes of reduction and oxidation.

Starting points
The Student Book section opener (pages 142–143) puts the ideas in the section into context and sets the scene. It also allows students to acknowledge and value their prior learning, and provides a benchmark against which future learning can be compared.

The questions provide a structure for introducing the section and can be used in a number of different ways:

- You could ask students to consider the questions as an introductory homework task.
- You could put students into groups to share their own ideas and understanding and then to report back to the whole class.
- Students could be given access to the Internet, preferably with a tight timescale, to find out the information required.

You could then use a spider chart or other form of wall chart to summarise everybody's ideas.

Recording these initial ideas allows you to retain them for reference as the individual topics are developed. In this way, your students' progress in learning can be readily acknowledged.

Topic 6.1: Rate of reaction

C6.1 Rate of reaction

Introduction

The core material focuses on describing how concentration, particle size, catalysts and temperature affect the rate of reactions.

Supplement The supplement material considers how a simple collision theory is used to explain how the rate of a reaction is affected by the factors mentioned above. The concept of a reaction pathway diagram/ energy profile can be used to explain the effect of a catalyst on a reaction.

This topic extends the idea of the particulate nature of matter to develop a simple collision theory that explains why certain factors can change the rate of a reaction. A study of catalysts provides links to the Haber process and the Contact process in Topic 6.2 *Reversible reactions and equilibrium*, catalytic cracking in Topic 11.4 *Alkenes* and fermentation in Topic 11d *Alcohols*. Activation energy provides a link with Topic 5.1 *Chemical energetics* and to Topic 6.2 *Reversible reactions and equilibrium.*

The topic lends itself to a range of different investigative activities. Once you have introduced the experimental techniques for measuring the rate of a reaction, the factors – particle size/surface area, concentration, temperature and catalysts – can be investigated.

Links to other topics

Section	Essential background knowledge	Useful links
1 States of matter	1.1 States of matter	
2 Atoms, elements and compounds	2.1 Atoms, elements and compounds	2.3 Molecules and covalent bonds
3 Stoichiometry	3.1 Stoichiometry	
5 Chemical energetics		5.1 Chemical energetics
6 Chemical reactions		6.2 Reversible reactions and equilibrium
11 Organic chemistry		11.4 Alkenes 11.5 Alcohols

Topic overview

C6.1a	**Orientation**
	This learning episode brings together a number of different ideas:
	• A recap on the students' current knowledge and understanding of the particulate nature of matter.
	• A quick demonstration of reactions that occur at different speeds.
	• An explanation of the difference between rate, speed and time.
	• **Supplement** An introduction to a simple collision theory.
C6.1b	**Monitoring the rate of a reaction**
	This learning episode involves practical work based on the reaction of marble chips with dilute hydrochloric acid and the reaction of magnesium with dilute hydrochloric acid. The rate of the two reactions is monitored either by measuring the loss in mass of the reaction mixture (as the carbon dioxide escapes) or by measuring the volume of (hydrogen) gas produced.
	Supplement The collision theory can be used to explain why the rate of reaction changes.

Topic 6.1: Rate of reaction

C6.1c	**Concentration of solutions**
	This learning episode involves practical work using the reaction between marble chips and dilute hydrochloric acid. The concentration of the hydrochloric acid is changed and the time taken to collect 40 cm^3 of carbon dioxide is measured.
	Supplement The collision theory can be used to explain why the rate of reaction is affected by the concentration of solutions.
C6.1d	**Temperature**
	This involves practical work using one of the reactions encountered in the topic.
	Supplement The collision theory explains why the rate of reaction is affected by temperature.
C6.1e	**Surface area of solids**
	This learning episode involves practical work using apparatus similar to that used in Learning episode C6.1b. The reaction of 'large' pieces of marble chip with dilute hydrochloric acid can be compared with the same reaction involving 'small' pieces of marble chip.
	Supplement The collision theory explains why the rate of reaction is affected by particle size/surface area of solids.
C6.1f	**Use of a catalyst**
	This involves practical work focused on identifying a good catalyst for the decomposition of hydrogen peroxide solution. In addition, the effect of changing the amount of the catalyst on the rate of the reaction is demonstrated.
	Supplement The effect of a catalyst on the reaction is explained in terms of a reaction pathway diagram.
C6.1g	**Consolidation and summary**
	There is an opportunity to briefly cover the effect of changing the pressure of gases. This is only mentioned briefly in the Student Book and a brief discussion should be sufficient. This learning episode allows for all the learning in the topic to be consolidated and for key ideas to be applied through tackling the end of topic questions in the Student Book.
	Supplement The effect of changing the pressure of gases on the rate of reaction.

Career links

These are some scientific careers that focus on this area of chemistry but careers in many other fields use the knowledge and skills gained studying science.

Chemical manufacturers need to understand the ways in which they can control the rate of reactions for safety and for maximising profits.

Topic 6.1: Rate of reaction

Learning episode C6.1a Orientation

Learning objective

- Identify physical and chemical changes and describe the differences between them.

Common misconceptions

Some students think that rate/speed and time are the same.

Some students think that all collisions between reacting particles result in a reaction.

Resources

Student Book pages 144–145

Worksheet C6.1a The particulate nature of matter

Resources for demonstration (see Technician's notes, following)

Approach

1. Recap on students' current knowledge and understanding of the particulate nature of matter

Introduce the topic using page 144 of the Student Book, concentrating on the introduction, knowledge check and learning outcomes. Start with the card sort activity on Worksheet C6.1a where small groups of students arrange the cards into 'true', 'false' and 'don't know'.

Join each group of students with another to discuss any differences in their card sorts. Take feedback and summarise the key differences between the arrangement and movement of the particles in solids, liquids and gases.

Check there is good understanding of the differences between physical and chemical changes.

2. Quick demonstration of reactions that occur at different speeds.

Use page 145 of the Student Book to illustrate the differences between physical changes and chemical changes (reactions).

Demonstrate a few reactions to show the different speeds at which the reactions take place **(see tech notes)**:

a) Almost instantaneous	Copper(II) nitrate solution and sodium carbonate solution (or alternative precipitation reaction)
b) Rapid once started	Burning magnesium ribbon in air (oxygen)
c) Quite slow	Calcium carbonate (marble chips) and dilute hydrochloric acid
d) Very slow	A shiny steel nail and moist air (no observable change during the lesson)

Ask the question: 'Why do some reactions happen very quickly and others are very slow?'.

SAFETY INFORMATION

Wear eye protection.

For longer lengths of magnesium ribbon burnt by the teacher or burning in oxygen, do not look directly at the flame. A welding filter or even viewing it through a 1mm gap between the fingers of one hand will offer protection. Magnesium burns with such brightness that viewing it directly may cause retinal damage.

Raising and lowering the crucible lid should not allow a direct view of the burning magnesium.

---

3. Explanation of the difference between speed, rate and time

Ask students what 'rate' is. Refer to a car: its speed in kilometres/hour is in fact the rate of travel of the car. Refer to the table on page 145 in the Student Book on speed, rate and time.

Topic 6.1: Rate of reaction

Supplement 4. Introduction to a simple collision theory

Although the idea of a collision theory is only required in the supplementary syllabus it is probably worth referring to it with all students, varying the detail to match the needs of the particular group that you are teaching. Explain the collision theory model that scientists use to explain the different rates at which reactions occur. Emphasise that there are two requirements:

- The reacting particles must collide.
- There must be sufficient energy involved in the collision to break chemical bonds. These collisions are called effective collisions.

Technician's notes

Be sure to check the latest safety notes on these resources before proceeding.

The following resources are needed for the demonstration of reaction speeds:

0.01 mol / dm^3 copper(II) nitrate solution (50 cm^3) – Moderate hazard
0.01 mol / dm^3 sodium carbonate solution (50 cm^3)
magnesium ribbon (2–5 cm)
5 g calcium carbonate (as marble chips)
0.2 mol / dm^3 hydrochloric acid (50 cm^3)
4 beakers (100 cm^3), crucible, tongs, Bunsen burner and heatproof mat
eye protection

Topic 6.1: Rate of reaction

Answers

Worksheet C6.1a

1. False; (the particles in a solid are vibrating and not stationary)
2. True
3. True
4. True
5. True
6. True
7. True
8. False
9. True
10. True
11. True. However, when ice melts the particles move closer together (due to the nature of the hydrogen bonds in the ice) – this is not the general occurrence when a solid melts.
12. False (the process is more accurately known as diffusion and not dispersion).

Page 147

1. In a physical change no new substances are made. In a chemical change at least one new substance is made.
2. The apparent change in mass is often because a gas has been either a reactant or a product (and is lost from the reaction vessel).
3. Supplement The particles must collide, and there must be sufficient energy in the collision (to break bonds).
4. Supplement An effective collision is one that results in a chemical reaction between the colliding particles.
5. Supplement A diagram like Fig. 6.3. It is an energy barrier. Only collisions that have enough energy to overcome this barrier will lead to a reaction.

Topic 6.1: Rate of reaction

Worksheet C6.1a The particulate nature of matter

Cut out the cards and then sort them into piles of 'True', 'False' or 'Not sure'.

1. In a solid the particles are not moving.	2. The particles in a gas are very far apart.	3. In a liquid the particles will be constantly bumping into each other.
4. The particles in a gas are moving at high speed.	5. The particles in a solid are held together by various types of forces.	6. Solid A has a higher melting point than solid B so the forces holding the particles together in A are stronger than those in B.
7. As a liquid is heated the particles move faster.	8. As a solid is heated the particles stay still.	9. The forces between gas particles are very small.
10. When a liquid evaporates, particles escape from the surface of the liquid.	11. When a solid melts and forms a liquid, in most cases at the melting point the particles will be further apart in the liquid.	12. When gas particles mix together this is known as dispersion.

Topic 6.1: Rate of reaction

Learning episode C6.1b Monitoring the rate of reaction

Learning objectives

- Describe practical methods for investigating the rate of a reaction including change in mass of a reactant or product and the formation of a gas.
- Interpret data, including graphs, from rate of reaction experiments.
- Supplement Describe collision theory in terms of:
   a) number of particles per unit volume
   b) frequency of collisions between particles
   c) kinetic energy of particles
   d) activation energy, E_a.
- Supplement Evaluate practical methods for investigating the rate of a reaction including change in mass of a reactant or a product and the formation of a gas.

Common misconceptions

Some students think that reactions proceed at a constant rate.

Resources

Student Book pages 145–149

Worksheet C6.1b Monitoring the rate of a reaction

Resources for demonstration and class practical (see Technician's notes, following)

Approach

Your choice of approach will depend on the apparatus available. You will need an electronic balance reading in grams accurate to two decimal places to accurately measure the loss in mass during the reaction between marble chips and dilute hydrochloric acid.

When measuring the volume of gas produced in a reaction, a gas syringe is ideal but an inverted measuring cylinder in a trough of water is an acceptable alternative. There are opportunities to practise all the practical skills.

One approach is to:

1. Demonstrate how the rate of the reaction between marble chips and hydrochloric acid can be monitored by measuring the loss in mass as the carbon dioxide escapes. The apparatus and method are given in the Student Book on pages 147. Record the class results and ask students to show them graphically. Discuss the different regions of the graph and link the steepness of the gradient to the rate of the reaction.

2. Use a class practical to explore the reaction between dilute hydrochloric acid and magnesium ribbon by measuring the volume of hydrogen produced. Full details are provided on Worksheet C6.1b

SAFETY INFORMATION
Wear eye protection.
Hydrogen gas is extremely flammable.
Ensure that there are no naked flames in the room.

3. You may use the graph from the class practical to reinforce the interpretation of the changing rate of reaction as a reaction proceeds.

Supplement Use simple collision theory to explain why the rate decreases – as the reactant particles are used up in the reaction, there will be fewer effective collisions in a given time.

Topic 6.1: Rate of reaction

Technician's notes

Be sure to check the latest safety notes on these resources before proceeding.

The following resources are needed for the demonstration of the reaction between marble chips and dilute hydrochloric acid:

5 g of marble chips (an excess)
30 cm^3 of 0.25 mol / dm^3 hydrochloric acid
measuring cylinder
electronic balance (reading in grams and accurate to 2 decimal places)
conical flask and cotton wool plug
stopwatch
eye protection

The following resources are needed for the class practical C6.1b, per group:

8 cm magnesium ribbon
25 cm^3 1 mol / dm^3 hydrochloric acid
conical flask, bung and delivery tube
gas syringe or 100 cm^3 measuring cylinder and trough of water
stand and clamp
eye protection

Answers

Page 149

1. A gas syringe will accurately measure the volume of gas produced.
2. No gas is being produced – the reaction hasn't started or it is finished.
3. The quicker reaction will have the steeper gradient.

Topic 6.1: Rate of reaction

Worksheet C6.1b Monitoring the rate of a reaction

What happens to the rate of a reaction as it proceeds? In this investigation you will be able to monitor the rate of the reaction between magnesium and hydrochloric acid.

$Mg(s) + 2HCl(aq) \rightarrow MgCl_2(aq) + H_2(g)$

Apparatus

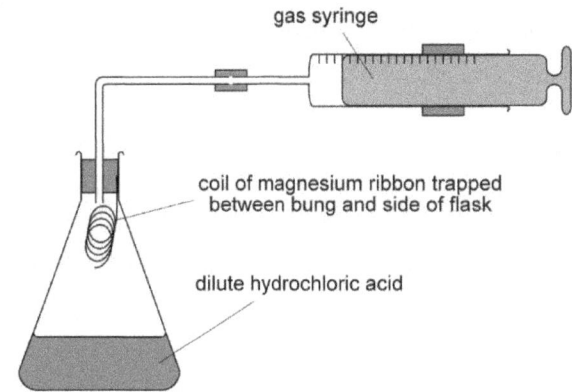

8 cm of magnesium ribbon

25 cm^3 of dilute hydrochloric acid

conical flask, bung and delivery tube

gas syringe or 100 cm^3 measuring cylinder and trough of water

stand and clamp

stopwatch

eye protection

SAFETY INFORMATION
Wear eye protection.
Hydrogen gas is extremely flammable.
Ensure that there are no naked flames in the room.

Method

1. Put on your eye protection.
2. Prepare a table of results as shown on the right.
3. Carefully transfer 25 cm^3 of hydrochloric acid into the conical flask.
4. Make a coil with the magnesium ribbon. Carefully trap it between the bung and the side of the flask (as shown in the diagram above).
5. Twist the bung until the magnesium ribbon falls into the acid, start the stopwatch immediately. Make sure that the bung fits tightly.
6. Measure the total volume of hydrogen collected in the syringe every 10 seconds.

Time / s	Total volume of hydrogen / cm^3
0	
10	
20	
30	
40	
50	
60	
70	
80	
90	

Handling experimental observations and data

7. Plot a graph of total volume of gas against time. Draw a smooth curved line of best fit through the points.
8. After how many seconds did the reaction finish?
9. How does the shape of the graph show that the reaction has finished?
10. What does the shape of the graph tell you about how the rate of reaction changes?
11. Use the idea of collisions between particles to explain why the rate changes during the reaction.

Topic 6.1: Rate of reaction

Learning episode C6.1c Concentration of solutions

Learning objectives

- Describe the effect on the rate of a reaction of changing the concentration of solutions.
- Supplement Describe and explain the effect on the rate of reaction of changing the concentration of solutions using collision theory.

Common misconceptions

Check that the difference between time and rate is understood.

Resources

Student Book pages 150–152

Resources for class practical (see Technician's notes, following)

Approach

The Developing Practical Skills on pages 151–152 of the Student Book relates directly to the experiment used in this learning episode.

Ask the student groups to base their experiment on the Developing Practical Skills experiment using exactly the same method and quantities. They could use the 5 different concentrations as in the Student Book or, if time is a consideration, 4 would be acceptable. Check whether measuring the production of 40 cm^3 of carbon dioxide is a sensible amount given the time allowed for the experiment. Change this if necessary. The students will need to create their own table to record their results.

Supplement Explain the results in terms of the collision theory: the more particles there are in a certain volume of solution the more effective collisions there will be.

SAFETY INFORMATION
Wear eye protection.

Technician's notes

Be sure to check the latest safety notes on these resources before proceeding.

The following resources are needed for the class practical C6.1c per group:

200 cm^3 0.2 mol / dm^3 hydrochloric acid
25 g calcium carbonate (marble chips)
50 cm^3 measuring cylinder or burette (hydrochloric acid)
50 cm^3 measuring cylinder or burette (water)
Stopwatch
eye protection
conical flask, delivery tube and gas syringe (as in Student Book diagram)

Topic 6.1: Rate of reaction

Answers

Supplement Developing Practical Skills, page 152

1. To ensure that it was a fair test – the amount of solution was constant so the volume of acid used is a measure of the concentration (directly proportional).

2. A burette or measuring cylinder. (The burette will be more accurate.)

3. Check that the axes are correctly labelled, the points plotted correctly and joined with a smooth curve.

4. The greater the volume of hydrochloric acid (that is, the greater the concentration of the solution) the greater the rate of the reaction.

5. 55 s (range 48–60 s).

6. Connecting the delivery tube to the syringe immediately after mixing the reagents. Attaching the delivery tube will cause some displacement of air from the flask.

Topic 6.1: Rate of reaction

Learning episode C6.1d Temperature

Learning objectives

- Describe the effect on the rate of reaction of changing the temperature.
- Interpret data, including graphs, from rate of reaction experiments.
- Describe practical methods for investigating the rate of a reaction including change in mass of a reactant or product and the formation of a gas.
- Supplement Describe and explain the effect on the rate of reaction of changing the temperature using collision theory.
- Supplement Evaluate practical methods for investigating the rate of a reaction including change in mass of a reactant or product and the formation of a gas.

Common misconceptions

The dramatic impact of temperature may come as a surprise to students – a 10 °C rise in temperature can double the rate of a reaction.

Resources

Student Book pages 152–154

Worksheet C6.1d Reaction rate and temperature

Resources for class practical (see Technician's notes, following)

Approach

Alternatively, reactions used previously could be used

This learning episode is a very good opportunity for students to devise and plan their own investigation. They will be familiar with the approach used in the previous learning episode, but will have to decide how to adapt it to allow an investigation of temperature. It is important to allow students to produce a plan without too much prompting.

Choosing the concentration of hydrochloric acid to use is a key aspect. If they choose the fastest reaction from the previous learning episode, they will find the reaction is too rapid to measure accurately. Choosing the slowest will be much more successful.

Supplement Once students have completed their investigation, their results can be explained in terms of the collision theory. A crucial point is that increasing temperature will not only ensure more collisions; it will significantly increase the energy of the collisions.

Make sure that students' plans have been checked before they start to carry them out.

SAFETY INFORMATION
Wear eye protection.

Topic 6.1: Rate of reaction

Technician's notes

Be sure to check the latest safety notes on these resources before proceeding.

150 cm^3 0.2 mol / dm^3 hydrochloric acid
25 g of calcium carbonate (marble chips)
50 cm^3 measuring cylinder or burette (hydrochloric acid)
50 cm^3 measuring cylinder or burette (water)
stopwatch
conical flask, delivery tube, gas syringe (as in Student Book)
eye protection (splash-proof goggles)
thermometer

Answers

Page 153

1. The units of concentration for solutions are mol / dm^3.

2. **Supplement** The particles are more closely packed together and so there will be more (effective) collisions per second.

3. a) Risk assessments included, quantities of magnesium and hydrochloric acid (concentration specified), apparatus, e.g. for collection of gas (gas syringe) or loss in mass (electronic balance).

    b) Appropriate sequence of steps in the method with a sensible number of different temperatures chosen.

    c) Appropriate table of results including the units of the measurements to be taken.

    (If possible, the students could then carry out their plan as a class practical)

4. **Supplement** Increasing temperature means the particles have more (kinetic) energy, more of the collisions will have energy greater than or equal to the activation energy and there will be more effective/successful collisions per second.

Science in Context, page 154

Explosions are usually caused by methane or coal dust. Often the methane explodes first and this ignites the coal dust.

Topic 6.1: Rate of reaction

Worksheet C6.1d Reaction rate and temperature

Rusting occurs slowly at room temperature but is much quicker at higher temperatures. How much difference does temperature actually make to the rate of a reaction?

Your task is to design and plan an investigation to find out the effect of temperature on the rate of a reaction.

Devise and plan the investigation

How are you going to change the temperature?

How are you going to control the other variables?

What range of temperatures would be safe and sensible? (The maximum temperature you should use is 40 °C.)

What are the hazards (what is your assessment of risk)?

How can the risks be reduced?

> **SAFETY INFORMATION**
> *Wear eye protection.*
> *Your teacher will provide safety information, depending on the reaction you are using.*

Using and organising techniques, apparatus and materials

1. Carry out your approach.

Observing, measuring and recording

2. Record your results.

Handling experimental observations and data

3. What do your results show?
4. Can you explain them using a simple collision theory?

Evaluating methods

5. Were any of your results inaccurate? If so, how did you recognise them and what were the likely causes?
6. How could the accuracy of your method be improved?

Topic 6.1: Rate of reaction

Learning episode C6.1e Surface area of solids

Learning objectives

- Describe the effect on the rate of reaction of changing the surface area of solids.
- Describe practical methods for investigating the rate of a reaction including the formation of a gas.
- Interpret data, including graphs, from rate of reaction experiments.
- Supplement Describe and explain the effect on the rate of reaction of changing the surface area of solids using collision theory.

Common misconceptions

Students may need convincing that the same mass of smaller particles will have a greater surface area than bigger particles. A sliced loaf of bread can be used to model why smaller pieces of a large lump will have a greater surface area.

Resources

Student Book pages 154–155

Worksheet C6.1e Reaction rate and surface area

Resources for the demonstration and class practical (see Technician's notes, following)

Approach

Whichever practical approach you use, students will be familiar with the apparatus from a previous learning episode. The reaction between marble chips and hydrochloric acid will be slower than that of magnesium ribbon and dilute hydrochloric acid, so you have to decide for how long students should take readings. If you choose to demonstrate the loss of mass method, then a video camera connected to a projector showing the balance display and the stopwatch allows students to take their own readings. This helps to keep them interested and motivated especially while the mass changes are slow.

It will be sufficient to compare the initial rates or early stages of the two reactions rather than waiting for the reaction to go to completion. Ideally, students should not be taking readings for more than 5 or 6 minutes for each experiment. (About 90 cm^3 of carbon dioxide should be produced at room temperature. If you want a quicker reaction you can increase the concentration of the acid, but make sure that the syringe is disconnected once the volume reaches 100 cm^3.)

The results can be shown graphically and the gradients of the two curves compared for the early stages of the reactions.

Supplement You may choose to use the collision theory to explain why the reaction has a greater rate with smaller particles. More marble surface and calcium carbonate 'particles' (ions) will be exposed to the hydrochloric acid particles (H$^+$ ions), so there will be more effective collisions in a given time.

SAFETY INFORMATION
Wear eye protection.
Ensure that the laboratory is well ventilated.

Technician's notes

Be sure to check the latest safety notes on these resources before proceeding.

The reaction between marble chips and dilute hydrochloric acid can be monitored by measuring the loss in mass or the volume of carbon dioxide produced as the reaction proceeds. The availability of accurate electronic balances (accurate to 0.01 g) will determine whether the loss of mass method is used, either as a demonstration **(see tech notes)** or a class practical. The method involving the collection of gas might be easier to resource. The marble chips can be categorised roughly into 'large' and 'small'.

Topic 6.1: Rate of reaction

The following resources are needed for the demonstration of the loss of mass method:

5 g of 'large' marble chips (an excess)
5 g of 'small' marble chips (an excess)
2 × 30 cm^3 of 0.25 M hydrochloric acid (allow 100 cm^3)
measuring cylinder
access to an electronic balance in grams accurate to 2 decimal places
conical flask and cotton wool plug
stopwatch
eye protection

The following resources are needed for the class practical C6.1e, per group:

5 g 'large' marble chips (an excess)
5 g 'small' marble chips (an excess)
2 × 30 cm^3 0.25 M hydrochloric acid (allow 100 cm^3)
conical flask, bung and delivery tube
gas syringe or 100 cm^3 measuring cylinder and trough of water
stand and clamp
stopwatch
eye protection

Topic 6.1: Rate of reaction

Worksheet C6.1e Reaction rate and surface area

What effect does the surface area of a solid have on the rate at which it reacts? In this investigation you are going to study the reaction between marble chips (calcium carbonate) and hydrochloric acid.

$$CaCO_3(s) + 2HCl(aq) \rightarrow CaCl_2(aq) + CO_2(g) + H_2O(l)$$

Apparatus

5 g 'large' marble chips (lower surface area) (an excess)

5 g 'small' marble chips (higher surface area) (an excess)

30 cm^3 0.25 M hydrochloric acid (for each experiment)

conical flask, bung and delivery tube

gas syringe or 100 cm^3 measuring cylinder and trough of water

stand and clamp

stopwatch

eye protection

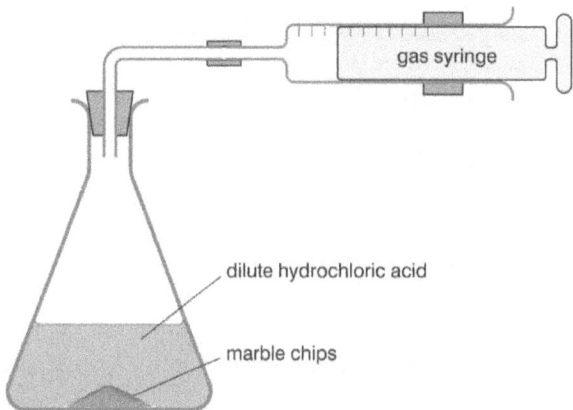

SAFETY INFORMATION
Wear eye protection.
Ensure that the laboratory is well ventilated.

Method

1. Put on your eye protection.
2. Add 30 cm^3 of the hydrochloric acid solution to 5 g of 'small' marble chips in a conical flask. Immediately connect to the gas syringe and start the stopwatch.
3. Take the total volume of gas produced every 30 seconds for about 5 minutes, recording your results in a table like the one shown here.
4. Carefully wash out the conical flask and then repeat the experiment with 5 g of 'large' marble chips. Record your results in the table.

Handling experimental observations and data

5. Plot the results to the two experiments on graph paper using the same axes.
6. What do the shapes of the two curves tell you about the differences in the rates of the reactions?
7. Use the idea of collisions between reacting particles to explain the differences in reaction rate.

Time / s	Total volume of gas ('small' marble chips) / cm^3	Total volume of gas ('large' marble chips) / cm^3
0	0	0

Topic 6.1: Rate of reaction

Learning episode C6.1f Use of a catalyst

Learning objectives

- Describe the effect on the rate of reaction of adding or removing a catalyst, including enzymes.
- State that a catalyst increases the rate of a reaction and is unchanged at the end of a reaction.
- Supplement Describe and explain the effect on the rate of reaction of adding or removing a catalyst including enzymes using collision theory.
- Supplement State that a catalyst decreases the activation energy, E_a, of a reaction.

Common misconceptions

Some students may have encountered inhibitors or negative catalysts. However, as far as this syllabus is concerned the focus is only on catalysts defined as increasing the rate of a reaction.

Resources

Student Book pages 155–156

Worksheet C6.1f Catalysts

Resources for class practical and demonstration (see Technician's notes, below)

Approach

Students should now be familiar with the experimental methods used to investigate the rate of various reactions. It may be that they do not need any further practice or experience. A suggested approach is as follows:

1. Students do a quick test tube investigation of possible catalysts for the decomposition of hydrogen peroxide (see Worksheet C6.1f). They add spatula measures of the solids to approximately 5 cm³ of hydrogen peroxide in a series of test-tubes. They observe the tubes to see if effervescence occurs (oxygen formation) and, if it does, at what rate.

> **SAFETY INFORMATION**
> *Wear eye protection.*
> *Hydrogen peroxide solution is an irritant – using 10 volume maximum solution is low hazard.*
> *Copper(II) oxide and manganese(IV) oxide are both harmful. Take care not to inhale.*
> *Copper(II) oxide is also hazardous to the aquatic environment and so needs to be carefully disposed of.*
> *Calcium oxide is a moderate hazard and corrosive.*

2. A teacher-led demonstration is used to reinforce the extent of the catalytic effect of manganese(IV) oxide on hydrogen peroxide – possibly comparing the effect of changing the amount of catalyst used **(see tech notes)**.

Supplement The way that a catalyst increases the rate of a reaction – by offering a reaction pathway with a lower activation energy – can be seen as an extension. The specificity of catalysts (and enzymes for that matter) is also worthy of attention. Enzymes are mentioned briefly in the Student Book (page 155) but some research on enzymes (and possibly enzyme inhibitors) would be a useful extension activity.

Topic 6.1: Rate of reaction

Technician's notes

Be sure to check the latest safety notes on these resources before proceeding.

The following resources are needed for the class practical C6.1f, per group:

40 cm³ of 10 volume hydrogen peroxide solution
a range of metal oxides:
copper(II) oxide
iron(III) oxide
manganese(IV) oxide
magnesium oxide
aluminium oxide
test-tubes and test-tube rack
teat pipette
spatula
eye protection

Dilute solutions deteriorate rapidly and may be more dilute than labelled. Check dilute solutions produce the expected result before the lesson.

The following resources are needed for the demonstration of a catalyst on hydrogen peroxide:

up to 100 cm³ of 20 volume hydrogen peroxide solution – only 20 cm³ needed for each demonstration
manganese(IV) oxide
conical flask with delivery tube to gas syringe
100 cm³ measuring cylinder
spatula
eye protection

Answers

Page 157

1. A catalyst is a substance that changes the rate of a chemical reaction.

2. A biological catalyst is called an enzyme.

3. A reaction involving gases (at least one gas).

4. **Supplement** The larger the surface area of the solid the greater the number of effective collisions with the acid particles and therefore the greater the rate of reaction.

Topic 6.1: Rate of reaction

Worksheet C6.1f Catalysts

Catalysts are substances that change the rate of a chemical reaction. In most cases they increase the rate of the reaction. Catalysts are often specific to one reaction; in other reactions they have little or no effect.

Your task is to find the best catalyst for increasing the rate of decomposition of hydrogen peroxide into water and oxygen:

$2H_2O_2(aq) \rightarrow 2H_2O(l) + O_2(g)$

The reaction is very slow at room temperature without a catalyst.

Apparatus

40 cm^3 of 10 volume hydrogen peroxide solution

copper(II) oxide, iron(III) oxide, manganese(IV) oxide, calcium oxide, magnesium oxide, aluminium oxide

test-tubes and test-tube rack

teat pipette

spatula

eye protection

SAFETY INFORMATION

Wear eye protection.

Hydrogen peroxide solution is an irritant.

Copper(II) oxide and manganese(IV) oxide are both harmful.

Copper(II) oxide is also hazardous to the aquatic environment and so needs to be carefully disposed of.

Calcium oxide is a moderate hazard and corrosive.

Method

1. Put on your eye protection.
2. Add a spatula measure of each solid to separate samples of 5 cm^3 of hydrogen peroxide solution in test-tubes.
3. Look for signs of oxygen being produced.

Handling experimental observations and data

4. Rank your solids in order from the most effective to the least effective at breaking down the hydrogen peroxide into oxygen and water.

MOST EFFECTIVE _____

_____

_____

_____

_____

LEAST EFFECTIVE _____

Topic 6.1: Rate of reaction

Learning episode C6.1g Consolidation and summary

Learning aims

- Review the learning points of the topic summarised in the end of topic checklist.
- Test understanding of the topic content by answering the end of topic questions.

Learning objectives

- Describe the effect on the rate of reaction of changing the pressure of gases.
- **Supplement** Describe and explain the effect on the rate of reaction of changing the pressure of gases using collision theory.

Resources

Student Book pages 156–160

Approach

The final factor to be discussed is the effect of changing the pressure of gases on the rate of reaction. Knowledge of the particulate nature of matter is key to understanding the effect.

Supplement Increasing the pressure of two reacting gases will force the gas particles closer together so increasing the number of effective collisions and so the rate of reaction. Reference can be made to the Haber and Contact processes if these have been covered already.

Ask students to work with a partner to make a list of key words from this topic. They could then work together to produce a spider diagram showing how the different concepts are linked. They could compare their list with the list of key terms given in the Student Book. Discuss the checklist and ask questions to see how much of the content students are comfortable with.

Students could make flashcards of the key content and then use the flashcards to quiz each other on the information.

Ask students to work individually through the end of topic questions in the Student Book without looking at the text. As they work, walk around the classroom observing their answers and questioning them as necessary to find out which questions are causing difficulties.

After a set period, ask students to stop working. Discuss any areas of difficulty you observed as you walked round the class.

Students should complete any unanswered questions for homework, but you should stress that they should answer the questions without looking at the text, so that they can see how much they have remembered.

Topic 6.1: Rate of reaction

End of topic questions mark scheme

The marks available for a question can indicate the level of detail you need to provide in your answer.

Question	Correct answer	Marks
1	D	1 mark
2 a)	Diagram similar to Fig 6.9:	
	Suitable reaction vessel.	1 mark
	Suitable apparatus for gas collection.	1 mark
2 b)	i) Increase the rate of reaction.	1 mark
	ii) Decrease the rate of reaction.	1 mark
	iii) Decrease the rate of reaction.	1 mark
3	The flour particles are very small.	1 mark
	When mixed well with air any sources of ignition will cause a very rapid reaction/explosion.	1 mark
4 a)	Carbon dioxide.	1 mark
4 b)	$CaCO_3(s) + 2HCl(aq) \rightarrow CaCl_2(aq) + CO_2(g) + H_2O(l)$	2 marks
	(1 mark for balanced equation; 1 mark for state symbols)	
4 c)	Marks for the graph:	
	Suitable scale for axes.	1 mark
	Points plotted correctly.	1 mark
	Smooth curve drawn.	1 mark
4 d)	i) 20 cm^3	1 mark
	ii) 16 cm^3	1 mark
	iii) 13 cm^3	1 mark
	iv) 0 cm^3	1 mark
Supplement 4 e)	The rate of reaction is greatest at the beginning of the reaction.	1 mark
	The rate decreases as the reaction proceeds and is zero after 70 seconds.	1 mark
Supplement 4 f)	The concentration of the reactants is greatest at the beginning of the reaction and so there will be more effective collisions.	1 mark
	As the reactants are used up there will be fewer effective collisions and so the rate of the reaction will decrease.	1 mark
4 g)	Marks for the graph:	
	The line should start from the origin.	1 mark
	The curve should be steeper/have a greater gradient and not cross the Graph 1 curve.	1 mark
	The curve should reach the same plateau as Graph 1 but sooner.	1 mark
4 h)	The question does not state which reactant is in excess so there are some possibilities.	
	Marks for the graph:	1 mark
	The line should start from the origin.	1 mark

Cambridge IGCSE Chemistry Teacher's Guide

Topic 6.1: Rate of reaction

Question	Correct answer	Marks
	The curve should be less steep/have a smaller gradient and not cross the first curve (Graph 1).	1 mark
	The curve should reach a plateau below or at the same level as the original plateau (Graphs 1 and 2) but after a longer time than Graph 1.	
Supplement 5	There is not enough energy in the collision.	1 mark
	To exceed the activation energy/break bonds.	1 mark
Supplement 6a	The activation energy is an energy barrier; it is the minimum energy required for a reaction to take place between colliding particles.	1 mark
Supplement 6b	Reaction A is likely to have the greater rate of reaction at a particular temperature.	1 mark
	It has a lower activation energy.	1 mark
Supplement 6c	A catalyst lowers the activation energy in a reaction.	1 mark
	More collisions between reacting particles will therefore have sufficient energy to exceed this activation energy.	1 mark
	Total:	35 marks

Topic 6.2: Reversible reactions and equilibrium

C6.2 Reversible reactions and equilibrium

Introduction

This short topic extends the basic ideas on chemical equations introduced in Topic 3.1 *Stoichiometry*. Reversible reactions are introduced through the action of heat on copper(II) sulfate crystals and cobalt(II) chloride crystals. This is followed by an extension activity focusing on how changing the conditions of a reaction affects the position of equilibrium. This is reinforced with the details of the conditions required in the Haber and Contact industrial processes.

There are some important links to other topics: the use of anhydrous copper(II) sulfate to identify the presence of water in Topic 10.1 *Chemistry of the environment*; hydrated salts in 7.1 *Acids, bases and salts*; exothermic and endothermic reactions in Topic 5.1 *Chemical energetics*; and catalysts in Topic 6.1 *Rate of reaction*.

Students have the opportunity to develop their practical skills in the Observing, measuring and recording category.

Links to other topics

Section	Essential background knowledge	Useful links
3 Stoichiometry	3.1 Stoichiometry	
5 Chemical energetics		5.1 Chemical energetics
6 Chemical reactions		6.1 Rate of reaction
7 Acids, bases and salts		7.1 Acids, bases and salts
10 Chemistry of the environment		10.1 Chemistry of the environment

Topic overview

C6.2a	Orientation
	This learning episode introduces reversible reactions by focusing on the action of heat on hydrated copper(II) sulfate and hydrated cobalt(II) chloride. In the case of the copper(II) sulfate, water is added to the residue (anhydrous copper(II) sulfate) to illustrate the reversibility of the reaction. Similarly, water is added to anhydrous cobalt(II) chloride.
C6.2b	**Supplement** **Changing the position of equilibrium**
	This learning episode introduces the expression 'dynamic equilibrium' and then considers how changing conditions can have an impact on the equilibrium position in reversible reactions. It also refers to the 'balancing act' between maximising the rate of a reaction and obtaining the best equilibrium position.
C6.2c	**Supplement** **The Haber and Contact industrial processes**
	This learning episode looks at two key industrial processes which illustrate the importance of choosing the right conditions for the reactions, both in terms of chemical energetics, the rate of reaction (both reactions are exothermic and so influence the optimum temperature) and in terms of equilibrium.
C6.2d	**Consolidation and summary**
	This learning episode recaps on the key ideas encountered in the topic. Time can be allocated to studying the end of topic checklist and then answering the end of topic questions in the Student Book.

Career links

These are some scientific careers that focus on this area of chemistry but careers in many other fields use the knowledge and skills gained studying science.

Production support chemists monitor the large scale processes used and evaluate the best reaction conditions to be used to keep the process safe but also allow them to make large quantities of the reaction products quickly.

Topic 6.2: Reversible reactions and equilibrium

Learning episode C6.2a Orientation

Learning objectives

- State that some chemical reactions are reversible as shown by the symbol ⇌.
- Describe how changing the conditions can change the direction of a reversible reaction for:
    (a) the effect of heat on hydrated compounds
    (b) the addition of water to anhydrous compounds
  limited to copper(II) sulfate and cobalt(II) chloride.

Resources

Student Book pages 161–163

Worksheet C6.2a Reversible reactions

Resources for a class practical (see Technician's notes, following)

Approach

Introduce reversible reactions as reactions that can go 'both ways', that is, from reactants to products and products back to reactants. Students may or may not be familiar with the action of heat on copper(II) sulfate and the terms 'hydrated' and 'anhydrous'.

Explain that the action of heat on copper(II) sulfate and cobalt(II) chloride can be used to demonstrate two reversible reactions.

Use Worksheet C6.2a to support the practical work and encourage students to produce full observations that include the appearance of the substances before, during and after the heating. Given the hazardous nature of cobalt(II) chloride it is recommended that this part of the experiment is done as a teacher demonstration **(see tech notes)**.

The hydrated copper(II) sulfate will lose its water of crystallisation and form anhydrous copper(II) sulfate. Adding water to the anhydrous copper(II) sulfate will reverse the change.

In the case of the cobalt(II) chloride, again water of crystallisation is lost and anhydrous cobalt(II) chloride is formed. Adding water reverses the change.

SAFETY INFORMATION
Wear eye protection.
Copper(II) sulphate is harmful. Cobalt(II) chloride is toxic by inhalation and a possible sensitiser by inhalation and skin contact.
Students with known sensitivities or allergies should wear disposable gloves.
It would be best for a technician to dispense the cobalt(II) chloride in test-tubes with mineral wool in the top of the test-tube.
Any spills should be reported and cleaned up quickly.

Topic 6.2: Reversible reactions and equilibrium

Technician's notes

Be sure to check the latest safety notes on these resources before proceeding.

The following resources are needed for the class practical C6.2a, per group:

test-tube
test-tube rack
spatula
Bunsen burner and heatproof mat
test-tube holder
copper(II) sulfate crystals
cobalt(II) chloride (no more than 5 g) in a test-tube with a mineral wool plug in the test-tube
eye protection
disposable gloves – for students who have known sensitivities or allergies

The cobalt(II) chloride and mineral wool plug should be put in the test-tube by a technician.

Answers

Page 164

1. The copper(II) sulfate crystals can be converted into anhydrous copper(II) sulfate by heating and removing the water in the crystals. When the water is re-added to anhydrous copper(II) sulfate the copper(II) sulfate crystals are reformed.

2. **Supplement** The concentration of each of the products and reactants remains constant unless a change is made to the reaction.

3. **Supplement** Reactants are constantly being converted into products and products are constantly being converted back into reactants. The rates of these two reactions are the same.

Topic 6.2: Reversible reactions and equilibrium

Worksheet C6.2a Reversible reactions

Some chemical reactions are reversible, which means that reactants can be changed into products but the products can change back into the reactants. You are going to observe two reversible reactions.

Apparatus

test-tubes, test-tube holder and test-tube rack

spatula

Bunsen burner and heatproof mat

copper(II) sulfate crystals (hydrated copper(II) sulfate)

cobalt(II) chloride crystals (hydrated cobalt(II) chloride)

eye protection

water bottle / water and pipette

SAFETY INFORMATION
Wear eye protection.
Copper(II) sulfate crystals are harmful. Cobalt(II) chloride is toxic.
If you have known allergies or sensitivities you should wear disposable gloves.
Avoid raising dusts of the two chemicals in the air. Report any spills immediately.

Method

1. Put on your eye protection.
2. Gently heat about a 1 cm depth of copper(II) sulfate crystals in a test-tube. When no further change occurs, allow the tube to cool for a few minutes (stop heating when it all turns white). Then add a few drops of water to the solid in the tube. Record your observations in the table below.
3. Gently heat about a 1 cm depth of cobalt(II) chloride crystals in a test-tube. When no further change occurs, allow the tube to cool for a few minutes. Then add a few drops of water to the solid in the tube. Record your observations in a table like the one below.

Observing, measuring and recording

Reaction	Observations
1. Copper(II) sulfate crystals	
a) Heating copper(II) sulfate crystals	
b) Cool and then add water to the solid produced	
2. Cobalt(II) chloride	
a) Heating cobalt(II) chloride crystals	
b) Cool and then add water to the solid produced	

Handling experimental observations and data

4. What does the term 'hydrated' mean?
5. What is the name of the solid formed when copper(II) sulfate crystals are heated?
6. Write equations for the two reactions.

Topic 6.2: Reversible reactions and equilibrium

Supplement Learning episode C6.2b Changing the position of equilibrium

Learning objectives

- Supplement State that a reversible reaction in a closed system is at equilibrium when:
    (a) the rate of the forward reaction is equal to the rate of the reverse reaction
    (b) the concentrations of reactants and products are no longer changing.
- Supplement Predict and explain, for any reversible reaction, how the position of equilibrium is affected by:
    (a) changing temperature
    (b) changing the pressure
    (c) changing concentration
    (d) using a catalyst.
  using information provided.

Common misconceptions

Students will often confuse rate and equilibria.

Resources

Student Book pages 163–166

Approach

Explain the concept of a dynamic equilibrium using analogies such as walking up an escalator that is moving down or running on a treadmill. Contrast this with a static equilibrium (such as a chair standing on a level floor), which is a more common experience in everyday life.

Explain that reversible reactions, or reactions in this state of dynamic equilibrium, are problematic if you are trying to make a product and don't want it to revert to the reactant as soon as it has formed.

Refer to the section on page 164 of the Student Book on changing the position of equilibrium. Concentrate on the impact of changing the concentration, pressure and temperature on a reaction in equilibrium.

Link exothermic and endothermic reactions to Topic 5.1 *Chemical energetics*. It is important to emphasise that these considerations are different from those relating to changing the rate of a reaction. In particular, stress that catalysts have no impact on equilibrium position – a catalyst will have equal impact on forward and reverse reactions.

Answers

Supplement Page 166

1. a) Low temperature.

   b) High pressure.

   c) Using a catalyst has no impact on the position of equilibrium.

2. a) The catalyst increases the rate of the reaction (but has no effect on the position of equilibrium).

   b) The rate of the reaction would be very low.

Topic 6.2: Reversible reactions and equilibrium

Supplement Learning episode C6.2c The Haber and Contact industrial processes

Learning objectives

- Supplement State the symbol equation for the production of ammonia in the Haber process, $N_2(g) + 3H_2(g) \rightleftharpoons 2NH_3(g)$
- Supplement State the sources of the hydrogen (methane) and nitrogen (air) in the Haber process.
- Supplement State the typical conditions in the Haber process as 450 °C, 20 000 kPa / 200 atm and an iron catalyst.
- Supplement State the symbol equation for the conversion of sulfur dioxide to sulfur trioxide in the Contact process, $2SO_2(g) + O_2(g) \rightleftharpoons 2SO_3(g)$
- Supplement State the sources of the sulfur dioxide (burning sulfur or roasting sulfide ores) and oxygen (air) in the Contact process.
- Supplement State the typical conditions for the conversion of sulfur dioxide to sulfur trioxide in the Contact process as 450 °C, 200 kPa / 2 atm and a vanadium(V) oxide catalyst.
- Supplement Explain, in terms of rate of reaction and position of equilibrium, why the typical conditions stated are used in the Haber process and in the Contact process, including safety considerations and economics.

Common misconceptions

Some students think that a catalyst changes not only the rate of a reaction but the yield as well.

Resources

Student Book pages 165–168

Resources for a demonstration (see Technician's notes, below)

Approach

Part 1

Demonstrate the production of ammonia by its displacement from ammonium salts by warming with dilute sodium hydroxide solution. Emphasise that ammonia is the only common alkaline gas and that it can be easily identified by testing with moist universal indicator paper. This will be studied further in Topic 12.2 Identification of ions and gases.

Explain why ammonia is such an important chemical, emphasising its use in the manufacture of fertilisers and nitric acid in particular. Refer to page 166 of the Student Book.

> **SAFETY INFORMATION**
>
> Wear eye protection.
>
> Ammonia gas is toxic. Carry out the investigation in a fume cupboard.
>
> Sodium hydroxide solution (0.4 mol/dm³) is irritating to the eyes and skin

You may wish to refer to the extreme conditions that are needed (particularly 200 atmospheres pressure) to make ammonia and the challenges that faced chemists like Fritz Haber in developing a viable process.

Topic 6.2: Reversible reactions and equilibrium

Technician's notes

Be sure to check the latest safety notes on these resources before proceeding.

The following resources are needed for the demonstration of the production of ammonia:

0.5 g ammonium chloride
0.4 mol / dm^3 sodium hydroxide solution
spatula, boiling tube, holder, universal indicator paper
Bunsen burner and heatproof mat
eye protection

Part 2

Explain why sulfuric acid is such an important chemical, emphasising its use in the manufacture of detergents, fertilisers and paints in particular.

Refer to the separate stages in the manufacture of sulfuric acid (Student Book pages 167–168). The key reaction is the oxidation of sulfur dioxide to sulfur trioxide. Consider the issue of getting the best balance of rate, equilibrium position and cost.

Again, emphasise that the catalyst does not affect the equilibrium position, because it increases the rates of both forward and backward reactions to the same extent. Explain why it is so important to dissolve sulfur trioxide in sulfuric acid before adding water, rather than adding water directly to sulfur trioxide.

Topic 6.2: Reversible reactions and equilibrium

Learning episode C6.2d Consolidation and summary

Learning aims

- Review the learning points of the topic summarised in the end of topic checklist.
- Test understanding of the topic content by answering the end of topic questions.

Resources

Student Book pages 169–171

Approach

Ask students to work with a partner to make a list of key words from this topic. They could then work together to produce a spider diagram showing how the different concepts are linked. They could compare their list with the list of key terms given in the Student Book. Discuss the checklist and ask questions to see how much of the content students are comfortable with.

Students could make flashcards of the key content and then use the flashcards to quiz each other on the information.

Ask students to work individually through the end of topic questions in the Student Book without looking at the text. As they work, walk around the classroom observing their answers and questioning them as necessary to find out which questions are causing difficulties.

After a set period, ask students to stop working. Discuss any areas of difficulty you observed as you walked round the class.

Students should complete any unanswered questions for homework, but you should stress that they should answer the questions without looking at the text, so that they can see how much they have remembered.

End of topic questions mark scheme

The marks available for a question can indicate the level of detail you need to provide in your answer.

Question	Correct answer	Marks
1	A reversible reaction is one in which the reactants form the products but the products can reform the reactants.	1 mark
2 a)	Hydrated copper(II) sulfate are blue crystals.	1 mark
	On heating, steam is given off and condenses as water on the cooler part of the tube.	1 mark
	A white/very pale blue powder remains.	1 mark
2 b)	On adding water steam is produced/the test-tube gets warm.	1 mark
	A blue solid is formed.	1 mark
3	$CuSO_4 \cdot 5H_2O(s) \rightleftharpoons CuSO_4(s) + 5H_2O(l)$ (1 mark for formulae; 1 mark for state symbols; 1 mark for reversible reaction sign)	3 marks
4	Purple solid.	1 mark
	Steam/condensation on cooler parts of tube formed on heating.	1 mark
	Blue solid remains.	1 mark
Supplement 5	B	1 mark

Topic 6.2: Reversible reactions and equilibrium

Question	Correct answer	Marks
Supplement 6	In a dynamic equilibrium the reactants are constantly being converted into products and products are constantly being converted back into reactants.	1 mark
	The rates of the forward and backward reactions are the same.	1 mark
Supplement 7 a	Nitrogen.	1 mark
	Hydrogen.	1 mark
Supplement 7 b	Nitrogen from the air.	1 mark
	Hydrogen from methane.	1 mark
Supplement 7 c	Temperature 450 °C	1 mark
	Pressure 20 000 kPa	1 mark
	Catalyst of iron	1 mark
Supplement 7 d	$N_2(g) + 3H_2(g) \rightleftharpoons 2NH_3(g)$ (1 mark for formulae and state symbols; 1 mark for reversible reaction sign)	2 marks
Supplement 8a)	The equilibrium moves to the right hand side/increasing yield of SO_3.	1 mark
	The equilibrium moves in the direction that reduces the amount of oxygen.	1 mark
Supplement 8 b)	The equilibrium moves to the right hand side/increasing yield of SO_3.	1 mark
	The equilibrium moves in the direction that produces fewer molecules.	1 mark
Supplement 8 c)	The equilibrium moves to the left hand side/decreasing yield of SO_3.	1 mark
	The equilibrium absorbs heat energy, the endothermic reverse reaction.	1 mark
Supplement 9 a)	The equilibrium moves to the right hand side/increasing yield of NO.	1 mark
	The equilibrium moves in the direction that reduces the amount of oxygen.	1 mark
Supplement 9 b)	There will be no impact on the equilibrium/no effect on amount of NO.	1 mark
	There are the same numbers of molecules/moles on each side of the equation.	1 mark
Supplement 9 c)	The equilibrium moves to the right hand side/increasing yield of NO.	1 mark
	The equilibrium absorbs heat energy, the endothermic forward reaction.	1 mark
	Total:	36 marks

C6.3 Redox reactions

Introduction

This is a short topic and many of the concepts are only suitable for the supplementary syllabus. When you teach the topic should depend on when it is most appropriate to your class. This Teacher's Guide recommends teaching this topic towards the end of the course, and so it may be seen as a consolidation or revision topic. Alternatively, you could approach the topic before students have encountered the definitions of oxidation and reduction as electron transfer in other topics (see below).

This topic builds on the understanding of ions from Topic 2.2 *Ions and ionic bonds* and oxidation and reduction gained from Topic 9.1 *Metals*, where the processes are defined in terms of gain or loss of oxygen.

The concept of combustion (oxidation) is covered in a number of topics, including Topic 10.1 *Chemistry of the environment*, Topic 11.2 *Fuels* and Topic 11.3 *Alkanes*. Students should be familiar with the use of oxidation states when naming compounds of transition metals (Topic 8.4 *Transition metals and noble gases*).

Supplement For the supplementary syllabus only, displacement reactions in Topic 8.3 *Group VII elements* and the discharge of ions in electrolysis in Topic 4.1 *Electrochemistry* extend the definitions to include loss and gain of electrons.

Links to other topics

Section	Essential background knowledge	Useful links
2 Atoms, elements and compounds	2.2 Ions and ionic bonds	
4 Electrochemistry		4.1 Electrochemistry
8 The Periodic Table		8.3 Group VII elements
		8.4 Transition elements and noble gases
9 Metals	9.1 Metals	
10 Chemistry of the environment	10.1 Chemistry of the environment	
11 Organic chemistry		11.2 Fuels
		11.3 Alkanes

Topic overview

C6.3a	Orientation
	This learning episode recaps on examples of oxidation and reduction encountered so far in the course. The extraction of metals from their oxides provides a suitable context to revise definitions of oxidation and reduction in terms of gain or loss of oxygen. The work is extended to the identification of oxidising and reducing agents. The terminology of oxidation states is introduced in the context of the naming of transition metal compounds.
C6.3b	**Supplement** Electron transfer
	This learning episode relates to the supplementary syllabus only and focuses on defining oxidation as loss of electrons and reduction as gain of electrons. Links are made to changes in oxidation state and the reduction of acidified potassium manganate(VII) and oxidation of potassium iodide are demonstrated. A worksheet provides an opportunity for the students to practise applying the definitions.

Topic 6.3: Redox reactions

C6.3c	**Consolidation and summary**
	This learning episode provides an opportunity for a quick recap of the ideas encountered in the topic.

Career links

These are some scientific careers that focus on this area of chemistry but careers in many other fields use the knowledge and skills gained studying science.

Dentists make use of redox chemistry with the use of hydrogen peroxide to whiten teeth.

Archaeologists can determine the composition of materials through redox analysis.

Topic 6.3: Redox reactions

Learning episode C6.3a Orientation

Learning objectives

- Use a Roman numeral to indicate the oxidation number of an element in a compound.
- Define redox reactions as involving simultaneous oxidation and reduction.
- Define oxidation as gain of oxygen and reduction as loss of oxygen.
- Identify redox reactions as reactions involving gain and loss of oxygen.
- Identify oxidation and reduction in redox reactions.

Common misconceptions

Some students think that there are reactions, such as combustion, where a substance is oxidised but nothing is reduced.

Resources

Student Book pages 172–174

Worksheet C6.3a Oxidation and reduction

Approach

This learning episode is likely to be relatively short, but this depends on the extent of students' background knowledge.

Ask students to define the processes of oxidation and reduction. Ask for examples of reactions where these processes take place.

Ask if the processes always go together as in the example of the reaction of copper(II) oxide and zinc on page 173 of the Student Book.

Define the term 'redox'. Then introduce the concept of an oxidation number, drawing on the examples provided in the Student Book (page 174).

Supplement Introduce the associated definitions of 'oxidising agent' and 'reducing agent', using copper(II) oxide and zinc as examples.

Use the worksheet provided to consolidate students' learning of these basic ideas. Question 3 on the combustion of carbon is intended to emphasise the nature of a redox reaction – if something is oxidised, then something must be reduced.

SAFETY INFORMATION
Wear eye protection.

Answers

Worksheet C6.3a

1. a) Magnesium.
   b) Lead(II) oxide.
   c) Lead(II) oxide.
   d) Magnesium.
   e) The oxidation number of the lead.

2. a) Carbon.
   b) Iron(III) oxide.
   c) Iron(III) oxide.
   d) Carbon.
   e) The oxidation number of the iron.

3. a) Carbon.
   b) Oxygen (its oxidation number has been reduced from 0 to –2)

Topic 6.3: Redox reactions

Worksheet C6.3a Oxidation and reduction

Oxidation is defined as the addition of oxygen in a chemical reaction.

Reduction is defined as the loss of oxygen in a chemical reaction.

A substance that brings about an oxidation reaction is called an oxidising agent.

A substance that brings about a reduction reaction is called a reducing agent.

1. Magnesium reacts with lead(II) oxide as shown in the equation below:

    magnesium + lead(II) oxide → magnesium oxide + lead

    $Mg(s)$ + $PbO(s)$ → $MgO(s)$ + $Pb(s)$

    a) Which substance has been oxidised?
    b) Which substance has been reduced?
    c) Which is the oxidising agent?
    d) Which is the reducing agent?
    e) What does the (II) represent in lead(II) oxide?

2. Carbon reacts with iron(III) oxide as shown in the equation below:

    carbon + iron(III) oxide → iron + carbon monoxide

    $3C(s)$ + $Fe_2O_3(s)$ → $2Fe(s)$ + $3CO(g)$

    a) Which substance has been oxidised?
    b) Which substance has been reduced?
    c) Which is the oxidising agent?
    d) Which is the reducing agent?
    e) What does the (III) represent in iron(III) oxide?

3. Carbon burns in oxygen to form carbon dioxide.

    carbon + oxygen → carbon dioxide

    $C(s)$ + $O_2(g)$ → $CO_2(g)$

    a) Which substance has been oxidised?
    b) Which substance has been reduced?

Topic 6.3: Redox reactions

Supplement Learning episode C6.3b Electron transfer

Learning objectives

- **Supplement** Define oxidation in terms of:
    (a) loss of electrons
    (b) an increase in oxidation number.
- **Supplement** Define reduction in terms of:
    (a) gain of electrons
    (b) a decrease in oxidation number.
- **Supplement** Identify redox reactions as reactions involving gain and loss of electrons.
- **Supplement** Identify redox reactions by changes in oxidation number using:
    (a) the oxidation number of elements in their uncombined state is zero
    (b) the oxidation number of a monatomic ion is the same as the charge on the ion
    (c) the sum of the oxidation numbers in a compound is zero
    (d) the sum of the oxidation numbers in a molecular ion is equal to the charge on the ion.
- **Supplement** Identify redox reactions by the colour changes involved when using acidified aqueous potassium manganate(VII) or aqueous potassium iodide.
- **Supplement** Define an oxidising agent as a substance that oxidises another substance and is itself reduced.
- **Supplement** Define a reducing agent as a substance that reduces another substance and is itself oxidised.
- **Supplement** Identify oxidising agents and reducing agents in redox reactions.

Resources

Student Book pages 172–176

Worksheet C6.3b Electron transfer

Resources for demonstration (see Technician's notes, following)

Approach

Introduce the definitions of oxidation and reduction in terms of electron transfer. Suggest to students that OILRIG is a useful way of remembering the definitions. Use page 173 of the Student Book, which translates the reaction of copper(II) oxide and zinc in terms of oxidation and reduction, to consider the changes to ions and atoms in this reaction. Other examples could be chosen from the discharge of ions in electrolysis (from Topic 4.1 *Electrochemistry*.)

Use page 174 of the Student Book to show how oxidation and reduction can also be defined in terms of changes in oxidation state.

Finally, demonstrate **(see tech notes)** the use of acidified potassium manganate(VII) as an oxidising agent (in its reaction with iron(II) ammonium sulfate solution and then with potassium iodide solution) and potassium iodide as a reducing agent (in its reaction with potassium manganate(VII) solution). The iron(II) ammonium sulfate solution is a useful source of $Fe^{2+}(aq)$ as the presence of the ammonium ions prevents the oxidation to Fe^{3+} (aq).

The worksheet can be used to consolidate the ideas encountered and provides an opportunity for students to practise using the new terminology. Refer to the Science in Context feature on photochromic glass as this reinforces the ideas encountered on electron transfer. The content of these Science in Context features is beyond the syllabus but provides the opportunity to explore the content more deeply.

Topic 6.3: Redox reactions

Technician's notes

Be sure to check the latest safety notes on these resources before proceeding.

The following resources are needed for the demonstration of oxidation and reduction:

25 cm^3 of 0.1 mol / dm^3 potassium manganate(VII) solution
25 cm^3 of 0.1 mol / dm^3 iron(II) ammonium sulfate solution
10 cm^3 0.1 mol / dm^3 sulfuric acid
25 cm^3 of 0.1 mol / dm^3 potassium iodide solution
beaker, dropping pipettes

Answers

Science in Context, page 176

a) 0

b) −1

c) 0

d) +1

Page 177

1. Reduction is the loss of oxygen or gain of electrons.

2. a) +2

   b) +3

   c) +7 (potassium has an oxidation number of +1)

3. Supplement The Cu^{2+} ion has been reduced. It has gained an electron and its oxidation state has been reduced.

4. Supplement The chromium atom has been oxidised. It has lost electrons and its oxidation state has been increased.

Supplement Worksheet C6.3b

1. a) Reduction.

   b) Oxidation.

   c) Reduction.

   d) Reduction.

2. a) Reduced.

   b) Oxidised.

   c) 0

   d) −1

3. a) Reduction.

   b) Oxidation.

   c) Reduction.

   d) Reduction.

Topic 6.3: Redox reactions

Supplement Worksheet C6.3b Electron transfer

Oxidation is defined as the loss of electrons.

Reduction is defined as the gain of electrons.

Oxidation is an increase in oxidation state.

Reduction is a decrease in oxidation state.

1. For each of the changes that occur in electrolysis below state whether the process involved is oxidation or reduction:

	Change at electrode	Oxidation or reduction
a)	The discharge of Al^{3+} ions at the cathode in the electrolysis of molten aluminium oxide.	
b)	The discharge of O^{2-} ions at the anode in the electrolysis of molten aluminium oxide.	
c)	The formation of lead at the cathode in the electrolysis of lead(II) bromide.	
d)	The formation of hydrogen at the cathode in the electrolysis of sodium chloride solution.	

2. The ionic equation below represents the reaction between chlorine and a solution of sodium bromide:

$$Cl_2(g) + 2Br^-(aq) \rightarrow 2Cl^-(aq) + Br_2(aq)$$

   a) Has the chlorine molecule been oxidised or reduced?

   b) Has the bromide ion been oxidised or reduced?

   c) What is the oxidation state of the chlorine in the Cl_2 molecule?

   d) What is the oxidation state of the bromide ion (Br^-)?

3. State whether the following changes involve oxidation or reduction:

	Change	Oxidation or reduction
a)	Carbon dioxide is converted into carbon monoxide.	
b)	Magnesium dissolves in dilute hydrochloric acid and forms Mg^{2+} ions in solution.	
c)	The oxidation state of manganese changes from +7 to +2.	
d)	The oxidation state of iodine changes from 0 to −1.	

Topic 6.3: Redox reactions

Learning episode C6.3c Consolidation and summary

Learning aims

- Review the learning points of the topic summarised in the end of topic checklist.
- Test understanding of the topic content by answering the end of topic questions.

Resources

Student Book pages 177–178

Approach

Ask students to work with a partner to make a list of key words from this topic. They could then work together to produce a spider diagram showing how the different concepts are linked. They could compare their list with the list of key terms given in the Student Book. Discuss the checklist and ask questions to see how much of the content students are comfortable with.

Students may find the concepts surrounding electron transfer difficult to grasp as they require familiarity with ionic equations and half-equations.

Students could make flashcards of the key content and then use the flashcards to quiz each other on the information.

Ask students to work individually through the end of topic questions in the Student Book without looking at the text. As they work, walk around the classroom observing their answers and questioning them as necessary to find out which questions are causing difficulties.

After a set period, ask students to stop working. Discuss any areas of difficulty you observed as you walked round the class.

Students should complete any unanswered questions for homework, but you should stress that they should answer the questions without looking at the text, so that they can see how much they have remembered.

Topic 6.3: Redox reactions

End of topic questions mark scheme

The marks available for a question can indicate the level of detail you need to provide in your answer.

Question	Correct answer	Marks
1	B CO_2 has been reduced (The answer could be A – the O_2 has been reduced)	1 mark
2 a)	The magnesium has been oxidised.	1 mark
2 b)	The zinc oxide has been reduced.	1 mark
2 c)	The reaction shows simultaneous oxidation and reduction.	1 mark
Supplement 2 d)	The oxidation number = 0	1 mark
Supplement 2 e)	Zinc oxide is the oxidising agent.	1 mark
Supplement 2 f)	Magnesium is the reducing agent.	1 mark
Supplement 3	The lead atom has lost electrons. So it has been oxidised.	1 mark 1 mark
Supplement 4 a)	Zero.	1 mark
Supplement 4 b)	+2	1 mark
Supplement 4 c)	Yes, it is a redox reaction. The copper has been oxidised (oxidation state from 0 to +2). The chlorine atoms in the Cl_2 molecule have been reduced (oxidation state from 0 to –1).	1 mark 1 mark
	Total:	13 marks

Section 7: Acids, bases and salts

Contents
C7.1 Acids, bases and salts

Overview of the section
Students should be familiar with some of the common acids such as hydrochloric acid, sulfuric acid and nitric acid but may not be aware of their industrial importance in today's world. Some may be familiar with organic acids such as formic acid (methanoic acid) as a result of stings and bites. Initially they will be less familiar with bases and salts (apart from common salt), although once these are introduced they are very likely to have encountered a number of these previously.

The industrial applications are not covered in this section but there are a relatively large number of links with other sections.

Starting points
The Student Book section opener (pages 180–181) puts the ideas in the section into context and sets the scene. It also allows students to acknowledge and value their prior learning, and provides a benchmark against which future learning can be compared.

The questions provide a structure for introducing the section and can be used in a number of different ways:
- You could ask students to consider the questions as an introductory homework task.
- You could put students into groups to share their own ideas and understanding and then to report back to the whole class.
- Students could be given access to the Internet, preferably with a tight timescale, to find out the information required.

You could then use a spider chart or other form of wall chart to summarise everybody's ideas.

Recording these initial ideas allows you to retain them for reference as the individual topics are developed. In this way, your students' progress in learning can be readily acknowledged.

Topic 7.1: Acids, bases and salts

C7.1 Acids, bases and salts

Introduction

This topic builds on knowledge of compounds introduced in Topic 2.1 *Atoms, elements and compounds*. The supplementary topic builds on knowledge of ions gained from Topic 2.2 *Ions and ionic bonds*. You will find opportunities to reinforce the concept of acids and bases in studying the alkali metals in Topic 8.2 *Group I elements,* and in Topic 10.1 *Chemistry of the environment*, which considers the production and impact of acid rain.

There are other links through neutralisation and enthalpy change in Topic 5.1 *Chemical energetics*, the industrial manufacture of sulfuric acid in Topic 6.2 *Reversible reactions and equilibrium*. Carboxylic acids are studied in Topic 11.6 *Carboxylic acids*.

The topic starts with the use of indicators to identify acids, alkalis and neutral substances. This is likely to be a revision for most students. You will then consider the characteristics of acids, bases and alkalis and then the types of oxides. The topic then focuses on soluble and insoluble salts, their nature and methods of preparation.

Supplement There is supplementary work on the preparation of insoluble salts.

Students have good opportunities to develop their practical/investigative skills, including accurate use of the titration technique.

Links to other topics

Section	Essential background knowledge	Useful links
2 Atoms, elements and compounds	2.1 Atoms, elements and compounds	2.2 Ions and ionic bonds
3 Stoichiometry		3.1 Stoichiometry
4 Electrochemistry		4.1 Electrochemistry
5 Chemical energetics		5.1 Chemical energetics
8 The Periodic Table		8.2 Group I elements
10 Chemistry of the environment		10.1 Chemistry of the environment
11 Organic chemistry		11.6 Carboxylic acids
12 Experimental techniques		12.1 Experimental techniques
		12.2 Identification of ions and gases

Topic overview

C7.1a	Orientation
	This learning episode seeks to revise and consolidate ideas on acids and alkalis, using indicators to classify them. Several indicators are used to emphasise the benefits of a universal indicator. The pH scale facilitates the classification of solutions as strongly or weakly acidic or strongly or weakly alkaline.
C7.1b	Acids, bases, alkalis and salts
	This learning episode considers the nature of acids, bases, alkalis and salts. The characteristic properties of acids and bases are considered and in this context the importance of controlling acidity in soil. A focus on the types of oxides is supported by a practical activity. Salts are introduced as the substances produced when the acidic hydrogen(s) of an acid is/are replaced by a metal.

Topic 7.1: Acids, bases and salts

	Supplement Acids are defined as sources of H⁺ ions and alkalis as sources of OH⁻ ions. The terms strong and weak are introduced in relation to the extent of dissociation of the acid or alkali into ions in aqueous solution. Finally, neutral and amphoteric oxides are introduced as part of a classification of oxides.	
C7.1c	**Making soluble salts**	
	This learning episode starts with considering four methods for producing soluble salts, and then focuses on the practical aspects of two methods. The first method is neutralisation, the reaction between an acid and an alkali and the titration technique. The second focuses on the preparation of hydrated magnesium sulfate by the reaction between magnesium carbonate and dilute sulfuric acid. Both preparation techniques provide students with opportunities for developing their practical skills.	
	The Developing Practical Skills feature on making copper(II) sulfate crystals (Student Book page 195) could be used as part of this learning episode, or it could be used as revision in learning episode C7.1e later in the topic.	
	Supplement The titration experiment can be extended to include mole calculations involving volumes and concentrations providing this work has already been covered in Topic 3 *Stoichiometry*.	
C7.1d	Supplement **Making insoluble salts**	
	This learning episode uses the rules provided in the Student Book for determining the solubility or insolubility of salts. Students perform a series of test-tube reactions to familiarise themselves with some precipitation reactions. They are also given practice at writing chemical equations for these reactions.	
C7.1e	**Consolidation and summary**	
	This learning episode recaps on the key ideas encountered in the topic. The Developing Practical Skills feature (page 195 of the Student Book) could be used as a means of revising the preparation of a soluble salt if it has not been used in learning episode C7.1c. Time can be allocated to answering the end of topic questions in the Student Book.	

Career links

These are some scientific careers that focus on this area of chemistry but careers in many other fields use the knowledge and skills gained studying science.

Water quality analysts check the purity and safety of drinking water and ensure that any impurities, such as salts, are below legal limits. Agronomists study the factors that affect crop growth including soil acidity, and work with farmers to improve plant yields.

Topic 7.1: Acids, bases and salts

Learning episode C7.1a Orientation

Learning objectives

- Describe acids in terms of their effect on:
  (a) litmus
  (b) thymolphthalein
  (c) methyl orange.

- Describe alkalis in terms of their effect on:
  (a) litmus
  (b) thymolphthalein
  (c) methyl orange.

Common misconceptions

Take care how you use the terms 'strong' and 'weak' in relation to acids and alkalis. The concept of strong and weak acids and strong and weak alkalis (that is, the extent of dissociation into ions) is covered in learning episode C7.1b. To avoid confusion later, it is helpful to use terms such as 'strongly acidic' rather than 'strong acid' etc. The terms 'strong' and 'weak' should not be confused with *concentration*, e.g. you can have a concentrated solution of a weak acid.

Resources

Student Book pages 182–184

Worksheet C7.1a Using indicators

Resources for class practical (see Technician's notes, following)

Approach

Your students are very likely to have existing experience and knowledge of acids and alkalis, and will probably have used indicators such as litmus and universal indicator. This learning episode will revise and consolidate their ideas.

Give them an overview of the topic; it provides a more detailed study of the nature of acids and alkalis as well as focusing on the class of compounds called salts.

Ask students to list their current knowledge of acids, alkalis and indicators. Take feedback and summarise on a chart. Explain that they are going to undertake a straightforward practical activity to consolidate their understanding, possibly including some indicators they are not familiar with: methyl orange and thymolphthalein.

In the context of pH and indicators ensure that students understand the meaning of the terms 'strongly acidic', 'weakly acidic', 'neutral', 'weakly alkaline' or 'strongly alkaline'.

Use Worksheet C7.1a *Using indicators* to support students in testing some 'everyday' chemicals. The advantages of using universal indicator and the pH scale will become obvious – it allows differentiation into strongly or weakly acidic and strongly or weakly alkaline.

SAFETY INFORMATION
Wear eye protection (splash-proof goggles).
Methyl orange is acutely toxic, corrosive, hazardous to the aquatic environment, a health hazard, a moderate hazard and flammable.
Universal indicator is flammable.
Thymolphthalein is flammable, a moderate hazard and a health hazard.

Topic 7.1: Acids, bases and salts

Technician's notes

Be sure to check the latest safety notes on these resources before proceeding.

The following resources are needed for the class practical C7.1a, per group:

test-tubes, test-tube rack
0.1 mol / dm^3 sodium hydroxide solution
0.1 mol / dm^3 hydrochloric acid
0.1 mol / dm^3 solution of bicarbonate of soda (sodium hydrogen carbonate)
soapy water, milk of magnesia, household 'ammonia' cleaner
grapefruit juice, vinegar, distilled water
solutions of methyl orange, thymolphthalein, universal indicator and chart
eye protection (splash-proof goggles)

Topic 7.1: Acids, bases and salts

Worksheet C7.1a Using indicators

Substances can be classified as acidic, alkaline or neutral. The colour that an indicator shows in a solution of the substance can be used to classify the substance.

Apparatus

test-tubes, test-tube rack

dilute hydrochloric acid, dilute sodium hydroxide, distilled water, soapy water, grapefruit juice, bicarbonate of soda, milk of magnesia, household ammonia cleaner, vinegar

solutions of methyl orange, thymolphthalein, universal indicator or universal indicator paper and chart

eye protection (splash-proof goggles)

SAFETY INFORMATION
Follow the instructions on the bottle of household ammonia cleaner
Wear eye protection (splash-proof goggles).

Method

Part 1

1. Put on your eye protection.
2. Test the dilute hydrochloric acid, distilled water and dilute sodium hydroxide with the indicators shown in the table. Record your observations.

Test solution	Colour of indicator in solution		
	Methyl orange	**Thymolphthalein**	**Universal indicator (pH)**
Dilute hydrochloric acid (A typical acid)			
Distilled water (Neutral)			
Dilute sodium hydroxide (A typical alkali)			

Page 1 of 2

Topic 7.1: Acids, bases and salts

Part 2

3. Test the solutions shown in the table with the indicators. Record your observations in each case.

Test solution	Colour of indicator when added to the test solution			Acid/alkali/ neutral pH
	Methyl orange	**Thymolphthalein**	**Universal indicator (pH)**	
Soapy water				
Grapefruit juice				
'Bicarbonate'				
Milk of magnesia				
Household 'ammonia' cleaner				
Vinegar				

Handling experimental observations and data

4. Complete the last column in your table of observations.
5. Which solution is:
   a) the most strongly acidic?
   b) the most strongly alkaline?
   c) neutral or the closest to being neutral?

Evaluating methods

6. What are the advantages of using universal indicator rather than methyl orange or thymolphthalein?

Topic 7.1: Acids, bases and salts

Learning episode C7.1b Acids, bases, alkalis and salts

Learning objectives

- Describe the characteristic properties of acids in terms of their reactions with: metals, bases, carbonates.
- State that bases are oxides or hydroxides of metals and that alkalis are soluble bases.
- Describe the characteristic properties of bases in terms of their reactions with: acids, ammonium salts.
- State that aqueous solutions of acids contain H^+ ions and aqueous solutions of alkalis contain OH^- ions.
- Describe how to compare hydrogen ion concentration, neutrality, relative acidity and relative alkalinity in terms of colour and pH using universal indicator paper.
- Describe the neutralisation reaction between an acid and an alkali to produce water,

    $H^+(aq) + OH^-(aq) \rightarrow H_2O(l)$.

- Classify oxides as acidic, including SO_2 and CO_2, or basic, including CuO and CaO, related to metallic and non-metallic character.
- Define a hydrated substance as a substance that is chemically combined with water and an anhydrous substance as a substance containing no water.
- Supplement Define acids as proton donors and bases as proton acceptors.
- Supplement Define a strong acid as an acid that is completely dissociated in aqueous solution and a weak acid as an acid that is partially dissociated in aqueous solution.
- Supplement State that hydrochloric acid is a strong acid, as shown by the symbol equation,

    $HCl(aq) \rightarrow H^+(aq) + Cl^-(aq)$.

- Supplement State that ethanoic acid is a weak acid, as shown by the symbol equation,

    $CH_3COOH(aq) \rightleftharpoons H^+(aq) + CH_3COO^-(aq)$.

- Supplement Describe amphoteric oxides as oxides that can react with acids and with bases to produce a salt and water.
- Supplement Classify Al_2O_3 and ZnO as amphoteric oxides.
- Supplement Define the term water of crystallisation as the water molecules present in hydrated crystals, including $CuSO_4 \cdot 5H_2O$ and $CoCl_2 \cdot 6H_2O$.

Resources

Student Book pages 184–189

Worksheet C7.1b Investigating oxides

Resources for class practical (see Technician's notes, following)

Approach

There is a large amount of information to cover in this learning episode. It would be helpful to spread it over more than one lesson, particularly if you are covering the supplementary work. Use the section in the Student Book to cover the learning objectives listed above.

After covering the properties of acids and bases, consider the classification of oxides – you may use a practical activity here. Spend some time clarifying the nature of a salt and the names of salts linked to the acids that they are formed from.

Topic 7.1: Acids, bases and salts

Explain that some salts are hydrated and contain water of crystallisation – show how this water of crystallisation is represented in the formula. (Students may have encountered the terms before if they have used anhydrous copper(II) sulfate to identify the presence of water.)

The sources of acidity in soil, the reasons for controlling this acidity and then the substances that are used could form the basis of a research task prior to feedback and discussion in the learning episode.

Supplement Introduce the definitions of acids and bases as proton donors and proton acceptors, respectively, and then how the degree of ionisation in water determines the strength of the acid or alkali. Your students may need a quick revision of ionic bonding at this point.

SAFETY INFORMATION
Wear eye protection (splash-proof goggles).
Sodium hydroxide and phosphoric acid are irritants.

Technician's notes

Be sure to check the latest safety notes on these resources before proceeding.

The following resources are needed for the class practical C7.1b, per group:

sodium hydroxide 0.1 mol / dm^3 (labelled 'sodium oxide (aq)')
phosphoric acid 0.1 mol / dm^3 (labelled 'phosphorus oxide (aq)')
sulfuric acid 0.1 mol / dm^3 (labelled 'sulfur oxide (aq)')
samples of magnesium oxide, aluminium oxide and silicon oxide (sand)
test-tubes, universal indicator and pH chart
distilled water, glass stirring rod
eye protection (splash-proof goggles)

Answers

Page 186

1. Both solutions are alkalis. Solution A is a weakly alkaline whereas solution B is a strongly alkaline.

2. The solution is acidic.

3. Calcium is a metal. The oxides (and hydroxides) of metals are bases.

4. Supplement Hydrochloric acid as a strong acid is completely ionised, all the HCl molecules are converted into H$^+$ and Cl$^-$ ions. Ethanoic acid as a weak acid is only partially ionised, only a few of the CH$_3$COOH molecules are converted into H$^+$ and CH$_3$COO$^-$ ions.

Science in Context, page 187

CaCO$_3$(s)	→	CaO(s)	+ CO$_2$(g)
1 mole	1 mole		
100 g	56 g		
1000 g	560 g		

560 g of quicklime (assuming 100% conversion)

Page 189

1. Potassium oxide is a basic oxide. Potassium is a metal (most metal oxides are basic).

2. Supplement A basic oxide will react with an acid to form a salt. An amphoteric oxide reacts with an acid or an alkali to form a salt.

Topic 7.1: Acids, bases and salts

Worksheet C7.1b Investigating oxides

Your task is to test the pH of a range of metal and non-metallic oxides and to identify any patterns in your results. Oxides which form alkaline solutions are known as **basic oxides**; oxides which form acidic solutions are known as **acidic oxides**. Some oxides when tested appear to be **neutral oxides** but this may be because they do not dissolve in water.

Apparatus

samples of magnesium oxide, aluminium oxide and silicon oxide

samples of sodium oxide/hydroxide (aq), phosphorus oxide (aq), sulfur oxide (aq)

test-tubes, glass stirring rod

universal indicator

pH chart, distilled water

eye protection (splash-proof goggles)

glass rods

distilled water

SAFETY INFORMATION
Wear eye protection (splash-proof goggles).
Sodium oxide (aq) and phosphorus oxide (aq) are irritants.

Method

1. Put on your eye protection.
2. You will have access to samples of the oxides given in the table below. Some will already be in solution, and others will be solids.
3. To test the solutions use universal indicator paper and the colour chart to determine the pH of the solution.
4. To test the solids, add a small amount of each to some distilled water in a test-tube and stir to try to dissolve the solid before testing with universal indicator paper.

Page 1 of 2

Topic 7.1: Acids, bases and salts

Observing, measuring and recording

5. Record your results in a table like this one.

	Sodium oxide (in solution exists as sodium hydroxide)	Magnesium oxide	Aluminium oxide	Silicon oxide	Phosphorus oxide	Sulfur oxide
Metal oxide or non-metal oxide						
State of matter	aq	s	s	s	aq	aq
pH of solution						
Acidic or neutral or basic (alkaline) oxide						

Handling experimental observations and data

6. What pattern can you identify in your results?
7. Are there any exceptions to this pattern?

Topic 7.1: Acids, bases and salts

Learning episode C7.1c Making soluble salts

Learning objectives

- Describe the preparation, separation and purification of soluble salts by reaction of an acid with:
  a) an alkali by titration
  b) excess metal
  c) excess insoluble base
  d) excess insoluble carbonate.

- Describe the general solubility rules for salts:
  a) sodium, potassium and ammonium salts are soluble
  b) nitrates are soluble
  c) chlorides are soluble, except lead and silver
  d) sulfates are soluble except barium, calcium and lead
  e) carbonates are insoluble, except sodium, potassium and ammonium
  f) hydroxides are insoluble, except sodium, potassium, ammonium and calcium (partially).

Resources

Student Book pages 189–192

Worksheet C7.1c(1) Making a soluble salt (1) – using a titration method

Worksheet C7.1c(2) Making a soluble salt (2)

Resources for class practical (see Technician's notes, following)

Approach

Introduce the rules for whether a salt is soluble or insoluble. Explain that the focus in this learning episode will be the preparation of soluble salts.

Look at the four general methods as listed on pages 190–191 of the Student Book. Explain to students that they will undertake some investigative work focused on Methods 1 and 3.

1. Acid and alkali

Students can use Worksheet C7.1c(1) to investigate Method 1 (acid + alkali). The focus is on the experimental technique; students do not actually produce a sample of a salt, although the worksheet indicates how this would be done.

Emphasise the importance of working carefully – the titration technique can give an accuracy of one drop. Also show how safely to use the equipment, for example fitting pipette fillers.

Explain that the first set of results should be considered as a trial. The first titration can be done relatively quickly to avoid drop-by-drop addition over a long period of time. Your students are likely to need to perform at least two further titrations to get the required agreement between results.

Topic 7.1: Acids, bases and salts

Supplement The worksheet provides an opportunity to use the titration results to calculate the concentration of the hydrochloric acid. Whether you ask students to tackle this will depend on whether you have covered this sort of calculation in Topic 3.1 *Stoichiometry*. Even if students are familiar with this sort of calculation, many of them will still find it difficult, so you will need to spend some time on this. The worksheet encourages a step-by-step approach to aid understanding.

SAFETY INFORMATION
Wear eye protection (splash-proof goggles).

2. Acid and carbonate

Students can use Worksheet C7.1c(2) to investigate Method 3 (acid + carbonate) by preparing a sample of hydrated magnesium sulfate. The method is the same as in the Student Book and may be applied to any soluble salt preparation involving a solid + acid.

Students may find it difficult to determine the crystallisation point. You might help them out with advice such as 'Don't reduce the volume of the evaporating solution by more than half'.

Supplement Some quantitative work is included, requiring students to work out a theoretical yield to compare with the actual yield obtained. Additionally, students should be able to suggest suitable starting chemicals to make a range of different soluble salts.

SAFETY INFORMATION
Wear eye protection (splash-proof goggles).
Dilute sulfuric acid is an irritant.

Technician's notes

Be sure to check the latest safety notes on these resources before proceeding.

The following resources are needed for the class practical C7.1c(1), per group:

burette and stand, 25 cm^3 pipette and bulb filler, conical flask, white tile, wash bottle containing distilled water
0.04 mol / dm^3 sodium hydroxide solution
0.15 mol / dm^3 hydrochloric acid, methyl orange
eye protection (splash-proof goggles)

The following resources are needed for the class practical C7.1c(2), per group:

250 cm^3 beaker, measuring cylinder, spatula, glass rod, filter funnel and filter paper, evaporating basin
Bunsen burner, tripod, gauze and heatproof mat, crystallising dish, microscope slide
0.5 mol / dm^3 sulfuric acid
magnesium carbonate
access to an electronic balance accurate to 1 decimal place

Topic 7.1: Acids, bases and salts

Answers

Page 192

1. A salt is formed when a replaceable hydrogen atom of an acid is replaced by a metal.
2. Sulfuric acid.
3. Potassium chloride will be soluble in water (as are all potassium salts).
4. Calcium nitrate.
5. Neutralisation is the reaction between an acid and an alkali or base to form a salt and water.
6. $H^+(aq)$.
7. $OH^-(aq)$.

Topic 7.1: Acids, bases and salts

Worksheet C7.1c(1) Making a soluble salt (1) – using a titration method

A soluble salt can be made by reacting an acid with an alkali – a neutralisation reaction. To ensure that the quantities of acid and alkali exactly neutralise each other (the end-point), the reaction is first performed using an indicator (a titration reaction) and can then be repeated without the indicator. Typically, the acid is put in the burette and the alkali is measured in a pipette.

This activity is about the titration technique and requires a high degree of care to obtain an accurate result.

Apparatus

burette and stand, 25 cm^3 pipette and bulb filler, conical flask, white tile

dilute hydrochloric acid, dilute sodium hydroxide, wash bottle containing distilled water, methyl orange

eye protection (splash-proof goggles)

SAFETY INFORMATION
Wear eye protection (splash-proof goggles).

Method

1. Put on your eye protection.
2. Rinse the burette first with distilled water and then with the dilute hydrochloric acid. Discard the solution used.
3. Rinse the pipette first with distilled water and then with dilute sodium hydroxide solution. Discard the solution used.
4. Following the instructions from your teacher, use the pipette bulb filler to transfer exactly 25.00 cm^3 of dilute sodium hydroxide to a conical flask. Add 3 drops of methyl orange indicator. Stand the conical flask on the white tile.
5. Following the instructions from your teacher, fill the burette with dilute hydrochloric acid and make sure that there are no air bubbles near to the jet.
6. Take the initial volume of the acid in the burette. Add the acid to the sodium hydroxide solution in the conical flask, swirling the flask all the time, until the indicator changes colour. Take the final volume of the acid.
7. Wash out the conical flask with distilled water and then repeat the titration until two of the readings agree to within 0.10 cm^3. (It is likely that your first titration will not be very accurate – it is difficult to know how close you are to the end-point at your first attempt.)

Note: The first result will give you a clear idea of the approximate amount of acid to add. In subsequent titrations you will be able to add the acid quickly until you are close to the end point and then add drop by drop. The indicator will change colour on the addition of 1 drop so you are aiming for accuracy of 1 drop!

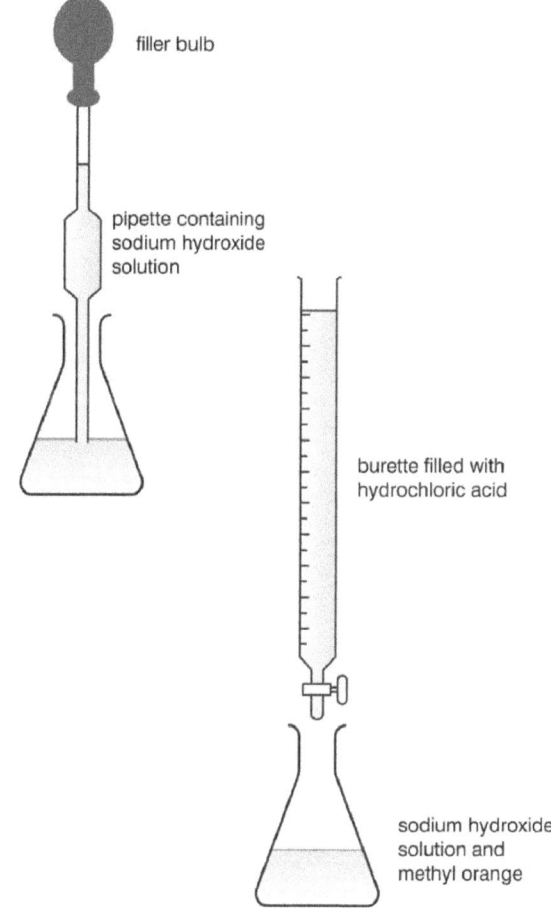

Topic 7.1: Acids, bases and salts

Observing, measuring and recording

Volume of sodium hydroxide solution used = 25.00 cm^3

Burette reading	1st titration	2nd titration	3rd titration	4th titration
2nd reading / cm^3				
1st reading / cm^3				
Difference / cm^3				

Accurate volume of hydrochloric acid for neutralisation = _____ cm^3 (x cm^3)

(Take the mean of the 'accurate' readings)

Supplement Handling experimental observations and data

The titration technique can also be used to work out the concentration of either the acid or alkali used in the reaction. The calculation needed is presented step by step below.

Assume the concentration of the sodium hydroxide solution = 0.1 mol / dm^3
Use your results to calculate the concentration of the hydrochloric acid. You know the accurate volume of solution used (shown as x above).

8. Write the equation for the reaction between hydrochloric acid and sodium hydroxide.

9. How many moles of hydrochloric acid react with 1 mole of sodium hydroxide?

10. The number of moles of sodium hydroxide used in 25.00 cm^3 of 0.1 M solution = _____

11. Therefore the number of moles of hydrochloric acid in x cm^3 of solution = _____

12. Therefore the number of moles of hydrochloric acid in 1000 cm^3 = _____

13. The concentration of the hydrochloric acid solution = _____ M

Topic 7.1: Acids, bases and salts

Worksheet C7.1c(2) Making a soluble salt (2)

Soluble salts can be made by adding an acid to a metal carbonate, in the following reaction:

acid + metal carbonate → salt + carbon dioxide + water

In this activity you are going to make a sample of hydrated magnesium sulfate, $MgSO_4 \cdot 7H_2O$

Apparatus

250 cm³ beaker, measuring cylinder, spatula, glass rod, filter funnel and filter paper, evaporating basin

Bunsen burner, tripod, gauze and heatproof mat, crystallizing dish, microscope slide

dilute sulfuric acid, magnesium carbonate, distilled water

access to an electronic balance

eye protection (splash-proof goggles)

SAFETY INFORMATION

Wear eye protection (splash-proof goggles).

Dilute sulfuric acid is an irritant.

Method

1. Put on your eye protection.

2. Put 50 cm³ of sulfuric acid solution into a beaker. Add magnesium carbonate powder a little at a time until no further reaction occurs. 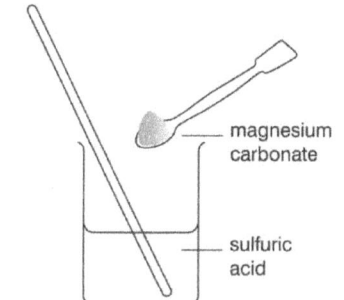	3. Filter the solution into an evaporating basin, leaving the unreacted magnesium carbonate on the filter paper. 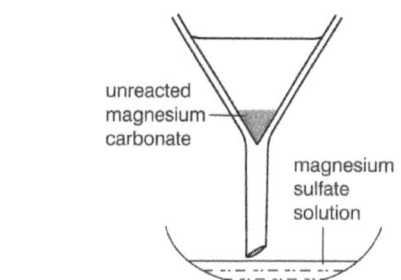
4. Heat the solution in the evaporating basin until it has reached crystallisation point (crystals form when the hot solution is added to a cold microscope slide). Stop heating at this point. 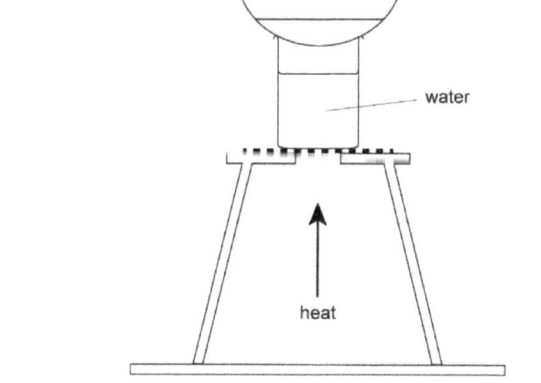	5. Pour the solution into a crystallising dish and leave to crystallise. 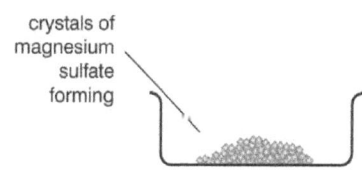

Page 1 of 2

Topic 7.1: Acids, bases and salts

Handling experimental observations and data

6. What gas is produced in the reaction?
7. What is the identification test for this gas? What would indicate a positive identification?
8. What does the term 'hydrated' mean?
9. Why isn't the evaporating basin that contains the solution heated until all the liquid has evaporated?
10. A solution that will crystallise on cooling is said to be 'saturated'. What is a saturated solution?

Supplement 11. The chemical equation for the reaction is:

$$MgCO_3(s) + H_2SO_4(aq) + 7H_2O(l) \rightarrow MgSO_4 \cdot 7H_2O(s) + CO_2(g) + H_2O(l)$$

(A_r: H = 1; C = 12; O = 16; Mg = 24; S = 32)

In this reaction 50 cm³ of 0.5 M sulfuric acid was reacted with excess magnesium carbonate. Calculate the mass of magnesium sulfate crystals that should be produced (the theoretical yield).

12. The actual yield will be less than the theoretical yield. Explain the reason for this.

Topic 7.1: Acids, bases and salts

Supplement Learning episode C7.1d Making insoluble salts

Learning objective

- Supplement Describe the preparation of insoluble salts by precipitation.

Resources

Student Book pages 193–194

Worksheet C7.1d Making an insoluble salt

Resources for class practical (see Technician's notes, below)

Approach

Explain that the method for preparing an insoluble salt involves a precipitation reaction. Introduce the learning episode by referring to page 193 in the Student Book and then use Worksheet C7.1d to enable students to carry out a number of different precipitation reactions.

The worksheet requires students to predict whether the combination of chemicals will produce an insoluble salt (thus revising the rules used to predict the solubility of a salt) and then to confirm or otherwise by trying the reaction. This is a good opportunity for students to practise writing chemical equations for the precipitation reactions.

Additionally, the students should be able to suggest suitable starting chemicals to make a range of different insoluble salts.

SAFETY INFORMATION
Wear eye protection (splash-proof goggles).
Silver nitrate causes skin and eye irritation.

Technician's notes

Be sure to check the latest safety notes on these resources before proceeding.

The following resources are needed for the class practical C7.1d, per group:

test-tubes, test-tube rack, droppers and eye protection (splash-proof goggles)
0.01 mol/dm^3 solutions of sodium carbonate, sodium sulfate
0.05 mol/dm^3 solution of silver nitrate
0.01 mol/dm^3 solutions of calcium nitrate, copper(II) sulfate
0.4 mol/dm^3 solution of sodium chloride
0.01 mol/dm^3 solution of potassium sulfate

Answers

Supplement Page 193

1. Precipitation is the formation of an insoluble salt as a result of a chemical reaction taking place in aqueous solution.

2. Filtration.

3. Washing with cold water will remove traces of any remaining soluble salts.

4. a) lead(II) nitrate + sodium chloride → lead(II) chloride + sodium nitrate

    b) $Pb(NO_3)_2(aq) + 2NaCl(aq) \rightarrow PbCl_2(s) + 2NaNO_3(aq)$

Topic 7.1: Acids, bases and salts

Supplement Worksheet C7.1d Making an insoluble salt

The following list will help you to predict whether a salt is soluble or insoluble:

All common sodium and potassium salts are soluble.

All nitrates are soluble.

Common chlorides are soluble except silver chloride.

Common sulfates are soluble, except those of barium and calcium.

Common carbonates are insoluble, except those of sodium and potassium.

Apparatus

test-tubes, test-tube rack, droppers

eye protection (splash-proof goggles)

solutions: sodium carbonate, sodium sulfate, silver nitrate, calcium nitrate, copper(II) sulfate, copper(II) nitrate, sodium chloride, potassium sulfate.

SAFETY INFORMATION
Wear eye protection (splash-proof goggles).
Silver nitrate causes skin and eye irritation.

Method

1. Put on your eye protection.
2. Look at the combinations of solutions in the table below. Predict which combinations are likely to react and produce an insoluble salt. If appropriate, give the name of the insoluble salt formed.
3. Mix about 1 cm depth of each of the pairs of solutions in separate test-tubes and record your observations in the table.

Solution A	Solution B	Do you predict the formation of an insoluble salt? If so, give the name of the insoluble salt	Observations on mixing the solutions
Sodium carbonate	Copper(II) sulfate		
Sodium sulfate	Copper(II) nitrate		
Silver nitrate	Sodium chloride		
Calcium nitrate	Potassium sulfate		

Handling experimental observations and data

4. How could a pure sample of an insoluble salt be separated from the remaining solutions?
5. Write chemical equations for the first two reactions occurring as you completed the table.

Topic 7.1: Acids, bases and salts

Learning episode C7.1e Consolidation and summary

Learning aims

- Review the learning points of the topic summarised in the end of topic checklist.
- Test understanding of the topic content by answering the end of topic questions.

Resources

Student Book pages 195–199

Approach

Ask students to work with a partner to make a list of key words from this topic. They could then work together to produce a spider diagram showing how the different concepts are linked. They could compare their list with the list of key terms given in the Student Book. Discuss the checklist and ask questions to see how much of the content students are comfortable with.

Students could make flashcards of the key content and then use the flashcards to quiz each other on the information.

Refer to the Science in Context feature, which provides additional information on some acids and alkalis. You could use the Developing Practical Skills feature on page 195 of the Student Book to revise the preparation of a soluble salt if you have not already used this as part of learning episode C7.1c.

Ask students to work individually through the end of topic questions in the Student Book without looking at the text. As they work, walk around the classroom observing their answers and questioning them as necessary to find out which questions are causing difficulties.

After a set period, ask students to stop working. Discuss any areas of difficulty you observed as you walked round the class.

Students should complete any unanswered questions for homework, but you should stress that they should answer the questions without looking at the text, so that they can see how much they have remembered.

Answers

Science in Context, page 195

A wasp sting needs to be treated with an acid (e.g. vinegar). The product contains ammonia which is an alkali and so this would not neutralise the liquid in the sting.

Developing Investigative Skills, page 195

1. Hydrated crystals contain water of crystallisation.
2. Diagram should show the apparatus shown in the filtering part of Fig. 7.9 on page 192 of the Student Book.
3. A filtrate passes through the filter paper.
4. Withdraw a sample of the hot solution using a glass rod and add to a cold microscope slide. If crystals form as the solution cools, the crystallisation point has been reached.
5. Copper(II) oxide is black.
6. Copper(II) sulfate solution is blue.
7. The powder is likely to be anhydrous copper(II) sulfate, the copper(II) sulfate has lost its water of crystallisation.
8. $CuO(s) + H_2SO_4(aq) \rightarrow CuSO_4(aq) + H_2O(l)$

Topic 7.1: Acids, bases and salts

End of topic questions mark scheme

The marks available for a question can indicate the level of detail you need to provide in your answer.

Question	Correct answer	Marks
1	D	1 mark
2 a)	An indicator is a substance that will distinguish between an acid and an alkali.	1 mark
2 b)	The pH scale shows how strongly acidic or how strongly alkaline a substance is.	1 mark
2 c)	i) Weakly acidic. ii) Weakly alkaline. iii) Strongly alkaline.	1 mark 1 mark 1 mark
3 a)	An acid is a substance that forms H^+ ions in water.	1 mark
3 b)	An alkali is a substance that forms OH^- ions in water.	1 mark
3 c)	Neutralisation.	1 mark
4 a)	A base.	1 mark
4 b)	A salt.	1 mark
4 c)	Soluble.	1 mark
4 d)	The calcium oxide is added to warm dilute hydrochloric acid with stirring. When no more solid will react filter the mixture. Heat the filtrate in an evaporating basin until it is saturated/reaches crystallisation point (remove a sample onto a cold watch glass to see if it crystallises). Leave the solution to cool and crystallise.	1 mark 1 mark 1 mark 1 mark
4 e)	$CaO(s) + 2HCl(aq) \rightarrow CaCl_2(aq) + CO_2(g) + H_2O(l)$ (1 mark for balanced equation; 1 mark for state symbols)	2 marks
Supplement 5 a)	Sulfuric acid.	1 mark
Supplement 5 b)	Barium chloride or barium nitrate.	1 mark
Supplement 5 c)	Mix solutions of dilute sulfuric acid and barium chloride/barium nitrate. Filter the suspension to isolate the solid. Wash the solid on the filter paper with distilled water and leave to dry/dry in a low temperature oven.	1 mark 1 mark 1 mark
Supplement 5 d)	$BaCl_2(aq) + H_2SO_4(aq) \rightarrow BaSO_4(s) + 2HCl(aq)$ or $Ba(NO_3)_2(aq) + H_2SO_4(aq) \rightarrow BaSO_4(s) + 2HNO_3(aq)$ (1 mark for balanced equation; 1 mark for state symbols)	2 marks
Supplement 6 a)	$K_2SO_4(aq) + 2H_2O(l)$ (1 mark for balanced equation; 1 mark for state symbols)	2 marks
Supplement 6 b)	$MgCl_2(aq) + H_2O(l)$ (1 mark for balanced equation; 1 mark for state symbols)	2 marks

Topic 7.1: Acids, bases and salts

Question	Correct answer	Marks
Supplement 6 c)	$Ba(NO_3)_2(aq) + CO_2(g) + H_2O(l)$ (1 mark for balanced equation; 1 mark for state symbols)	2 marks
Supplement 6 d)	$ZnCl_2(aq) + H_2(g)$ (1 mark for balanced equation; 1 mark for state symbols)	2 marks
Supplement 6 e)	$ZnCO_3(s) + 2KCl(aq)$ (1 mark for balanced equation; 1 mark for state symbols)	2 marks
Supplement 7	$CoCl_2$ is anhydrous cobalt(II) chloride.	1 mark
	$CoCl_2 \cdot 6H_2O$ is hydrated cobalt(II) chloride (it contains water of crystallisation)	1 mark
	Total:	37 marks

Sections 4, 5, 6 and 7: Exam-style questions mark scheme

Exam-style questions and sample answers have been written by the authors. In examinations, the way marks are awarded may be different. References to assessment and/or assessment preparation are the publisher's interpretation of the syllabus requirements and may not fully reflect the approach of Cambridge Assessment International Education.

The marks available for a question can indicate the level of detail you need to provide in your answer.

Question	Correct answer	Marks
2	C	1 mark
3 a)	i) Correctly plotted graph. 5 points plotted correctly = 3 marks, 3–4 points plotted correctly = 2 marks, 1–2 points plotted correctly = 1 mark ii) Point at 44 °C circled. iii) Any one sensible source of error: incorrect measurement of temperature, loss in mass or even volume.	3 marks 1 mark 1 mark
3 b)	58 ± 2 s 35 ± 2 s	1 mark 1 mark
3 c)	i) 0.017 ± 0.01 0.029 ± 0.02 ii) g s^{-1} iii) The rate increases. iv) When the temperature increases the particles will move faster and collide more frequently. There will also be more energy involved in the collision and so more collisions will lead to a reaction.	1 mark 1 mark 1 mark 1 mark 1 mark
3 d)	Put the acid in a fridge or freezer until the temperature falls to 5 °C.	1 mark
Supplement 4 a)	Reversible reaction.	1 mark
Supplement 4 b)	The reaction is exothermic.	1 mark
Supplement 4 c)	A low temperature will give a high yield. A high temperature will give a good rate of reaction. 450 °C provides an optimum balance of reasonable yield at reasonable rate.	1 mark 1 mark 1 mark
Supplement 4 d)	i) A catalyst provides an alternative pathway for the reaction with a lower activation energy. ii) Vanadium(V) oxide is the catalyst.	1 mark 1 mark 1 mark
5 a)	There are mobile electrons between the layers of carbon atoms.	1 mark
5 b)	The lead and bromide ions will not be able to move when lead(II) bromide is a solid.	1 mark 1 mark
Supplement 5 c)	First row: cathode (B). Reduction.	1 mark

Sections 4, 5, 6 and 7: Exam-style questions mark scheme

Question	Correct answer	Marks
	Second row: anode (A). Oxidation.	1 mark
6 a)	To measure the acid you should use a measuring cylinder.	1 mark
6 b)	The nickel(II) carbonate is added in excess so that all of the sulfuric acid is used up.	1 mark
6 c)	The fizzing is because carbon dioxide gas is given off.	1 mark
6 d)	Correctly drawn diagram showing filter paper in a filter funnel over a beaker.	2 marks
	Labels for filter funnel, filter paper and beaker.	1 mark
6 e)	Filtrate.	1 mark
6 f)	To obtain pure dry crystals you would evaporate off some of the water	1 mark
	and allow it to crystallise in a warm place.	1 mark
6 g)	i) $7H_2O$	1 mark
	ii) The sign means equilibrium or a reversible reaction.	1 mark
6 h)	To obtain green nickel(II) sulfate from white you would add water.	1 mark
7 a)	iron + sulfuric acid →	1 mark
	iron sulfate + hydrogen	1 mark
7 b)	i) Cathode.	1 mark
	ii) It allows conduction so that ions can move through the solution.	1 mark
	iii) The iron object is coated with a layer of copper.	2 marks
	The rod of copper loses copper and gets smaller.	2 marks
7 c)	Chromium is used because it protects the iron so that it does not rust.	1 mark
7 d)	Most reactive iron, chromium, copper least reactive	1 mark
	Total:	49 marks

Section 8: The Periodic Table

Contents

C8.1 The Periodic Table

C8.2 Group I elements

C8.3 Group VII elements

C8.4 Transition elements and noble gases

Overview of the section

The Periodic Table could be considered to be the foundation of inorganic chemistry. Students will already be familiar with the link between electronic structure and the arrangement of elements in the Periodic Table. This section starts with a brief recap on the structure of the Periodic Table before a more detailed study of two groups of metals, the Group 1 metals and the transition metals, providing a sharp contrast of the properties of these two groups. Similarly there is a detailed study of two groups of non-metals, the Group VII elements and the noble gases, which again provide a sharp contrast in chemical properties. There is unsurprisingly this section links to a relatively large number of other sections.

Starting points

The Student Book section opener (pages 208–209) puts the ideas in the section into context and sets the scene. It also allows students to acknowledge and value their prior learning, and provides a benchmark against which future learning can be compared.

The questions provide a structure for introducing the section and can be used in a number of different ways:

- You could ask students to consider the questions as an introductory homework task.
- You could put students into groups to share their own ideas and understanding and then to report back to the whole class.
- Students could be given access to the Internet, preferably with a tight timescale, to find out the information required.

You could then use a spider chart or other form of wall chart to summarise everybody's ideas.

Recording these initial ideas allows you to retain them for reference as the individual topics are developed. In this way, your students' progress in learning can be readily acknowledged.

Topic 8.1: The Periodic Table

C8.1 The Periodic Table

Introduction

This topic builds on students' understanding of Topic 2.1 *Atoms, elements and compounds*, which covered atomic structure and elements as substances that cannot be broken down by chemical means.

The Periodic Table is introduced as a very useful way to arrange the elements and to separate metals from non-metals. This topic provides the basis for studying groups and arrangements in the Periodic Table, including Topic 8.2 *Group I elements*, Topic 8.3 *Group VII elements* and Topic 8.4 *Transition elements and noble gases*.

The topic concentrates on how elements are arranged in the Periodic Table and how their arrangement is linked to their atomic structures. You will consider how reactivity changes within a group of metals and a group of non-metals. Later topics in this section provide more detailed study of this.

Links to other topics

Section	Essential background knowledge	Useful links
2 Atoms, elements and compounds	2.1 Atoms, elements and compounds 2.2 Ions and ionic bonds	2.3 Molecules and covalent bonds 2.4 Metallic bonding
8 The Periodic Table		8.2 Group I elements 8.3 Group VII elements 8.4 Transition elements and noble gases
9 Metals		9.1 Metals

Topic overview

C8.1a	**Orientation**
	The purpose of this short learning episode is to recap students' understanding of the nature of elements and atomic structure. You may use demonstrations to set the scene for this topic and some of the subsequent topics on particular groups of elements.
C8.1b	**Arrangement of the elements**
	This learning episode concentrates on the structure of the Periodic Table, the use of the proton number to order the elements and how they are arranged in groups and periods. It also covers the link between the position of an element in the Periodic Table and its likely metal/non-metal classification and electron arrangement.
	The relationship between the group number and the number of outer electrons and ion charge will act as a revision of the ideas covered in Topic 2.2 *Ions and ionic bonds*.
C8.1c	**Consolidation and summary**
	This learning episode provides an opportunity for a quick recap on the ideas encountered in the topic and time for the students to answer the end of topic questions in the Student Book.

Career links

These are some scientific careers that focus on this area of chemistry but careers in many other fields use the knowledge and skills gained studying science.

A knowledge of the periodic table underpins many careers in science. For example, solar energy research chemists and technicians use non-metals to improve the efficiency of solar panels; computational toxicologists use computer models to assess the risks of different elements and compounds; and geochemists investigate the elements present in different rocks and minerals.

Topic 8.1: The Periodic Table

Learning episode C8.1a Orientation

Learning objectives

- Describe the differences between elements, compounds and mixtures.
- Describe the structure of the atom as a central nucleus containing neutrons and protons surrounded by electrons in shells.
- Determine the electronic configuration of elements with proton number 1 to 20, e.g. 2,8,3.

Resources

Resources for demonstration (see Technician's notes, following)

Approach

This introductory learning episode can be very short, particularly if students show a good knowledge and understanding of previous work on atoms and atomic structure. You could use a quick quiz of 10 questions to probe their understanding of the nature of an element (as opposed to a compound or a mixture) and the arrangement of protons, neutrons and electrons in an atom.

You can then justify the study of the Periodic Table by a quick demonstration of the nature of three elements: sodium (symbol Na; a shiny, soft element stored under oil), copper (symbol Cu; a hard, shiny metal with high melting point) and chlorine (symbol Cl, a pale yellow-green gas) **(see tech notes)**.

Cut a small piece of sodium with a sharp knife on filter paper to show how soft it is. Show students the samples of the other two elements.

These elements are clearly very different from each other. Where are they found in the Periodic Table? Perhaps there is a clear link between the properties of different elements and their position in the Periodic Table? Perhaps the Periodic Table as an arrangement of elements might be a really useful way of simplifying the study of all these elements?

> **SAFETY INFORMATION**
>
> *Wear eye protection (splash-proof goggles).*
>
> *Keep chlorine gas in fume cupboard.*
>
> *Chlorine is oxidising, toxic and hazardous to the environment.*
>
> *Small amounts of Cl_2, which can cause respiratory distress in some people, may be produced.*
> **The laboratory must be well ventilated.**

Technician's notes

Be sure to check the latest safety notes on these resources before proceeding.

The following resources are needed for the demonstration of sodium, copper and chlorine:

bottle of sodium
copper foil
gas jar of chlorine (should be kept in a fume cupboard)
sharp knife, tongs and filter paper
eye protection (splash-proof goggles)

Topic 8.1: The Periodic Table

Learning episode C8.1b Arrangement of the elements

Learning objectives

- Describe the Periodic Table as an arrangement of elements in periods and groups and in order of increasing proton number / atomic number.
- Describe the change from metallic to non-metallic character across a period.
- Describe the relationship between group number and the charge on the ions formed from elements in that group.
- Explain similarities in the chemical properties of elements in the same group of the Periodic Table in terms of their electron configuration.
- Explain how the position of an element in the Periodic Table can be used to predict its properties.
- Supplement Identify trends in groups, given information about the elements.

Resources

Student Book page 210–214

Approach

Refer briefly to the historical development of the Periodic Table and the work of Mendeleev, who is generally credited with being the leading originator of the modern Periodic Table. Emphasise the following aspects of the arrangement of the table:

1. The labelling of groups and periods.

2. The relative positions of metals, non-metals and metalloids.

Supplement 3. Trends in reactivity for metals and non-metals. The Student Book explains these trends, based on an understanding of the formation of ions. For metals, the further the outer electrons are from the attractive force of the nucleus the more readily the atom will lose an electron and form a positive ion; for non-metals, the smaller the atom the more an 'incoming' electron will experience the attractive force of the nucleus and so the more readily the atom will form a negative ion.

4. The relationship between group number, number of electrons in the outer electron shell and ion charge.

Answers

Page 212

1. a) 20
   b) The proton number is the number of protons (which equals the number of electrons) in an atom of the element. Calcium has 20 protons and 20 electrons.
   c) Group II.   d) Period 4.   e) Calcium is a metal.

2. Halogens.

3. Halogens are non-metals.

Page 214

1. Aluminium has 3 electrons in the outer shell.
2. Oxygen will form an O^{2-} ion (the oxide ion) with a 2− charge.
3. Supplement Fluorine (F).
4. Supplement Barium (Ba).

Science in Context, page 214

An atom of Am has 95 electrons, 95 protons and 148 neutrons.

Topic 8.1: The Periodic Table

Learning episode C8.1c Consolidation and summary

Learning aims

- Review the learning points of the topic summarised in the end of topic checklist.
  - Test understanding of the topic content by answering the end of topic questions.

Resources

Student Book pages 215–217

Approach

Ask students to work with a partner to make a list of key words from this topic. They could then work together to produce a spider diagram showing how the different concepts are linked. They could compare their list with the list of key terms given in the Student Book. Discuss the checklist and ask questions to see how much of the content students are comfortable with.

Students could make flashcards of the key content and then use the flashcards to quiz each other on the information.

Ask students to work individually through the end of topic questions in the Student Book without looking at the text. As they work, walk around the classroom observing their answers and questioning them as necessary to find out which questions are causing difficulties.

After a set period, ask students to stop working. Discuss any areas of difficulty you observed as you walked round the class.

Students should complete any unanswered questions for homework, but you should stress that they should answer the questions without looking at the text, so that they can see how much they have remembered.

Supplement Ideas on trends in reactivity will feature strongly in Topic 8.2 *Group I elements*, Topic 8.3 *Group VII elements* and Topic 9.1 *Metals*.

Topic 8.1: The Periodic Table

End of topic questions mark scheme

The marks available for a question can indicate the level of detail you need to provide in your answer.

Question	Correct answer	Marks
1 a)	C	1 mark
1 b)	A	1 mark
1 c)	D	1 mark
1 d)	C	1 mark
1 e)	b, d and f	1 mark
1 f)	D	1 mark
2 a)	2,8,1	1 mark
2 b)	2,8,4	1 mark
2 c)	2,7	1 mark
3	As you move from the left to the right along Period 3, the elements change from metals to non-metals.	1 mark
4	Elements in the same group have the same number of electrons in their outer electron shell.	1 mark
5 a)	Na^+	1 mark
5 b)	Cl^-	1 mark
6	The noble gases have a full outer shell of electrons or 8 electrons in their outer electron shells.	1 mark
	They do not easily gain or lose electrons.	1 mark
Supplement 7 a)	Reactivity increases as you go down a group of metals.	1 mark
Supplement 7 b)	Reactivity decreases down a group of non-metals.	1 mark
	Total:	17 marks

C8.2 Group I elements

Introduction

This topic follows on naturally from Topic 8.1 *The Periodic Table*. Students will know that Group I is a group of metals and will probably know that sodium is an unusual metal, as it is stored under oil in the laboratory. As the topic is very short, you could easily cover the first two learning episodes in the same lesson.

The topic centres on the reactions of the Group I elements with water. The Student Book also covers reactions of Group I elements with chlorine to illustrate their high reactivity, although this is not required by the course syllabus. Alkali metals have obvious links with Topic 7.1 *Acids, bases and salts* and the reactivity of metals in Topic 8.4 *Transition elements and noble gases*.

Links to other topics

Section	Essential background knowledge	Useful links
2 Atoms, elements and compounds		2.2 Ions and ionic bonds
3 Stoichiometry	3.1 Stoichiometry	
7 Acids, bases and salts		7.1 Acids, bases and salts
8 The Periodic Table	8.1 The Periodic Table	8.4 Transition elements and noble gases
9 Metals		9.1 Metals

Topic overview

C8.2a	Orientation
	This is a very short learning episode re-emphasising the position of the Group I elements in the Periodic Table and introducing the elements lithium, sodium and potassium. These are very unusual metals, as they are soft and stored under oil in the laboratory. As metals they have very low densities and melting points. The trend in reactivity of the elements is emphasised and equations for the reaction of the elements with oxygen are introduced.
C8.2b	**Reactions of the Group I elements**
	This learning episode involves demonstrating the reactions of lithium, sodium and potassium with water. It emphasises the formation of hydrogen gas and an alkaline solution. An explanation of the trend in reactivity is provided in terms of the ease of removal of the outermost electron. Equations for the reactions are developed. Reference is also made to the reactions with chlorine.
C8.2c	**Consolidation and summary**
	This is another short learning episode that provides an opportunity for a quick recap on learning points, as well as giving students time to answer the end of topic questions in the Student Book.

Career links

These are some scientific careers that focus on this area of chemistry but careers in many other fields use the knowledge and skills gained studying science.

Soil scientists conduct research to study the effects of potassium and sodium deficiencies in plants.

Neuroscientists and researchers study the effect of the Group I ions on brain activity in the drive to find treatments for diseases such Alzheimer's and epilepsy.

Topic 8.2: Group I elements

Learning episode C8.2a Orientation

Learning objective

- Describe the Group I alkali metals, lithium, sodium and potassium, as relatively soft metals with general trends down the group, limited to:
  (a) decreasing melting point
  (b) increasing density
  (c) increasing reactivity.

Resources

Student Book pages 218–219

Resources for a demonstration (see Technician's notes, below)

Approach

Quickly recap on previous work on the Periodic Table. Ask students what they already know about the Group I elements. Show samples of the elements in bottles. Ask students why the elements are stored in oil. Explain that the melting points of the elements decrease down the group (indicating that the strength of the metallic bonding decreases) and overall the densities of the metals increase down the group. You can also cut small samples of the metals on a filter paper with a sharp knife. *Make sure that pieces of metal that are not to be used immediately are returned to their bottles and so are kept under oil* **(see tech notes)**.

Refer to the Student Book (page 219), which shows that the reactivity of the Group I elements increases down the group. Construct equations for the reactions of the metals with oxygen (from the air).

SAFETY INFORMATION
Wear eye protection (splash-proof goggles).
Dispense only the quantity of each metal required, and keep the remainder under oil.

Technician's notes

Be sure to check the latest safety notes on these resources before proceeding.

The following resources are needed for the demonstration of the Group I metals:

lithium – one piece, 5 mm cube; sodium – one piece, 4 mm cube; potassium – one piece, 3 mm cube
forceps, filter paper and knife, eye protection (splash-proof goggles or a face shield)

Answers

Page 219

1. They react with water to form alkaline solutions.

2. They have one electron in the outer shell.

3. They are soft to cut (also have very low melting points).

4. The melting point of potassium will be lower than that for sodium as melting points decrease down Group 1.

5. Potassium is more reactive than lithium because the outer electron is further from the attraction of the nucleus and can be more easily removed.

Topic 8.2: Group I elements

Learning episode C8.2b Reactions of the Group I elements

Learning objective

- Predict the properties of other elements in Group I, given information about the elements.

Resources

Student Book pages 220–222

Resources for a demonstration (see Technician's notes, below)

Approach

Demonstrate the reaction of lithium, sodium and potassium with water **(see tech notes)**. The oil must be wiped off the metal once it has been cut. A 500 cm^3 beaker can be used for lithium. For sodium and potassium, a small trough of water on an overhead projector provides good visibility. Alternatively, you may use a large trough of water.

Use a safety screen and carefully control the size of the metal samples. In a small trough of water, use samples no bigger than 1 mm × 1 mm; in a large trough of water the metal samples must be no bigger than 2 mm × 2 mm. Demonstrate the reactions in turn, using fresh water each time. Add universal indicator to the solution to illustrate how an alkaline solution forms – hence the family name 'alkali metals'.

The increased reactivity down the group should be easy to observe from lithium (which doesn't usually melt) to sodium (which melts into a sphere instantaneously) to potassium (which melts and catches fire on contact with the water). Re-emphasise the reason for the increased reactivity – the increasing distance of the outer electron from the nucleus.

On the Internet there are many video clips of rubidium reacting with water. This can form a stimulating conclusion to the demonstrations. Ask students to predict what will happen before they watch the clip.

More detailed observations are provided in the Student Book. Introduce equations for the reactions.

> **SAFETY INFORMATION**
>
> Wear eye protection (splash-proof goggles).
>
> Use safety screens. The screens should be positioned close to the trough to avoid the risk of sodium or potassium shooting out of the trough.
>
> In a small trough of water, use samples no bigger than 1 mm × 1 mm; in a large trough of water the metal samples must be no bigger than 2 mm × 2 mm.

Technician's notes

Be sure to check the latest safety notes on these resources before proceeding.

The following resources are needed for the demonstration of the reactions of Group I metals:

lithium
sodium
potassium
forceps, filter paper and sharp knife (all dry)
500 cm^3 beaker (for lithium); glass trough (for sodium and potassium)
universal indicator paper or solution
overhead projector and 2 safety screens
goggles or face shield

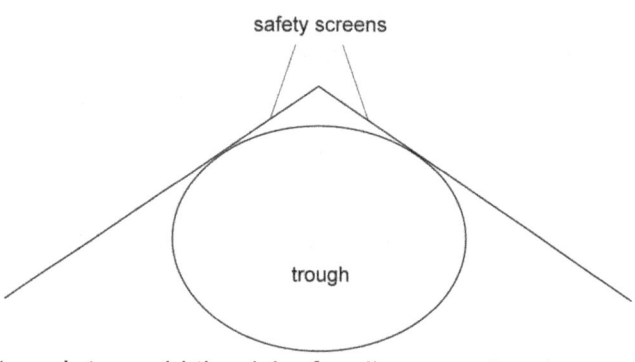

The safety screens should be positioned close to the trough to avoid the risk of sodium or potassium shooting out of the trough, as shown in the diagram above. Take steps to prevent theft.

Answers

Science in Context, page 221

Li_2CO_3 and LiOH.

Page 221

1. Sodium oxide is white.

2. Hydrogen. The solution formed is potassium hydroxide.

3. The compounds are soluble.

4. a) A period is a horizontal row of elements in the Periodic Table. All the elements in the same period have the same number of electron shells.

    For example: Period 1 elements: hydrogen (1) to helium (2) – 1 electron shell.

    Period 2 elements: lithium (2,1) to neon (2,8) – 2 electron shells.

    Period 3 elements sodium (2,8,1) to argon (2,8,8) – 3 electron shells.

    b) Magnesium is in the third period of the Periodic Table.

    c) Sodium has only 1 electron in its outer shell and this is relatively easily removed as it is shielded from the nucleus by the other shells. Argon has a full shell of electrons and so is very unreactive.

5. a) A group is a vertical column of elements having similar chemical properties because of their outer shell electronic structure.

    b) Lithium, sodium, potassium.

    c) All the elements in Group I have one electron in the outer shell.

    d) The reactivity of these elements depends upon the ease at which the outer electrons are lost. One electron can easily be lost to form positive ions. The ease with which it can be lost increases down the group because the electron is less tightly held in the atom and therefore reactivity increases down the group.

Science in Context, page 222

Compared to sodium, caesium will have a lower melting point, higher density and higher reactivity.

Topic 8.2: Group I elements

Learning episode 8.2c Consolidation and summary

Learning aims

- Review the learning points of the topic summarised in the end of topic checklist.
  - Test understanding of the topic content by answering the end of topic questions.

Resources

Student Book pages 223–224

Approach

Approach

Ask students to work with a partner to make a list of key words from this topic. They could then work together to produce a spider diagram showing how the different concepts are linked. They could compare their list with the list of key terms given in the Student Book. Discuss the checklist and ask questions to see how much of the content students are comfortable with.

Students could make flashcards of the key content and then use the flashcards to quiz each other on the information.

Ask students to work individually through the end of topic questions in the Student Book without looking at the text. As they work, walk around the classroom observing their answers and questioning them as necessary to find out which questions are causing difficulties.

After a set period, ask students to stop working. Discuss any areas of difficulty you observed as you walked round the class.

Students should complete any unanswered questions for homework, but you should stress that they should answer the questions without looking at the text, so that they can see how much they have remembered.

Topic 8.2: Group I elements

End of topic questions mark scheme

The marks available for a question can indicate the level of detail you need to provide in your answer.

Question	Correct answer	Marks
1	A	1 mark
2 a)	Potassium.	1 mark
2 b)	To prevent reaction with air (oxygen) or water.	1 mark
2 c)	Potassium.	1 mark
2 d)	The elements react with the oxygen in the air.	1 mark
2 e)	Sodium is less dense than water.	1 mark
3	The Group I elements react with water to form alkalis.	1 mark
	The alkalis are hydroxides, such as sodium hydroxide.	1 mark
4 a)	lithium + oxygen → lithium oxide	1 mark
	$4Li(s) + O_2(g) \rightarrow 2Li_2O(s)$	2 marks
	(1 mark for correct formulae; 1 mark for balancing)	
4 b)	potassium + water → potassium hydroxide + hydrogen	1 mark
	$2K(s) + 2H_2O(l) \rightarrow 2KOH(aq) + H_2(g)$	2 marks
	(1 mark for correct formulae; 1 mark for balancing)	
4 c)	potassium + chlorine → potassium chloride	1 mark
	$2K(s) + Cl_2(g) \rightarrow 2KCl(s)$	2 marks
	(1 mark for correct formulae; 1 mark for balancing)	
Supplement 5 a)	Rubidium is a solid.	1 mark
Supplement 5 b)	i) Hydrogen.	1 mark
	ii) Rubidium hydroxide would be formed.	1 mark
	Universal indicator would show the presence of an alkali.	1 mark
Supplement 5 c)	Rubidium would be more reactive than potassium.	1 mark
	The outer electron in rubidium is further away from the nucleus than that in potassium and so it will be more easily transferred in a reaction.	1 mark
Supplement 6	Potassium is a larger atom than sodium.	1 mark
	The outer electron in potassium is further away from the nucleus than the outer electron in sodium.	1 mark
	The outer electron in potassium is easier to remove (as in a reaction) than the outer electron in sodium.	1 mark
	Total:	20 marks

C8.3 Group VII elements

Introduction

This is a short topic that is likely to follow on from Topic 8.1 *The Periodic Table* and Topic 8.2 *Group I elements*. Students should be familiar with the position of non-metals in the Periodic Table, so they should recognise Group VII elements as non-metals.

The topic concentrates on the appearance of the three common halogens (chlorine, bromine and iodine), their relative reactivities and how these are confirmed by displacement reactions involving the halogen and solutions of their salts. There is an opportunity to practice the redox nature of these reactions if the section on Redox has been covered.

Topic 12.2 *Identification of ions and gases* covers the test for halide ions. There is an opportunity for some student practical work on displacement reactions.

Links to other topics

Section	Essential background knowledge	Useful links
2 Atoms, elements and compounds		2.2 Ions and ionic bonds
3 Stoichiometry	3.1 Stoichiometry	
8 The Periodic Table	8.1 The Periodic Table	8.2 Group I elements
12 Experimental techniques		12.2 *Identification of ions and gases*

Topic overview

C8.3a	**Orientation**
	This learning episode very briefly recaps on the structure of the Periodic Table, followed by an introduction to the elements of chlorine, bromine and iodine. Fluorine and astatine are briefly mentioned in the context of predicting their physical states and relative reactivities.

C8.3b	**Displacement reactions of the halogens**
	This learning episode focuses on the potential reactions of chlorine, bromine and iodine with solutions of their salts.
	Supplement Students investigate the redox nature of these reactions, using the definitions of oxidation and reduction in terms of electron loss/gain. (If the Redox section has been covered).

C8.3c	**Consolidation and summary**
	This learning episode allows a quick recap on the ideas encountered in the topic, particularly displacement reactions, and an opportunity for students to answer the end of topic questions in the Student Book.

Career links

These are some scientific careers that focus on this area of chemistry but careers in many other fields use the knowledge and skills gained studying science.

Laboratory technicians and science teachers need to have a good understanding of the properties and dangers of the halogens in order to plan practical work that can be done safely by students when using them.

Topic 8.3: Group VII elements

Learning episode C8.3a Orientation

Learning objectives

- Describe the Group VII halogens, chlorine, bromine and iodine, as diatomic non-metals with general trends down the group, limited to: increasing density, decreasing reactivity.
- State the appearance of the halogens at r.t.p. as: chlorine, a pale yellow-green gas; bromine, a red-brown liquid; iodine, a grey-black solid.
- Predict the properties of other elements in Group VII, given information about the elements.

Resources

Student Book pages 225–226

Resources for a demonstration (see Technician's notes, following)

Approach

Ask students to tell you what they already know about the Group VII elements – they should know that they are non-metals, that they all have seven electrons in their outer electron shells and that reactivity (for non-metals) decreases as you descend the group.

Explain that the elements have the family name 'halogens', which means 'salt maker'. In other words, these elements react with metals to form salts (such as chlorides, bromides and iodides).

Show students samples of the three halogens: chlorine is a pale green gas; bromine is a red-brown liquid and iodine is a black solid **(see tech notes)**. Explain that because chlorine and bromine are toxic in the laboratory they are often used in solution – chlorine solution is colourless; bromine solution is orange.

Put the three elements in order of reactivity and then put cards for fluorine and astatine in the correct positions. Ask students to predict the appearance and reactivity of these other two elements (fluorine – a pale yellow gas; astatine a black solid). Refer students to the Science in Context feature on fluorine on page 229 of the Student Book. The content of these Science in Context features is beyond the syllabus but provides the opportunity to explore the content more deeply.

Finally, explain the trend in reactivity: the smallest atom most easily gains an electron to achieve the electron configuration of the nearest noble gas (the 'incoming' electron would feel a greater attraction from the nucleus).

SAFETY INFORMATION
Wear eye protection (splash-proof goggles).
Chlorine is oxidising, toxic and hazardous to the environment.
Small amounts of Cl_2, which can cause respiratory distress in some people, may be produced. **The laboratory must be well ventilated.**
Keep all the samples in a fume cupboard.

Technician's notes

Be sure to check the latest safety notes on these resources before proceeding.

The following resources are needed for the demonstration of the Group VII elements:

a gas jar of chlorine (in a fume cupboard)
bromine liquid in a bottle/gas jar (in a fume cupboard) and iodine solid (0.25 g)
eye protection (splash-proof goggles)

Topic 8.3: Group VII elements

Learning episode C8.3b Displacement reactions of the halogens

Learning objectives

- Describe and explain displacement reactions of halogens with other halide ions.
- Predict the properties of other elements in Group VII, given information about the elements.

Resources

Student Book pages 227–228

Worksheet C8.3b Displacement reactions of halogens

Resources for demonstration (see Technician's notes, following)

Approach

Explain displacement reactions in terms of the halogen atoms competing for a metal. Demonstrate the practical shown on Worksheet C8.3b. Students should not use cyclohexane in the classroom, so this must be a teacher demonstration. Students can record observations during the demonstration using the worksheet. Explain that halogens are used in solution to reduce the risks posed by these chemicals. Cyclohexane, a non-polar solvent, is used to distinguish more precisely between solutions containing bromine and those containing iodine. You will need to spend time on developing the equations for the reactions.

The Developing Practical Skills box on page 228 of the Student Book deals with displacement reactions. You could use this as a consolidation after the practical activity or leave it for the consolidation and summary learning episode at the end of the topic.

Supplement Page 227 of the Student Book explains the redox nature of these reactions with an ionic equation and then with half-equations. Students are expected to understand that reduction is the gain of electrons and oxidation is the loss of electrons.

SAFETY INFORMATION

Wear eye protection (splash-proof goggles).

The non-polar/ hydrocarbon solvent is highly flammable and harmful, and irritating to skin.

Chlorine solution, bromine solution and iodine solution are all irritants.

Warn asthmatics.

Ensure that there are no naked flames.

Ensure that the laboratory is well ventilated.

Cyclohexane highly flammable and harmful and should not be used by students.

Topic 8.3: Group VII elements

Technician's notes

Be sure to check the latest safety notes on these resources before proceeding.

The following resources are needed for the class practical C8.3b, per group:

chlorine solution (0.1% w/v) – diluted until the colour is just visible
bromine solution (0.3% w/v) – diluted until the colour is just visible
iodine solution (0.5% w/v) – diluted until the colour is just visible
0.1 mol / dm³ solution sodium chloride
0.1 mol / dm³ solution sodium bromide
0.1 mol / dm³ solution sodium iodide
cyclohexane
test-tubes, droppers, glass rods
eye protection (splash-proof goggles)
beaker for waste chemicals

Answers

Page 228

1. 7 electrons in the outer shell.

2. The atoms only need to gain one electron to achieve 8 in the outer shell.

3. The chlorine molecule is made up of two atoms combined/bonded together, Cl_2.

4. Astatine is probably a solid at room temperature. Group VII elements show trends in their physical and chemical properties. At room temperature, fluorine and chlorine are gases, bromine is a liquid and iodine is a solid. Astatine is below iodine in Group VII; therefore it is also likely to be a solid.

5. A displacement reaction is where one Group VII element takes the place of another in a metallic compound.

6. **Supplement** The displacement reaction involves one Group VII element being reduced (gaining electrons) and one being oxidised (losing electrons).

Developing Practical Skills, page 229

1. Make sure there are no naked flames in the room.

   Work in a fume cupboard or make sure the room is well ventilated.

   Don't dispose of the liquid mixture containing the non-polar solvent down the sink.

2. Chlorine is more reactive than bromine (it displaced the bromine in sodium bromide).

   Chlorine is more reactive than iodine (it displaced the iodine in sodium iodide).

3. $Br_2(aq) + 2NaI(aq) \rightarrow 2NaBr(aq) + I_2(aq)$

4. Tube 6. Iodine is less reactive than bromine and so cannot displace bromine from sodium bromide. (The non-polar solvent layer should have been violet.)

Science in Context, page 230

a) CaF_2

b) $Ca^{2+}F^-$

c) Anode

Page 230

1. Chlorine is very effective at killing bacteria that are often present in water supplies.
2. Iodine is used as an antiseptic.
3. The plastic is heat resistant and also provides a non-stick surface.
4. a) Supplement

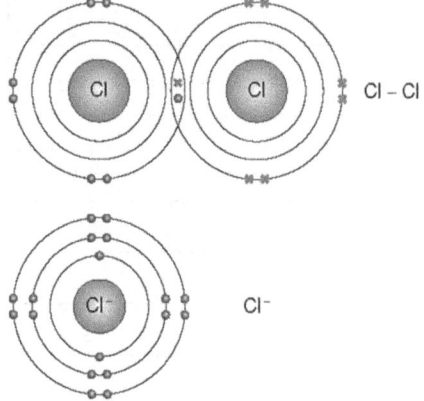

   b) Supplement $2Cl^-(aq) \rightarrow Cl_2(g) + 2e^-$. The chloride ions lose electrons.

   c) Supplement $2NaOH(aq) + Cl_2(g) \rightarrow NaCl(aq) + NaClO(aq) + H_2O(l)$

   d) Supplement Chlorine is a more reactive halogen than bromine. Chlorine will displace bromine from a solution of bromide ions. (Chlorine will oxidise bromide ions to bromine.)

   Observations: chlorine water is pale green. When this is added to a colourless solution of potassium bromide the resulting solution will turn orange due to the presence of bromine.

5. a) Supplement The reactivity of fluorine is due to its electronic structure 2,7. Fluorine only needs to gain one electron to form a fluoride ion. This is very easy because of its small size and high attractive force of the nucleus.

   b) Supplement $F_2(aq) + 2e^- \rightarrow 2F^-(aq)$

   c) Supplement Both chlorine and iodine are less reactive than fluorine. Fluorine could only be displaced from fluoride ions by a more reactive halogen. As there are no halogens that are more reactive than fluorine, fluorine will not be displaced from fluoride ions.

Topic 8.3: Group VII elements

Worksheet C8.3b Demonstration of displacement reactions of the halogens

Under the right conditions, the halogen elements will compete with each other to form compounds with metals. For example, if bromine is added to sodium iodide solution there are two possibilities:

1. Bromine solution + sodium iodide solution → no change
2. Bromine solution + sodium iodide solution → sodium bromide solution + iodine solution

If as in 1 there is no change, then iodine is more reactive than bromine.

If the reaction in 2 takes place then bromine is more reactive than iodine.

From your knowledge of the trend in reactivity of the halogen elements, you should be able to predict which is more likely: 1 or 2.

Apparatus

solutions of chlorine, bromine and iodine

solutions of sodium chloride, sodium bromide and sodium iodide

non-polar solvent (cyclohexane)

test-tubes, glass rod

eye protection (splash-proof goggles)

SAFETY INFORMATION
Wear eye protection (splash-proof goggles).
Cyclohexane is highly flammable and harmful.
Chlorine solution, bromine solution and iodine solution are all irritants.
If you are asthmatic, you should take care.
Ensure that there are no naked flames.
Ensure that the laboratory is well ventilated.

Method (demonstrated by teacher)

Part 1

1. Put on your eye protection.
2. Samples of chlorine solution, bromine solution and iodine solution are put in separate test-tubes.
3. 1 cm depth of the cyclohexane is added to each tube and stirred carefully with a glass rod.
4. Record the colour of the cyclohexane layer in the table.

TAKE CARE: Do not pour the cyclohexane mixtures into the sink.

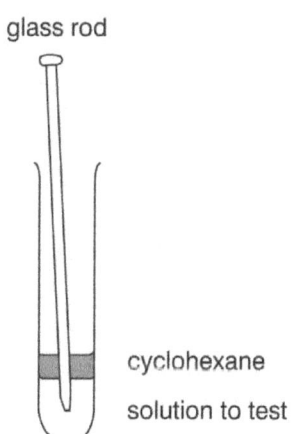

Page 1 of 2

Observing, measuring and recording

Table 1

Solution	Colour of non-polar solvent layer
Chlorine	
Bromine	
Iodine	

Method

Part 2

5. Now observe the tests shown in Table 2.
6. 0.5 cm depth of solution A is put in a test-tube. About 1 cm depth of solution B is added. Finally about 1 cm depth of the cyclohexane is added and the mixture is stirred with a glass rod.
7. Record the colour of the cyclohexane layer in the table.

Observing, measuring and recording

Table 2

Solution A	Solution B	Colour of non-polar solvent layer	Which halogen remains in the non-polar solvent layer?
Chlorine	Sodium bromide		
Chlorine	Sodium iodide		
Bromine	Sodium chloride		
Bromine	Sodium iodide		
Iodine	Sodium chloride		
Iodine	Sodium bromide		

Handling experimental observations and data

8. Write word equations for any reactions that occurred.
9. What is the order of reactivity of the halogen elements as indicated by these displacement reactions?
10. **Supplement** Write fully balanced chemical equations for any reactions that occurred. In each case identify the reactant that has been oxidised and the reactant that has been reduced.
11. **Supplement** Would you expect a reaction between astatine and sodium bromide solution? Explain your answer.

Topic 8.3: Group VII elements

Learning episode C8.3c Consolidation and summary

Learning aims

- Review the learning points of the topic summarised in the end of topic checklist.
  - Test understanding of the topic content by answering the end of topic questions.

Resources

Student Book pages 232–233

Approach

Ask students to work with a partner to make a list of key words from this topic. They could then work together to produce a spider diagram showing how the different concepts are linked. They could compare their list with the list of key terms given in the Student Book. Discuss the checklist and ask questions to see how much of the content students are comfortable with.

Students could make flashcards of the key content and then use the flashcards to quiz each other on the information.

Revisit displacement reactions and, if not already covered, ask students to answer the questions related to the Developing Practical Skills feature on page 229 of the Student Book.

Ask students to work individually through the end of topic questions in the Student Book without looking at the text. As they work, walk around the classroom observing their answers and questioning them as necessary to find out which questions are causing difficulties.

Supplement Spend some time revising the equations for displacement reactions and the redox nature of these reactions.

After a set period, ask students to stop working. Discuss any areas of difficulty you observed as you walked round the class.

Students should complete any unanswered questions for homework, but you should stress that they should answer the questions without looking at the text, so that they can see how much they have remembered.

Topic 8.3: Group VII elements

End of topic questions mark scheme

The marks available for a question can indicate the level of detail you need to provide in your answer.

Question	Correct answer	Marks
1	C	1 mark
2 a)	Chlorine.	1 mark
2 b)	Bromine.	1 mark
2 c)	Iodine.	1 mark
2 d)	Bromine is a red-brown liquid.	1 mark
3 a)	The Group VII elements have 7 electrons in the outer electron shell.	1 mark
	The Group VII elements only need to gain 1 electron in a reaction to achieve a full outer electron shell or 8 electrons in their outer electron shell.	1 mark
3 b)	Fluorine is the smallest of the Group VII atoms and so its outer electrons feel the strongest attraction to the nucleus.	1 mark
	Fluorine therefore can gain an electron (in a reaction) more easily than the other elements can.	1 mark
4 a)	sodium + chlorine → sodium chloride	1 mark
	$2Na(s) + Cl_2(g) \rightarrow 2NaCl(s)$	2 marks
	(1 mark for formulae; 1 mark for balancing)	
4 b)	magnesium + bromine → magnesium bromide	1 mark
	$Mg(s) + Br_2(l) \rightarrow MgBr_2(s)$	2 marks
	(1 mark for formulae; 1 mark for balancing)	
4 c)	hydrogen + fluorine → hydrogen fluoride	1 mark
	$H_2(g) + F_2(g) \rightarrow 2HF(g)$	2 marks
	(1 mark for formulae; 1 mark for balancing)	
5 a)	This is a displacement reaction.	1 mark
5 b)	$Br_2(l) + 2NaI(aq) \rightarrow 2NaBr(aq) + I_2(aq)$	2 marks
	(1 mark for formulae; 1 mark for balancing)	
Supplement 5 c)	i) Oxidation is the loss of electrons.	1 mark
	The iodide ions have lost electrons and been oxidised.	1 mark
	ii) Reduction is the gain of electrons.	1 mark
	The bromine has gained electrons and been reduced.	1 mark
	Total:	25 marks

C8.4 Transition elements and noble gases

Introduction

This topic completes the systematic study of the Periodic Table. The two aspects are combined because they represent two important 'regions' of the Periodic Table, not because they are particularly similar.

There are clear links to Topic 8.1 *The Periodic Table*, Topic 8.2 *Group I elements* and Topic 8.3 *Group VII elements*, and Topic 9.1 *Metals*. Students should be familiar with the position of metals and non-metals in the Periodic Table. They should know the significance of the electron configuration of noble gases in chemical bonding as explored in Topic 2.2 *Ions and ionic bonds* and Topic 2.3 *Molecules and covalent bonds*.

The characteristic colours of the transition metal compounds, and specifically their hydroxides, link to Topic 12.2 *Identification of ions and gases*. There is also a link to Topic 6.1 *Rate of reaction* through the use of transition metals as catalysts.

After a brief recap on the Periodic Table's structure and organisation, the topic concentrates on the properties of the transition metals, including their variable oxidation states. There is a brief look at the noble gases, focusing primarily on their electronic structures and uses. The topic provides an opportunity for developing the practical/ investigative skills of Observing, measuring and recording.

Links to other topics

Section	Essential background knowledge	Useful links
2 Atoms, elements and compounds		2.2 Ions and ionic bonds
		2.3 Molecules and covalent bonds
6 Chemical reactions		6.1 Rate of reaction
8 The Periodic Table	8.1 The Periodic Table	8.2 Group I elements
		8.3 Group VII elements
9 Metals		9.1 Metals
12 Experimental techniques		12.2 Identification of ions and gases

Topic overview

C8.4a	Orientation
	This learning episode very briefly recaps on the structure of the Periodic Table and highlights the positions of the transition metals and the noble gases. The transition metals are contrasted with the Group I metals and the noble gases are contrasted with the Group VII elements.
C8.4b	**The transition elements**
	This learning episode focuses on the properties of the transition metals (high densities and high melting points), the variable oxidation states exhibited by many of the transition metals (for those students following the supplementary syllabus) and the use of transition metals and their compounds as catalysts. A class practical is used to emphasise the fact that many transition metals form coloured compounds.
	Supplement The variable oxidation numbers of the transition elements are highlighted.

Topic 8.4: Transition elements and noble gases

C8.4c	**The noble gases**
	The unreactive nature of the noble gases provides the core of this short learning episode, with links being made to the students' knowledge of ionic and covalent bonding. The monatomic nature of the noble gases is emphasised, as are their uses.
C8.4d	**Consolidation and summary**
	This learning episode allows a quick recap on the ideas encountered in the topic and an opportunity for students to answer the end of topic questions in the Student Book.

Career links

These are some scientific careers that focus on this area of chemistry but careers in many other fields use the knowledge and skills gained studying science.

Aircraft engineers work with transition metals such as titanium to design aircraft which are strong but lightweight.

Anaesthesiologists use some noble gases such as xenon in general anaesthetics and welders often do their job in an atmosphere of inert argon to keep them safe.

Topic 8.4: Transition elements and noble gases

Learning episode C8.4a Orientation

Learning aims

- To review the significance of the positioning of the transition metals in the Periodic Table.
- To review the significance of the positioning of the noble gases in the Periodic Table.
- Know the positions of the transition metals and noble gases in the Periodic Table.
- Know some of the key differences between the transition metals and the Group I metals.
- Know some of the key differences between the noble gases and the Group VII elements.

Resources

Resources for a demonstration (see Technician's notes, following)

Approach

Ask students to consider the element copper, Cu. What does the position of copper in the Periodic Table indicate about the element? In what ways is copper similar to, and different from, a Group I element such as sodium?

Show students samples of a selection of transition metals and compare with a sample of the element sodium **(see tech notes)**.

SAFETY INFORMATION
Wear eye protection (splash-proof goggles).
Warn students who have allergies to heavy metals, such as nickel not to handle it unless they are wearing disposable gloves.

Ask students about the element argon, Ar. What does the position of argon in the Periodic Table indicate about the element? In what ways is argon similar to, and different from, a Group VII element such as chlorine?

Ask students about the electronic structure of the noble gases. What is the significance of the noble gas electron structure when atoms combine to form ionic or covalent bonds?

Technician's notes

Be sure to check the latest safety notes on these resources before proceeding.

The following resources are needed for the demonstration of transition metals:

samples of transition metals, e.g. chromium, iron, copper, nickel, zinc
a bottle of sodium, with the metal stored in oil

Topic 8.4: Transition elements and noble gases

Learning episode C8.4b The transition elements

Learning objectives

- Describe the transition elements as metals that:
(a) have high densities
(b) have high melting points
(c) form coloured compounds
(d) often act as catalysts as elements and in compounds
- Supplement Describe transition elements as having ions with variable oxidation numbers, including iron(II) and iron(III).

Resources

Student Book pages 234–236

Worksheet C8.4b Transition metal compounds

Resources for a class practical (see Technician's notes, following)

Approach

Ask students to look up the densities and melting points of the following transition metals and to compare with the corresponding data for magnesium and aluminium:

- titanium, vanadium, chromium, iron, nickel, copper, silver, gold, mercury.

Refer to the comparison on page 234 of the Student Book between the transition metals and the Group I metals. Students could research the use of transition metals as catalysts as a homework task.

Introduce the class practical, which highlights the characteristic colours of some transition metal compounds. It also provides a link to the identification of cations by precipitation reactions. (See Topic 12.2 *Identification of ions and gases* and Worksheet C8.4b (Using a flame test to identify metal ions) to check that you are happy with the amount of overlap between these practical activities.)

The worksheet suggests that zinc is not a typical transition metal – this could be the focus of a short discussion. Stress the use of Roman numerals to indicate the oxidation number of the metal. Ask students why Roman numerals tend *not* to be used when naming zinc compounds.

Supplement A common characteristic of transition elements is that they have variable oxidation numbers.

Supplement Page 235 of the Student Book will reinforce the outcomes of the practical work and provides an opportunity for those students following the supplementary syllabus to consider ionic equations for the precipitation reactions.

SAFETY INFORMATION

Wear eye protection (splash-proof goggles).

Solutions of copper(II) sulfate, iron(II) ammonium sulfate, iron(III) chloride, zinc sulfate and ammonia are irritants. 0.1 M sodium hydroxide solution is an irritant.

If students are allergic to nickel they should wear disposable gloves.

Topic 8.4: Transition elements and noble gases

Technician's notes

Be sure to check the latest safety notes on these resources before proceeding.

The following resources are needed for the class practical C3d.2a, per group:

0.1 mol/dm^3 solutions of copper(II) sulfate, iron(II) ammonium sulfate, iron(III) chloride, zinc sulfate
0.1 mol/dm^3 sodium hydroxide solution
0.5 mol/dm^3 ammonia solution
test-tubes, droppers, glass rods
eye protection (splash-proof goggles)

Answers

Page 236

1. No. Copper is very unreactive (below hydrogen in reactivity series/used for hot and cold water pipes).
2. Supplement The number indicates the oxidation number of the chromium.
3. a) $FeSO_4(aq) + 2NaOH(aq) \rightarrow Fe(OH)_2(s) + Na_2SO_4(aq)$

    b) Green.

Topic 8.4: Transition elements and noble gases

Worksheet C8.4b Transition metal compounds

The transition metals form compounds with characteristic colours that contrast with those of the Group I and Group II elements. You are going to produce some hydroxides of transition metals to investigate their characteristic colours.

Apparatus

0.1 M solutions of copper(II) sulfate, iron(II) ammonium sulfate, iron(III) chloride, zinc sulfate

0.1 M sodium hydroxide solution

0.5 M ammonia solution

droppers and glass rods

test-tubes

eye protection (splash-proof goggles)

SAFETY INFORMATION
Wear eye protection (splash-proof goggles).
Solutions of copper(II) sulfate, iron(II) ammonium sulfate, iron(III) chloride, zinc sulfate and ammonia are irritants
Sodium hydroxide solution is an irritant.

Method

1. Put on your eye protection.
2. To a 2 cm depth of the transition metal compound in solution add 5 drops of sodium hydroxide solution and record your observations in the table below.
3. Continue to add sodium hydroxide solution until you have added a 2 cm depth in total (an excess). Stir the mixture with a glass rod and then record your observations.
4. Repeat the above procedure using ammonia solution instead of sodium hydroxide. Record your results in the table.

Observing, measuring and recording

Transition metal compound solution	Observations on adding 5 drops of sodium hydroxide solution	Observations on adding excess sodium hydroxide solution	Observations on adding 5 drops of ammonia solution	Observations on adding excess ammonia solution
Copper(II) sulfate				
Iron(II) ammonium sulfate				
Iron(III) chloride				
Zinc sulfate				

Page 1 of 2

Handling experimental observations and data

5. Complete the table below to show the colours of the transition metal hydroxides.

Transition metal hydroxide	Colour
Copper(II) hydroxide	
Iron(II) hydroxide	
Iron(III) hydroxide	
Zinc hydroxide	

6. Write the word and symbol equation for the reaction between copper(II) sulfate and sodium hydroxide solution.

7. Zinc hydroxide is not a typical transition metal hydroxide. Give two reasons to explain this statement.

8. Which transition metal compound shows a different reaction with ammonia solution to that with sodium hydroxide solution?

Topic 8.4: Transition elements and noble gases

Learning episode C8.4c The noble gases

Learning objective

- Describe the Group VIII noble gases as unreactive, monatomic gases and explain this in terms of electronic configuration.

Resources

Student Book page 236

Approach

Students might be interested to know that there is more argon (0.9%) in the air than there is carbon dioxide (0.04%).

Students should be very familiar with the unreactive nature of the noble gases and should be able to explain this in terms of full outer electron shells (or 8 electrons in the outer electron shell).

Ask students to undertake some independent research on the uses of the noble gases and on any reactions that they do undergo. This will make the point that they are not totally unreactive and will react with other elements under certain circumstances, e.g. xenon will react with the highly reactive element fluorine.

Topic 8.4: Transition elements and noble gases

Learning episode C8.4d Consolidation and summary

Learning aims

- Review the learning points of the topic summarised in the end of topic checklist.
  - Test understanding of the topic content by answering the end of topic questions.

Resources

Student Book pages 237–239

Approach

Ask students to work with a partner to make a list of key words from this topic. They could then work together to produce a spider diagram showing how the different concepts are linked. They could compare their list with the list of key terms given in the Student Book. Discuss the checklist and ask questions to see how much of the content students are comfortable with.

Students could make flashcards of the key content and then use the flashcards to quiz each other on the information.

Ask students to work individually through the end of topic questions in the Student Book without looking at the text. As they work, walk around the classroom observing their answers and questioning them as necessary to find out which questions are causing difficulties.

After a set period, ask students to stop working. Discuss any areas of difficulty you observed as you walked round the class.

Students should complete any unanswered questions for homework, but you should stress that they should answer the questions without looking at the text, so that they can see how much they have remembered.

Topic 8.4: Transition elements and noble gases

End of topic questions mark scheme

The marks available for a question can indicate the level of detail you need to provide in your answer.

Question	Correct answer	Marks
1	B	1 mark
2 a)	Transition metals have higher densities.	1 mark
	Transition metals have higher melting points.	1 mark
2 b)	A catalyst is a substance that increases the rate of a chemical reaction.	1 mark
2 c)	The alkali metals only have 1 electron in the outer electron shell (one valency electron).	1 mark
	They only need to lose one electron when they react to form compounds.	1 mark
3 a)	Compound B – it is coloured/blue.	1 mark
3 b)	Copper.	1 mark
3 c)	$CuSO_4(aq) + 2NaOH(aq) \rightarrow Cu(OH)_2(s) + Na_2SO_4(aq)$ (1 for correct formula; 1 for balancing)	2 marks
Supplement 4 a)	The iron ions have variable oxidation numbers of 2 and 3.	2 marks
Supplement 4 b)	$Fe(OH)_2$ and $Fe(OH)_3$	2 marks
5	The noble gases have full outer electron shells (or have 8 electrons in the outer shell).	1 mark
	They therefore don't need to gain or lose electrons to achieve this state.	1 mark
6	They exist as single atoms.	1 mark
7	Xenon.	1 mark
	Total:	18 marks

Section 9: Metals

Contents
C9.1 Metals

Overview of the section
Metals are common everyday materials and students will be very familiar with the common metals. Awareness of the nature of alloys may also be present although this section will extend this by looking in more detail at the structure of alloys and how this affects their properties. Their properties then link to their uses. A major part of this section is a study of the reactivity series which brings together the chemical properties of a range of metals. The corrosion of iron and ways of reducing/preventing this corrosion are studied. The final part of the section focuses on the extraction of iron and aluminium from their ores with the supplementary study concentrating on the associated chemical and ionic equations.

Starting points
The Student Book section opener (pages 240–241) puts the ideas in the section into context and sets the scene. It also allows students to acknowledge and value their prior learning, and provides a benchmark against which future learning can be compared.

The questions provide a structure for introducing the section and can be used in a number of different ways:
- You could ask students to consider the questions as an introductory homework task.
- You could put students into groups to share their own ideas and understanding and then to report back to the whole class.
- Students could be given access to the Internet, preferably with a tight timescale, to find out the information required.

You could then use a spider chart or other form of wall chart to summarise everybody's ideas.

Recording these initial ideas allows you to retain them for reference as the individual topics are developed. In this way, your students' progress in learning can be readily acknowledged.

C9.1 Metals

Introduction

This topic is extensive and you will need to give it a relatively large amount of time.

Students will be aware of the differences in the reactivity of metals from their work in Topic 8.1 *The Periodic Table* and Topic 8.2 *Group I elements*. The reduction of metal oxides to form metals provides a link to Topic 6.3 *Redox reactions*. There are also links to Topic 7.1 *Acids, bases and salts* through the reactions of metals with acid to produce hydrogen.

This topic starts with a section on the physical properties of metals, which is extended to include the structure and uses of alloys. The next learning episode focuses on the reactivity series of metals, concentrating on the reaction of metals with water and hydrochloric acid.

The reduction of oxides with carbon leads to a consideration of the extraction of metals, using iron and zinc as examples. Reference is made to the extraction of aluminium in this topic, but a more detailed study of this process is included in Topic 4.1 *Electrochemistry*. Finally, you will consider the uses of metals such as aluminium and iron or steel. The uses of copper and zinc are restricted to the extended curriculum.

There are some opportunities for students to develop their practical skills.

Links to other topics

Section	Essential background knowledge	Useful links
2 Atoms, elements and compounds		2.4 Metallic bonding
4 Electrochemistry		4.1 Electrochemistry
6 Chemical reactions		6.3 Redox reactions
7 Acids, bases and salts		7.1 Acids, bases and salts
8 The Periodic Table	8.1 The Periodic Table 8.2 Group I elements	8.4 Transition metals and noble gases

Topic overview

C9.1a	**Orientation**
	This learning episode provides an opportunity to revise the reactions of the Group I metals with water, in comparison with the relative lack of reactivity of the transition metals. You might like to demonstrate the reaction of sodium and water and compare this with adding a piece of copper to water.
	Explain that the topic will not only concentrate on the reactivity series of metals but how this can be used to predict ways of extracting metals from their ores. Some consideration will also be given to alloys, particularly those of aluminium and iron (steel).
C9.1b	**Properties of metals**
	This learning episode focuses on the characteristic physical properties of metals. The nature and structure of alloys are explored and a simple model is provided to explain why alloys are stronger than the pure metal from which they are made. A straightforward practical activity using Worksheet C9.1b can be used to emphasise the characteristic properties of metals and how they differ from those of typical non-metals.

Topic 9.1: Metals

C9.1c	**Reactivity series**
	This learning episode starts with reference to reactions of metals with oxygen and then focuses on the reaction of metals with water (or steam) and hydrochloric acid. The reaction of magnesium with steam can be demonstrated; Worksheet C9.1c(1) can be used as a student practical to investigate the reaction of a range of metals with dilute hydrochloric acid.
	Displacement reactions involving heating a metal oxide with carbon feature in Worksheet C9.1c(2) can be used to help develop a greater understanding of the reduction of metal oxides using carbon. These reactions can be used to introduce or revise the concept of a redox reaction.
	Supplement Displacement reactions in solution involving a metal and a solution of a metal salt are then considered. Worksheet C9.1c(3) reinforces the concept of a displacement reaction and provides an opportunity to use chemical equations to summarise the outcomes of these reactions. The apparent unreactivity of aluminium is explained in terms of its impermeable oxide coating.
C9.1d	**Extraction of metals**
	This learning episode focuses on the manufacture of iron in a blast furnace, showing the different stages of the process together with the overall equation for the reduction of the iron(III) oxide. Understanding of the processes involved in the blast furnace can be checked using Worksheet C9.1d. The conversion of iron into the alloy steel provides a link to the next learning episode on the uses of metals. Reference is made to the extraction of aluminium from bauxite (considered in detail in Topic 4.1 *Electrochemistry*).
C9.1e	**Uses of metals**
	The uses of aluminium and steel provide the starting point for this learning episode. The focus then switches to the problems caused by the rusting of iron and steel and the relative merits of the methods used to prevent or limit such corrosion.
	Worksheet C9.1e provides students with a relatively straightforward plan and design activity relating to the corrosion of metals.
	The uses of the different steel alloys are considered. The use of copper in electrical wiring and cooking utensils is also covered.
	Supplement The use of zinc in galvanising is considered.
C9.1f	**Consolidation and summary**
	This learning episode provides an opportunity for a quick recap on the ideas encountered in the topic and time for the students to answer the end of topic questions in the Student Book.

Career links

These are some scientific careers that focus on this area of chemistry but careers in many other fields use the knowledge and skills gained studying science.

Some environmental chemists analyse soil and water samples for contamination from heavy metals. Powder metallurgy engineers create components and equipment from metal powders to reduce waste.

Topic 9.1: Metals

Learning episode C9.1a Orientation

Learning objective

- Explain how the position of an element in the Periodic Table can be used to predict its properties.

Common misconceptions

Some students think that alloys are pure metals.

Some students think that alloys are always a mixture of metals (e.g. discounting the use of carbon in steel)

Resources

Student Book page 243

Resources for a demonstration (see Technician's notes, following)

Approach

If appropriate, you may demonstrate the reaction of sodium with water to revise the highly reactive nature of the Group I metals **(see tech notes)**. Compare this reaction with the lack of reactivity of copper. Explain that metals have a range of reactivity: sodium is one of the most reactive metals and copper is one of the least reactive.

SAFETY INFORMATION
Wear eye protection (splash-proof goggles).
Use safety screens. The screens should be positioned close to the trough to avoid the risk of the sodium shooting out of the trough.
In a small trough of water, use a sample no bigger than 1 mm × 1 mm; in a large trough of water the metal sample must be no bigger than 2 mm × 2 mm.
Sodium reacts violently with water, releasing flammable hydrogen gas that may ignite spontaneously.

Ask students to name a metal that is more reactive than sodium and a metal that is less reactive than copper (metals like silver and gold are so unreactive they are found in their native state). Explain that chemists have found it useful to produce a reactivity series for the most common metals: the reactivity series indicates the method that is needed to extract the metal from its ore.

Ask students to find out the name of an ore of iron and how the iron is extracted from this ore. (The Student Book is a quick source for this information, or students could use the Internet.)

Ask students to find bronze and brass (two common 'metals') in the Periodic Table. Why are these substances not included in the Periodic Table? Are they metals? How is a metal different from an alloy? You could set a homework task of a focused piece of research on the nature of alloys, the names of some common alloys and their uses.

Technician's notes

Be sure to check the latest safety notes on these resources before proceeding.

The following resources are needed for the demonstration of the reaction of sodium with water:

sodium
large glass trough of water
2 safety screens
forceps

| filter paper and sharp knife (all dry) |
| eye protection (splash-proof goggles) (goggles or face shield) |

The safety screens should be positioned close to the trough to avoid the risk of sodium shooting out of the trough, as shown in the diagram.

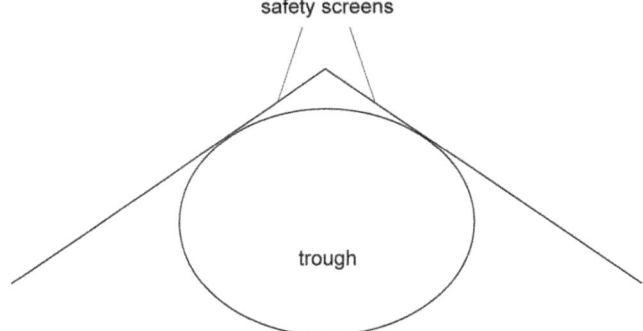

Topic 9.1: Metals

Learning episode C9.1b Properties of metals

Learning objectives

- Compare the general physical properties of metals and non-metals, including:
  (a) thermal conductivity
  (b) electrical conductivity
  (c) malleability and ductility
  (d) melting points and boiling points.
- Describe the general chemical properties of metals, limited to their reactions with:
  (a) dilute acids
  (b) cold water and steam
  (c) oxygen.
- Describe an alloy as a mixture of a metal with other elements, including:
  (a) brass as a mixture of copper and zinc
  (b) stainless steel as a mixture of iron and other elements, such as chromium, nickel and carbon.
- State that alloys can be harder or stronger than the pure metals and are more useful.
- Describe the uses of alloys in terms of their physical properties, including stainless steel in cutlery because of its hardness and resistance to rusting.
- Identify representations of alloys from diagrams of structure.
- Supplement Explain in terms of structure how alloys can be harder or stronger than the pure metals because the different sized atoms in alloys mean the layers can no longer slide over each other.

Common misconceptions

Some students think that all metals are magnetic. There are only three: iron, nickel and cobalt.

Resources

Student Book pages 242–246

Worksheet C9.1b Physical properties of metals and non-metals

Resources for a class practical (see Technician's notes, below)

Approach

Worksheet C9.1b gives students an opportunity to explore the physical properties of some elements and identify some of the properties of metals in comparison with those of non-metals.

The worksheet will require you to demonstrate a comparison of the conduction of heat by the different elements **(see tech notes)**.

The characteristic physical properties of metals are summarised on page 243 of the Student Book.

Pages 244–246 of the Student Book consider the uses of some common alloys and include some structural diagrams to explain why alloys are stronger than the metals from which they are formed. If students researched alloys as a homework task they could present their findings and then the information in the Student Book could be used as a summary.

SAFETY INFORMATION

Wear eye protection (splash-proof goggles).

Wash hands after handling lead.

Lead metal will rub off on skin. Lead metal can be wrapped in plastic wrap.

Topic 9.1: Metals

Technician's notes

Be sure to check the latest safety notes on these resources before proceeding.

The following resources are needed for the class practical C3e.2a, per group:

samples (3 cm × 1 cm strips, where possible) of aluminium, carbon, copper, iron, lead, sulfur, zinc; avoid sharp edges
electrical circuit – power supply (6 V)
6 V lamp in holder
leads
magnet
eye protection (splash-proof goggles)

The following resources are needed for the demonstration of heat conduction:

Bunsen burner, tripod, gauze (or access to hotplate), heatproof mat
longer strips of aluminium, carbon, copper, iron, zinc (all the same length)
candle wax or petroleum jelly

SAFETY INFORMATION
Ensure that the petroleum jelly is low hazard.

Answers

Page 246

1. A ductile metal can be drawn into wires.

2. A malleable metal can be hammered into shape.

3. An alloy is a mixture of a metal with one or more other elements.

4. Cupronickel is used for making coins.

5. **Supplement** The element added in the alloy disrupts the rows of aluminium atoms making them less likely to slide over each other when under strain.

Topic 9.1: Metals

Worksheet C9.1b Physical properties of metals and non-metals

Your task is to identify the characteristic physical properties of metals and non-metals.

Apparatus

samples of the following elements: aluminium, carbon, copper, iron, lead, sulfur and zinc

electrical circuit (as shown in the diagram)

magnet

SAFETY INFORMATION
Wash hands after handling lead.
Lead metal will rub off on skin. Lumps of lead can be wrapped in plastic wrap.

Method

1. You will be provided with small samples of the following elements: aluminium, carbon, copper, iron, lead, sulfur, zinc. By observation and testing record your results in the table below.

To test for conduction of heat

2. Your teacher will demonstrate a simple way of comparing the rate of conduction of heat. Equal lengths of the elements will have a drawing pin attached to one end by some candle wax or petroleum jelly. The other ends of the elements will be heated on a hotplate or in a Bunsen burner flame. As heat is conducted down the element the wax or petroleum jelly will soften and the drawing pin will fall off.

    Lead and sulfur cannot be tested in this way (the lead will melt and the sulfur will catch fire).

To test for conduction of electricity

3. Use the circuit shown in the diagram below and test each element in turn.

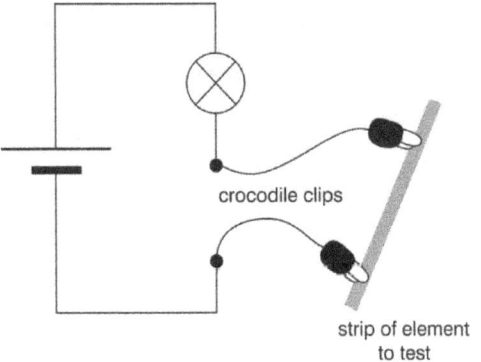

To test if material is magnetic or not

4. Use a magnet to see if the material is magnetic or not.

Topic 9.1: Metals

Observing, measuring and recording

Element	Metal or non-metal	Appearance	Dull or shiny	Flexible or brittle	Good / poor conductor of heat	Good / poor conductor of electricity	Magnetic / non-magnetic
Aluminium							
Carbon							
Copper							
Iron							
Lead							
Sulfur							
Zinc							

Handling experimental observations and data

5. Use your results to complete this summary chart.

Physical property	Metal	Non-metal
Appearance		
Conduction of heat		
Conduction of electricity		
Magnetism		

6. List any exceptions to the conclusions that you have drawn.

Topic 9.1: Metals

Learning episode C9.1c Reactivity series

Learning objectives

- State the order of the reactivity series as: potassium, sodium, calcium, magnesium, aluminium, carbon, zinc, iron, hydrogen, copper, silver, gold.
- Describe the reactions, if any, of:
  (a) potassium, sodium and calcium with cold water
  (b) magnesium with steam
  (c) magnesium, zinc, iron, copper, silver and gold with dilute hydrochloric acid.
      and explain these reactions in terms of the position of the metals in the reactivity series.
- Deduce an order of reactivity from a given set of experimental results.
- **Supplement** Describe the relative reactivities of metals in terms of their tendency to form positive ions, by displacement reactions, if any, with the aqueous ions of magnesium, zinc, iron, copper and silver.
- **Supplement** Explain the apparent unreactivity of aluminium in terms of its oxide layer.

Resources

Student Book pages 247–250

Worksheet C9.1c(1) The reactivity of metals

Worksheet C9.1c(2) Obtaining metals from metal oxides

Worksheet C9.1c(3) Metals and displacement reactions

Resources for demonstrations and class practicals (see Technician's notes, below)

Approach

This is a long learning episode with three main parts, and is likely to span a number of lessons.

Part 1

Refer to the reactions of metals with oxygen – the Student Book contrasts the reaction of calcium with oxygen, with the fact that there is no reaction of gold with oxygen (page 247). Students will have seen the reaction of sodium with water. Demonstrate the reaction of magnesium with steam. This reaction can most easily be demonstrated using a hard-glass test-tube with a plug of water-soaked mineral wool in the bottom, a coil of magnesium ribbon in the middle and with a bung and small jet positioned in the open end of the tube. Do not use magnesium powder **(see tech notes)**.

The tube is clamped horizontally and the magnesium is heated strongly with the flame occasionally being directed for a few seconds to the mineral wool. When the reaction starts, hydrogen can be ignited at the jet.

Remind students of the reactions of metals with dilute hydrochloric to produce hydrogen (this was covered in Topic 7.1 *Acids, bases and salts*). Use Worksheet C9.1c(1) to support a student practical activity. Refer to the equation for the reaction between zinc and hydrochloric acid on page 248 of the Student Book and then to the reactivity series on page 248. Point out that the metals at the bottom of the series are very unreactive and are found in nature in their native states.

Supplement Focus on the apparent, and surprising, unreactivity of aluminium in relation to its position in the reactivity series. See Student Book page 250.

SAFETY INFORMATION
Wear eye protection (goggles or face shield).
Magnesium is highly flammable. Dilute hydrochloric acid and dilute sulfuric acid are corrosive.

Topic 9.1: Metals

Part 2

This part focuses on displacement reactions involving the reduction of metal oxides by more reactive metals or by carbon. It provides an opportunity to revise the definitions of oxidation and reduction in terms of oxygen gain or loss.

Introduce Worksheet C9.1c(2). This is a practical activity to reinforce ideas about the reduction of metal oxides, this time using carbon. Explain that carbon is used in these reduction (redox) reactions on an industrial scale rather than using more reactive metals. Ask students why carbon is a suitable reducing agent to be used on an industrial scale as opposed to, for example, magnesium.

> **SAFETY INFORMATION**
>
> Wear eye protection (splash-proof goggles).
>
> Copper(II) oxide is harmful. Zinc oxide is dangerous to the environment.
>
> Good ventilation is important when heating metals and oxides, particularly when lead is used if anyone may be pregnant.

Supplement Part 3

Use Worksheet C9.1c(3) to support student practical work on displacement reactions involving a metal and a solution containing the ions of another metal. As part of the activity, ask students to use the reactivity series to make predictions about displacement reactions.

The Developing Practical Skills feature on page 250 also focuses on displacement reactions in solution. You could leave this until the consolidation and summary learning episode, where you could use it as a revision exercise.

> **SAFETY INFORMATION**
>
> Wear eye protection (splash-proof goggles).
>
> Magnesium is highly flammable. Copper(II) sulfate and iron(II) sulfate are harmful.

Technician's notes

Be sure to check the latest safety notes on these resources before proceeding.

The following resources are needed for the demonstration (Part 1):

magnesium ribbon
Bunsen burner and heatproof mat
mineral wool, test-tube, bung and jet
eye protection (splash-proof goggles)

The following resources are needed for the class practical, C9.1c(1), per group:

test-tubes, test-tube rack, wooden splint and droppers
1 cm strip of magnesium ribbon (pre-cut)
1 cm strip of each of the following metals: aluminium, copper and lead foil
1 spatula of granulated zinc
1 spatula of iron powder
about 50 cm^3 0.5 mol/dm^3 hydrochloric acid
about 50 cm^3 0.5 mol/dm^3 sulfuric acid
eye protection (splash-proof goggles)

Topic 9.1: Metals

The following resources are needed for the class practical, C9.1c(2), per group:

about 1 g copper(II) oxide
about 1 g each of magnesium oxide, zinc oxide, iron(III) oxide
about 100 cm³ limewater, about 1 g carbon powder. Label botte of limewater as a moderate hazard.
eye protection (splash-proof goggles)
7 test-tubes, delivery tube, spatula, test-tube holder, clamp and stand
Bunsen burner and heatproof mat

The following resources are needed for the class practical, C9.1c(3), per group:

1 cm length of magnesium ribbon
1 cm lengths or squares of copper, iron and zinc
about 5 cm³ 0.1 mol / dm³ copper(II) sulfate
about 5 cm³ 0.1 mol / dm³ iron(II) ammonium sulfate labelled iron(II) sulfate
about 5 cm³ 0.1 mol / dm³ magnesium sulfate and 0.1 mol / dm³ zinc sulfate
test-tubes and test-tube racks
eye protection (splash-proof goggles)

Answers

Page 249

1. No. Copper is below hydrogen in the reactivity series.
2. Risk assessments included quantities of metals and hydrochloric acid (concentration specified) and apparatus.

    a) Appropriate sequence of steps in the method.

    b) Appropriate table of results including the units of the measurements to be taken.

    (If possible, the students could then carry out their plan as a class practical)
3. $2K(s) + 2H_2O(l) \rightarrow 2KOH(aq) + H_2(g)$
4. No. Carbon is below magnesium in the reactivity series.
5. **Supplement** $Mg(s) + Pb^{2+}(s) \rightarrow Mg^{2+}(s) + Pb(s)$

Developing Practical Skills, page 250

1. A metal cannot displace itself from a solution of its salt.
2. She already knows that metal D cannot displace the other three metals and so must be the least reactive metal.
3. B, C, A, D
4. 10 – Yes, 11 – Yes, 12 – Yes.
5. $B(s) + C(NO_3)_2(aq) \rightarrow B(NO_3)_2(aq) + C(s)$
6. Copper.

Topic 9.1: Metals

Worksheet C9.1c(1) The reactivity of metals

Hydrogen can be prepared by the reaction between a metal and dilute hydrochloric acid or dilute sulfuric acid. In this activity you will be able to compare the reactivity of some different metals with these two dilute acids.

The quantities of hydrogen produced will be relatively small and so will not pose a significant hazard.

Apparatus

small samples of aluminium, copper, iron, lead, magnesium and zinc

dilute hydrochloric acid, dilute sulfuric acid

test-tubes and test-tube rack, wooden splint

eye protection (splash-proof goggles)

SAFETY INFORMATION

Wear eye protection (splash-proof goggles).

Lead and its compounds are toxic. The copper(II) compounds are harmful.

Report any spills to your teacher and wash your hands after handling lead.

Method

1. Put on your eye protection.
2. Put a sample of each metal in a separate test-tube and add about a 2 cm depth of dilute hydrochloric acid. Record your observations in the table.
3. Repeat the procedure using the metals and dilute sulfuric acid.
4. Where the reaction is sufficiently vigorous, collect some gas by putting a bung in the end of the test-tube for 30 seconds and then remove it and apply a lighted splint to the mouth of the test-tube.

Observing, measuring and recording

Metal	Observations	
	Dilute hydrochloric acid	**Dilute sulfuric acid**
Aluminium		
Copper		
Iron		
Lead		
Magnesium		
Zinc		

Page 1 of 2

Topic 9.1: Metals

Handling experimental observations and data

5. Use your observations to put the metals in an order of reactivity:

    Most reactive   _____

    _____

    _____

    _____

    _____

    Least reactive   _____

6. Complete the table below:

Test for hydrogen gas	
What you use for the test	The results that confirm the presence of hydrogen

7. Write equations for the following reactions:
    a) zinc with dilute hydrochloric acid
    b) magnesium with dilute sulfuric acid

Evaluating methods

8. The method you have used may not produce the correct order of reactivity for the metals you tested. Suggest how your method could be improved to give greater accuracy.

Topic 9.1: Metals

Worksheet C9.1c(2) Obtaining metals from metal oxides

Many metals can be extracted from their ores by heating the ore with carbon. The reaction can be summarised by the word equation:

metal oxide + carbon → metal + carbon dioxide

In this reaction the metal oxide is reduced. This only happens if the metal is less reactive than carbon.

Apparatus

7 test-tubes, delivery tube, spatula, test-tube holder, Bunsen burner, clamp stand and heatproof mat

carbon powder, copper(II) oxide, magnesium oxide, iron(III) oxide, zinc oxide, a solution of limewater

eye protection (splash-proof goggles)

SAFETY INFORMATION
Wear eye protection (splash-proof goggles).
Copper(II) oxide is harmful and zinc oxide is harmful to the environment.
Report any spills to your teacher.
Ensure that the laboratory is well ventilated.

Method

1. Put on your eye protection.
2. Mix 1 g (spatula) measures of carbon powder with 1 g (spatula) of copper(II) oxide in a dry test-tube and set up the apparatus as shown.
3. Heat the test-tube strongly for about 2 minutes.

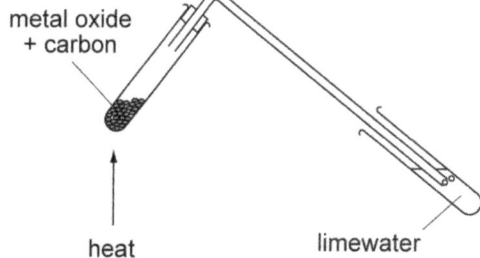

When you stop heating, make sure the delivery tube is removed immediately from the lime water.

4. When the test-tube has cooled down, carefully examine the solid mixture and the lime water and record your results in the table.
5. Repeat the procedure for all the other metal oxides.

NOTE: Room must be well ventilated.

Using and organising techniques, apparatus and materials

6. Why is the delivery tube removed from the limewater as soon as the heating is stopped?
7. Why is the limewater used?

Page 1 of 2

Topic 9.1: Metals

Observing, measuring and recording

Name of metal oxide	Changes in solid mixture	Changes in the lime water
Copper(II) oxide		
Magnesium oxide		
Iron(III) oxide		
Zinc oxide		

Handling experimental observations and data

8. Which of the metal oxides appear to have been reduced by the carbon? Explain why you have selected each of these metal oxides.
9. Write fully balanced equations, including state symbols, for each of the reactions that leads to the reduction of the metal oxide.
10. Why didn't reactions occur with all four metal oxides?

Supplement Worksheet C9.1c(3) Metals and displacement reactions

A more reactive metal will displace a less reactive metal from a solution containing ions of the less reactive metal. These reactions have been used to confirm the order of metals in the reactivity series.

In this activity you should be able to use your knowledge of the reactivity series to make predictions about the likelihood of a displacement reaction taking place.

Apparatus

small samples of the following metals: copper, iron, magnesium and zinc

solutions of copper(II) sulfate, iron(II) sulfate, magnesium sulfate, zinc sulfate

test-tubes and test-tube rack

eye protection (splash-proof goggles)

SAFETY INFORMATION
Wear eye protection (splash-proof goggles).
Magnesium is flammable.
Copper(II) sulfate and iron(II) sulfate are harmful.

Method

1. Put on your eye protection.
2. Put a tick in the upper box for each combination of metal/solution where you expect a displacement reaction to take place. Alternatively, put a cross in the upper box for each combination where you don't expect a displacement reaction to take place.
3. Put about a 2 cm depth of each solution in four separate test-tubes.
4. Add a different sample of metal to each tube.
5. Wait for about 5 minutes and then look for any changes to the metal or to the solution. Changes might include a coating on the metal or bubbles forming around the metal. You may need to tip the metal out of the solution and examine it closely to see any change.
6. Record your observations in the table below using the lower box for each combination.

Topic 9.1: Metals

Observing, measuring and recording

Metal	Copper(II) sulfate solution $CuSO_4(aq)$	Magnesium sulfate solution $MgSO_4(aq)$	Iron(II) sulfate solution $FeSO_4(aq)$	Zinc sulfate solution $ZnSO_4(aq)$
Copper Cu				
Magnesium Mg				
Iron Fe				
Zinc Zn				

Handling experimental observations and data

7. Why have some of the boxes in the table been shaded?
8. Which combinations did not match the prediction you made? Can you suggest a reason for this?
9. Write equations for all the displacement reactions that took place.

Topic 9.1: Metals

Learning episode C9.1d Extraction of metals

Learning objectives

- Describe the ease of obtaining metals from their ores, related to the position of the metal in the reactivity series.
- Describe the extraction of iron from hematite in the blast furnace, limited to:
  (a) the burning of carbon (coke) to provide heat and produce carbon dioxide
  (b) the reduction of carbon dioxide to carbon monoxide
  (c) the reduction of iron(III) oxide by carbon monoxide
  (d) the thermal decomposition of calcium carbonate / limestone to produce calcium oxide
  (e) the formation of slag.
  Symbol equations are **not** required.
- State that the main ore of aluminium is bauxite and that aluminium is extracted by electrolysis.
- Supplement State the symbol equations for the extraction of iron from hematite:
  (a) $C + O_2 \rightarrow CO_2$
  (b) $C + CO_2 \rightarrow 2CO$
  (c) $Fe_2O_3 + 3CO \rightarrow 2Fe + 3CO_2$
  (d) $CaCO_3 \rightarrow CaO + CO_2$
  (e) $CaO + SiO_2 \rightarrow CaSiO_3$.
- Supplement Describe the extraction of aluminium from purified bauxite / aluminium oxide, including:
  (a) the role of cryolite
  (b) why the carbon anode needs to be regularly replaced
  (c) the reactions at the electrodes, including ionic half-equations.
  Details of the purification of bauxite are **not** required.

Resources

Student Book pages 252–258

Worksheet C9.1d Extracting iron

Approach

Remind students that most metals exist as ores, and when a pure metal is needed, the metal must be extracted from its ore. Refer to the Student Book (page 252), which relates the reactivity of a metal to its method of extraction. Students should be familiar with the use of carbon as a reducing agent from learning episode C9.1c. They will consider the use of electricity and electrolysis when they study Topic 4.1 *Electrochemistry*.

Introduce the industrial process used to extract iron from its ore, hematite (iron(III) oxide). Ask why electrolysis is not used to extract iron. (It is too expensive; reduction with carbon (coke) is much cheaper.)

Consider the diagram of the blast furnace (page 254) and look at the stages given in the Student Book. Emphasise that the overall process is reduction.

Supplement For students following the supplementary syllabus spend some time on the chemical equations for the main reactions.

Reinforce these ideas using Worksheet C9.1d.

Explain that the iron produced in the blast furnace has limited use – it contains too high a proportion of carbon, which means it is brittle and cannot be easily shaped. Instead, most iron is converted into steel, which is an alloy.

Revise the term 'alloy', a mixture of a metal with another element. By reducing the proportion of carbon in iron obtained from a blast furnace, a much more versatile and useful substance can be made.

Topic 9.1: Metals

Use the Student Book to look at the different compositions of the various steel alloys and their uses. Refer also to the Science in Context section on page 252 of the Student Book. The content of these Science in Context features is beyond the syllabus but provides the opportunity to explore the content more deeply.

Supplement Emphasise also that the main aluminium ore is bauxite (aluminium oxide) and the extraction of aluminium from bauxite is undertaken by electrolysis. A diagram of the electrolytic cell is included in the Student Book on page 257. Explain the role of cryolite and the reactions taking place at the electrodes. The equations and ionic half-equations provide a good opportunity to revise these ideas.

Answers

Page 255

1. Iron ore (hematite), coke and limestone.
2. Iron(III) oxide.
3. Carbon dioxide, carbon monoxide, nitrogen (from the air).
4. Supplement $2Fe_2O_3(s) + 3C(s) \rightarrow 4Fe(s) + 3CO_2(g)$
5. a) An alloy is a mixture of a metal and another element.
   b) The pig iron is brittle. Steel is more flexible and more resistant to corrosion.
6. a) Oxygen + water.
   b) Chromium protects iron from oxygen and water/used as it is shiny – good decorative effect.
   c) Aluminium forms a thin layer of aluminium oxide, which acts as a protective layer – does not react with the air.
7. a) Supplement $2Al(s) + Fe_2O_3(s) \rightarrow 2Fe(s) + Al_2O_3(s)$
   b) Supplement Aluminium is higher in the reactivity series than iron, therefore it is more reactive. Aluminium is able to displace the less reactive iron from its oxide and so forms iron and aluminium oxide.
   c) Supplement Any metal which is higher than iron in the reactivity series can be selected. The higher the metal in the series, the more reactive the metal and the more reactive the reaction will be. If the chosen metal is above aluminium, for example, magnesium, the reaction is more reactive. If the metal is below aluminium, for example, zinc, the reaction will be less reactive. In practice this is not feasible.
   d) Supplement Aluminium is displacing iron in iron(III) oxide and becoming aluminium oxide by losing electrons. Iron(III) oxide is gaining electrons to become iron metal.

   Redox is when oxidation and reduction occur. Aluminium is losing electrons (oxidation). Iron(III) oxide is gaining electrons (reduction).

Science in Context, page 256

Metals should be recycled. The maxim Reduce, Recycle, Reuse is important:
- The supplies of metal ores will eventually be exhausted.
- In the longer term, advances in recycling should reduce costs.
- There is a limit to the amount of waste that can be put into landfill sites – potential damages to water supplies, etc.

Topic 9.1: Metals

Science in Context, page 258

a) TiO_2

b) Carbon can only be used to extract titanium from titanium oxide if carbon is more reactive than titanium. In fact, titanium is more reactive than carbon but less reactive than magnesium so in some processes magnesium is used.

Worksheet C9.1d

1. hematite – iron oxide; coke – carbon; limestone – calcium carbonate; hot air – oxygen and nitrogen
2. a) i) hot air   ii) molten iron   iii) slag   iv) iron ore, coke and limestone.
   b) Iron ore (iron oxide) + carbon → iron + carbon monoxide (carbon dioxide)
3. a), b)

Carbon monoxide reduces iron oxide.	iron oxide + carbon monoxide → iron + carbon dioxide	$Fe_2O_3(s) + 3CO(g) \rightarrow 2Fe(s) + 3CO_2(g)$
Limestone decomposes to form calcium oxide (which reacts with impurities to form molten slag).	calcium carbonate → calcium oxide + carbon dioxide	$CaCO_3(s) \rightarrow CaO(s) + CO_2(g)$
Blast of hot air oxidises coke.	carbon + oxygen → carbon monoxide	$2C(s) + O_2(g) \rightarrow 2CO(g)$

c) An oxidation reaction involves the addition of oxygen, e.g. carbon → carbon dioxide.

A reduction reaction involves the removal of oxygen, e.g. iron oxide → iron.

Topic 9.1: Metals

Worksheet C9.1d Extracting iron

1. Iron is made from iron ore in a blast furnace. There are four raw materials. Draw lines to match them to the main chemical substances in them.

raw material
hematite (iron ore)
coke
limestone
hot air

main chemical substances
carbon
oxygen and nitrogen
iron oxide
calcium carbonate

2. a) Use the words below to label the parts (i) to (iv) of a blast furnace.

   iron ore   molten iron   slag

   hot air   coke   limestone

   b) Write a word equation to summarise the overall change that happens in a blast furnace.

3. a) Match each of the reactions A, B, and C to its word equation and balanced symbol equation.

   b) Supplement Match each of the reactions A, B, and C to its balanced symbol equation.

   Reaction

   A Carbon monoxide reduces iron oxide.

   B Limestone decomposes to form calcium oxide (which reacts with impurities to form molten slag).

   C blast of hot air oxidises coke.

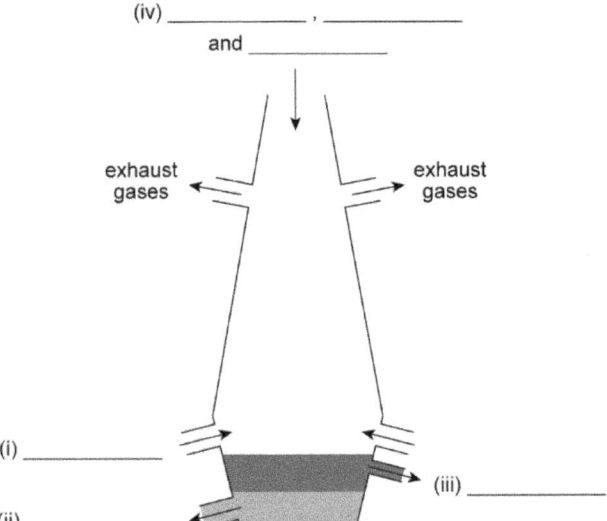

Word equation	Balanced symbol equation
1. carbon + oxygen → carbon monoxide	i) $CaCO_3(s) \rightarrow CaO(s) + CO_2(g)$
2. iron oxide + carbon monoxide → iron + carbon dioxide	ii) $2C(s) + O_2(g) \rightarrow 2CO(g)$
3. calcium carbonate → calcium oxide + carbon dioxide	iii) $Fe_2O_3(s) + 3CO(g) \rightarrow 2Fe(s) + 3CO_2(g)$

c) Explain the difference between an oxidation reaction and a reduction reaction, using reactions in a blast furnace as examples.

Topic 9.1: Metals

Learning episode C9.1e Uses of metals

Learning objectives

- Describe the uses of metals in terms of their physical properties, including:
  (a) aluminium in the manufacture of aircraft because of its low density
  (b) aluminium in the manufacture of overhead electrical cables because of its low density and good electrical conductivity
  (c) aluminium in food containers because of its resistance to corrosion
  (d) copper in electrical wiring because of its good electrical conductivity and ductility.
- State the conditions required for the rusting of iron and steel to form hydrated iron(III) oxide.
- State some common barrier methods, including painting, greasing and coating with plastic.
- Describe how barrier methods prevent rusting by excluding oxygen or water.
- Supplement Describe the use of zinc in galvanising as an example of a barrier method and sacrificial protection.
- Supplement Explain sacrificial protection in terms of the reactivity series and in terms of electron loss.

Common misconceptions

Some students think that steel does not corrode (they may be confusing steel with stainless steel).

Resources

Student Book pages 244–252

Worksheet C9.1e Preventing corrosion

Resources for a class practical (see Technician's notes, following)

Approach

Start by considering the uses of aluminium and steel, referring to the section on pages 244–245 of the Student Book. Then concentrate on corrosion or rusting of iron and steel (page 251).

Ask students to say under what conditions iron will rust. Ask why iron might rust more rapidly in seawater. Use the information on page 251 of the Student Book to look at the different ways of protecting the corrosion or rusting of iron.

Ask students to work in small groups and to plan an investigation to compare the effectiveness of different ways of limiting the rusting of iron.

Worksheet C9.1e provides a structure for students to plan and then put their plan into practice. The task is very straightforward. You will need to judge whether students need additional prompting about the things that they should consider as they plan.

Students will need to consider the best ways of attaching the magnesium and zinc to the iron nails. It is likely that they will need to record observations after about 48 hours.

Finally, refer to the uses of copper, reflecting its properties as a very good conductor of heat (use in cooking utensils) and a very good conductor of electricity (use in electrical wiring).

Supplement Consider the variety of steel alloys and how their properties are dependent on the amount of carbon and other elements mixed with the iron. Finally use the results of the practical activity as a way of introducing the use of zinc in galvanising and sacrificial protection – a much better solution to the problems of rusting than some of those considered earlier.

SAFETY INFORMATION
Wear eye protection (splash-proof goggles)
Magnesium ribbon is flammable.

Topic 9.1: Metals

Technician's notes

Be sure to check the latest safety notes on these resources before proceeding.

The following resources are needed for the class practical C9.1e, per group:

shiny iron/mild steel nails
sodium chloride and spatula
grease
oil
2 cm length of magnesium ribbon
2 cm square of zinc foil – avoid sharp edges
test-tubes and test-tube rack
eye protection (splash-proof goggles)

Answers

Science in Context, page 252

$4Fe(s) + 3O_2(g) \rightarrow 2Fe_2O_3(s)$

Page 252

1. Air (oxygen) and water must be present.

2. The grease can be easily removed or wiped away.

3. a) Supplement Galvanising involves coating iron or steel with zinc.

    b) Supplement As zinc is more reactive than iron, moist air will react with zinc in preference to the iron.

Topic 9.1: Metals

Worksheet C9.1e Preventing corrosion

Iron and steel corrode or rust quite quickly when exposed to moist air. The rusting is an oxidation process and the iron is converted into iron(III) oxide. The iron(III) oxide is porous and so rusting will continue even after the surface is covered in rust.

Apparatus

shiny iron or steel nails

common salt, grease, oil, magnesium ribbon, zinc foil

test-tubes and test-tube rack

eye protection (splash-proof goggles)

> **SAFETY INFORMATION**
> *Wear eye protection (splash-proof goggles).*
> *Magnesium ribbon is highly flammable.*

Planning experiments and investigations

1. Plan an investigation to find out which is the best method for preventing the corrosion or rusting of iron nails when in contact with air and salt water.

    The methods of prevention you are going to test are:

    A Smearing the iron with grease

    B Coating the iron with oil

    C Putting the iron in contact with magnesium

    D Putting the iron in contact with zinc

2. Decide on your method and how you will record your results.

3. Carry out your method, analyse your results and then evaluate your approach.

Method

4. Write your method.

Observing, measuring and recording

5. Draw a table to record your results.

Handling experimental observations and data

6. What conclusions can you draw from your observations?

Evaluating methods

7. How would you rate the success of your plan and method? What problems did you encounter? How could the design have been improved?

Topic 9.1: Metals

Learning episode 9.1f Consolidation and summary

Learning aims

- Review the learning points of the topic summarised in the end of topic checklist.
- Test understanding of the topic content by answering the end of topic questions.

Resources

Student Book pages 250, 267, 259–263

Approach

Ask students to work with a partner to make a list of key words from this topic. They could then work together to produce a spider diagram showing how the different concepts are linked. They could compare their list with the list of key terms given in the Student Book. Discuss the checklist and ask questions to see how much of the content students are comfortable with.

Students could make flashcards of the key content and then use the flashcards to quiz each other on the information.

The Science in Context feature on the extraction of metals on page 257 of the Student Book could be referred to if this were not used in learning episode C9.1d. The content of these Science in Context features is beyond the syllabus but provides the opportunity to explore the content more deeply.

Supplement The Developing Practical Skills feature (page 250 of the Student Book) can be used to revise the work on displacement reactions if this was not used in learning episode C9.1c.

Ask students to work individually through the end of topic questions in the Student Book without looking at the text. As they work, walk around the classroom observing their answers and questioning them as necessary to find out which questions are causing difficulties.

After a set period, ask students to stop working. Discuss any areas of difficulty you observed as you walked round the class.

Students should complete any unanswered questions for homework, but you should stress that they should answer the questions without looking at the text, so that they can see how much they have remembered.

Topic 9.1: Metals

End of topic questions mark scheme

The marks available for a question can indicate the level of detail you need to provide in your answer.

Question	Correct answer	Marks
1	B	1 mark
2	Sodium, calcium, magnesium, zinc, copper. (minus 1 for each misplaced metal)	2 marks
3 a)	Y, Q, Z, X. (minus 1 mark for each misplaced metal)	2 marks
3 b)	i) Y	1 mark
	ii) Q oxide.	1 mark
	iii) Q oxide.	1 mark
	iv) Y	1 mark
4	Gold and silver are found in their pure state. They are not combined with other elements (as compounds).	1 mark
5 a)	$2Fe_2O_3(s) + 3C(s) \rightarrow 4Fe(s) + 3CO_2(g)$ (1 mark for formulae; 1 mark for balancing)	2 marks
5 b)	The iron(III) oxide is reduced – it has lost oxygen.	1 mark
5 c)	The limestone forms calcium oxide.	1 mark
	The calcium oxide combines with impurities such as sand (silicon dioxide) to form a slag (calcium silicate).	1 mark
6 a)	It is strong.	1 mark
	It has a low density.	1 mark
6 b)	It resists corrosion.	1 mark
7	Ceramic discs are not metals or carbon.	1 mark
	They do not conduct electricity (they are an insulator).	1 mark
Supplement 8 a)	Displacement reaction (redox reaction).	1 mark
Supplement 8 b)	Zinc is more reactive than copper.	1 mark
Supplement 9 a)	$Mg(s) + PbO(s) \rightarrow MgO(s) + Pb(s)$ (1 mark for correct formulae; 1 mark for balancing)	2 marks
Supplement 9 b)	Magnesium.	1 mark
Supplement 9 c)	A redox reaction is one involving reduction and oxidation.	1 mark
Supplement 10 a)	$2ZnO(s) + C(s) \rightarrow 2Zn(s) + CO_2(g)$ (1 mark for formulae; 1 mark for balancing) (Also allow: $ZnO(s) + C(s) \rightarrow Zn(s) + CO(g)$.)	2 marks
Supplement	The electrolysis requires the zinc oxide to be in a molten state.	1 mark

Topic 9.1: Metals

Question	Correct answer	Marks
10 b)	This requires considerable amounts of energy (so the process is very expensive).	1 mark
Supplement 11 a)	In solid aluminium oxide the ions cannot move to the electrodes.	1 mark
	When molten or in solution the ions can move to the electrodes.	1 mark
Supplement 11 b)	$2O^{2-} \rightarrow O_2 + 4e^-$	2 marks
Supplement 11 c)	Oxygen is produced in the electrolysis.	1 mark
	The oxygen will react with the carbon to form carbon dioxide.	1 mark
Supplement 11 d)	$Al^{3+} + 3e^- \rightarrow Al$	2 marks
Supplement 11 e)	The electrolysis process requires large quantities of electricity.	1 mark
	Hydroelectric power generates electricity in a carbon friendly way.	1 mark
Supplement 12 a)	Galvanising.	1 mark
Supplement 12 b)	The zinc is more reactive than the iron.	1 mark
	The zinc reacts with oxygen in the air before the iron does.	1 mark
Supplement 12 c)	Painting, applying grease, plastic coating (1 mark for each).	3 marks
	Total:	46 marks

Section 10: Chemistry of the environment

Contents
C10.1 Chemistry of the environment

Overview of the section
This section is focuses on the global and local issues that are regularly in the news. The students following this syllabus are going to be a generation which will be aware of the issues possibly more than previous generations. The importance of limiting, or removing, the sources of pollution for the water supplies and the air is the central issue of this section. The sources of pollution are now generally very well-known, as are the potential strategies to reduce or eliminate the impact they are having. Action is being taken and time will tell whether the pace of change is rapid enough. This section provides a detailed context and a rationale for acting.

Starting points
The Student Book section opener (pages 264–265) puts the ideas in the section into context and sets the scene. It also allows students to acknowledge and value their prior learning, and provides a benchmark against which future learning can be compared.

The questions provide a structure for introducing the section and can be used in a number of different ways:
- You could ask students to consider the questions as an introductory homework task.
- You could put students into groups to share their own ideas and understanding and then to report back to the whole class.
- Students could be given access to the Internet, preferably with a tight timescale, to find out the information required.

You could then use a spider chart or other form of wall chart to summarise everybody's ideas.

Recording these initial ideas allows you to retain them for reference as the individual topics are developed. In this way, your students' progress in learning can be readily acknowledged..

C10.1 Chemistry of the environment

Introduction

This topic focuses essentially on the environmental factors governing the quality of our water and air.

Students will have encountered hydrated salts in Topic 7 *Acids, bases and salts* and so will be aware of the reactions of anhydrous copper(II) sulfate and anhydrous cobalt(II) chloride with water. These reactions are also referred to in Topic 6b *Reversible reactions and equilibrium*.

The study of carbon dioxide and pollutants such as sulfur dioxide links to the combustion of fuels in Topic 11a *Fuels* and Topic 11b *Alkanes*.

The topic starts with a section on chemical tests for water, the water cycle and water purification methods. This extends to consider water from natural sources and variety of substances that it contains, some beneficial and some harmful. The focus then switches to the air and the issues relating to climate changes, including the greenhouse effect. The carbon cycle and parts of the nitrogen cycle are considered as they provide overall context for issues being addressed.

For students following the supplementary syllabus there is a more detailed focus on global warming and an explanation how catalytic converters address some of the issues caused by the exhaust gases produced by car engines.

There are some opportunities for students to develop their practical/investigative skills.

Links to other topics

Section	Essential background knowledge	Useful links
2 Atoms, elements and compounds	2.1 Atoms, elements and compounds	
6 Chemical reactions		6.1 Rate of reaction 6.2 Reversible reactions and equilibrium
7 Acids, bases and salts	7.1 Acids, bases and salts	
11 Organic chemistry		11.2 Fuels 11.3 Alkanes
12 Experimental techniques		12.2 Identification of ions and gases

Topic overview

C10.1a	Orientation
	As this topic will come near the beginning of the course, this learning episode focuses on the students' knowledge and prior learning about air and water. It is likely that many students will already have a good knowledge of the composition of the air and the water cycle, from previous study in geography if not in science.
C10.1b	**Water**
	The learning episode has three parts. In part 1 the focus is the use of anhydrous copper(II) sulfate and anhydrous cobalt(II) chloride to detect the presence of water. In part 2 the focus is on the water cycle and water purification. In part 3 the focus is on NPK fertilisers.

Topic 10.1: Chemistry of the environment

C10.1c	**The composition of the air**
	This learning episode looks at the composition of pure air and in outline the processes in the carbon and nitrogen cycles that maintain that composition. The nature and impact of pollutants on the composition of the air is covered in the next section.
	Supplement This part involves a more detailed consideration of photosynthesis.
C10.1d	**Air quality and climate**
	This learning episode considers the sources and impact of common pollutants such as carbon monoxide, sulfur dioxide, oxides of nitrogen and lead compounds. There is a particular focus on acid rain and the greenhouse effect (distinguishing the greenhouse effect from the enhanced greenhouse effect).
	Supplement This part of the learning episode considers in more detail the production of the oxides of nitrogen when burning fuel in cars and the use of catalytic convertors.
C10.1e	**Consolidation and summary**
	This learning episode provides an opportunity for a quick recap on the ideas encountered in the topic and time for the students to answer the end of topic questions in the Student Book.

Career links

These are some scientific careers that focus on this area of chemistry but careers in many other fields use the knowledge and skills gained studying science.

Some atmospheric chemists study the changes in atmospheric pollutants which can be harmful to life. Analytical technicians may look for micro-plastic pollution in samples taken from different ecosystems. Environmental consultants advise companies on how to reduce the impact of their products on the environment.

Topic 10.1: Chemistry of the environment

Learning episode C10.1a Orientation

Learning aims

- To review knowledge on the composition of the air.
- To revise understanding of hydrated salts.
- To highlight the content areas in the topic.
- Know that oxygen is a key component of the air and that it reacts with elements and compounds to form oxides.
- Know that a hydrated substance is a substance that is chemically combined with water.
- Supplement Know that water of crystallisation is the water molecules present in hydrated crystals.

Common misconceptions

Some students think that oxygen is the major component of the air.

Some students think that the percentage of carbon dioxide in the air is much greater than 0.04%.

Some students think there are significant amounts of hydrogen in the air.

There may be confusion between the greenhouse effect and the enhanced greenhouse effect. The greenhouse effect is the trapping of heat under the atmosphere, which is a natural effect caused by greenhouse gases. However, when greenhouse gas concentrations are too high, they trap too much heat and increase the temperature of the Earth, causing the enhanced greenhouse effect.

Approach

The main purpose of this introductory learning episode is to map out the main areas of study in the topic. Although it may come near the beginning of the course, certain aspects will build on previous learning in science, and it is important to acknowledge this learning.

Ask questions to elicit students' prior knowledge, and prompt links to other topics where appropriate. Key points might include:

1. Water

- A simple test for water (link to hydrated salts?)
- The water cycle (link to experimental techniques: evaporation and condensation?)
- Water purification (link to chlorination?)
- The substances that affect water purity (link to the impact of plastics on aquatic life?)

2. The air

- The composition of the air (the gases and their proportions? Oxygen the 'active' ingredient?)
- How the composition remains approximately constant (respiration, photosynthesis?)
- Substances that act as pollutants (sources of pollution – cars, power stations, factories?)
- Carbon dioxide as a greenhouse gas (greenhouse effect?)

Topic 10.1: Chemistry of the environment

Learning episode C10.1b Water

Learning outcomes

- Describe chemical tests for the presence of water using anhydrous cobalt(II) chloride and anhydrous copper(II) sulfate.
- Describe how to test for the purity of water using melting point and boiling point.
- Explain that distilled water is used in practical chemistry rather than tap water because it contains fewer chemical impurities.
- State that water from natural sources contains a variety of substances, including:
  (a) dissolved oxygen
  (b) metal compounds
  (c) plastics
  (d) sewage
  (e) harmful microbes
  (f) nitrates from fertilisers
  (g) phosphates from fertilisers and detergents.
- State that some of these substances are beneficial, including:
  (a) dissolved oxygen for aquatic life
  (b) some metal compounds provide essential minerals for life.
- State that some of these substances are potentially harmful including:
  (a) some metal compounds are toxic
  (b) some plastics harm aquatic life
  (c) sewage contains harmful microbes which cause disease
  (d) nitrates and phosphates lead to deoxygenation of water and damage to aquatic life.
  Details of the eutrophication process are **not** required.
- Describe the treatment of the domestic water supply in terms of:
  (a) sedimentation and filtration to remove solids
  (b) use of carbon to remove tastes and odours
  (c) chlorination to kill microbes.
- State that ammonium salts and nitrates are used as fertilisers.
- Describe the use of NPK fertilisers to provide the elements nitrogen, phosphorus and potassium for improved plant growth.

Resources

Student Book pages 267–270

Resources for a demonstration (see Technician's notes, below)

Worksheet C10.1b

Topic 10.1: Chemistry of the environment

Approach

The learning episode has three parts.

Part 1

Demonstrate the action of water on anhydrous copper(II) sulfate and anhydrous cobalt(II) chloride (powder or paper form) **(see tech notes)**. Explain that these tests will indicate that water is present but do not prove that the liquid tested is pure water (determining the boiling point is one way of doing this). Worksheet C10.1b could be used.

Ask students to write equations for the two reactions and revise the terms 'hydrated' and 'anhydrous'.

> **SAFETY INFORMATION**
>
> *Wear eye protection (splash-proof goggles).*
>
> Copper(II) sulfate is harmful. Cobalt(II) chloride is toxic by inhalation and a possible sensitiser by inhalation and skin contact. Avoid handling paper if possible, wash hands if papers are handled.

Part 2

Use the Student Book to introduce the water cycle (Student Book page 268) and a common method of water treatment (page 270). It is very likely that students will have studied the water cycle before, if not in science then in geography. They should be familiar with the terms 'evaporation' and 'condensation'.

In water treatment, emphasise the importance of the filtration through sand before the process of chlorination. Students could research other methods of water treatment (in particular desalination), as well as the sorts of water-borne diseases and the problems caused by drinking 'dirty' or untreated water. Use the Student Book page 269 as a basis for discussing the beneficial or harmful effects of the substances found in natural water supplies.

Part 3

Use the Student Book (page 270) to introduce the use of NPK fertilisers and the impact these fertilisers can have on water sources.

Technician's notes

Be sure to check the latest safety notes on these resources before proceeding.

The following resources are needed for the demonstration of water and anhydrous copper(II) sulfate and anhydrous cobalt(II) chloride:

anhydrous copper(II) sulfate, anhydrous cobalt(II) chloride and cobalt(II) chloride (powder or paper)
test-tubes, eye protection (splash-proof goggles)

Topic 10.1: Chemistry of the environment

Worksheet C10.1b Testing the purity of water samples

You are provided with 3 samples of water: A, B and C. Your task is to plan an experiment that will enable you to put the water samples in order of purity.

Your plan should:

a) Show how to safely use techniques, apparatus and materials.
b) Show in detail the procedure you would use.
c) Show how you would record your observations and measurements.
d) Show how you would use your results to put the three samples in order of purity.
e) List the possible sources of errors in your method.

Topic 10.1: Chemistry of the environment

Learning episode 10.1c The composition of the air

Learning objectives

- State the composition of clean, dry air as approximately 78% nitrogen, N_2, 21% oxygen, O_2, and the remainder as a mixture of noble gases and carbon dioxide, CO_2.
- Describe photosynthesis as the reaction between carbon dioxide and water to produce glucose and oxygen in the presence of chlorophyll and using energy from light.
- State the word equation for photosynthesis, carbon dioxide + water → glucose + oxygen.
- Supplement State the symbol equation for photosynthesis, $6CO_2 + 6H_2O \rightarrow C_6H_{12}O_6 + 6O_2$

Common misconceptions

Some students think that oxygen is the major component of the air.
Some students think that the percentage of carbon dioxide in the air is much greater than 0.04%.

Resources

Student Book pages 271–273

Approach

The learning episode concentrates on the percentage composition of 'clean, dry' air and the cycles that keep it approximately constant. Exact details of the carbon cycle (shown on page 273 of the Student Book) are not needed but they provide a useful context for discussion.

Student Book page 271 provides information about the composition of the air – the proportion of oxygen at 21% (approximately one-fifth) is also emphasised in the Developing Practical Skills box on page 271.

The apparently surprising low proportion of carbon dioxide can lead to a general discussion of the processes that maintain this proportion. The effect of carbon dioxide as a greenhouse gas is covered in learning episode C10.1d.

The high proportion of nitrogen in the atmosphere poses the question: 'Is nitrogen an important component of the air?' Emphasise that it is very unreactive (inert) and that some plants (leguminous – 'pod' plants, for example, peas) can 'fix' the nitrogen and form protein.

In lightning storms nitrogen is converted into a useful compound that has benefit for the soil and plants. However, particularly in intensive agriculture, these processes do not produce enough accessible nitrogen for plants to grow healthily. This provides a link to the use of fertilisers.

The Science in Context feature on page 272 of the Student Book can be used to explore the process used in the industrial manufacture of oxygen and nitrogen. Stress the important uses of oxygen and nitrogen and how they are stored as liquids under pressure. The content of these Science in Context features is beyond the syllabus but provides the opportunity to explore the content more deeply.

Supplement Look in more detail at the carbon cycle (page 273 of the Student Book) and, in particular, at the processes of combustion, respiration and photosynthesis. Emphasise that, of these processes, only photosynthesis removes carbon dioxide from the atmosphere (dissolving in the oceans is another removal process).

Topic 10.1: Chemistry of the environment

Answers

Developing practical skills, page 271

1. The iron filings would start to rust. The colour of the filings would change in colour to orange/brown.

2. The iron is being oxidised to iron(III) oxide.

   $4Fe(s) + 3O_2(g) \rightarrow 2Fe_2O_3(s)$

3. The air contains at least 15% oxygen.

4. The amount of iron filings used by students may have been different. For example, students may have used less than the required excess needed to obtain a result close to 20%.

5. To ensure there is equal gas pressure in and outside the tube.

Science in context, page 272

The boiling point of oxygen is −183 °C which is greater than −185 °C so the oxygen will be in a liquid state not a gas. The boiling point of nitrogen is −196 °C, so at a higher temperature of −190 °C the nitrogen will be a gas.

Page 273

1. Anhydrous means without water (water of crystallisation).

2. Cobalt(II) chloride will change from pink to blue.

3. Finding the melting point (or freezing point) or boiling point of a sample of water will determine its purity. Pure water will freeze at 0 °C and boil at 100 °C (under conditions of standard pressure).

4. a) The first filter is coarse gravel. The second filter is fine sand.

   b) Chlorine is used to kill bacteria.

5. a) Nitrogen is 78%.

   b) Carbon dioxide is 0.04%.

6. Photosynthesis removes carbon dioxide from the air.

Topic 10.1: Chemistry of the environment

Learning episode C10.1d Air quality and climate

Learning objectives

- State the source of each of these air pollutants, limited to:
  (a) carbon dioxide from the complete combustion of carbon-containing fuels
  (b) carbon monoxide and particulates from the incomplete combustion of carbon-containing fuels
  (c) methane from the decomposition of vegetation and waste gases from digestion in animals
  (d) oxides of nitrogen from car engines
  (e) sulfur dioxide from the combustion of fossil fuels which contain sulfur compounds.
- State the adverse effects of these air pollutants, limited to:
  (a) carbon dioxide: higher levels of carbon dioxide leading to increased global warming, which leads to climate change
  (b) carbon monoxide: toxic gas
  (c) particulates: increased risk of respiratory problems and cancer
  (d) methane: higher levels of methane leading to increased global warming, which leads to climate change
  (e) oxides of nitrogen: acid rain, photochemical smog and respiratory problems
  (f) sulfur dioxide: acid rain
- State and explain strategies to reduce the effects of these environmental issues, limited to:
  (a) climate change: planting trees, reduction in livestock farming, decreasing use of fossil fuels, increasing use of hydrogen and renewable energy, e.g. wind, solar.
  (b) acid rain: use of catalytic converters in vehicles, reducing emissions of sulfur dioxide by using low-sulfur fuels and flue gas desulfurisation with calcium oxide.
- Supplement Describe how the greenhouse gases carbon dioxide and methane cause global warming, limited to:
  (a) the absorption, reflection and emission of thermal energy
  (b) reducing thermal energy loss to space.
- Supplement Explain how oxides of nitrogen form in car engines and describe their removal by catalytic converters, e.g. $2CO + 2NO \rightarrow 2CO_2 + N_2$.

Common misconceptions

Damage to the ozone layer may be seen to be the greatest cause of global warming.

There may be confusion between the greenhouse effect and the enhanced greenhouse effect. The greenhouse effect is the trapping of heat under the atmosphere, which is a natural effect caused by greenhouse gases. However, when greenhouse gas concentrations are too high, they trap too much heat and increase the temperature of the Earth, causing the enhanced greenhouse effect.

Resources

Student Book pages 274–279

Worksheet C10.1d Air pollution

Approach

The focus of this learning episode includes the main pollutants in the atmosphere, acid rain and the impact of greenhouse gases. Detailed information is provided in the Student Book and other resources can be used to provide additional evidence.

This learning episode lends itself to student enquiry, either individually or in groups. Worksheet C10.1d provides a template that the students could use. It includes an additional piece of research into carbon footprints, carbon trading (carbon credits) and carbon offsetting.

Supplement Refer to the use of catalytic convertors as a means of reducing the emission of nitrogen oxides from car exhausts. The section on page 277 of the Student Book provides the equation for the reduction of nitrogen monoxide using a catalytic converter.

Answers

Science in Context, page 277

In many parts of the world cows are a very important food source, for milk and meat (beef). Replacing cows could seriously damage the food chain in these places. One solution may be to develop feed additives and supplements given to cows which suppress the enzyme which accelerates the production of methane in a cow's gut. There are claims that this approach could reduce methane emissions from cows by 30%. For people who have a vegetarian diet the reduction in the number of cows would not be seen as a problem.

Page 279

1. A major source of carbon monoxide is the incomplete combustion of fuels, e.g. in a motor car.
2. a) Methane is the major component of natural gas. It is also produced by decaying vegetable matter and by ruminant animals such as cows.
   b) Carbon dioxide is another greenhouse gas.
3. a) Sulfur dioxide and nitrogen oxide(s) are gases that cause acid rain.
   b) Sulfur dioxide forms sulfuric acid; nitrogen oxide forms nitric acid.
   c) Environmental problems include harming plants and fish in lakes, damaging buildings made of metal, marble or limestone.
4. a) Supplement $N_2(g) + O_2(g) \rightarrow 2NO(g)$
   b) Supplement $2NO(g) + 2CO(g) \rightarrow N_2(g) + 2CO_2(g)$
5. Supplement $6CO_2(g) + 6H_2O(l) \rightarrow C_6H_{12}O_6(aq) + 6O_2(g)$

Topic 10.1: Chemistry of the environment

Worksheet C10.1d Air pollution

This worksheet provides a grid for you to summarise the findings of your research into air pollution.

1. Common pollutants

Name of pollutant	What is the source of the pollutant and how does it get into the air?	What damage does the pollutant cause?	How can the pollutant be removed or its impact reduced?
Carbon monoxide			
Sulfur dioxide			
Oxides of nitrogen			
Particulates			

Topic 10.1: Chemistry of the environment

2. The greenhouse effect
   a) List some greenhouse gases
   b) What is the greenhouse effect and how is it caused?

3. Air pollution terms
What do you understand by the following terms below?

Term	What it involves
Flue gas desulfurisation	
Photochemical smog	

Topic 10.1: Chemistry of the environment

Learning episode 10.1e Consolidation and summary

Learning aims

- Review the learning points of the topic summarised in the end of topic checklist.
- Test understanding of the topic content by answering the end of topic questions.

Resources

Student Book pages 274–279

Approach

Ask students to work with a partner to make a list of key words from this topic. They could then work together to produce a spider diagram showing how the different concepts are linked. They could compare their list with the list of key terms given in the Student Book. Discuss the checklist and ask questions to see how much of the content students are comfortable with.

Students could make flashcards of the key content and then use the flashcards to quiz each other on the information.

Ask students to work individually through the end of topic questions in the Student Book without looking at the text. As they work, walk around the classroom observing their answers and questioning them as necessary to find out which questions are causing difficulties.

After a set period, ask students to stop working. Discuss any areas of difficulty you observed as you walked round the class.

Students should complete any unanswered questions for homework, but you should stress that they should answer the questions without looking at the text, so that they can see how much they have remembered.

End of topic questions mark scheme

The marks available for a question can indicate the level of detail you need to provide in your answer.

Question	Correct answer			Marks
1	A			1 mark
2	Distilled water contains no dissolved impurities.			1 mark
3 a)	Anhydrous copper(II) sulfate or anhydrous cobalt(II) chloride.			1 mark
3 b)	White powder or pink powder			1 mark
	to blue.			1 mark
4	Nitrates and phosphates increase plant growth in the stream or river.			1 mark
	The plant growth reduces levels of dissolved oxygen needed by fish.			1 mark
5	Chlorine is used in water purification to kill microbes.			1 mark
6 a)	21%			1 mark
6 b)	0.04%			1 mark
7	Knowledge about lead is not part of the syllabus. In this question it is included to show how the table should be completed.			
	Pollutant	What is the source of the pollutant?	How does the pollutant get into the air?	
	Lead compounds	Lead additives in	Burning petrol in a	
				2 marks

Topic 10.1: Chemistry of the environment

Question	Correct answer			Marks
		petrol	car	2 marks
	Carbon monoxide	Carbon in fuels	Incomplete combustion	2 marks
	Sulfur dioxide	Sulfur compounds in fuels	Combustion of the fuel	
	Oxides of nitrogen	Nitrogen in the air	Burning petrol in a car	
8	Process	What is removed from the air in the process?	What is put into the air in the process?	2 marks
	Combustion	Oxygen	Carbon dioxide	2 marks
	Respiration	Oxygen	Carbon dioxide	2 marks
	Photosynthesis	Carbon dioxide	Oxygen	
Supplement 9 a)	Short-wave radiation from the Sun heats the ground and the warm Earth gives off heat as long-wave radiation. The radiation is prevented from escaping from the Earth by greenhouse gases.			1 mark / 1 mark
Supplement 9 b)	Carbon dioxide. Methane.			1 mark / 1 mark
Supplement 10	The oxides of nitrogen are converted into nitrogen by the carbon monoxide in the exhaust gases. $2CO + 2NO \rightarrow 2CO_2 + N_2$			1 mark / 1 mark
	Total:			28 marks

Sections 8, 9 and 10: Exam-style questions mark scheme

Exam-style questions and sample answers have been written by the authors. In examinations, the way marks are awarded may be different. References to assessment and/or assessment preparation are the publisher's interpretation of the syllabus requirements and may not fully reflect the approach of Cambridge Assessment International Education.

The marks available for a question can indicate the level of detail you need to provide in your answer.

Question	Correct answer	Marks
2	C	1 mark
3 a)	Si	1 mark
3 b)	S	1 mark
3 c)	Group I.	1 mark
3 d)	Group II.	1 mark
3 e)	Group VII.	1 mark
4 a)	2,8,7	1 mark
4 b)	7	1 mark
4 c)	Brown fumes to colourless gas.	1 mark
4 d)	i) Red.	1 mark
	Hydrogen iodide forms an acid in water.	1 mark
	ii) Green.	1 mark
	Hydrogen iodide will not form an acid unless dissolved in water – it would be neutral.	1 mark
5 a)	Magnesium, zinc, iron.	1 mark
5 b)	magnesium + sulfuric acid → magnesium sulfate + hydrogen	1 mark
5 c)	$Mg(s) + H_2SO_4(aq) \rightarrow MgSO_4(aq) + H_2(g)$	1 mark
5 d)	Copper (also silver or gold).	1 mark
5 e)	The reaction with water/steam or the reaction with oxygen.	1 mark
6 a)	hematite.	1 mark
	molten iron	1 mark
	slag.	1 mark
6 b)	i) $C(s) + O_2(g) \rightarrow CO_2(g)$	1 mark
	ii) $CO_2(g) + C(s) \rightarrow 2CO(g)$	1 mark
6 c)	The limestone decomposes to form calcium oxide (CaO).	1 mark
	The calcium oxide then combines with sand (silica) to form a slag.	1 mark
6 d)	The iron(III) oxide has lost oxygen.	1 mark
6 e)	i) Aluminium is higher in the reactivity series than carbon.	1 mark
	ii) Any two of the following use/property combinations: packaging (non-toxic), in aeroplanes (high strength to weight ratio – low density), electrical cables (good electrical conductivity), kitchen utensils (shiny appearance/non-toxic). (1 mark for each of two correct use and property combinations)	2 marks

Sections 8, 9 and 10: Exam-style questions mark scheme

Question	Correct answer	Marks
7 a)	X is nitrogen.	1 mark
7 b)	i) octane + oxygen → carbon dioxide + water	2 marks
	ii) Hydrocarbons contain carbon and hydrogen.	1 mark
	iii) Alkanes.	1 mark
7 c)	Carbon monoxide is the product of incomplete combustion.	1 mark
7 d)	i) $N_2 + 2O_2 \rightarrow 2NO_2$	1 mark
	ii) NO_2 causes breathing difficulties and illness because it dissolves in water in the lungs.	1 mark
7 e)	i) The main source is burning coal or other fossil fuels.	1 mark
	ii) Oxidation means addition of oxygen.	1 mark
	iii) sulfuric acid + iron → iron(II) sulfate + hydrogen	2 marks
	iv) Acid rain erodes calcium carbonate.	1 mark
8 a)	Chlorine, argon, potassium, bromine, iodine. (Allow symbols.)	1 mark
8 b)	Chlorine, potassium, argon, bromine, iodine. (Allow symbols.)	1 mark
8 c)	B.	1 mark
8 d)	Chlorine, bromine, iodine. (Allow symbols.)	1 mark
8 e)	i) Potassium/K.	1 mark
	ii) Argon/Ar.	1 mark
8 f)	A.	1 mark
	D.	1 mark
9 a)	The density increases	1 mark
	down the group.	1 mark
9 b)	A temperature between about 670 °C and 710 °C (rubidium is predicted to boil between 670 °C and 714 °C).	1 mark
9 c)	A value between about 0.26 and 0.30 nm (the radius of a caesium atom is likely to be between 0.260 and 0.300 nm).	1 mark
9 d)	Lithium would react less rapidly.	1 mark
9 e)	Three of: conduct heat, conduct electricity, malleable, ductile, shiny, sonorous. (1 mark for each of three correct answers.)	3 marks
9 f)	i) The other product is sodium hydroxide.	1 mark
	ii) Test for hydrogen is to put in a lighted splint.	1 mark
	The result is that there will be a pop.	1 mark
9 g)	i) The positively charged particle is a proton.	1 mark
	ii) These atoms are called isotope(s).	1 mark
	iii) There are three nucleons in tritium.	1 mark
	iv) Radioactivity can be used as a radioactive tracer or in treating cancer.	1 mark

Sections 8, 9 and 10: Exam-style questions mark scheme

Question	Correct answer	Marks
Supplement 10	Atoms in a metal / Atoms in an alloy (with foreign atoms labelled)	2 marks
	In a pure metal the layers of atoms can easily slide over each other.	1 mark
	In an alloy the added elements stop the layers of metal atoms from sliding.	1 mark
Supplement 11	Greenhouse gases absorb and reflect heat (long-wave radiation) from the Earth's surface.	2 marks
	They therefore stop heat loss to space.	1 mark
	Total	73 marks

Topic 11.2: Fuels

Section 11: Organic chemistry

Contents
C11.1 General introduction to organic chemistry
C11.2 Fuels
C11.3 Alkanes
C11.4 Alkenes
C11.5 Alcohols
C11.6 Carboxylic acids
C11.7 Polymers

Overview of the section
This section covers the organic chemistry content of the course. It is unlikely that students will have studied organic chemistry before starting this course. You will need to spend time developing their understanding of organic formulae, functional groups and the general terminology they are likely to meet during the section. The naming of organic compounds and improving their familiarity with terms such as homologous series, 'saturated', and 'unsaturated'.

Supplement In addition, structural formulae and 'isomerism' (for the supplementary syllabus only) can be introduced and then these ideas can be reinforced during the study of individual topics.

After the general introduction hydrocarbon fuels are the focus before concentrating on the four homologous series: alkanes, alkenes, alcohols and carboxylic acids (mainly for the supplementary syllabus only). In the case of alcohols, the content is mostly a study of ethanol. The study of alkenes links to later work on addition polymerisation, while knowledge of carboxylic acids supports an understanding of the formation of condensation polymers.

Supplement The polymers topic is for the most part only required for the supplementary syllabus.

All the topics in the section require a good understanding of atomic structure, covalent bonding and the properties of simple covalent compounds. Discussion of the combustion of hydrocarbons links to pollution in Topic 10.1 *Chemistry of the environment*. In the suggested teaching sequence, all the topics are included in the second year of the course. As with other sections, it is important to use orientation to establish the extent of your students' prior knowledge.

Starting points
The Student Book section opener (pages 292–293) puts the ideas in the section into context and sets the scene. It also allows students to acknowledge and value their prior learning, and provides a benchmark against which future learning can be compared.

The questions provide a structure for introducing the section and can be used in a number of different ways:
- You could ask students to consider the questions as an introductory homework task.
- You could put students into groups to share their own ideas and understanding and then to report back to the whole class.
- Students could be given access to the Internet, preferably with a tight timescale, to find out the information required.

You could then use a spider chart or other form of wall chart to summarise everybody's ideas.

Recording these initial ideas allows you to retain them for reference as the individual topics are developed. In this way, your students' progress in learning can be readily acknowledged.

C11.1 General introduction to organic chemistry

Introduction

This topic as its name implies is a general introduction. Its contents are replicated in the subsequent topics in this section. Emphasis is placed on drawing displayed formulae of organic compounds, interpreting the general formulae of compounds in a homologous series and appreciating that in a homologous series all the compounds will have similar chemical properties.

Links to other topics

Section	Essential background knowledge	Useful links
2 Atoms, elements and compounds	2.3 Molecules and covalent bonds	
11 Organic chemistry		11.2 Fuels
		11.3 Alkanes
		11.4 Alkenes
		11.5 Alcohols
		11.6 Carboxylic acids
		11.7 Polymers

Topic overview

C11.1a	Orientation
	This learning episode introduces and defines the terminology that will be used throughout the section. There are no further activities and you can move straight to Topic 11.2 *Fuels*.

Career links

These are some scientific careers that focus on this area of chemistry but careers in many other fields use the knowledge and skills gained studying science.

Forensic analysts, environmental chemists and food scientists are just three examples of careers which make use of a wide range of knowledge on organic chemistry.

Pharmaceutical chemists develop active ingredients to improve or create new medicines.

Topic 11.1: General introduction to organic chemistry

Learning episode C11.1a Orientation

Learning objectives

- Draw and interpret the displayed formula of a molecule to show all the atoms and all the bonds.
- Write and interpret general formulae of compounds in the same homologous series, limited to:
  (a) alkanes, C_nH_{2n+2}
  (b) alkenes, C_nH_{2n}
  (c) alcohols, $C_nH_{2n+1}OH$
  (d) carboxylic acids, $C_nH_{2n+1}COOH$.
- Identify a functional group as an atom or group of atoms that determine the chemical properties of a homologous series.
- State that a homologous series is a family of similar compounds with similar chemical properties due to the presence of the same functional group.
- State that a saturated compound has molecules in which all carbon–carbon bonds are single bonds.
- State that an unsaturated compound has molecules in which one or more carbon–carbon bonds are not single bonds.
- Supplement State that a structural formula is an unambiguous description of the way the atoms in a molecule are arranged, including $CH_2=CH_2$, CH_3CH_2OH, CH_3COOCH_3
- Supplement Describe the general characteristics of a homologous series as:
  (a) having the same functional group
  (b) having the same general formula
  (c) differing from one member to the next by a $-CH_2-$unit
  (d) displaying a trend in physical properties
  (e) sharing similar chemical properties.

Resources

Student Book pages 290–293

Approach

Students should be familiar with some organic compounds from their study of Topic 2.3 *Molecules and covalent bonds*. By revising some of the molecules they have encountered already it should be possible to provide a quick introduction to some functional groups and homologous series, as well as saturated and unsaturated compounds. The time spent on this will depend on your overall strategy for studying organic chemistry. You may decide to introduce these ideas in the context of the other topics.

C11.2 Fuels

Introduction

This topic introduces organic chemistry as well as a very direct link to Topic 11.3 *Alkanes* and Topic 11.4 *Alkenes*. Fractional distillation features in Topic 12.1 *Experimental techniques*. In Topic 2.3 *Molecules and covalent bonds* students explored the nature of bonding in hydrocarbon molecules and learned the physical properties associated with simple molecular compounds. The problems of the combustion and incomplete combustion of hydrocarbon fuels are covered in Topic 10.1 *Chemistry of the environment*.

The topic starts with a general introduction to the fossil fuels coal, natural gas and petroleum (crude oil) before looking in some detail at separating petroleum into its components by fractional distillation. Cracking is covered in Topic 11.4 *Alkenes* to emphasise that cracking is needed to convert larger petroleum fractions into more useful smaller fractions. Finally, the continuing use of fossil fuels is considered.

There is some opportunity for developing practical skills in this topic.

Links to other topics

Sections	Essential background knowledge	Useful links
2 Atoms, elements and compounds	2.3 Molecules and covalent bonds	
10 Chemistry of the environment	10.1 Chemistry of the environment	
11 Organic chemistry		11.3 Alkanes 11.4 Alkenes
12 Experimental techniques	12.1 Experimental techniques	

Topic overview

C11.2a	Orientation
	This learning episode provides an opportunity to revise or reinforce ideas on the main fossil fuels and their non-renewable nature. An opportunity is taken to revise the nature of covalent bonding and to draw some dot-and-cross diagrams of hydrocarbons. Reference is also made to fractional distillation as a process of separating liquids with different boiling points.
C11.2b	**The fractional distillation of petroleum**
	This learning episode focuses on the industrial use of the fractional distillation of petroleum (crude oil). The process is demonstrated and the fractions obtained are compared for colour, viscosity and flammability. Emphasis is placed on the nature and uses of the major fractions obtained from the fractional distillation.
C11.2c	**Consolidation and summary**
	This learning episode considers the advantages and disadvantages of using fossil fuels before recapping the key ideas encountered in the topic. Time can be allocated to studying the end of topic checklist and then answering the end of topic questions in the Student Book.

Career links

These are some scientific careers that focus on this area of chemistry but careers in many other fields use the knowledge and skills gained studying science. Policy advisors for the government use their knowledge and understanding of chemistry to brief politicians on scientific research to inform changes that may be needed to their policies. Petroleum geologists find sources of crude oil by analysing structures underground using geological and geophysical methods.

Topic 11.2: Fuels

Learning episode C11.2a Orientation

Learning objectives

- Name the fossil fuels: coal, natural gas and petroleum.
- Name methane as the main constituent of natural gas.
- State that hydrocarbons are compounds that contain hydrogen and carbon only.
- State that petroleum is a mixture of hydrocarbons.

Resources

Student Book page 294

Approach

Students should be very familiar with the names of the common fossil fuels – coal, natural gas and petroleum (crude oil). They should also be familiar with the term 'non-renewable'.

Check the level of this existing knowledge with a few questions. Refer to page 294 of the Student Book. Ask students what they understand by the term 'hydrocarbon', which they should have met in the earlier Topic 10.1 *Chemistry of the environment*.

Ask students to draw a dot-and-cross diagram for the simplest hydrocarbon: methane, CH_4. Revise ideas on covalent bonding if and as required.

Supplement Ask students to draw a dot-and-cross diagram for ethene, C_2H_4.

Explain the terms saturated and unsaturated in the context of methane and ethene. Explain also that methane belongs to a family of organic compounds called alkanes, whereas ethene belongs to a family of organic compounds called alkenes (both of which will be studied later in the course). Ask what the characteristic properties of simple covalent substances are.

Explain that petroleum is a mixture of a large number of organic compounds, many of which are used as fuels. Ask what process can be used to separate a mixture of liquids – if necessary, remind students about fractional distillation. Explain that the next learning episode will look in more detail at the fractional distillation of petroleum.

Topic 11.2: Fuels

Learning episode C11.2b The fractional distillation of petroleum

Learning objectives

- Describe the separation of petroleum into useful fractions by fractional distillation.
- Describe how the properties of fractions obtained from petroleum change from the bottom to the top of the fractionating column, limited to:
  (a) decreasing chain length
  (b) higher volatility
  (c) lower boiling points
  (d) lower viscosity.
- Name the uses of the fractions as:
  (a) refinery gas fraction for gas used in heating and cooking
  (b) gasoline / petrol fraction for fuel used in cars
  (c) naphtha fraction as a chemical feedstock
  (d) kerosene / paraffin fraction for jet fuel
  (e) diesel oil / gas fraction for fuel used in diesel engines
  (f) fuel oil fraction for fuel used in ships and home heating systems
  (g) lubricating oil fraction for lubricants, waxes and polishes
  (h) bitumen fraction for making roads.

Resources

Student Book pages 295–297

Worksheet C11.2b The fractional distillation of petroleum (crude oil)

Resources for a demonstration (see Technician's notes, following)

Approach

Ask students what process can be used to separate a mixture of liquids with different boiling points (fractional distillation). Explain that petroleum (crude oil) can be separated into components using fractional distillation, but rather than separating liquid by liquid (or compound by compound), it is separated into fractions with a range of boiling points. These fractions are therefore likely to contain more than one compound.

Demonstrate the fractional distillation of a petroleum or crude oil substitute **(see tech notes)**. Explain that petroleum or crude oil is too dangerous to be allowed in schools and that the technician has made up a safer substitute, though it is still harmful.

Use Worksheet C11.2b so that students can record the observations and measurements and analyse their findings. Trends in boiling points, colour, viscosity, ease of burning and smokiness of the flame for the fractions are given on pages 295–297 of the Student Book.

It is important that students know some of the key components of the fractions (refinery gases, gasoline, kerosene, diesel, fuel oil and bitumen), where they are produced in the fractionating column and the approximate number of carbon atoms they have in their molecules.

SAFETY INFORMATION
Wear eye protection (splash-proof goggles).
Petroleum/crude oil substitute is highly flammable and harmful.
Ventilate room well to remove smoke, and only use small amounts

Topic 11.2: Fuels

Technician's notes

Be sure to check the latest safety notes on these resources before proceeding.

You will need the following resources for the demonstration of fractional distillation:

100 cm³ petroleum/crude oil substitute made from: • 55 cm³ liquid paraffin; 20 cm³ paraffin oil (kerosene)   • 11 cm³ white spirit; 4 cm³ petroleum ether (100–120 °C)   • 4 cm³ petroleum ether (80–100 °C); 6 cm³ of petroleum ether (60–80 °C)   • black artists' oil paint (to provide colour)   about 6 cm³ is needed for the demonstration
Bunsen burner and heatproof mat
mineral wool
tongs
side-arm borosilicate glass boiling tube, delivery tube and rubber connection tubing
thermometer (0–360 °C), teat pipette, beaker, watch glass
small test-tubes to collect fractions and test-tube holder
eye protection (splash-proof goggles)
SAFETY INFORMATION   *Crude oil must not be used in schools.*

Answers

Page 297

1. The supplies of petroleum/crude oil are limited – it takes millions of years for crude oil to be formed.
2. Natural gas or methane. It is trapped in pockets above the oil.
3. Small chain of carbon atoms.
4. Long chain of carbon atoms.
5. These fractions readily form a vapour.

Topic 11.2: Fuels

Worksheet C11.2b The fractional distillation of petroleum (crude oil)

Petroleum or crude oil is a mixture of many different liquids. Because these liquids have different boiling points, they can be separated by fractional distillation.

You will be shown a demonstration of how crude oil can be separated into fractions with different boiling points. These fractions will then be compared to see how their properties vary.

Apparatus

Bunsen burner and heatproof mat

mineral wool

tongs

clamp and stand

side-arm borosilicate glass test-tube, delivery tube and rubber connection tubing

thermometer (0–360 °C), teat pipette, beaker, watch glass

petroleum or crude oil substitute

eye protection (splash-proof goggles)

small test-tubes to collect fractions and test-tube holder

SAFETY INFORMATION

Wear eye protection (splash-proof goggles).

Petroleum/crude oil substitute is highly flammable and harmful.

Ventilate room well to remove smoke, and only use small amounts

---

Method

1. Put on your eye protection.
2. The petroleum will be heated slowly and four or five different fractions collected with boiling points in different temperature ranges.
3. The different fractions will then be observed and tested. Record your observations in the table below.

Note: viscosity is a measure of the runniness (mobility) of the liquid.

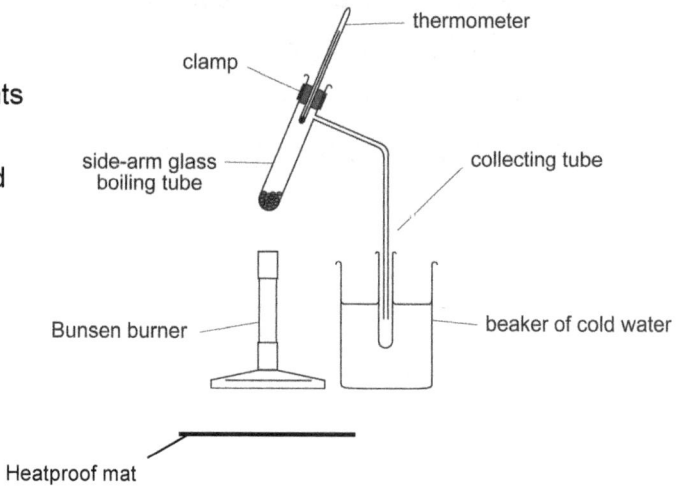

Topic 11.2: Fuels

Observing, measuring and recording

Fraction	Boiling point range / °C	Colour	Viscosity	Observations on burning (flammability)
1				
2				
3				
4				
5				

Handling experimental observations and data

4. Summarise the trends in properties from fraction 1 to fraction 5.

Property	Trend from fraction 1 to fraction 5
Colour	
Viscosity	
Flammability	

5. What colour flame indicates that a hydrocarbon fuel has sufficient oxygen to burn completely?
6. What products are formed when a hydrocarbon fuel burns completely in oxygen?
7. What colour flame indicates that a hydrocarbon fuel has insufficient oxygen to burn completely?
8. What products could be formed when a hydrocarbon fuel burns in an insufficient supply of oxygen?

Topic 11.2: Fuels

Learning episode C11.2c Consolidation and summary

Learning aims

- Review the learning points of the topic summarised in the end of topic checklist.
- Test understanding of the topic content by answering the end of topic questions.

Common misconceptions

Some students think that all fossil fuels will run out in the next few years. (Supplies of coal are relatively large.)

Resources

Student Book pages 295–301

Approach

Ask students to work with a partner to make a list of key words from this topic. They could then work together to produce a spider diagram showing how the different concepts are linked. They could compare their list with the list of key terms given in the Student Book. Discuss the checklist and ask questions to see how much of the content students are comfortable with.

Students could make flashcards of the key content and then use the flashcards to quiz each other on the information.

Use the Science in Context box, *The Fossil Fuel Dilemma*, on page 297 of the Student Book to consider the advantages and disadvantages of using fossil fuels to generate energy. Are alternative forms of energy the answer? Should coal be used more extensively? The content of these Science in Context features is beyond the syllabus but provides the opportunity to explore the content more deeply.

Ask students to work individually through the end of topic questions in the Student Book without looking at the text. As they work, walk around the classroom observing their answers and questioning them as necessary to find out which questions are causing difficulties.

After a set period, ask students to stop working. Discuss any areas of difficulty you observed as you walked round the class.

Reinforce the point that students will do further work on alkanes and alkenes, and on the concept of saturated and unsaturated hydrocarbons, in topics that follow this one.

Students should complete any unanswered questions for homework, but you should stress that they should answer the questions without looking at the text, so that they can see how much they have remembered.

Answers

Science in Context, page 298

Options available include:

- Reduce global energy consumption.
- Continue to develop sources of energy from renewable energy sources.
- Produce better filters in coal fired power stations to reduce the production of particulates, carbon monoxide and carbon dioxide.

Topic 11.2: Fuels

End of topic questions mark scheme

The marks available for a question can indicate the level of detail you need to provide in your answer.

Question	Correct answer	Marks
1	C	1 mark
2 a)	Petroleum/crude oil is formed from the remains of animals.	1 mark
	Pressed together under layers of rock (over millions of years).	1 mark
2 b)	It takes millions of years to form – crude oil used cannot be replaced.	1 mark
3 a)	Fractional distillation.	1 mark
3 b)	The boiling point decreases.	1 mark
3 c)	Some parts of the mixture condense and form liquids (which are drained off).	1 mark
	The parts that do not condense (temperature above the boiling point) pass up the column.	1 mark
4 a)	Carbon dioxide.	1 mark
	Water.	1 mark
4 b)	$2C_8H_{18}(l) + 25O_2(g) \rightarrow 16CO_2(g) + 18H_2O(l)$	2 marks
	(1 mark for formulae; 1 mark for balancing)	
4 c)	Carbon monoxide is highly poisonous.	1 mark
	It reduces the capacity of the blood to transport oxygen around the body.	1 mark
	Total:	14 marks

C11.3 Alkanes

Introduction

Students should already be familiar with electronic structure from Topic 2.1 *Atoms, elements and compounds* and with covalent bonding from Topic 2.3 *Molecules and covalent bonds*. There are also links to methane as a greenhouse gas and the incomplete combustion of fuels in Topic 10.1 *Chemistry of the environment*. This topic builds on the introduction to organic chemistry provided in Topic 11.1 *General introduction to organic chemistry* and Topic 11.2 *Fuels*. It is also the basis for the subsequent study of Topic 11.4 *Alkenes*.

The topic explains the nature of a homologous series and reaffirms terms such as 'hydrocarbon' and 'saturated', followed by the use of the names of alkanes in naming all organic compounds. Students will have another opportunity, if needed, to revise dot and cross diagrams.

Supplement Combustion and (mainly for the supplementary syllabus) substitution reactions are highlighted as the main reactions of alkanes.

Supplement Structural isomerism is introduced for the supplement syllabus.

Links to other topics

Section	Essential background knowledge	Useful links
2 Atoms, elements and compounds	2.1 Atoms, elements and compounds 2.3 Molecules and covalent bonds	
10 Chemistry of the environment	10.1 Chemistry of the environment	
11 Organic chemistry	11.1 General introduction to organic chemistry 11.2 Fuels	11.4 Alkenes

Topic overview

C11.3a	Orientation
	This learning episode starts with a revision of covalent bonding and introduces the concept of a homologous series within the organic chemistry branch of chemistry. The names of the first five alkanes are introduced, together with information about their states of matter at room temperature and their uses as fuels. The terms 'hydrocarbon' and 'saturated' are revised. The general characteristics of a homologous series are introduced.
C11.3b	**The chemical properties of alkanes**
	This learning episode starts with the combustion of alkanes, re-emphasising their general use as fuels. The concept of complete and incomplete combustion is revised (first encountered in Topic 10.1 *Chemistry of the environment*) and the potential dangers associated with incomplete combustion.
	Supplement Substitution is then introduced as another reaction of alkanes, with the reaction between methane and chlorine as the example.
C11.3c	Supplement **The structure of alkanes**
	This is a short learning episode that focuses on the existence of structural isomers for alkanes with four or more carbon atoms.
C11.3d	**Consolidation and summary**
	This learning episode provides an opportunity for a quick recap of the ideas encountered in the topic and time for the students to answer the end of topic questions in the Student Book.

Topic 11.3: Alkanes

Career links

These are some scientific careers that focus on this area of chemistry but careers in many other fields use the knowledge and skills gained studying science.

Gas engineers service boilers and fires to make sure that combustion of the fuel is complete and does not produce the toxic gas carbon monoxide, or particulates which can be harmful to human health.

Car designers work with scientists to design car engines which use the fuel in the most efficient ways.

Topic 11.3: Alkanes

Learning episode C11.3a Orientation

Learning objectives

- Write and interpret general formulae of compounds in the same homologous series:
  (a) alkanes, C_nH_{2n+2}
- Supplement Define structural isomers as compounds with the same molecular formula, but different structural formulae, including C_4H_{10} as $CH_3CH_2CH_2CH_3$ and $CH_3CH(CH_3)CH_3$.
- Name and draw the displayed formulae of methane and ethane.
- Supplement Name and draw the structural and displayed formulae of unbranched alkanes containing up to four carbon atoms per molecule.
- State the type of compound present, given a chemical name ending in –ane or from a molecular formula or displayed formula.
- State that the bonding in alkanes is single covalent and that alkanes are saturated hydrocarbons.

Resources

Student Book pages 302–306

Worksheet C11.3a Covalent bonding in alkanes

Resources for demonstration (see Technician's notes, below)

Approach

Explain that alkanes are a 'family' or homologous series of organic chemicals. Show how the formulae of alkanes match the general formula C_nH_{2n+2}.

Show samples of alkanes: methane (natural gas/Bunsen burner), propane (camping gas canister), butane (lighter fuel) and pentane. Mention that they are all fuels and that their physical properties vary from methane as a gas, through to propane and butane as gases that are often liquefied under pressure, to pentane, a liquid. Emphasise the meaning of the term 'hydrocarbon'. The samples are just shown to illustrate their everyday use – photos could be used instead.

Ask students what they can recall about the nature of covalent bonding. Use molecular models to illustrate the structure of alkanes and Worksheet C11.3a to recap on dot-and-cross bonding diagrams.

SAFETY INFORMATION
Wear eye protection (splash-proof goggles).

Technician's notes

Be sure to check the latest safety notes on these resources before proceeding.

The following resources are needed for the demonstration of alkanes:

a bottle or canister of camping gas (propane)
lighter fuel (butane)
bottle of pentane

Answers

Worksheet C11.3a

Methane Ethane Propane

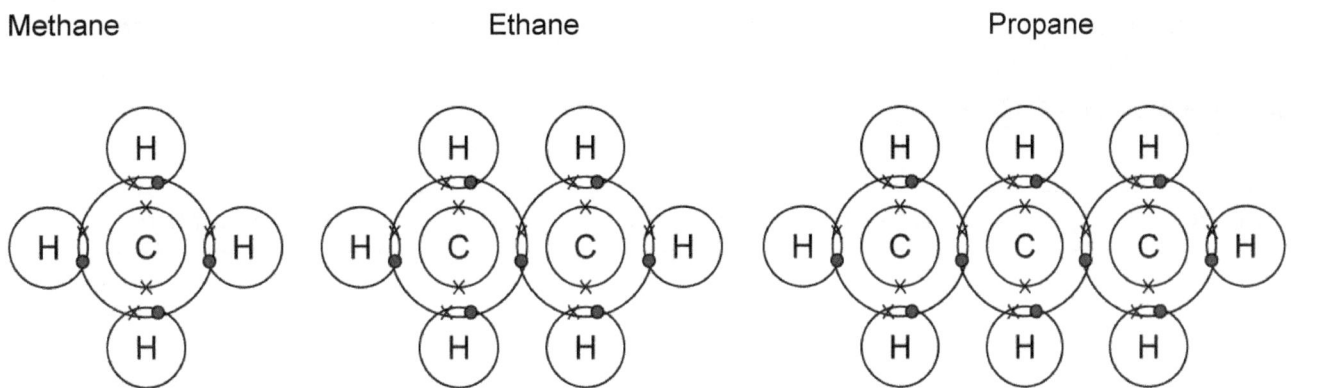

Topic 11.3: Alkanes

Worksheet C11.3a Covalent bonding in alkanes

Methane, ethane and propane are compounds in the alkane homologous series. They are covalently bonded.

Draw dot-and-cross diagrams showing the bonding in each of these compounds. In each case the displayed formula has been inserted in the table.

(Proton numbers: H = 1; C = 6)

Alkane	Dot-and-cross diagram	Displayed formula
Methane		H—C(H_4 structure: H above, H below, H left, H right of C)
Ethane		H₃C—CH₃ (displayed)
Propane		H₃C—CH₂—CH₃ (displayed)

Topic 11.3: Alkanes

Learning episode C11.3b The chemical properties of alkanes

Learning objectives

- Describe the properties of alkanes as being generally unreactive, except in terms of combustion and substitution by chlorine.
- Supplement State that in a substitution reaction one atom or group of atoms is replaced by another atom or group of atoms.
- Supplement Describe the substitution reaction of alkanes with chlorine as a photochemical reaction, with ultraviolet light providing the activation energy, E_a, and draw the structural or displayed formulae of the products, limited to monosubstitution.

Resources

Student Book pages 305–307

Approach

Students will be familiar with the combustion of alkane fuels. Explain that hydrocarbons burn in a plentiful supply of air or oxygen to form carbon dioxide and water (as shown by the blue flame on a Bunsen burner).

Ask what happens if the air supply is restricted. (This is demonstrated by the yellow flame on the Bunsen burner.) Emphasise that incomplete combustion can produce carbon and carbon monoxide, and that carbon monoxide is toxic.

Let students practise writing equations for the complete and incomplete combustion of simple hydrocarbons. Refer to the equations on page 305 of the Student Book.

Supplement Introduce students to the substitution reaction of alkanes. Emphasise what conditions are needed (chlorine in the presence of ultraviolet light) and why the reaction is called a substitution reaction. Refer to page 306 of the Student Book.

Answers

Page 305

1. a) Contains no C=C double bonds.

   b) A compound containing hydrogen and carbon only.

2. a) $C_{15}H_{32}$

   b) Carbon dioxide and water.

Page 306

1. The fuel will burn with a yellow (rather than blue) flame.

2. Carbon and carbon monoxide.

3. It combines with the haemoglobin to form carboxyhaemoglobin, which prevents the haemoglobin from combining with oxygen.

4. Wind, wave, solar and nuclear power are alternative ways of generating energy.

5. Supplement A reaction in which one atom or group of atoms is replaced by an atom or group of atoms.

Topic 11.3: Alkanes

Supplement Learning episode C11.3c The structure of alkanes

Learning objective

- Supplement Define structural isomers as compounds with the same molecular formula, but different structural formulae, including C_4H_{10} as $CH_3CH_2CH_2CH_3$ and $CH_2CH(CH_3)CH_3$.

Resources

Student Book pages 306–307

Approach

Explain that alkanes have been shown as straight-chain molecules so far. Introduce the concept of structural isomers and branched-chain molecules with the same molecular formulae.

Show molecular models of butane and 2-methylpropane. Explain how the names of these structural isomers relate to the number of carbon atoms in the longest chain.

Page 307 of the Student Book shows the three structural isomers of pentane. Emphasise that although the molecules have the same formula, they have different structures and therefore different physical properties, as shown by their different boiling points.

One of the questions on page 307 of the Student Book refers to hexane and some of its isomers. All the isomers contain C–C single bonds. Explain that this type of molecule is said to be 'saturated' (students may be familiar with saturated and unsaturated fats in food). Mention that unsaturated hydrocarbons contain C=C double bonds (this will be covered in more detail in the next topic).

Answers

Page 307

1. Supplement

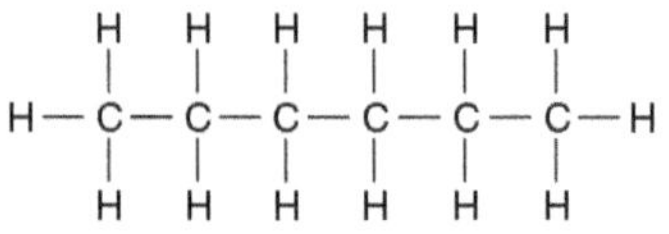

[Structural formula of hexane showing six carbons in a chain, each with appropriate hydrogens]

The molecular formula is C_6H_{14}.

2. Hexane will be a liquid. Its physical properties will most closely resemble those of pentane.

3. Supplement Structural isomers are molecules with the same molecular formula but different structural formulae.

4. Supplement Any two of the following:

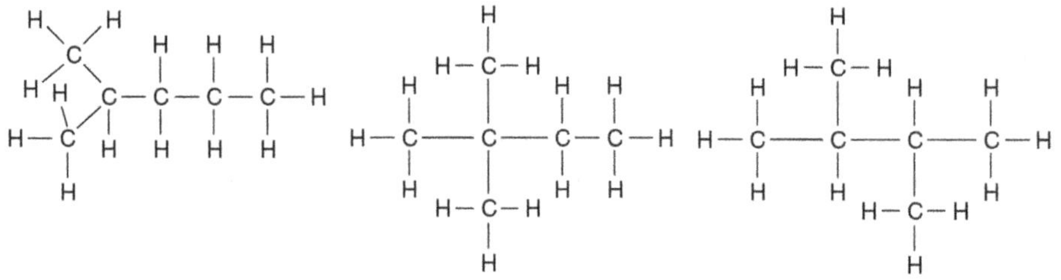

[Three structural formulae of hexane isomers shown]

Topic 11.3: Alkanes

Learning episode C11.3d Consolidation and summary

Learning aims

- Review the learning points of the topic summarised in the end of topic checklist.
- Test understanding of the topic content by answering the end of topic questions.

Resources

Student Book pages 277, 308–310

Approach

Ask students to work with a partner to make a list of key words from this topic. They could then work together to produce a spider diagram showing how the different concepts are linked. They could compare their list with the list of key terms given in the Student Book. Discuss the checklist and ask questions to see how much of the content students are comfortable with.

Students could make flashcards of the key content and then use the flashcards to quiz each other on the information.

Refer to the Science in Context feature on methane on page 277 of the Student Book (used in Topic 10.1 *Chemistry of the environment*), to highlight that methane is a greenhouse gas and that it contributes to global warming. The content of these Science in Context features is beyond the syllabus but provides the opportunity to explore the content more deeply.

Ask students to work individually through the end of topic questions in the Student Book without looking at the text. As they work, walk around the classroom observing their answers and questioning them as necessary to find out which questions are causing difficulties.

After a set period, ask students to stop working. Discuss any areas of difficulty you observed as you walked round the class.

Students should complete any unanswered questions for homework, but you should stress that they should answer the questions without looking at the text, so that they can see how much they have remembered.

End of topic questions mark scheme

The marks available for a question can indicate the level of detail you need to provide in your answer.

Question	Correct answer	Marks
1	B	1 mark
2	A homologous series is group of organic compounds with the same general formula, similar chemical properties and physical properties, which change gradually from one member to the next.	1 mark
3	$C_{10}H_{22}$	1 mark
4	No. This compound does not have the general formula of C_nH_{2n+2}.	1 mark
5 a)	C_2H_6	1 mark
5 b)	Carbon dioxide.	1 mark
	Water.	1 mark
5 c)	Blue flame.	1 mark
5 d)	$2C_2H_6(g) + 7O_2(g) \rightarrow 4CO_2(g) + 6H_2O(l)$ (1 mark for formulae; 1 mark for balancing)	2 marks

Topic 11.3: Alkanes

Question	Correct answer	Marks
5 e)	Carbon.	1 mark
	Carbon monoxide.	1 mark
5 f)	Yellow flame.	1 mark
Supplement 6	Structural isomerism is the existence of compounds with the same molecular formula but different structural formulae.	1 mark
Supplement 7 a)	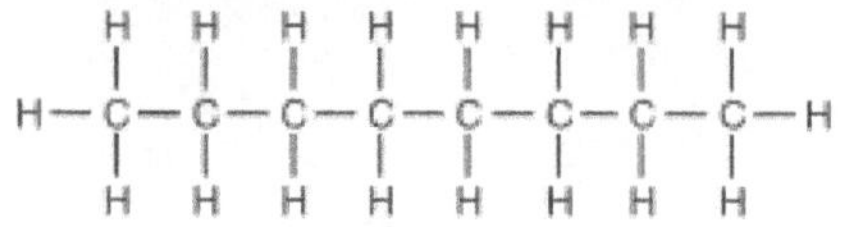 Structural diagram of octane (straight chain C8H18).	1 mark
Supplement 7 b)	Diagram must have 8 carbon atoms and 18 hydrogen atoms with at least one branch. Some examples are shown here. 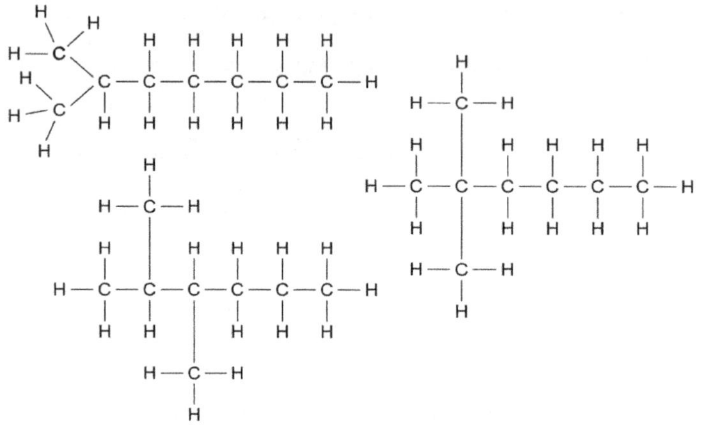 (1 mark for any of the above, or other correctly drawn isomers)	1 mark
Supplement 7 c)	Liquid.	1 mark
Supplement 7 d)	Octane is a saturated hydrocarbon – it contains only C–C single bonds (no C=C bonds).	1 mark
Supplement 8 a)	Substitution.	1 mark
Supplement 8 b)	In the presence of ultraviolet (UV) light.	1 mark
Supplement 8 c)	Bromomethane.	1 mark
	Total:	21 marks

C11.4 Alkenes

Introduction

This is a short topic that extends understanding of covalent bonding from Topic 2.3 *Molecules and covalent bonds*, Topic 11.1 *General introduction to organic chemistry* and the introductory work on alkanes in Topic 11.3 *Alkanes*. It also provides the basis for a more detailed consideration of addition polymerisation in Topic 11.7 *Polymers*.

The topic focuses on three aspects of alkenes: the use of catalytic cracking to produce alkenes from larger petroleum fractions, their structures and their chemical reactions, including combustion and the addition reactions with bromine water and in the formation of poly(ethene).

Supplement The supplementary syllabus includes addition reactions with bromine, hydrogen and steam. The preparation of ethanol by the catalytic addition of steam features in Topic 11.5 *Alcohols*.

Links to other topics

Section	Essential background knowledge	Useful links
2 Atoms, elements and compounds	2.1 Atoms, elements and compounds 2.3 Molecules and covalent bonds	
11 Organic chemistry	11.1 General introduction to organic chemistry 11.2 Fuels 11.3 Alkanes	11.5 Alcohols 11.7 Polymers

Topic overview

C11.4a	**Orientation**
	This learning episode picks up on many of the ideas covered in Topic 4b *Alkanes*, including the distinction between a saturated and unsaturated hydrocarbon and the covalent bonding associated with a C=C double bond.
	The characteristics of a homologous series are revised and the general formula for an alkene is introduced.
C11.4b	**Cracking crude oil fractions**
	The reason for the importance of the catalytic cracking of the 'heavier' crude oil fractions is emphasised (converting the less useful longer-chain hydrocarbons into more useful shorter-chain hydrocarbons).
C11.4c	**The chemical properties of alkenes**
	This learning episode focuses on the combustion of alkenes as typical hydrocarbons, the addition reaction with bromine water and the formation of poly(ethene). The decolourisation of bromine water is introduced as a way of identifying an alkene as an unsaturated hydrocarbon.
	Supplement Addition reactions with bromine, hydrogen and steam are introduced.
C11.4d	**Consolidation and summary**
	This learning episode recaps on the ideas encountered in the topic, as well as considering a Science in Context feature, *Saturated and Unsaturated Fats* in the Student Book. Time can be allocated to answering the end of topic questions in the Student Book.

Career links

These are some scientific careers that focus on this area of chemistry but careers in many other fields use the knowledge and skills gained studying science.

Petrochemical engineers develop ways that crude oil can be broken down into smaller fractions which are used to make plastics and fuels.

Topic 11.4: Alkenes

Learning episode C11.4a Orientation

Learning objectives

- Write and interpret general formulae of compounds in the same homologous series, (b) alkenes, C_nH_{2n}
- **Supplement** Define structural isomers as compounds with the same molecular formula, but different structural formulae, including C_4H_8 as $CH_3CH_2CH=CH_2$ and $CH_3CH=CHCH_3$.
- Name and draw the displayed formula of ethene.
- **Supplement** Name and draw the structural and displayed formulae of unbranched alkenes, including but-1-ene and but-2-ene, containing up to four carbon atoms per molecule.
- State the type of compound present, given a chemical name ending in –ene or from a molecular formula or displayed formula.
- State that the bonding in alkenes includes a double carbon–carbon covalent bond and that alkenes are unsaturated hydrocarbons.

Resources

Student Book pages 311–312

Approach

Ask students to name the first two members of the alkane homologous series and to draw the displayed formulae for these.

Illustrate that the alkenes contain a C=C double bond as the functional group, that is, the alkenes are unsaturated hydrocarbons. Ask students to draw the displayed formula for ethene and then propene.

Ask students if they can remember the characteristics of a homologous series (general formula, gradual trend in physical properties and common chemical properties). Explain that alkenes have a general formula C_nH_{2n} and ask them to draw the displayed formula for butene (C_4H_8).

Supplement Use Table 11.4 on page 312 of the Student Book to look at the trend in boiling points, and the subsequent states of matter at room temperature and pressure, of the alkene series.

Topic 11.4: Alkenes

Learning episode C11.4b Cracking crude oil fractions

Learning objectives

- Describe the manufacture of alkenes and hydrogen by the cracking of larger alkane molecules using a high temperature and a catalyst.
- Describe the reasons for the cracking of larger alkane molecules.

Resources

Student Book pages 313–314

Worksheet C11.4b Cracking liquid paraffin

Resources for a class practical (see Technician's notes, below)

Approach

Refer to Table 11.5 on page 313 of the Student Book, which shows the typical percentages of the different fractions produced by the fractional distillation of crude oil. Explain that the fractions most easily used are the 'lighter' fractions, such as gasoline (13%), and so the 'heavier' fractions must be converted into the lighter fractions.

Emphasise that one of the products of cracking is always an alkene. Alkenes are much more reactive than alkanes, so they can be converted (by addition reactions) into a much wider range of useful chemicals.

Worksheet C11.4b provides details of a class practical involving the cracking of liquid paraffin. **Warn students to be careful that a 'suck back' does not take place**. This process also features in the Developing Practical Skills box on page 314 of the Student Book.

You will need to decide whether to refer to both and, if so, in what order you will introduce them.

SAFETY INFORMATION
Wear eye protection (splash-proof goggles).
Aqueous bromine (bromine water) is harmful.
Ensure that the laboratory is well ventilated.

Topic 11.4: Alkenes

Technician's notes

Be sure to check the latest safety notes on these resources before proceeding.

The following resources are needed for the class practical C11.4b, per group:

medicinal paraffin (sometimes called liquid paraffin)
aqueous bromine (bromine water (0.02 M)) – diluted until the colour is barely visible – 5 cm^3
pot fragments
Bunsen burner and heatproof mat
stand and clamp, boiling tube, bung and delivery tube with Bunsen valve (see below for details on how to make a Bunsen valve)
mineral wool and tongs
water basin, test-tubes, 2 dropping pipettes
eye protection (splash-proof goggles)

It is recommended that a Bunsen valve is fitted to the end of the delivery tube to reduce the risk of suck-back. Bunsen valves can be made easily as follows.

You will need a piece of clean, unused soft rubber tubing, about 3 cm long and a piece of glass rod, 1–2 cm long. Attach the rubber tubing to the end of the delivery tube and then attach the glass rod to the other end of the tubing, as shown in the diagram. Make a slit along one side of the rubber tubing, about 1 cm in length.

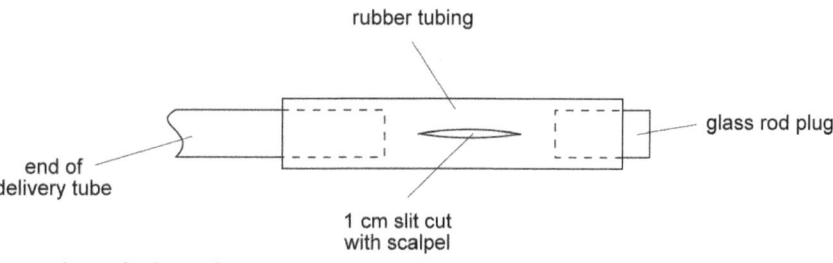

Answers

Page 313

1. The fractional distillation of crude oil produces a high proportion of long-chain hydrocarbons, which are not as useful as short-chain hydrocarbons. Cracking converts the long-chain hydrocarbons into more useful shorter chain hydrocarbons.

2. The conditions required for cracking oil fractions are a temperature of between 600 and 700 °C and a catalyst of silica or alumina.

Developing Practical Skills, page 314

1. The gases must be insoluble in water.

2. Water would otherwise be sucked back into the very hot glass tube, which may shatter and cause injuries.

3. Liquid paraffin is flammable. Care must be taken to make sure the apparatus is assembled securely. The boiling tube could crack while it is being heated. Safety glasses should be worn.
   There is danger of a 'suck-back' when heating is stopped. This can be prevented by removing the delivery tube from the trough of water before stopping the heating.

4. The first test-tube would contain a large volume of air displaced from the apparatus.

5. $C_{14}H_{30}(g) \rightarrow C_{12}H_{26}(g) + C_2H_4(g)$

Topic 11.4: Alkenes

Worksheet C11.4b Cracking liquid paraffin

Liquid paraffin contains long-chain hydrocarbons. These long-chain hydrocarbons can be broken down into shorter chain hydrocarbons by a process known as cracking. Cracking needs a high temperature and a catalyst to give a suitable rate of reaction. In this experiment pieces of pot will act as the catalyst.

Apparatus

pot fragments

Bunsen burner and heatproof mat

stand and clamp, boiling tube, bung and delivery tube with Bunsen valve

mineral wool, tongs, water basin,

test-tubes, two dropping pipettes,

liquid paraffin, aqueous bromine

eye protection (splash-proof goggles)

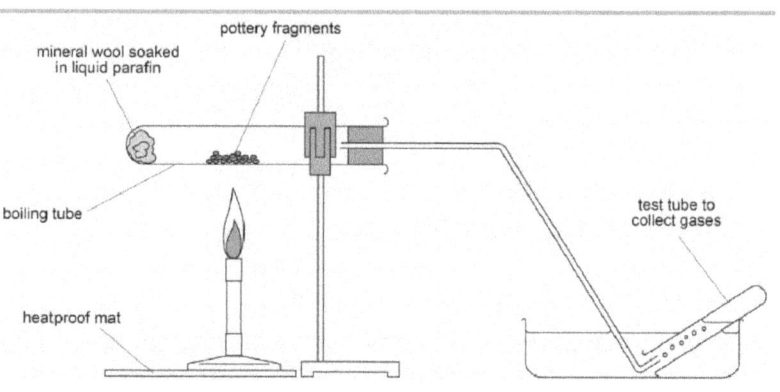

SAFETY INFORMATION
Wear eye protection (splash-proof goggles).

Aqueous bromine (bromine water) is harmful.

Method

1. Put on your eye protection.
2. Put some mineral wool in the bottom of a boiling tube. Using a dropping pipette, add a few drops of liquid paraffin to soak the mineral wool.
3. Clamp the boiling tube horizontally as shown in the diagram and place a pile of pot fragments in the centre of the tube. Then complete the setting up of the apparatus.
4. Fill three or four test-tubes with water and place them in the trough ready to collect the gas.
5. Heat the pot fragments strongly and occasionally heat the mineral wool for a second or two.
6. Collect the gas produced in the test-tubes.
7. When all the test-tubes are full of gas, **remove the delivery tube from the water by raising the apparatus, and then stop heating, to avoid the risk of suck back**.

Evaluating methods

8. Why is the delivery tube removed from the water before heating is stopped?

Page 1 of 2

Topic 11.4: Alkenes

Observing, measuring and recording

9. Test the gas you have produced and record your observations in the table.

Test	Observations
Add a lighted splint	
Add 5 or 6 drops of aqueous bromine	

Handling experimental observations and data

10. What conclusions can you make about the gas you collected in the experiment?

Topic 11.4: Alkenes

Learning episode C11.4c The chemical properties of alkenes

Learning objectives

- Describe the test to distinguish between saturated and unsaturated hydrocarbons by their reaction with aqueous bromine.
- **Supplement** State that in an addition reaction only one product is formed.
- **Supplement** Describe the properties of alkenes in terms of addition reactions with:
  (a) bromine or aqueous bromine
  (b) hydrogen in the presence of a nickel catalyst
  (c) steam in the presence of an acid catalyst.
  and draw the structural or displayed formulae of the products.

Resources

Student Book pages 315–318

Resources for demonstration (see Technician's notes following)

Approach

Revise the combustion of hydrocarbons and the products that are formed by burning hydrocarbons in a plentiful supply of air (carbon dioxide and water) and in a limited supply of air (carbon and carbon monoxide). What observation would suggest that the hydrocarbon was burning in a limited supply of air? (A yellow flame.)

Demonstrate the reaction of an alkene (hexene or cyclohexene) with aqueous bromine (CARE). Students are not allowed to use cyclohexene in the classroom, so this must be a teacher demonstration **(see tech notes)**. The bromine water is decolourised as an addition reaction takes place. Use Fig. 11.17 on page 315 of the Student Book to illustrate the displayed formula of the product of the reaction and the reason for describing the reaction as 'addition'.

Explain that this reaction is used to identify alkenes (or more accurately any unsaturated hydrocarbon, including alkynes, which contain a C≡C triple bond). Tell students that they will have an opportunity to use this identification test later in the course.

Supplement You could illustrate how ethene molecules can join together, as monomers, in an addition reaction to make poly(ethene), a polymer. Emphasise how the polymer has a repeating unit. Explain that this reaction will be studied in detail in Topic 11.7 *Polymers*.

Supplement Explain the addition reactions of ethene with bromine, hydrogen and steam. In each case ask students to write the displayed formula of the product formed.

SAFETY INFORMATION
Wear eye protection (splash-proof goggles).
Aqueous bromine is harmful.
Hexene and cyclohexene are highly flammable.
Ensure that the laboratory is well ventilated.

Technician's notes

Be sure to check the latest safety notes on these resources before proceeding.

The following resources are needed for the demonstration of an alkene reacting with bromine:

an alkene (such as hexene or cyclohexene)
0.005 mol / dm^3 concentration of aqueous bromine
test-tube, droppers, test-tube holder
eye protection (splash-proof goggles)

Answers

Page 316

1. It contains at least one C=C double bond.

2. The manufacture of ethene involves the catalytic cracking of larger alkane molecules at high temperature.

3. Fractional distillation produces fractions containing molecules with high numbers of carbon atoms. These large molecules have limited use. Cracking produces small molecules, including alkenes, which are much more useful. They can be used to manufacture a range of useful products, for example, polymers.

4. Supplement

   [Structural diagrams showing two pentene isomers: pent-1-ene and pent-2-ene]

Science in Context, page 317

A saturated compound only contains carbon to carbon single bonds.

An unsaturated compound contains one or more carbon to carbon double bonds (or triple bonds).

Page 318

1. a) Alkane: C_6H_{14}, alkene C_6H_{12}. The position of the double bond can be between any pair of carbon atoms, but there should be one less hydrogen attached to the double-bonded carbons.

   [Structural diagrams of hexane and hexene showing carbon-hydrogen single covalent bonds, carbon-carbon single covalent bonds, and the carbon=carbon double covalent bond]

   b) Supplement Isomers of hexene

   [Structural diagrams of hex-1-ene, hex-2-ene, and hex-3-ene]

   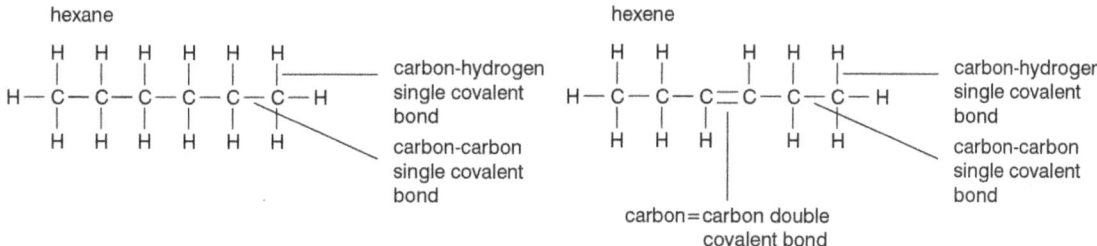

   c) Supplement Hexane undergoes a substitution reaction with bromine (any H can be substituted with Br/can have more than one substitution). HBr is also formed in the reaction. The diagram shows 1-bromohexane.

   [Structural diagram of 1-bromohexane]

Topic 11.4: Alkenes

Hexene undergoes an addition reaction with aqueous bromine (note aqueous bromine loses its colour – this is a test for unsaturation). The bromine will add across the double bond. Example shows addition of bromine to hex-1-ene to form 1,2-dibromohexane.

```
     Br  Br  H   H   H   H
     |   |   |   |   |   |
H —  C — C — C — C — C — C — H
     |   |   |   |   |   |
     H   H   H   H   H   H
```

2. a) Fuels are substances that provide heat energy. Alkanes burn readily in air, combining with oxygen to produce carbon dioxide and water vapour and large quantities of heat.

   b) Incomplete combustion leads to the formation of carbon monoxide instead of carbon dioxide. It is a very poisonous gas and particularly dangerous as it has no odour and causes drowsiness. Carbon monoxide is poisonous because it reacts with the haemoglobin in the blood, forming carboxyhaemoglobin. The haemoglobin is no longer available to carry oxygen to the body and death results from oxygen starvation.

   c) Short-chain hydrocarbons are more likely to form carbon dioxide and water as their main products as there is less carbon per molecule in these hydrocarbons to react with the available oxygen. Longer-chain hydrocarbons often burn with a smoky flame and leave black carbon deposits as there is insufficient oxygen to form carbon dioxide, with the many carbons in the longer chains. Carbon monoxide is also formed.

Topic 11.4: Alkenes

Learning episode C11.4d Consolidation and summary

Learning aims

- Review the learning points of the topic summarised in the end of topic checklist.
- Test understanding of the topic content by answering the end of topic questions.

Resources

Student Book pages 317–321

Approach

Ask students to work with a partner to make a list of key words from this topic. They could then work together to produce a spider diagram showing how the different concepts are linked. They could compare their list with the list of key terms given in the Student Book. Discuss the checklist and ask questions to see how much of the content students are comfortable with.

Students could make flashcards of the key content and then use the flashcards to quiz each other on the information.

Use the Science in Context feature on saturated and unsaturated fats on page 317 of the Student Book to emphasise the importance of recognising this distinction in a healthy diet. The content of these Science in Context features is beyond the syllabus but provides the opportunity to explore the content more deeply.

Ask students to work individually through the end of topic questions in the Student Book without looking at the text. As they work, walk around the classroom observing their answers and questioning them as necessary to find out which questions are causing difficulties.

After a set period, ask students to stop working. Discuss any areas of difficulty you observed as you walked round the class.

Students should complete any unanswered questions for homework, but you should stress that they should answer the questions without looking at the text, so that they can see how much they have remembered.

End of topic questions mark scheme

The marks available for a question can indicate the level of detail you need to provide in your answer.

Question	Correct answer	Marks
1	C	1 mark
2 a)	Carbon dioxide.	1 mark
	Water.	1 mark
2 b)	i) $C_2H_4(g) + 3O_2(g) \rightarrow 2CO_2(g) + 2H_2O(l)$	2 marks
	(1 mark for formulae; 1 mark for balancing)	
	ii) Blue flame.	1 mark
2 c)	i) $C_2H_4(g) + O_2(g) \rightarrow 2C(s) + 2H_2O(l)$	2 marks
	(1 mark for formulae; 1 mark for balancing)	
	ii) Yellow flame.	1 mark
3 a)	Diagrams of butane (left) and but-1-ene (right), e.g.	2 marks

Topic 11.4: Alkenes

Question	Correct answer	Marks
	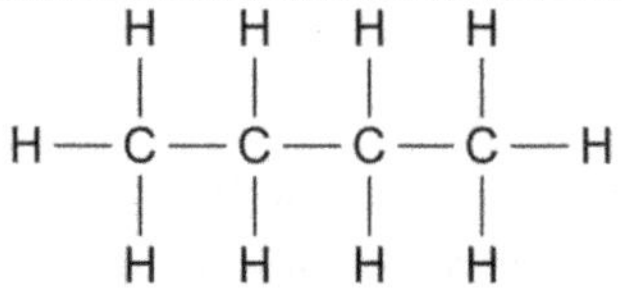 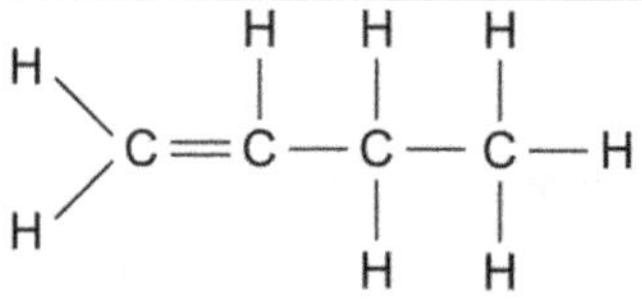 [Structural diagrams: butane (H-C-C-C-C-H with all H) and but-1-ene (H₂C=C-C-C-H with H's)]	
3 b)	Butene (but-1-ene).	1 mark
3 c)	Bromine water.	1 mark
4a	A hydrocarbon is a substance that contains carbon and hydrogen atoms only.	1 mark
4b	A catalyst (silica or alumina).	1 mark
	High temperature.	1 mark
4c	C_8H_{18}	1 mark
4d	The alkane series.	1 mark
4e	Cracking converts the less useful longer chain molecules	1 mark
	into more useful shorter chain molecules.	1 mark
5 a)	Orange.	1 mark
	To colourless/decolourised.	1 mark
5 b)	$C_3H_6(g) + Br_2(aq) \rightarrow C_3H_6Br_2(l)$	2 marks
	(1 mark for formulae; 1 mark for balancing)	
5 c)	An addition reaction.	1 mark
Supplement 6 a)	Unsaturated. It has the general formula of an alkene – a series of unsaturated hydrocarbons (contain C=C double bonds).	1 mark
Supplement 6 b)	Heptene.	1 mark
Supplement 6 c)	Isomers of heptene: diagrams should have seven carbon atoms with a double bond between two carbon atoms as shown below. 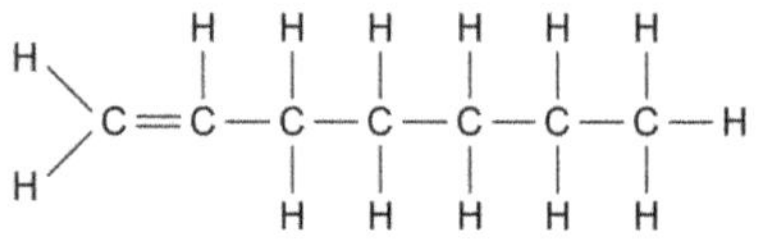 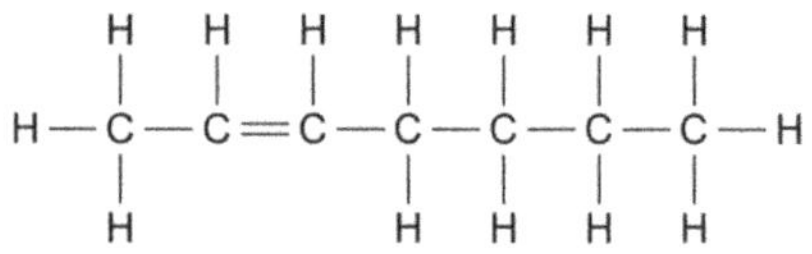 [Two structural diagrams of heptene isomers]	2 marks
Supplement 7 a)	C_8H_{16}	1 mark
Supplement 7 b)	Liquid – pentene with 5 carbon atoms is a liquid so octane is likely to be a liquid.	1 mark
	Total:	31 marks

C11.5 Alcohols

Introduction

This topic introduces alcohols, the third homologous series in the *Organic Chemistry* section, although the focus is almost exclusively on ethanol. It is likely that this topic will come near to the end of the course. It provides an opportunity to revise some of the common features of organic compounds and homologous series.

As with Topic 11.3 *Alkanes* and Topic 11.4 *Alkenes*, covalent bonding in alcohols can be linked back to Topic 2.3 *Molecules and covalent bonds*. However, you may not need to emphasise this link if this topic follows on closely after Topics 11.3 and 11.4.

The use of ethanol as a fuel links to the problems of burning other fuels, such as fossil fuels, covered in Topic 10.1 *Chemistry of the environment* and Topic 11.2 *Fuels*. Topic 11.6 *Carboxylic acids* covers the oxidation of ethanol to form ethanoic acid, both as an often unwanted product of fermentation and in the laboratory by the use of acidified potassium manganate(VII). Topic 11.6 also covers the formation of esters by the reaction between an alcohol and a carboxylic acid.

The topic builds on the concept of a homologous series. It compares the manufacture of ethanol by fermentation, including the use of fractional distillation to separate the ethanol from water, with that from ethene and steam. The merits and problems of using ethanol as a fuel are considered, along with its use as a solvent.

Links to other topics

Section	Essential background knowledge	Useful links
2 Atoms, elements and compounds	2.1 Atoms, elements and compounds 2.3 Molecules and covalent bonds	
10 Chemistry of the environment	10.1 Chemistry of the environment	
11 Organic chemistry	11.2 Fuels 11.3 Alkanes 11.4 Alkenes	11.6 Carboxylic acids

Topic overview

C11.5a	Orientation
	This short learning episode revises the concept of a homologous series and introduces the general formula for the alcohol series. The focus quickly centres on ethanol, often referred to simply as 'alcohol', and some of its important uses.
C11.5b	The manufacture of ethanol
	This learning episode is in three parts. The first part involves the manufacture of ethanol by fermentation and the use of fractional distillation to separate ethanol from water. The second part considers the manufacture of ethanol from ethene, obtained from crude oil.
	The Developing Practical Skills box feature on page 326 of the Student Book could be used here to consolidate understanding of fermentation, or it could be used as revision in learning episode C11.5d at the end of the topic.
	Supplement Finally, the two methods for manufacturing ethanol are compared, along with the factors that might determine the preferred method of manufacture.

Topic 11.5: Alcohols

C11.5c	**Reactions of ethanol**
	Initially the learning episode focuses on the combustion of ethanol and its use as a fuel for motor cars. The Science in Context feature on page 328 of the Student Book is used to stimulate discussion of the issues arising from using the fermentation of sugar to generate a fuel.
C11.5d	**Consolidation and summary**
	This learning episode recaps on the key ideas encountered in the topic. Time may be allocated to answering the end of topic questions in the Student Book. The Developing Practical Skills section could be used for revision if not already used in learning episode C11.5b.

Career links

These are some scientific careers that focus on this area of chemistry but careers in many other fields use the knowledge and skills gained studying science.

Ethanol engineers work with the management teams to develop the most efficient process for manufacturing ethanol.

Chemists working in the biofuels industry work to make more efficient fuels such as ethanol produced from sugar cane.

Topic 11.5: Alcohols

Learning episode C11.5a Orientation

Learning objectives

- Write and interpret general formulae of compounds in the same homologous series, (c) alcohols, $C_nH_{2n+1}OH$
- Name and draw the displayed formula of ethanol.
- State the type of compound present, given a chemical name ending in –ol or from a molecular formula or displayed formula.
- **Supplement** Name and draw the structural and displayed formulae of unbranched alcohols, including propan-1-ol, protan-2-ol, butan-1-ol and butan-2-ol, containing up to four carbon atoms per molecule.
- State the uses of ethanol as:
  (a) a solvent
  (b) a fuel.

Common misconceptions

Some students think that there is only one alcohol, that it is a single substance and not the name of a homologous series.

Resources

Student Book pages 322–324

Approach

Introduce alcohols as the third homologous series covered in the course. Look at the displayed formula for ethanol and, if necessary, revise the nature of the covalent bonding in the molecule.

Use page 324 of the Student Book to consider the common uses of ethanol. Compare the burning of ethanol with some of the fossil fuels. Ask students why ethanol is an attractive fuel for use in motor cars.

Supplement Provide the general formula for an alcohol and ask students to work out the molecular formula and then draw the displayed and structural formula of the first four alcohols of the series.

Demonstrate that propanol and butanol have structural isomers by asking students to draw different structures for the two alcohols.

Answers

Page 324

1. C_4H_9OH

2. It is a relatively 'clean' fuel, releasing carbon dioxide and water into the atmosphere. It does not release sulfur dioxide and nitrogen oxides which are the main causes of acid rain, as petrol does when it burns. Increasingly, however, the production of carbon dioxide and its impact on global warming is becoming a very big issue. It is a renewable fuel as it can be made from plant material.

3. A solvent is a liquid that dissolves other substances (solutes) to form solutions.

Topic 11.5: Alcohols

Learning episode C11.5b The manufacture of ethanol

Learning objectives

- Describe the manufacture of ethanol by:
  (a) fermentation of glucose solution at 25–35 °C in the presence of yeast and in the absence of oxygen
  (b) catalytic addition of steam to ethene at 300 °C and 6000 kPa / 60 atm in the presence of an acid catalyst.
- Supplement Describe the advantages and disadvantages of the manufacture of ethanol by:
  (a) fermentation
  (b) catalytic addition of steam to ethene.

Common misconceptions

Some students think that the ethanol produced by fermentation is different than that produced from ethene.

Resources

Student Book pages 324–327

Resources for demonstration (see Technician's notes, following)

Approach

The learning episode conveniently splits into three parts:

1. Fermentation demonstration

Set up a demonstration of the fermentation method for making ethanol from sugar, using apparatus similar to that shown in the Developing Practical Skills box on page 326 of the Student Book **(see tech notes)**.

Alongside this, demonstrate how fractional distillation can be used to separate the ethanol from water after fermentation is complete. Use apparatus similar to that shown on page 325 of the Student Book and emphasise that the collected product can be determined from the temperature of the thermometer at the top of the column (ethanol has a boiling point of 78 °C) **(see tech notes)**.

The ethanol can be identified by burning a small quantity on a borosilicate watch glass or in a crucible. This should be a demonstration only **(see tech notes)**.

SAFETY INFORMATION
Wear eye protection (splash-proof goggles).
Ethanol is extremely flammable.
The ethanol must not be consumed or taken home.
Ensure that the laboratory is well ventilated.

You could use Developing Practical Skills on page 326 to consolidate understanding of the fermentation process. Alternatively, you might use it as a revision task at the end of the topic.

2. Manufacture of ethanol

Use page 327 of the Student Book to illustrate the conditions required to make ethanol from ethene (which is obtained by cracking fractions obtained from crude oil). Remind students that this is an example of an addition reaction, which they encountered in Topic 11.4 *Alkenes*.

Emphasise that the extreme conditions required (300 °C and 60 atmospheres pressure) mean that the production costs are relatively high.

Topic 11.5: Alcohols

Supplement 3. Which method of manufacture?

Use the table on page 327 of the Student Book to stimulate a discussion about the factors that determine which method of ethanol manufacture is chosen. (The use of sugar as a renewable source is also considered in the next learning episode in the context of: 'Is this the best way of using a foodstuff such as sugar?')

Technician's notes

Be sure to check the latest safety notes on these resources before proceeding.

The following resources are needed for the demonstration of fermentation:

simple fermentation apparatus:
conical flask, water-bath, bung and delivery tube, test-tube (page 326 in Student Book)
sugar (glucose), yeast, limewater. Limewater is a moderate hazard.
fractional distillation apparatus:
Bunsen burner and heatproof mat, clamps and stands, circular flask, fractionating column containing glass beads (or specially designed), condenser and tubes (page 325 in Student Book)
ethanol
anti-bumping granules
eye protection (splash-proof goggles)

Answers

Page 326

1. Fermentation is the process in which ethanol is made from sugar, yeast and water.
2. The optimum temperature is in the range 25 °C to 35 °C.
3. The yeast contains enzymes that increase the rate of the reaction.
4. The fractional distillation will separate the ethanol from the water present.

Developing Practical Skills, page 326

1. Use a thermostatically controlled heater in the water-bath or leave the apparatus near to a heater to maintain the temperature within the range needed or heat gently with a Bunsen burner or add hot water to maintain temperature.
2. To show that gas was being produced (by the bubbles) and to identify the gas as carbon dioxide (turns the limewater cloudy).
3. Frothing in the flask/bubbles in the limewater/limewater turning milky/turning cloudy/a white precipitate forms (all of these three descriptions are correct so any are acceptable).
4. No more bubbles through the limewater.
5. Ethanol. The boiling point of ethanol is 78 °C, which is below that of water (100 °C).

Topic 11.5: Alcohols

Learning episode C11.5c Reactions of ethanol

Learning objectives

- Describe the combustion of ethanol.
  - (a) State the uses of ethanol as: a solvent, a fuel.
  - (a) Supplement Describe the advantages and disadvantages of the manufacture of ethanol by: fermentation, catalytic addition of steam to ethene.

Resources

Student Book page 328

Resources for demonstration (see Technician's notes, below)

Worksheet C11.5c

Approach

Students may be familiar with the use of ethanol in spirit burners. If not, you can demonstrate this use.

Recap the combustion of hydrocarbons and ask students what products they would expect to be formed when ethanol is burned in a plentiful supply of air. Ask what colour flame they would expect to see.

Then consider the burning of ethanol in a limited supply of air. What would be the colour of the flame in this context? Ask students to write word and chemical equations for these reactions.

Use the Science in Context feature on page 328 of the Student Book to support a discussion of the issues associated with using ethanol obtained by fermentation as a fuel. The content of these Science in Context features is beyond the syllabus but provides the opportunity to explore the content more deeply.

SAFETY INFORMATION
Extreme care is needed with spirit burners
Check that the lid on the spirit burner is secured and that the wick is not loose.
Fill the spirit burner or fill the extra space with cotton wool.
Spirit burners should be for dedicated use with a specific alcohol only.
Wear eye protection (splash-proof goggles).

Technician's notes

Be sure to check the latest safety notes on these resources before proceeding.

The following resources are needed for the demonstration of burning ethanol:

spirit burner containing ethanol

Answers

Science in Context, page 328

Issues to discuss include:

- Sugar cane can be used to produce sugar as a foodstuff.
- Using land to produce fuel rather than food will have a negative impact on food production.
- Reduction in forests to create land suitable for growing will reduce the amount of carbon dioxide removed from the atmosphere by photosynthesis.

Topic 11.5: Alcohols

Worksheet C11.5c Comparing the amount of energy produced when alcohols burn

You are provided with samples of three alcohols: ethanol, propan-1-ol and butan-1-ol. Your task is to plan an experiment to compare the amount of energy produced when these alcohols burn in air. As a measure of the energy produced you can use:

the temperature rise of a fixed volume of water per gram of alcohol burnt

Your plan should:

a) Show how to safely use techniques, apparatus and materials.
b) Show in detail the procedure you would use.
c) Show how you would record your observations and measurements.
d) Show how you would use your results to calculate the temperature rise of the water per gram of alcohol burnt (H = 1, C = 12, O = 16).
e) List the possible sources of errors in your method.

Topic 11.5: Alcohols

Learning episode C11.5d Consolidation and summary

Learning aims

- Review the learning points of the topic summarised in the end of topic checklist.
- Test understanding of the topic content by answering the end of topic questions.

Resources

Student Book pages 329–331

Approach

You could use the Developing Practical Skills feature on fermentation (Student Book 326) to revise the ideas encountered in learning episode C11.5b, if you did not use it in that learning episode.

Ask students to work with a partner to make a list of key words from this topic. They could then work together to produce a spider diagram showing how the different concepts are linked. They could compare their list with the list of key terms given in the Student Book. Discuss the checklist and ask questions to see how much of the content students are comfortable with.

Students could make flashcards of the key content and then use the flashcards to quiz each other on the information.

Ask students to work individually through the end of topic questions in the Student Book without looking at the text. As they work, walk around the classroom observing their answers and questioning them as necessary to find out which questions are causing difficulties.

After a set period, ask students to stop working. Discuss any areas of difficulty you observed as you walked round the class.

Students should complete any unanswered questions for homework, but you should stress that they should answer the questions without looking at the text, so that they can see how much they have remembered.

Topic 11.5: Alcohols

End of topic questions mark scheme

The marks available for a question can indicate the level of detail you need to provide in your answer.

Question	Correct answer	Marks
1	D	1 mark
2	$C_nH_{2n+1}OH$	1 mark
3	Sugar cane.	1 mark
	Sugar beet.	1 mark
4 a)	Enzymes present in the yeast speed up the fermentation process.	1 mark
	Enzymes are denatured at temperatures above about 35 °C.	1 mark
4 b)	Fermentation is an anaerobic process and takes place in the absence of oxygen.	1 mark
	If oxygen were present the ethanol would be oxidised (to ethanoic acid).	1 mark
5 a)	Ethene is obtained from crude oil.	1 mark
5 b)	The phosphoric acid is a catalyst.	1 mark
5 c)	Temperature 300 °C.	1 mark
	Pressure 6000 kPa	1 mark
5 d)	$C_2H_4(g) + H_2O(g) \rightarrow C_2H_5OH(g)$	1 mark
Supplement 6 a)	Fermentation uses renewable resources/ethanol has suitable flavour for alcoholic drinks.	1 mark
Supplement 6 b)	The method involving ethene is a much faster process than fermentation.	1 mark
Supplement 7 a)	$C_5H_{11}OH$	1 mark
Supplement 7 b)	Pentanol:	1 mark
Supplement 7 c)	i) A structural isomer is a molecule with the same molecular formula as another molecule but a different structural formula.	1 mark
	ii) Pentan-3-ol:	1 mark
	Total:	19 marks

C11.6 Carboxylic acids

Introduction

This topic introduces the carboxylic acids, the last homologous series in the *Organic Chemistry* section, although the focus is almost exclusively on ethanoic acid. This topic is likely to come near to the end of the course. It provides an opportunity to revise some of the common features of organic compounds and homologous series. Most of the topic is intended for students following the supplement syllabus.

Covalent bonding in acids can be linked back to Topic 2.3 *Molecules and covalent bonds*, although you may not need to emphasise this link if this topic follows on closely after Topic 11.5 *Alcohols*. Students will have studied the concept of a weak acid in Topic 7.1 *Acids, bases and salts*. There are links to Topic 11.5 *Alcohols* with the reaction to produce esters and with Topic 11.7 *Polymers* in the preparation of condensation polymers such as nylon (a polyamide) and terylene (a polyester). The oxidation of ethanol using potassium manganate(VII) provides a link to Topic 6.3 *Redox reactions* and changes of oxidation numbers.

The topic looks at the formation of ethanoic acid from the oxidation of ethanol via two processes: as an (often unwanted) product of fermentation, and in the laboratory by the oxidation of ethanol using acidified aqueous potassium manganate(VII). The properties of ethanoic acid are limited to those general properties of an acid, its nature as a typical weak acid and its reaction with alcohols to form esters.

Links to other topics

Section	Essential background knowledge	Useful links
2 Atoms, elements and compounds	2.1 Atoms, elements and compounds 2.3 Molecules and covalent bonds	
6 Chemical reactions	6.3 Redox reactions	
7 Acids, bases and salts	7.1 Acids, bases and salts	
11 Organic chemistry	11.3 Alkanes 11.5 Alcohols	11.7 Polymers

Topic overview

C11.6a	Orientation
	This short learning episode revises the concept of a homologous series and introduces the general formula for the acid series. The focus quickly centres on ethanoic acid, which is recognisable in dilute solution as vinegar.
C11.6b	Supplement The formation of ethanoic acid
	This is a short learning episode and relates to the formation of ethanoic acid by the oxidation of ethanol • By bacterial oxidation during vinegar production • using acidified aqueous potassium manganate(VII) solution.

Topic 11.6: Carboxylic acids

C11.6c	**The properties of ethanoic acid**
	The learning episode is in two parts.
	Part 1 allows a revision of the typical reactions of an acid, e.g. the reactions with metals, bases and carbonates and the formation of salts.
	Supplement The concept of a weak acid is then introduced, as an acid that only partially dissociates into ions in aqueous solution.
	Supplement Part 2 involves the preparation of esters to illustrate the range of smells used in flavourings and perfumes. Given the dangers of concentrated sulfuric acid it is recommended that the preparation of different esters is demonstrated rather than offered as a class practical.
C11.6d	**Consolidation and summary**
	This learning episode recaps on the key ideas encountered in the topic. Time may be allocated to answering the end of topic questions in the Student Book.

Career links

These are some scientific careers that focus on this area of chemistry but careers in many other fields use the knowledge and skills gained studying science.

Food scientists work to improve the preservation and taste of food through the addition of flavourings such as carboxylic acids and esters.

The uses of carboxylic acids and esters are also studied by scientists in the pharmaceutical and medical industries.

Topic 11.6: Carboxylic acids

Learning episode C11.6a Orientation

Learning objectives

- Write and interpret general formulae of compounds in the same homologous series, (d) $C_nH_{2n+1}COOH$.
- Name and draw the displayed formula of ethanoic acid.
- State the type of compound present, given a chemical name ending in –oic acid or from a molecular formula or displayed formula.
- Supplement Name and draw the structural and displayed formulae of unbranched carboxylic acids, containing up to four carbon atoms per molecule.

Resources

Student Book pages 332–333

Approach

This is a very short learning episode.

Introduce acids as the fourth homologous series covered in the course. Look at the displayed formula of methanoic acid and, if necessary, revise the nature of the covalent bonding in the molecule. Emphasise that the second member of the homologous series is ethanoic acid, which in dilute solution is vinegar (old name acetic acid). Give students the general formula and ask them to work out the molecular formula.

Supplement Then draw the structural and displayed formulae of the next two acids in the series, propanoic acid and butanoic acid. Use molecular models to illustrate the functional group of the acids.

Topic 11.6: Carboxylic acids

Supplement Learning episode C11.6b The formation of ethanoic acid

Learning objective

- Supplement Describe the formation of ethanoic acid by the oxidation of ethanol:
  (a) with acidified aqueous potassium manganate(VII)
  (b) by bacterial oxidation during vinegar production.

Resources

Student Book page 333

Approach

This learning episode is very short.

Refer to the process of fermentation encountered in Topic 11.5 *Alcohols*. Ask students what conditions are necessary for fermentation.

Ask what the term 'anaerobic' means. Explain that if oxygen or air comes in contact with the fermenting mixture as part of the fermentation process, yeast can catalyse the oxidation of the ethanol into ethanoic acid.

Explain that in the laboratory ethanoic acid can be made by oxidising ethanol with acidified aqueous potassium manganate(VII) solution. Students will have encountered potassium manganate(VII) in Topic 6.3 *Redox reactions*.

Ask students what the manganate(VII) ion is reduced to when it behaves as an oxidising agent (Mn^{2+}). Then ask them to work out the oxidation numbers of manganese in the two compounds. Ask students to explain the redox reaction in terms of changes in oxidation numbers of the manganese.

Note: It is probably not worth demonstrating this reaction, because refluxing will be required to produce a significant yield of ethanoic acid.

Topic 11.6: Carboxylic acids

Learning episode C11.6c The properties of ethanoic acid

Learning objectives

- Describe the reaction of ethanoic acid with:
  a) metals
  b) bases
  c) carbonates
  including names and formulae of the salts produced..
- Supplement Describe the reaction of a carboxylic acid with an alcohol using an acid catalyst to form an ester.
- Supplement Name and draw the displayed formulae of the unbranched esters which can be made from unbranched alcohols and carboxylic acids, each containing up to four carbon atoms.

Resources

Student Book pages 333–334

Resources for demonstration (see Technician's notes, following)

Approach

This learning episode is in two parts:

Part 1

Ask students to list the typical reactions of an acid – the Student Book gives the reaction of the acid with magnesium, copper(II) oxide and sodium carbonate. Concentrate on what would be observed in these reactions and refer to the formula of the ethanoate ion (compare it with the NO_3^- ion formed when nitric acid forms a salt with sodium carbonate).

Supplement Revise the definition of a weak acid. Ask students which hydrogen atom in the ethanoic molecule they think dissociates.

Look at the equation on page 334 of the Student Book showing the partial ionisation of ethanoic acid.

Supplement Part 2

This part involves demonstrating the formation of a number of esters, which are produced when a carboxylic acid reacts with an alcohol in the presence of concentrated sulfuric acid as a catalyst. Explain that esters are commonly used in flavourings and perfumes.

This practical lends itself to teacher demonstration **(see tech notes)**. The method is as follows:

1. Wear eye protection and chemical protective gloves.

2. Place 1 cm^3 of ethanol and 1 cm^3 of ethanoic acid in a boiling tube. Carefully add a few drops of concentrated sulfuric acid.

3. Place the boiling tube in a hot water-bath (at about 80 °C) for about 5 minutes.

4. Carefully pour the contents of the boiling tube into cold water in a beaker.

5. Carefully smell the beaker of water – the ester should be floating on the surface of the water.

6. Repeat the method with the combinations of alcohols and acids shown in the table.

Alcohol	Acid	Ester (smell)
Ethanol	Ethanoic acid	Ethyl ethanoate (glue)
Pentanol	Ethanoic acid	Pentyl ethanoate (pears)
Octanol	Ethanoic acid	Octyl ethanoate (bananas)
Methanol	Salicylic acid (3 g)	Methyl salicylate (oil of wintergreen)

Topic 11.6: Carboxylic acids

The students do not need to know the names of all these esters but the demonstration should illustrate the range of esters they encounter in everyday life.

SAFETY INFORMATION
Wear eye protection (splash-proof goggles).
Ethanol is extremely flammable; ethanoic acid is an irritant and concentrated sulfuric acid is corrosive.
Salicylic acid can cause burns on the skin.
Wear chemical protective gloves.
Ensure that the laboratory is well ventilated.

Technician's notes

Be sure to check the latest safety notes on these resources before proceeding.

The following resources are needed for the demonstration of the formation of esters:

eye protection (splash-proof goggles) and chemical protective gloves.
concentrated sulfuric acid
methanol, ethanol, pentanol, octanol
2 mol / dm^3 ethanoic acid
salicylic acid and spatula
boiling tubes
water-bath or large beaker
0–100 °C thermometer
10 cm^3 measuring cylinders
access to a kettle
dropper

Topic 11.6: Carboxylic acids

Learning episode C11.6d Consolidation and summary

Learning aims

- Review the learning points of the topic summarised in the end of topic checklist.
- Test understanding of the topic content by answering the end of topic questions.

Resources

Student Book pages 335–336

Approach

Revise the functional groups of carboxylic acids and esters. Students will need to know these in Topic 11.7 *Polymers* when they study condensation polymerisation to produce nylon (an amide made from an acid) and terylene (a polyester).

Ask students to work with a partner to make a list of key words from this topic. They could then work together to produce a spider diagram showing how the different concepts are linked. They could compare their list with the list of key terms given in the Student Book. Discuss the checklist and ask questions to see how much of the content students are comfortable with.

Students could make flashcards of the key content and then use the flashcards to quiz each other on the information.

Ask students to work individually through the end of topic questions in the Student Book without looking at the text. As they work, walk around the classroom observing their answers and questioning them as necessary to find out which questions are causing difficulties.

After a set period, ask students to stop working. Discuss any areas of difficulty you observed as you walked round the class.

Students should complete any unanswered questions for homework, but you should stress that they should answer the questions without looking at the text, so that they can see how much they have remembered.

Topic 11.6: Carboxylic acids

End of topic questions mark scheme

The marks available for a question can indicate the level of detail you need to provide in your answer.

Question	Correct answer	Marks
1	C	1 mark
2	The functional group in an acid is –COOH.	1 mark
3 a)	Propanoic acid.	1 mark
Supplement 3 b)	Structural formula of propanoic acid: H-C(H)(H)-C(H)(H)-C(=O)-O-H	1 mark
4 a)	Effervescence/bubbling.	1 mark
	Sodium carbonate disappears/powder reduces in quantity.	1 mark
	Colourless solution remains.	1 mark
4 b)	$2CH_3COOH(aq) + Na_2CO_3(s) \rightarrow 2CH_3COONa(aq) + H_2O(l) + CO_2(g)$.	2 marks
	(1 mark for correct formulae; 1 mark for balancing)	
Supplement 5	In the presence of air/oxygen	1 mark
	ethanol is oxidised to ethanoic acid.	1 mark
Supplement 6	Acidified	1 mark
	potassium manganate(VII).	1 mark
Supplement 7	It is only partially ionised in water.	1 mark
	$CH_3COOH(aq) \rightleftharpoons CH_3COO^-(aq) + H^+(aq)$	1 mark
	Total:	15 marks

C11.7 Polymers

Introduction

This topic is mainly required for the supplementary syllabus. It is likely to come very close to the end of the course and to be the last topic studied in the *Organic Chemistry* section.

As with all the organic chemistry topics, this topic builds on knowledge of covalent bonding covered in Topic 2.3 *Molecules and covalent bonds*. In addition, there are links to Topic 11.4 *Alkenes* in relation to addition polymerisation, to Topic 11.5 *Alcohols* in relation to the formation of natural and synthetic polymers and fermentation and to Topic 11.6 *Carboxylic acids* in relation to condensation polymerisation and the structure of natural polymers.

The topic starts with a recap on the functional groups and characteristic properties of alkenes, alcohols and carboxylic acids. After this revision, the topic focuses on addition polymerisation and condensation polymerisation. The differences between the two processes are emphasised. There are opportunities to consider some of the environmental aspects of the manufacture and use of synthetic polymers, particularly recycling and disposal. Proteins as natural polymers are then considered.

There are few opportunities for students to develop their investigative skills.

Links to other topics

Section	Essential background knowledge	Useful links
2 Atoms, elements and compounds	2.3 Molecules and covalent bonds	
11 Organic chemistry	11.4 Alkenes	
	11.5 Alcohols	
	11.6 Carboxylic acids	

Topic overview

C11.7a	**Orientation**
	This learning episode provides an opportunity to revise the organic chemistry of alkenes, alcohols and carboxylic acids, focusing on the functional groups and characteristic reactions. The terms 'monomer', 'polymer' and 'polymerisation' are introduced.
C11.7b	**Synthetic polymers**
	This learning episode is in three parts.
	Part 1 Addition polymerisation
	This part focuses on how single alkene monomers, or substituted alkene monomers, can combine to form addition polymer molecules. It emphasises how the monomers combine to form the repeating unit of polymers. The reverse process identifies the monomer molecule from the structural formula of the polymer. Examples are given of common addition polymers and their uses. A possible practical activity is included on the identification of addition polymers.
	Supplement Deducing the structure of the repeat unit in an addition polymer is a supplementary activity.
	Supplement **Part 2 Condensation polymerisation**
	This part introduces condensation polymerisation as a contrast to addition polymerisation. Some detail is provided of the structures of the monomers and the repeating units in the polymers. Emphasis is also placed on the formation of a small molecule (often water)

Topic 11.7: Polymers

	when two different monomer molecules combine.
	Part 3 The problems of plastics
	Using the Science in Context feature in the Student Book provides a focus for discussion of the problems posed by the non-biodegradability of many synthetic polymers.
C11.7c	Supplement **Proteins**
	Proteins are introduced as a natural polyamide. Consideration is given to how amino acids link together to form the protein.
C11.7d	**Consolidation and summary**
	This learning episode is an opportunity to recap on the key ideas of the topic. Time can be allocated to studying the end of topic checklist and then answering the end of topic questions in the Student Book.

Career links

These are some scientific careers that focus on this area of chemistry but careers in many other fields use the knowledge and skills gained studying science.

Plastics engineers research ways in which plastics can be made to be more biodegradable as well as the best ways to recycle them.

Evolutionary biologists study proteins to try and better understand the beginnings of life on earth.

Topic 11.7: Polymers

Learning episode C11.7a Orientation

Learning objective

- Define polymers as large molecules built up from many smaller molecules called monomers.

Resources

Student Book pages 337–338

Approach

Ask students to write the general formula for an alkene, an alcohol and a carboxylic acid. In each case ask them to identify the functional group. Ask students to draw the structural formulae of the first three members of the alkene, alcohol and carboxylic acid series. Check that they can remember the names of the compounds that they have drawn.

Introduce the terms 'monomer', 'polymer' and 'polymerisation'. Explain that the topic will consider some synthetic polymers, together with polymers that are often referred to as plastics, and proteins as natural polymers. Ask students, in groups, to make a list of as many things as they know about polymers – allow only a few minutes to do this. Review the lists. Disposal of plastics and recycling will be common emerging themes.

Explain that the topic focuses on two different ways of making synthetic polymers. The first method involves alkenes and makes use of their reactivity and ability to undergo addition reactions. The second method involves a very different type of reaction. The disposal and recycling of plastics will also be considered.

Students who study biology may already know something about proteins. Challenge students, working in pairs, to write down four things that they know about proteins. Again, review the lists.

Topic 11.7: Polymers

Learning episode C11.7b Synthetic polymers

Learning objectives

- Describe the formation of poly(ethene) as an example of addition polymerisation using ethene monomers.
- State that plastics are made from polymers.
- Describe how the properties of plastics have implications for their disposal.
- Describe the environmental challenges caused by plastics, limited to:
  (a) disposal in land fill sites
  (b) accumulation in oceans
  (c) formation of toxic gases from burning.
- Supplement Identify the repeat units and/or linkages in addition polymers and in condensation polymers
- Supplement Deduce the structure or repeat unit of an addition polymer from a given alkene and vice versa
- Supplement Deduce the structure or repeat unit of a condensation polymer from given monomers and vice versa, limited to:
  (a) polyamides from a dicarboxylic acid and a diamine
  (b) polyesters from a dicarboxylic acid and a diol.
- Supplement Describe the differences between addition and condensation polymerisation
- Supplement Describe and draw the structure of:
  (a) nylon, a polyamide

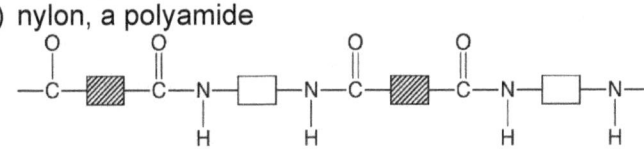

  (b) PET, a polyester

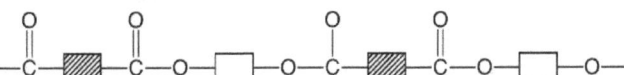

  The full name for PET, polyethylene terephthalate, is **not** required.
- Supplement State that PET can be converted back into monomers and re-polymerised

Resources

Student Book pages 338–342

Worksheet C11.7b Identifying addition polymers

Resources for a class practical (see Technician's notes, following)

Approach

Part 1 Addition polymerisation

Introduce the definition of an addition polymer. Use structural formulae to illustrate how alkene molecules can undergo addition reactions to form a polymer chain. Show how substituted alkenes such as chloroethene can similarly form addition polymers.

Use page 339 of the Student Book to show some of the addition polymers in common use. Consider the uses of the common addition polymers.

Supplement Let students practise deducing the repeating unit of an addition polymer from the structure of the monomer and then the reverse – that is, working out the structure of the monomer from the structural formula of part of an addition polymer.

Topic 11.7: Polymers

Use worksheet C11.7b to support a class practical activity in which students identify three different samples of addition polymers or plastics, essentially by working out the approximate density of the plastic sample.

SAFETY INFORMATION
Wear eye protection (splash-proof goggles).
Ethanol is extremely flammable.
Solutions of potassium carbonate are irritants.

Supplement Part 2 Condensation polymerisation

You may take a simple approach to condensation polymerisation. The structural formulae of the monomer molecules are complicated, sometimes involving functional groups that are beyond the scope of this course. Simple 'block' representations can be used for the two different monomers involved in the condensation process, as shown in the Student Book.

Demonstrate the nylon 'rope trick' to show how nylon can be made from two monomers – referred to simply as monomer A and monomer B. Explain that the term 'condensation' results from the fact that water is often formed when the two monomers combine together. Contrast this with addition polymerisation, where the only product is the polymer.

SAFETY INFORMATION
Decanedioyl dichloride is corrosive and hydrolysed by water forming hydrogen chloride gas.
Cyclohexane is highly flammable.
Wear eye protection (splash-proof goggles).

Part 3 The problems of plastics

Rehearse some of the familiar problems of using plastics, both in terms of their disposal and recycling. Emphasise and explain the non-biodegradability of many addition polymers.

Refer to the 'three Rs' (Reduce, Reuse, Recycle) and ask the students how these three Rs are being used, or could be used more effectively, to prevent waste.

Use the Science in Context section *The Challenges of Recycling Plastics*, on page 342 of the Student Book to explain that recycling is complicated, not just because different plastic materials need to be separated but also because some plastic materials cannot be melted down and recycled (thermosetting plastics). The content of these Science in Context features is beyond the syllabus but provides the opportunity to explore the content more deeply.

Technician's notes

Be sure to check the latest safety notes on these resources before proceeding.

The following resources for the class practical C11.7b, per group:

liquid 1 (ethanol)
liquid 2 (596 cm^3 ethanol + 439 cm^3 distilled water)
liquid 3 (448 cm^3 ethanol + 586 cm^3 distilled water)
liquid 4 (distilled water)
liquid 5 (184 g potassium carbonate dissolved in 965 cm^3 distilled water)
liquid 6 (513 g potassium carbonate dissolved in 866 cm^3 distilled water)
scissors, boiling tubes, boiling tube racks, glass stirring rod

Topic 11.7: Polymers

| plastic samples labelled A, B and C |
| eye protection (splash-proof goggles) |

The following resources for the demonstration of condensation polymerisation:

| solution A (2.2 g 1,6-diaminohexane in 50 cm^3 distilled water) |
| solution B (1.5 g decanedioyl chloride (sebacoyl chloride) in 50 cm^3 cyclohexane) |
| 50 cm^3 beaker, tweezers |
| eye protection (splash-proof goggles) (goggles or face shield) |

Answers

Page 340

1. The individual beads are like monomer molecules. The string of beads is like a polymer made by joining together many of these monomers.

2. Poly(ethene)/polythene is used to make plastic bags.

3. a) Supplement

   $$\begin{array}{c} H \quad Cl \\ \diagdown \diagup \\ C=C \\ \diagup \diagdown \\ H \quad H \end{array} + \begin{array}{c} H \quad Cl \\ \diagdown \diagup \\ C=C \\ \diagup \diagdown \\ H \quad H \end{array} \longrightarrow \begin{array}{c} H \quad Cl \quad H \quad Cl \\ | \quad | \quad | \quad | \\ -C-C-C-C- \\ | \quad | \quad | \quad | \\ H \quad H \quad H \quad H \end{array}$$

   b)

   $$\begin{array}{c} H \quad Cl \\ | \quad | \\ -C-C- \\ | \quad | \\ H \quad H \end{array}$$

4. Supplement Poly(chloroethene) is an addition polymer.

Supplement Page 341

1. Nylon is made from two monomers and a small molecule is eliminated when the two monomers combine. An addition polymer has only one monomer.

2. To produce a polymer chain the monomers need to be able to join together at both ends of the molecules.

Science in Context, page 342

Issues related to biodegradable plastics include:
- Advantages: reduced long-term environmental effects; could use specific landfill sites so they could be constantly re-used.
- Disadvantages: the relatively long timescale for decomposition; problems of plastic particles in the sea; the production of methane.
- Reducing the use of all plastics could be the best solution.

Topic 11.7: Polymers

Worksheet C11.7b Identifying addition polymers

There are many addition polymers in everyday use, as the table below shows:

Polymer	Alternative name	Density / g/cm^3	Common use
Expanded poly(phenylethene)	Expanded polystyrene	0.02–0.06	burger box
Poly(propene)	Polypropylene	0.89–0.91	soft cheese tub
Low density poly(ethene)	Low density polythene (LDPE)	0.91–0.93	branded lemon juice container
High density poly(ethene)	High density polythene (HDPE)	0.94–0.96	fabric conditioner bottle
Poly(phenylethene)	Polystyrene	1.04–1.11	yoghurt pot
Poly(chloroethene)	Polyvinylchloride (PVC)	1.20–1.55	guttering on a house

You are going to use a 'float' test to help identify 3 unknown samples of addition polymers or plastics.

Apparatus

scissors

boiling tubes, boiling tube rack, glass rod

samples of plastic A, B and C

liquids labelled 1, 2, 3, 4, 5 and 6

> **SAFETY INFORMATION**
> *Wear eye protection (splash-proof goggles).*
> *Liquids 1, 2 and 3 are highly flammable.*
> *Liquids 5 and 6 are irritants.*
> *Ensure that there are no naked flames.*

Method

1. Put on your eye protection.
2. Pour 20 cm^3 of each of the liquids 1–6 into a separate boiling tube.
3. Cut out samples of the plastics A, B and C into 4 mm × 4 mm squares. Add a sample of A to each of the liquids. Push the sample with the stirring rod to see whether it sinks or floats.
4. Repeat the procedure with samples B and C. Record your results in the table below.

Topic 11.7: Polymers

Observing, measuring and recording

Liquid	Density / g/cm³	Observations on adding plastic (✓ = floats; x = sinks)		
		A	B	C
1	0.79			
2	0.91			
3	0.94			
4	1.00			
5	1.15			
6	1.38			

Handling experimental observations and data

5. Use your observations and the table of information at the beginning of the worksheet to identify the plastics in samples A, B and C.

Plastic sample	Name of the addition polymer in the plastic material
A	
B	
C	

Topic 11.7: Polymers

Supplement Learning episode C11.7c Proteins

Learning objectives

- **Supplement** Describe proteins as natural polyamides and that they are formed from amino acid monomers with the general structure:

$$\begin{array}{c} H \quad R \quad O \\ | \quad | \quad \| \\ N=C-C \\ | \quad | \quad | \\ H \quad H \quad O-H \end{array}$$

where R represents different types of side chain

- **Supplement** Describe and draw the structure of proteins as:

[block diagram showing protein structure with alternating N-H and C=O groups linked through block repeat units]

Resources

Student Book pages 343–344

Approach

Students may find this learning episode difficult as it involves potentially complex functional groups and repeat units. It is important to keep structural diagrams as simple as possible and to use block diagrams, as in the Student Book. Students who are studying biology are likely to be much more familiar with proteins than students who are not.

Students need to understand the nature of the monomer units (amino acids) that make up the protein and the characteristic bonding or link unit within a protein. Draw out the similarities between a protein and nylon in terms of the linking structure.

Answers

Science in Context, page 344

Starch, a polymer, is formed when monomers combine and small molecules (water) are produced – this is the condensation process. In forming an addition polymer no small molecules are produced as well as the polymer.

Page 344

1. A non-biodegradable plastic cannot be broken down by bacteria in the soil.
2. a) **Supplement** A carboxylic acid (–COOH) and an amine (–NH$_2$).
   b) **Supplement** A condensation polymer. A polyamide.
   c) **Supplement** Protein is broken down by a process known as hydrolysis. In the body this can be achieved by stomach acid.

Topic 11.7: Polymers

Learning episode C11.7d Consolidation and summary

Learning aims

- Review the learning points of the topic summarised in the end of topic checklist.
- Test understanding of the topic content by answering the end of topic questions.

Resources

Student Book pages 345–347

Approach

Ask students to work with a partner to make a list of key words from this topic. They could then work together to produce a spider diagram showing how the different concepts are linked. They could compare their list with the list of key terms given in the Student Book. Discuss the checklist and ask questions to see how much of the content students are comfortable with.

Students could make flashcards of the key content and then use the flashcards to quiz each other on the information.

Take the opportunity to revise aspects of the chemistry of alkenes, alcohols and acids, particularly if students had limited recall of these at the start of this topic.

Ask students to work individually through the end of topic questions in the Student Book without looking at the text. As they work, walk around the classroom observing their answers and questioning them as necessary to find out which questions are causing difficulties.

After a set period, ask students to stop working. Discuss any areas of difficulty you observed as you walked round the class.

Students should complete any unanswered questions for homework, but you should stress that they should answer the questions without looking at the text, so that they can see how much they have remembered.

End of topic questions mark scheme

The marks available for a question can indicate the level of detail you need to provide in your answer.

Question	Correct answer	Marks
1	A	1 mark
2 a)	A monomer is a molecule that can combine with other molecules to form a polymer.	1 mark
2 b)	A polymer is a giant (large) molecule made up of one or more monomers.	1 mark
Supplement 3 a)	An addition polymer is formed when molecules of a single monomer join together in large numbers.	1 mark
Supplement 3 b)	A C=C double bond.	1 mark
Supplement 3 c)	[Diagram showing three propene monomers with C=C double bonds joining to form a polymer chain with single C–C bonds]	2 marks
Supplement 3 d)	Propane is a saturated hydrocarbon and does not contain a C=C double bond.	1 mark
	It cannot undergo addition reactions and so cannot form a polymer.	1 mark

Topic 11.7: Polymers

Question	Correct answer	Marks
Supplement 4	Completed table as shown below: <table><tr><th>Addition polymer</th><th>Use</th></tr><tr><td>Poly(ethene)</td><td>Buckets/bowls/plastic bags</td></tr><tr><td>Poly(propene)</td><td>Packaging/ropes/carpets</td></tr><tr><td>Poly(chloroethene)</td><td>Plastic sheets/artificial leather</td></tr></table> (1 mark for one correct answer for each polymer)	1 mark 1 mark 1 mark
5 a)	Addition polymers cannot be broken down by the bacteria in the soil.	1 mark 1 mark
5 b)	Plastics have to be separated from other recyclable materials. There are different types of plastic – they need to be separated. Only some (thermoplastic) plastics can be melted and reformed; others (thermosetting) decompose on strong heating.	1 mark 1 mark 1 mark
Supplement 6 a)	A condensation polymer is made from two different monomers. A small molecule (such as water) is also produced when two monomers combine.	1 mark 1 mark
Supplement 6 b)	i) Nylon/terylene (allow polyester/polyurethane). (Any one for 1 mark) ii) Nylon/terylene/polyester used in clothing. (Accept other sensible alternatives; any one for 1 mark)	1 mark 1 mark
Supplement 7 a)	i) $-\overset{\overset{\displaystyle O}{\|}}{C}-\underset{\underset{\displaystyle H}{\|}}{N}-$ ii) Proteins.	1 mark 1 mark
Supplement 7 b)	i) Amino acids. ii) A protein can be broken down by acid hydrolysis.	1 mark 2 marks
	Total:	26 marks

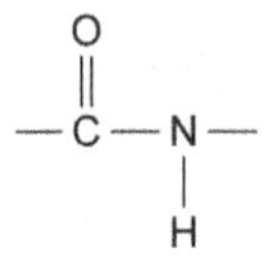

Section 11: Exam-style questions mark scheme

Exam-style questions and sample answers have been written by the authors. In examinations, the way marks are awarded may be different. References to assessment and/or assessment preparation are the publisher's interpretation of the syllabus requirements and may not fully reflect the approach of Cambridge Assessment International Education.

The marks available for a question can indicate the level of detail you need to provide in your answer.

Question	Correct answer	Marks
2	B	1 mark
3 a)	i) True. ii) False. iii) True. iv) False. v) False. (1 mark for each correct answer)	5 marks
3 b)	i) A compound/molecule containing carbon and hydrogen only.	1 mark
	ii) A compound/molecule containing only C-to-C single bonds.	1 mark
3 c)	i) C_3H_8	1 mark
	ii) Diagram as shown in Table 11.4 on page 312 of Student Book.	2 marks
4 a)	i) Bitumen.	1 mark
	ii) Gasoline.	1 mark
	iii) Bitumen.	1 mark
4 b)	(Catalytic) cracking.	1 mark
	The long-chain hydrocarbon is passed at high temperature (600–700 °C)	1 mark
	over a catalyst of silica or alumina.	1 mark
4 c)	i) $2CH_4(g) + 3O_2(g) \rightarrow 2CO(g) + 4H_2O(l)$	2 marks
	ii) Carbon monoxide molecules attach themselves to the haemoglobin in the blood and this prevents the haemoglobin from transporting oxygen.	1 mark 1 mark
5 a)	The alkene homologous series.	1 mark
5 b)	Monomer.	1 mark
Supplement 5 c)	As in Fig. 11.36 on page 338 of the Student Book but with the Cl atoms replaced by CH_3 units.	2 marks
Supplement 5 d)	As in Table 11.11 on page 339 of the Student Book for the repeat unit.	2 marks
5 e)	Addition polymer.	1 mark
5 f)	Packaging/ropes/carpets. (Any two for 1 mark each.)	2 marks
5 g)	They are non-biodegradable.	1 mark
	They are not easily broken down by bacteria in the soil.	1 mark
Supplement 5 h)	i) It is a condensation polymer.	1 mark
	ii) It is made from two different monomers.	1 mark
6 a)	The ethene molecules are monomers.	1 mark

Section 11: Exam-style questions mark scheme

Question	Correct answer	Marks
6 b)	Ethane cannot be polymerised because it does not have a double bond.	1 mark
6 c)	Diagram as in Fig. 1.61 on page 54 of Student Book.	1 mark
6 d)	i) Cracking means breaking down of long-chain hydrocarbons into smaller molecules.	1 mark
	ii) A high temperature is needed.	1 mark
	iii) C_8H_{18}	1 mark
6 e)	i) H_2	1 mark
	ii) Fractional distillation creates a temperature gradient in the fractionating column so that the smaller/lighter molecules (rise) higher in the column and different fractions condense at particular places depending on their boiling points.	1 mark / 1 mark
	iii) Petrol/gasoline is used as fuel.	1 mark
	Lubricating fraction is used for lubricating oils.	1 mark
Supplement 7 a)	i) A is glutamic acid.	1 mark
	B is alanine.	1 mark
	ii) The locating agent must be used because the acids are colourless.	1 mark
	iii) Diagram as shown in Fig. 11.40 on page 341 of the Student Book. The picture should show an amide linkage and continuation at the ends.	3 marks
Supplement 7 b)	i) $2C_2H_5OH$	1 mark
	$2CO_2$	1 mark
	ii) The reaction stops because glucose is used up or the yeast is 'killed' by ethanol.	1 mark
	iii) If there was any oxygen it would oxidise the ethanol to ethanoic acid and water.	1 mark
	iv) The ethanol can be concentrated by fractional distillation.	1 mark
Supplement 8 a)	i) Equilibrium means there is no change in concentration of reagents.	1 mark
	ii) It must be lower because the reverse reaction	1 mark
	is endothermic (OR the forward reaction is exothermic).	1 mark
	iii) Advantage: increased rate.	1 mark
	Reason: because molecules collide more frequently.	1 mark
	Advantage: increased yield.	1 mark
	Reason: high pressure favours side with few molecules.	1 mark
Supplement 8 b)	i) $2CH_3OH + 3O_2 \rightarrow 2CO_2 + 4H_2O$	2 marks
	ii) methyl ethanoate + water.	2 marks
	iii) Methanoic acid.	1 mark
	Total:	68 marks

Section 12: Experimental techniques

Contents
C12.1 Experimental techniques
C12.2 Identification of ions and gases

Overview of the section
As the title of this section indicates the focus is very much on practical activities that the students can actively take part in and consider the related risk assessments. Some of the practical work may have featured in earlier study but, nevertheless, a revision or recap could prove beneficial. You will need to decide whether you approach the whole section at one time or you decide to split it so that it links more closely with some of the other sections.

Chemical analysis focuses on simple identification tests that can readily be performed in a school/college laboratory. Essentially it involves the identification of common anions, cations and gases.

Supplement The work on chromatography includes R_f values at supplementary level and the acid–base titration content could well introduce calculations, also at supplementary level.

Starting points
The Student Book section opener (pages 354–355) puts the ideas in the section into context and sets the scene. It also allows students to acknowledge and value their prior learning, and provides a benchmark against which future learning can be compared.

The questions provide a structure for introducing the section and can be used in a number of different ways:
- You could ask students to consider the questions as an introductory homework task.
- You could put students into groups to share their own ideas and understanding and then to report back to the whole class.
- Students could be given access to the Internet, preferably with a tight timescale, to find out the information required.

You could then use a spider chart or other form of wall chart to summarise everybody's ideas.

Recording these initial ideas allows you to retain them for reference as the individual topics are developed. In this way, your students' progress in learning can be readily acknowledged.

C12.1 Experimental techniques

Introduction

You may find that this topic overlaps significantly with what students have already learned. After the orientation learning episode you will find it easier to judge how much teaching time to devote to the topic.

There are some useful links to other topics: the use of filtration and crystallisation in the preparation of soluble salts in Topic 7.1 *Acids, bases and salts*, and the use of distillation and fractional distillation in Topic 11.2 *Fuels* and Topic 11.5 *Alcohols*.

This topic focuses first on measurement, then on the criteria for purity and finally on some familiar methods of purification, including filtration, distillation and fractional distillation.

Links to other topics

Section	Essential background knowledge	Useful links
7 Acids, bases and salts		7.1 Acids, bases and salts
11 Organic chemistry		11.2 Fuels
		11.5 Alcohols

Topic overview

C12.1a	Orientation
	Students will be familiar with a range of laboratory measuring equipment and are also likely to have some prior knowledge of ways of separating mixtures. The purpose of this learning episode is to assess their prior knowledge, identify any misconceptions and then decide how much teaching time will be needed on the rest of the topic.
C12.1b	Criteria for purity
	This learning episode considers purity, initially using chromatography to separate pure substances from a mixture. Finding the melting and boiling points of substances are then considered as other measures of purity.
	Supplement The use of R_f values is introduced to identify the components separated in chromatography, together with the use of locating agents when colourless substances are being separated using chromatography.
C12.1c	Methods of purification
	This learning episode is intended to make sure that the students are familiar with the following separation processes: simple distillation, fractional distillation, filtration, crystallisation and chromatography. These aspects may be very familiar to students and so the learning episode may be quite short.
C12.1d	Consolidation and summary
	This learning episode provides a quick recap of the key ideas of the topic.

Career links

These are some scientific careers that focus on this area of chemistry but careers in many other fields use the knowledge and skills gained studying science.

Experimental skills also underpin all careers in chemistry and not only specifically in the lab. Analytical chemists develop analytical and purification methods to purify compounds such as medicines before they are used in biological tests. Water purification chemists analyse drinking water to make sure that it is suitable for human use and consumption.

Topic 12.1: Experimental techniques

Learning episode C12.1a Orientation

Learning objectives

- Name appropriate apparatus for the measurement of time, temperature, mass and volume, including:
  (a) stopwatches
  (b) thermometers
  (c) balances
  (d) burettes
  (e) volumetric pipettes
  (f) measuring cylinders
  (g) gas syringes.
- Suggest advantages and disadvantages of experimental methods and apparatus.
- Describe a:
  (a) solvent as a substance that dissolves a solute
  (b) solute as a substance that is dissolved in a solvent
  (c) solution as a mixture of one or more solutes dissolved in a solvent
  (d) saturated solution as a solution containing the maximum concentration of a solute dissolved in the solvent at a specified temperature
  (e) residue as a substance that remains after evaporation, distillation, filtration or any similar process
  (f) filtrate as a liquid or solution that has passed through a filter.

Resources

Student Book pages 356–363

Resources for demonstration (see Technician's notes, below)

Approach

Start with a quick quiz in which students have to name some common laboratory measuring equipment. This could include a stopwatch, thermometer, electronic scales or balance, burettes, dropping pipettes, volumetric pipettes and measuring cylinders.

Set up demonstrations of distillation, fractional distillation, filtration, crystallisation and chromatography **(see tech notes)**. As students observe each process, ask them to identify which states of matter are being separated in each process. You will need to judge whether students have enough prior knowledge to omit learning episode C12.1c.

SAFETY INFORMATION
Wear eye protection (splash-proof goggles).
Ethanol is highly flammable.

Technician's notes

Be sure to check the latest safety notes on these resources before proceeding.

The following resources are needed for a demonstration of methods of purification:

stopwatch, thermometer, electronic balance, burette, dropping pipette and measuring cylinder
distillation apparatus (Student Book page 362), with dilute blue washable ink, for example
fractional distillation apparatus (Student Book page 363), with ethanol and water, for example
filtration, with sand and water, for example
crystallisation apparatus (Student Book page 362), with salt solution, for example
chromatography apparatus (Student Book page 358), with black soluble ink, for example

Topic 12.1: Experimental techniques

Learning episode C12.1b Criteria for purity

Learning objectives

- Describe how paper chromatography is used to separate mixtures of soluble coloured substances, using a suitable solvent.
- Interpret simple chromatograms to identify:
  (a) unknown substances by comparison with known substances
  (b) pure and impure substances.
- Supplement Describe how paper chromatography is used to separate mixtures of soluble colourless substances, using a suitable solvent and a locating agent.
  Knowledge of specific locating agents is **not** required.
- Supplement State and use the equation for R_f:

$$R_f = \frac{\text{distance travelled by substance}}{\text{distance travelled by solvent}}$$

Resources

Student Book pages 358–360

Worksheet C12.1b Paper chromatography

Resources for a class practical (see Technician's notes, following)

Approach

From the Orientation learning episode you will be able to judge whether it is appropriate to provide some practical investigation of the separation of mixtures. If so, chromatography lends itself to class practical work.

Worksheet C12.1b can be used to support this work. Instructions are given on the worksheet.

SAFETY INFORMATION
Wear eye protection (splash-proof goggles).

Technician's notes

Be sure to check the latest safety notes on these resources before proceeding.

The following resources are needed for the class practical C12.1b:

paper chromatography apparatus as shown in Student Book page 359
250 cm³ beaker, strips of paper, clip to hold paper, pencil (to sit across top of beaker), sticky tape
4 samples of black (water soluble) ink labelled A, B, C and D – two of the inks should be the same, so 3 different inks are needed

Topic 12.1: Experimental techniques

Answers

Page 361

1. A baseline drawn in pencil will not dissolve in the solvent.
2. If the solvent were above the baseline the substances would just dissolve and form a solution in the beaker.
3. The dye may be insoluble/does not dissolve in the solvent.
4. The boiling point will be higher than that of pure water/above 100 °C, at normal pressure.
5. Supplement The R_f factor is the distance travelled by the compound divided by the distance travelled by the compound = $\frac{1.7}{10}$ = 0.17

Worksheet C12.1b

1. A baseline and labels drawn in pencil will not dissolve in the water.
2. To make sure that the level of the water was below the line on which the inks have been 'spotted' (otherwise the inks will simply dissolve in the water).
3. Supplement To measure the R_f values accurately the exact distance travelled by the water must be known. If the water soaked to the top of the filter paper the inks would continue to move up the paper but the position reached by the water would not change.

Topic 12.1: Experimental techniques

Worksheet C12.1b Paper chromatography

This experiment allows you to identify which two of four different samples of black ink (A, B, C and D) are the same.

Apparatus

beaker

strip of filter paper

four samples of black ink

4 glass rods

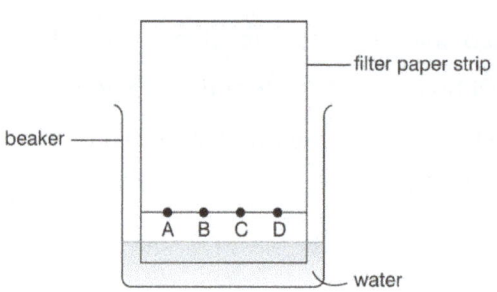

SAFETY INFORMATION
Wear eye protection (splash-proof goggles).

Method

1. Draw a pencil line about 2 cm from the bottom of the filter paper strip.
2. In pencil, on this line, mark the positions (A, B, C and D) where the four samples of ink will be 'spotted'.
3. Use a different glass rod for each ink. Add a small drop of each ink onto the mark made on the paper for that ink.
4. Put a 1 cm depth of water in a beaker and carefully place the filter paper into the beaker.
5. When the water has soaked three-quarters of the way up the filter paper strip, remove the strip from the water, mark on the filter paper, using a pencil, how far the solvent has travelled and let it dry on a paper towel.

Using and organising techniques, apparatus and materials

1. Why was a pencil used to draw the line and label the positions of the ink on the filter paper strip?
2. Why was only 1 cm depth of water put into the beaker?
3. Supplement Why was the filter paper strip paper removed when the water was soaking up close to the top of the paper?

Handling experimental observations and data

4. Which coloured dye was the most soluble in water?
5. Which two inks were the same? Explain how you came to your decision.

Supplement 6. Work out the R_f values for each of the dyes in each of the inks A, B, C and D.

Topic 12.1: Experimental techniques

Learning episode C12.1c Methods of purification

Learning objectives

- Describe and explain methods of separation and purification using:
  (a) a suitable solvent
  (b) filtration
  (c) crystallisation
  (d) simple distillation
  (e) fractional distillation.
- Suggest suitable separation and purification techniques, given information about the substances involved.
- Identify substances and assess their purity using melting point and boiling point information.

Common misconceptions

Some students may think that these methods of purification involve chemical changes.

Resources

Student Book pages 361–364

Worksheet C12.1c Methods of purification

Resources for class practical in worksheet C12.1c (see below)

Approach

Review the following processes, making use of the relevant sections in the Student Book:

dissolving, filtration, crystallisation, distillation and fractional distillation.

You will know from learning episode C12.1a whether it is appropriate to give students some practical opportunities to investigate purification/separation of mixtures. If so, then a simple distillation lends itself to class practical work.

Worksheet C12.1c can be used to support this work.

SAFETY INFORMATION
Wear eye protection (splash-proof goggles).

Technician's notes

Be sure to check the latest safety notes on these resources before proceeding.

The following resources are needed for the class practical C12.1c:

a dilute solution of washable blue ink
eye protection (splash-proof goggles)
simple distillation apparatus as shown on Worksheet C12.1c: boiling tube and test-tube, bung with delivery tube, porcelain pieces, 250 cm^3 beaker, Bunsen burner, heatproof mat, clamp and stand

Topic 12.1: Experimental techniques

Answers

Page 364

1. A solvent is a liquid that will dissolve a substance (solute).

2. If a substance is soluble in a solvent, it dissolves in that solvent.

3. Distillation.

4. b) boiling points.

Worksheet C12.1c

4. The porcelain pieces act as anti-bumping granules and help to prevent the liquid from boiling so vigorously that it boils over and into the delivery tube.

5. The cold water helps the test-tube to act as a condenser.

6. The liquid collected in the second test-tube is known as the distillate.

7. The ink contains a colourless liquid (water) as well as at least one coloured dye.

8. Efficiency could be improved if a condenser were used rather than a test-tube standing in a beaker of cold water (the water will slowly warm up as the distillation proceeds).

Topic 12.1: Experimental techniques

Worksheet C12.1c Methods of purification

Simple distillation

This experiment allows you to separate some of the components of ink.

Apparatus

Bunsen burner and heatproof mat
blue ink
boiling tube with bung
delivery tube
test-tube
250 cm³ beaker
clamp and stand
eye protection (splash-proof goggles)
porcelain pieces

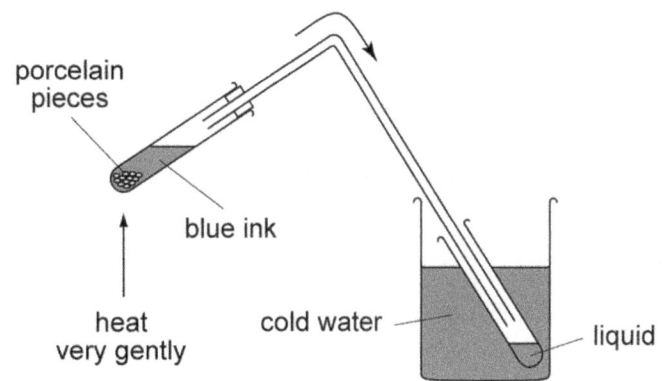

SAFETY INFORMATION
Wear eye protection (splash-proof goggles).

Method

1. Put on eye protection.
2. Set up the apparatus as shown in the diagram, adding a few porcelain pieces to the blue ink in the boiling tube.
3. Heat the ink slowly with a Bunsen burner until you have collected a 1 cm depth of liquid in the test-tube.

Using and organising techniques, apparatus and materials

4. What was the purpose of adding the porcelain pieces to the ink before heating?
5. What is the function of the cold water in the beaker?
6. What is the general name given to liquids like the one collected in the second test-tube?

Handling experimental observations and data

7. What evidence is there to suggest that the ink was not a pure substance?

Panning and evaluating investigations

8. How could the efficiency of this separation of the components in ink be improved?

Topic 12.1: Experimental techniques

Learning episode C12.1d Consolidation and summary

Learning aims

- Review the learning points of the topic summarised in the end of topic checklist.
- Test understanding of the topic content by answering the end of topic questions.

Learning outcomes

- Describe an acid–base titration to include the use of a:
  (a) burette
  (b) volumetric pipette
  (c) suitable indicator.
- Describe how to identify the end-point of a titration using an indicator.

Resources

Student Book pages 365–367

Approach

It would seem sensible that work on acid-base titrations takes place as part of Topic 7.1 *Acids, bases and salts.* As this topic is likely to be covered before Topic 7.1 it is probably sufficient to mention that work on titrations will be covered later in the course.

Ask students to work with a partner to make a list of key words from this topic. They could then work together to produce a spider diagram showing how the different concepts are linked. They could compare their list with the list of key terms given in the Student Book. Discuss the checklist and ask questions to see how much of the content students are comfortable with.

Students could make flashcards of the key content and then use the flashcards to quiz each other on the information.

Ask students to work individually through the end of topic questions in the Student Book without looking at the text. As they work, walk around the classroom observing their answers and questioning them as necessary to find out which questions are causing difficulties.

After a set period, ask students to stop working. Discuss any areas of difficulty you observed as you walked round the class.

Students should complete any unanswered questions for homework, but you should stress that they should answer the questions without looking at the text, so that they can see how much they have remembered.

Topic 12.1: Experimental techniques

End of topic questions mark scheme

The marks available for a question can indicate the level of detail you need to provide in your answer.

Question	Correct answer	Marks
1	A	1 mark
2	Draw a pencil line about 1 cm from the bottom of a strip of filter paper. Spot the four samples of ink onto the line leaving space between each.	1 mark 1 mark
	Put the filter paper into a beaker containing a small amount of water (making sure the level of the water is below the line).	1 mark
	Identify the 2 inks that produce the same pattern and positions of dyes on the chromatogram.	
3 a)	The ink may not dissolve in the water.	1 mark
3 b)	Use another solvent, e.g. alcohol.	1 mark
4	The boiling point will be higher than 78 °C, e.g. 80 °C.	1 mark
5	Impurities will lower the melting point of ice.	1 mark
6	The condenser is kept cool (by the constant flow of water).	1 mark
7	Heat the sodium chloride solution in an evaporating basin.	1 mark
	Evaporate all the water/leave to crystallise (once saturated).	1 mark
Supplement 8 a)	Compound A.	1 mark
Supplement 8 b)	Compound D.	1 mark
Supplement 8 c)	R_f = approx. 0.50	1 mark
	The solvent has travelled twice as far as the compound (allow measurements).	1 mark
Supplement 8 d)	The substance cannot travel further than the solvent (or travel exactly the same distance).	1 mark
	Total:	16 marks

C12.2 Identification of ions and gases

Introduction

This may be approached as a stand-alone topic, although there is a strong link to Topic 7.1 *Acids, bases and salts* through the precipitation reactions used to identify metal ions in solution. In this context there are also links to Topic 8.4 *Transition elements and noble gases*. Students will probably have already encountered the tests for oxygen, carbon dioxide and hydrogen in Topic 9.1 *Metals* and Topic 10.1 *Chemistry of the environment*. The use of the terms 'cation' and 'anion' link to Topic 4.1 *Electrochemistry*.

The topic focuses on identification of cations by flame tests and then tests for cations in solutions and includes the test for the ammonium ion. It then considers tests for anions, which are essentially solution tests with the possible exception of the test for the carbonate ion. The topic concludes with the tests for gases.

There are plenty of opportunities for students to practise and develop their practical skills through qualitative analysis and identification activities.

Links to other topics

Section	Essential background knowledge	Useful links
2 Atoms, elements and compounds	2.2 Ions and ionic bonds	
3 Stoichiometry	3.1 Stoichiometry	
4 Electrochemistry		4.1 Electrochemistry
7 Acids, bases and salts	7.1 Acids, bases and salts	
8 The Periodic Table		8.1 The Periodic Table 8.3 Group VII elements 8.4 Transition elements and noble gases
9 Metals		9.1 Metals
10 Chemistry of the environment		10.1 Chemistry of the environment

Topic overview

C12.2a	Orientation
	This short introductory learning episode can be used to revise ideas on ionic bonding and the charges on ions. You may link this to Topic 8.1 *The Periodic Table* if this topic has already been taught. In addition, you may revise some of the tests for gases already encountered. You may introduce the terms 'cation' and 'anion', particularly if students are unfamiliar with them.
C12.2b	Identifying cations
	This learning episode has three themes: the identification of metal ions using a flame test, the identification of metal ions in solution using sodium hydroxide solution and ammonia solution, and the identification of the ammonium ion.
	Worksheets C12.2b(1) and C12.2b(2) support student practical work.

Topic 12.2: Identification of ions and gases

C12.2c	**Identifying anions**
	This learning episode has five themes: the identification of solid carbonates by reaction with dilute hydrochloric acid, the identification of the halide ions (chloride, bromide and iodide) using acidified silver nitrate solution, the use of acidified barium nitrate solution to identify the sulfate ion in solution, the use of aqueous sodium hydroxide and aluminium to identify the nitrate ion, and the use of a dilute acid (and manganate(VII) ions) to identify the sulfite ion.
	Worksheet C12.2c supports the identification of the halide and sulfate ions in solution.
C12.2d	**Identifying gases**
	This learning episode brings together information about individual confirmatory tests for gases, including tests for hydrogen, oxygen, carbon dioxide, sulfur dioxide, chlorine and ammonia. Most of these tests should be familiar to students.
	Worksheet C12.2d provides a key that supports a systematic approach to identifying the five gases.
C12.2e	**Consolidation and summary**
	This learning episode provides an opportunity for a quick recap of the ideas encountered in the topic and time for the students to answer the end of topic questions in the Student Book.

Career links

These are some scientific careers that focus on this area of chemistry but careers in many other fields use the knowledge and skills gained studying science.

Astrochemists design probes used to study the atmosphere and surface composition of other plants in the solar system through gas and ion analysis, among other techniques.

Topic 12.2: Identification of ions and gases

Learning episode C12.2a Orientation

Learning aims

- To recap on existing knowledge of ions and identification tests for gases.
- Know that metals form positive ions which are called cations.
- Know that non-metals form negative ions which are called anions.
- Know the identification tests for hydrogen, oxygen and carbon dioxide.

Approach

This is a short learning episode. Ask students to summarise in three or four points what they know about ionic bonding. If they have studied Topic 8.1 *The Periodic Table*, ask them how the Periodic Table can help them to work out the charges on ions.

Explain that the topic has three main sections. The first looks at some tests that can be used to identify positive ions (also called cations), mainly metal ions but also the ammonium ion. The second section deals with tests for non-metal ions (also called anions). These tests together will identify the composition of some simple compounds. The third looks at the test for gases.

Recap on the terms 'cation' and 'anion'. Relate these to how ions behave in electrolysis.

Ask students to write down any gas identification tests they already know about. Explain that in this topic the following gases will be considered: hydrogen, oxygen, carbon dioxide, chlorine, sulfur dioxide and ammonia. Students will probably not have encountered the tests for sulfur dioxide and ammonia.

Topic 12.2: Identification of ions and gases

Learning episode C12.2b Identifying cations

Learning outcomes

- Describe tests using aqueous sodium hydroxide and aqueous ammonia to identify the aqueous cations:
  (a) aluminium, Al^{3+}
  (b) ammonium, NH_4^+
  (c) calcium, Ca^{2+}
  (d) chromium(III), Cr^{3+}
  (e) copper(II), Cu^{2+}
  (f) iron(II), Fe^{2+}
  (g) iron(III), Fe^{3+}
  (h) zinc, Zn^{2+}.
- Describe the use of a flame test to identify the cations:
  (a) lithium, Li^+
  (b) sodium, Na^+
  (c) potassium, K^+
  (d) calcium, Ca^{2+}
  (e) barium, Ba^{2+}.
  (f) copper(II), Cu^{2+}.

Resources

Student Book pages 368–371

Worksheet C12.2b(1) Using a flame test to identify metal ions

Worksheet C12.2b(2) Identifying metal ions in solution

Resources for a demonstration and a class practical (see Technician's notes, following)

Approach

There are three parts to this learning episode:

1. Identifying metal ions using a flame test

This part is supported by Worksheet C12.2b(1). Demonstrate the flame test technique, emphasising the importance of 'cleaning' the nichrome wire between tests **(see tech notes)**. Allow students to test the solids provided, including unknown solids A and B.

SAFETY INFORMATION
Wear eye protection (splash-proof goggles).
Copper(II) nitrate is corrosive, a moderate hazard and hazardous to the aquatic environment.
Copper(II) chloride is a moderate hazard and hazardous to the aquatic environment.
Lithium chloride is a moderate hazard.
Some of the solids are hazardous to the aquatic environment and so great care is needed with disposal

Topic 12.2: Identification of ions and gases

2. Identifying metal ions in solution

This part is supported by Worksheet C12.2b(2). The basis of the test is the precipitation of insoluble metal hydroxides. The hydroxides of aluminium and zinc are amphoteric and so will dissolve in excess sodium hydroxide solution. In addition, if ammonia solution is used copper(II) hydroxide will dissolve in excess ammonia forming a deep blue solution of a complex ion.

Students have to use their results to identify the metal ions present in two unknown solutions. It is worth spending time checking that the students are able to write equations for these precipitation reactions.

> **SAFETY INFORMATION**
>
> *Wear eye protection (splash-proof goggles).*
>
> *Sodium hydroxide solution is caustic and ammonia solution is an irritant and releases toxic vapour even at low concentrations.*
>
> *Ensure that the laboratory is well ventilated.*

3. Identifying the ammonium ion

Demonstrate the test using sodium hydroxide solution as described on page 370 of the Student Book **(see tech notes)**. Make the point that the ammonia gas is the only common alkaline gas and use of this fact will be made later in the topic when identifying gases.

> **SAFETY INFORMATION**
>
> *Wear eye protection (splash-proof goggles).*

Technician's notes

Be sure to check the latest safety notes on these resources before proceeding.

The following resources are needed for the class practical C12.2b(1) per group:

nichrome wire in holder (cork or hard glass)
Bunsen burner and heatproof mat
watch glasses, spatula
1 mol / dm^3 hydrochloric acid
copper(II) chloride, lithium chloride
calcium chloride, magnesium chloride, potassium chloride, sodium chloride
potassium sulfate (or other potassium salt) labelled as 'substance A'
copper(II) nitrate (or other copper salt) labelled as 'substance B'
eye protection (splash-proof goggles)

The following resources are needed for the class practical C12.2b(2), per group:

beakers, droppers, test-tubes, test-tube rack
0.1 mol / dm^3 sodium hydroxide solution, 0.1 mol / dm^3 ammonia solution
0.1 mol / dm^3 solutions of aluminium nitrate, calcium nitrate, chromium(III) chloride, copper(II) sulfate, iron(III) chloride, zinc nitrate
0.1 mol / dm^3 solutions of iron(II) ammonium sulfate (labelled iron(II) sulfate)
0.1 mol / dm^3 solutions of copper(II) chloride (labelled as 'solution A')
0.1 mol / dm^3 iron(II) ammonium sulfate (labelled as 'solution B')
eye protection (splash-proof goggles)

Topic 12.2: Identification of ions and gases

SAFETY INFORMATION

Some of the solids are hazardous to the aquatic environment and so great care is needed with disposal.

Copper(II) nitrate is corrosive, a moderate hazard and hazardous to the aquatic environment.

Copper(II) chloride is a moderate hazard and hazardous to the aquatic environment.

Lithium chloride is a moderate hazard.

The following resources are needed for the demonstration of identifying the ammonium ion:

test-tube, dropper
Bunsen burner and heatproof mat
universal indicator paper and chart
0.1 mol / dm³ ammonium chloride solution
0.1 mol / dm³ sodium hydroxide

Note: iron(II) ammonium sulfate is used because the solution of iron(II) ions with ammonium ions is more stable than iron(II) sulfate

Answers

Page 371

1. a) A white precipitate forms which does not dissolve in excess sodium hydroxide solution.
   b) A white precipitate forms which does dissolve in excess sodium hydroxide solution.
2. Add sodium hydroxide solution. Fe^{2+} produces a green precipitate; Fe^{3+} produces a red-brown precipitate.

Topic 12.2: Identification of ions and gases

Worksheet C12.b(1) Using a flame test to identify metal ions

Some metal ions (cations) can be identified from the characteristic colours they produce when heated in a Bunsen flame. You will test a number of compounds containing known metal ions and then use your results to identify the metal ions present in solids A and B.

Apparatus

Bunsen burner and heatproof mat

1 M hydrochloric acid

compounds A and B

watch glasses, spatula

flame test wire and holder

eye protection (splash-proof goggles)

compounds containing the following metal ions: calcium, copper, lithium, magnesium, potassium, sodium

SAFETY INFORMATION

Wear eye protection (splash-proof goggles).

1 M hydrochloric acid is corrosive.

Copper(II) chloride and lithium chloride are harmful.

Method

1. Put on your eye protection.
2. Heat a flame test wire in the hottest part of a Bunsen burner flame until the only colour produced in the flame is a faint orange.
3. Put a spatula measure of the solid you are going to test on a watch glass.
4. Dip the wire into some clean 1 M hydrochloric acid on a watch glass and then into the solid sample. Put the flame test wire into the hottest part of the Bunsen burner flame. Record the colour of the flame produced in the table below.
5. Repeat the procedure for each of the solids you are testing. Remember to clean the wire after each test by heating it in the flame and to use fresh hydrochloric acid each time.

Observing, measuring and recording

Metal ion (cation)	Flame colour
Calcium (Ca^{2+})	
Copper (Cu^{2+})	
Lithium (Li^+)	
Magnesium (Mg^{2+})	
Potassium (K^+)	
Sodium (Na^+)	
Solid A	
Solid B	

Interpreting observations and data

6. Identify the metal ions present in solid A and solid B.

Topic 12.2: Identification of ions and gases

Worksheet C12.2b(2) Identifying metal ions in solution

Many metal ions (cations) can be detected in solution from the colour of the precipitate they form when sodium hydroxide solution or ammonia solution is added. This test is only successful when the hydroxide of the metal ion is insoluble in water – that is, if it forms a precipitate in the solution.

Apparatus

beaker, dropper, sodium hydroxide solution, ammonia solution, test-tubes, test-tube rack, eye protection (splash-proof goggles)

solutions containing the following metal ions: aluminium, calcium, chromium(III), copper, iron(II), iron(III), zinc and potassium, solutions A and B

SAFETY INFORMATION
Wear eye protection.
Sodium hydroxide solution is caustic and ammonia solution is an irritant and releases toxic vapour even at low concentrations.
Ensure that the laboratory is well ventilated.

Method

1. Put on your eye protection.
2. Put about a 2 cm depth of the solution to be tested in a test-tube.
3. Using a dropper, carefully add several drops of sodium hydroxide solution and then excess. Record your observations in the table below.
4. Repeat steps 2 and 3 using clean test-tubes, and adding ammonia solution instead of sodium hydroxide solution to the solution to be tested.

Observing, measuring and recording

Metal ion (cation) in solution	Observations on adding sodium hydroxide solution (drop by drop and then to excess)	Observations on adding ammonia solution (drop by drop and then to excess)
Aluminium (Al^{3+})		
Calcium (Ca^{2+})		
Copper (Cu^{2+})		
Iron(II) (Fe^{2+})		
Iron(III) (Fe^{3+})		
Zinc (Zn^{2+})		
Chromium (Cr^{3+})		
Solution A		
Solution B		

Page 1 of 2

Topic 12.2: Identification of ions and gases

Interpreting observations and data

5. Which metal ion did not produce a precipitate? Why was a precipitate not formed in this case?
6. Which metal ions formed a precipitate that dissolved in excess sodium hydroxide?
7. Which metal ions formed a precipitate that dissolved in excess ammonia solution?
8. Identify the metal ions present in solutions A and B.

    A

    B

9. Write word equations and chemical equations for the following reactions:

    a) Copper(II) sulfate solution and sodium hydroxide solution.

    b) Iron(III) chloride solution and sodium hydroxide solution.

Topic 12.2: Identification of ions and gases

Learning episode C12.2c Identifying anions

Learning objective

- Describe tests to identify the anions:
  (a) carbonate, CO_3^{2-}, by reaction with dilute acid and then testing for carbon dioxide gas
  (b) chloride, Cl^-, bromide, Br^-, and iodide I^-, by acidifying with dilute nitric acid then adding aqueous silver nitrate
  (c) nitrate, NO_3^-, by reduction with aluminium foil and aqueous sodium hydroxide and then testing for ammonia gas
  (d) sulfate, SO_4^{2-}, by acidifying with dilute nitric acid then adding aqueous barium nitrate
  (e) sulfite, SO_3^{2-}, by reaction with acidified aqueous potassium manganate(VII).

Resources

Student Book pages 372–374

Worksheet C12.2c Identifying non-metal ions in solution

Resources for a demonstration and a class practical (see Technician's notes, below)

Approach

There are five parts to the learning episode.

1. Identifying the carbonate ion

Students should be familiar with the test to identify carbon dioxide. Demonstrate the reaction of a carbonate, such as calcium carbonate, with dilute hydrochloric acid and bubble the gas through limewater **(see tech notes)**. You may use apparatus similar to that on page 372 of the Student Book.

Give students time to write equations for this carbonate + acid reaction. Refer also to the equations given in the Student Book (page 372).

2. Identifying halide ions

Use the first part of Worksheet C12.2c. In this part students test four unknown solutions A–D, record their observations and then identify the halide ion present using the information given on colours of halide precipitates.

SAFETY INFORMATION
Wear eye protection (splash-proof goggles).
Silver nitrate solution is harmful.
Nitric acid causes skin and eye irritation.
Sodium sulfite is corrosive and a moderate hazard.
Sodium nitrate is oxidising and a moderate hazard.
Aluminium powder is flammable.

Mention that the precipitates are light sensitive and so may darken if left to stand.

3. Identifying sulfate ions

Use the second part of Worksheet C12.2c. Using the information provided on what constitutes a positive sulfate ion test, students test four unknown solutions E–H, record their results and then identify which solutions contain sulfate ions.

Again, it is worth spending some time on writing chemical equations for these reactions.

Topic 12.2: Identification of ions and gases

SAFETY INFORMATION

Wear eye protection (splash-proof goggles).

Barium nitrate solution is harmful.

Nitric acid causes skin and eye irritation.

---

4. Identifying nitrate ions

Demonstrate the reaction to test for nitrate ions as indicated in the Student Book (page 373) **(see tech notes)**. Again mention the significance of obtaining an alkaline gas (ammonia).

5. Identifying sulfite ions

Demonstrate the reaction to test for the sulfite ion as indicated in the Student Book (page 373) **(see tech notes)**.

The Student Book includes some ionic equations that are only relevant to the students following the supplementary syllabus.

Technician's notes

Be sure to check the latest safety notes on these resources before proceeding.

The following resources are needed for a demonstration (parts 1, 4 and 5):

test-tube, bung and delivery tube, test-tube
0.1 mol/dm^3 hydrochloric acid, calcium carbonate, limewater. Limewater is a moderate hazard.
0.1 mol/dm^3 sodium hydroxide solution, sodium nitrate, aluminium powder, universal indicator paper
boiling tube, spatula, filter
sodium sulfite, 1 mol/dm^3 hydrochloric acid, 0.1 mol/dm^3 potassium manganate(VII) solution (15 cm^3).

The following resources are needed for the class practical C12.2c (parts 2 and 3), per group:

test-tubes, test-tube rack, droppers
0.05 mol/dm^3 silver nitrate solution, 0.1 mol/dm^3 nitric acid
0.1 mol/dm^3 potassium iodide (labelled as 'solution A'), 0.1 mol/dm^3 sodium chloride (labelled as 'solution B')
0.1 mol/dm^3 sodium bromide (labelled as 'solution C'), 0.1 mol/dm^3 sodium iodide (labelled as 'solution D')
0.1 mol/dm^3 sodium chloride (labelled as 'solution E'), 0.1 mol/dm^3 sodium sulfate (labelled as 'solution F')
0.1 mol/dm^3 potassium sulfate (labelled as 'solution G'), 0.1 mol/dm^3 sodium chloride (labelled as 'solution H')
0.1 mol/dm^3 barium nitrate solution
0.1 mol/dm^3 nitric acid
eye protection (splash-proof goggles)

SAFETY INFORMATION

Wear eye protection (splash-proof goggles).

Barium nitrate solution is harmful.

Nitric acid causes skin and eye irritation.

Answers

Page 374

1. Add dilute sodium hydroxide and heat. An alkaline gas (turns red litmus paper blue) indicates the presence of an ammonium compound.

2. a) Carbon dioxide.

   b) Bubble the gas through limewater. A white precipitate forms.

3. The Fe^{3+} ion is present in solution X.

4. The Cl^- ion is present in solution Y.

5. Plan needs to check for testing of both anion and cation for each sample and should include practical instructions.

   i) Blue compound.

   Test for copper(II) – sodium hydroxide: result blue precipitate.

   $Cu^{2+}(aq) + 2OH^-(aq) \rightarrow Cu(OH)_2(s)$

   Test for sulfate – nitric acid/barium nitrate: result white precipitate.

   $Ba^{2+}(aq) + SO_4^{2-}(aq) \rightarrow BaSO_4(s)$

   ii) White compound.

   Flame test for Na^+ – yellow.

   Test for carbonate – add dilute acid: effervescence/carbon dioxide evolved – turns limewater milky.

   $CO_3^{2-}(s) + 2H^+(aq) \rightarrow H_2O(l) + CO_2(g)$

6. a) Range of possible answers:

Name of cation	Colour of precipitate
Aluminium, Zinc or Calcium	White
Copper(II)	Blue
Iron(II)	Green/turns brown slowly
Iron(III)	Rust brown/orange
Chromium (III)	Green

   b) Supplement $Ag^+(aq) + X^-(aq) \rightarrow AgX(s)$, where X^- is Cl^-, Br^-, I^-.

Topic 12.2: Identification of ions and gases

Worksheet C12.2c Identifying non-metal ions in solution

You need to be able to identify four non-metal ions or anions in solution:

a) the halide ions (Group VII): chloride, bromide and iodide

b) the sulfate ion.

You will need to use two separate tests. In each case you will be given some solutions containing unknown non-metal ions. You will have to use your observations and the information provided to identify the non-metal ions.

Apparatus

test-tubes, test-tube rack, droppers

silver nitrate solution and dilute nitric acid

barium nitrate solution and dilute nitric acid

solutions A, B, C, D, E, F, G and H

eye protection (splash-proof goggles)

SAFETY INFORMATION
Wear eye protection (splash-proof goggles).
Barium nitrate solution is harmful.
Nitric acid causes skin and eye irritation.

Method

1. Put on your eye protection.

Test 1

2. Put approximately a 2 cm depth of the test solution in a test-tube. Add approximately a 1 cm depth of dilute nitric acid followed by approximately a 1 cm depth of silver nitrate solution. Record your observations in Table 1.

Test 2

3. Put approximately a 2 cm depth of the test solution in a test-tube. Add approximately a 1 cm depth of dilute nitric acid followed by approximately a 1 cm depth of barium nitrate solution. Record your observations in Table 2.

Observing, measuring and recording

Table 1

Test solution	Observations on adding dilute nitric acid and silver nitrate solution	Non-metal ion (anion) present
A		
B		
C		
D		

Page 1 of 2

Topic 12.2: Identification of ions and gases

Table 2

Test solution	Observations on adding dilute nitric acid and barium nitrate solution	Is the sulfate ion (anion) present?
E		
F		
G		
H		

Handling experimental observations and data

4. Use the information in the table below to identify the non-metal ions present in Test 1. Complete the last column of Table 1 above.

Non-metal ion	Observations on adding dilute nitric acid followed by silver nitrate solution
Chloride (Cl^-)	A white precipitate forms.
Bromide (Br^-)	A cream coloured precipitate forms.
Iodide (I^-)	A yellow precipitate forms.

5. Write a chemical equation for the reaction of solution B with silver nitrate solution (you can assume that solution B is a solution of a sodium compound).

6. Use the information in the table below to identify which solutions contain the sulfate ion. Complete the last column of Table 2.

Non-metal ion	Observations on adding dilute nitric acid followed by barium nitrate solution
Sulfate (SO_4^{2-})	A white precipitate forms.

7. Write a chemical equation for the reaction of solution F with barium nitrate solution (you can assume that solution F is a solution of a sodium compound).

Topic 12.2: Identification of ions and gases

Learning episode C12.2d Identifying gases

Learning objective

- Describe tests to identify the gases:
    a) ammonia, NH_3, using damp red litmus paper
    b) carbon dioxide, CO_2, using limewater
    c) chlorine, Cl_2, using damp litmus paper
    d) hydrogen, H_2, using a lighted splint
    e) oxygen, O_2, using a glowing splint
    f) sulfur dioxide, SO_2, using acidified aqueous potassium manganate(VII).

Resources

Student Book page 375

Worksheet C12.2d Identifying gases

Resources for a class practical (see Technician's notes, below)

Approach

This learning episode reinforces or revises the tests for the gases in this topic. Students should be familiar with these. Worksheet C12.2d provides a key for identifying some samples of unknown gases.

The flow diagram uses a glowing splint to distinguish between hydrogen and oxygen. The syllabus requires students to know that a glowing splint is used to detect oxygen.

SAFETY INFORMATION
Wear eye protection (splash-proof goggles).
Chlorine is oxidising, toxic and hazardous to the environment.
Small amounts of Cl_2, can cause respiratory distress in some people. **The laboratory must be well ventilated.**
Ammonia gas is flammable and toxic by inhalation, and should be used in a fume cupboard.
Ensure that the laboratory is well ventilated. If you are asthmatic, take care when handling these chemicals.

Technician's notes

Be sure to check the latest safety notes on these resources before proceeding.

The following resources are needed for the class practical C12.2d, per group:

universal indicator paper and chart, splints
Bunsen burner and heatproof mat
Limewater is a moderate hazard.
samples of gases (labelled A–D) in stoppered test-tubes: A – hydrogen, B – carbon dioxide, C – ammonia, D – chlorine, E – oxygen
eye protection (splash-proof goggles), water to dampen litmus paper

Answers

Page 375

1. Damp red litmus/ universal indicator paper turns blue.

2. Oxygen.   3. Chlorine.

Topic 12.2: Identification of ions and gases

Worksheet C12.2d Identifying gases

You need to know the identification tests for the following gases:

    hydrogen   oxygen   carbon dioxide   ammonia   chlorine   sulfur dioxide

You will be provided with samples of 5 unknown gases to identify. (None of the samples is sulfur dioxide.)

Apparatus

universal indicator paper and charts	limewater solution
splints	Bunsen burner and heatproof mat
access to gas samples A, B, C, D and E	eye protection (splash-proof goggles)

SAFETY INFORMATION

Wear eye protection (splash-proof goggles).

Chlorine is oxidising, toxic and hazardous to the environment.

Small amounts of Cl_2, can cause respiratory distress in some people. **The laboratory must be well ventilated.**

Ammonia gas is flammable and toxic by inhalation. Ammonia should be used in a fume cupboard, and ensure that the laboratory is well ventilated. If you are asthmatic, take particular care when handling these chemicals.

Hydrogen is extremely flammable. Oxygen is an oxidiser. Keep oxygen and hydrogen away from Bunsen flames. Use wooden splints at a distance from the Bunsen burner.

Method

1. Put on your eye protection.
2. Use the key below to identify the gases. Record your observations in the table.

Identification key

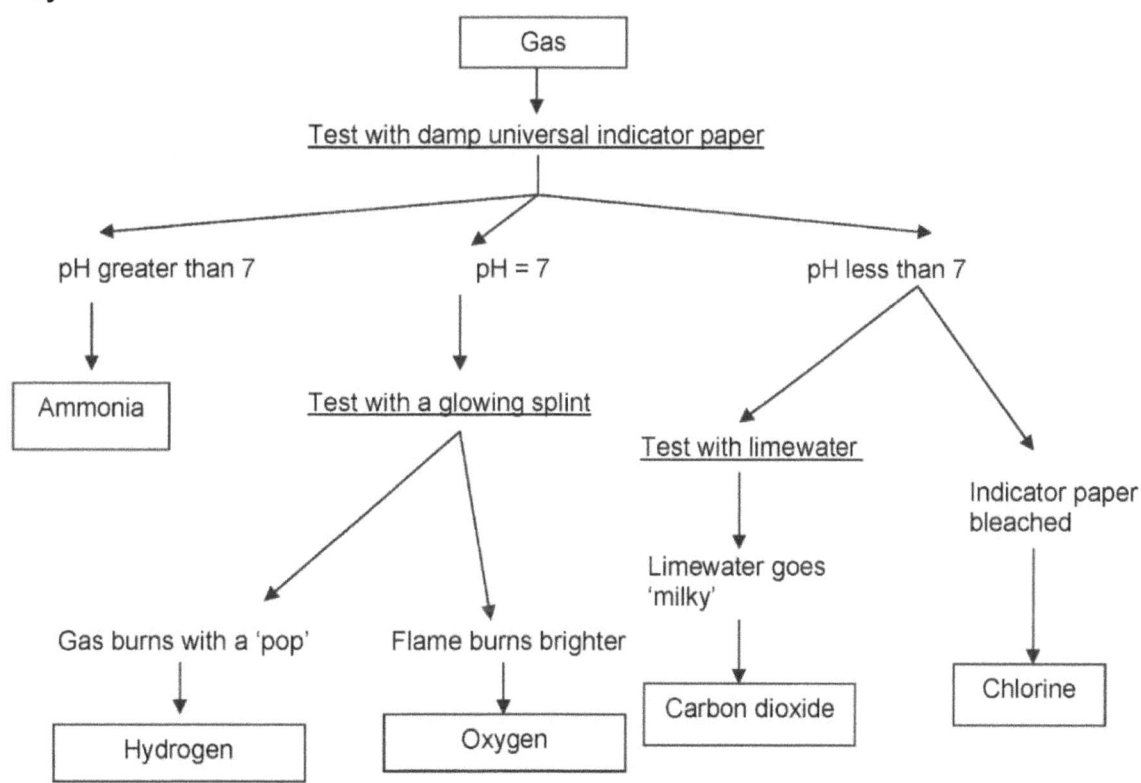

Page 1 of 2

Topic 12.2: Identification of ions and gases

Observing, measuring and recording

Gas	Result of tests used	Gas identification
A		
B		
C		
D		
E		

Handling experimental observations and data

3. Use your observations to identify the gas present in each sample. Complete the last column of the table above.
4. Write an equation for the reaction that occurs when a lighted splint is applied to hydrogen.
5. Write an equation for the reaction between carbon dioxide and limewater.

Topic 12.2: Identification of ions and gases

Learning episode C12.2e Consolidation and summary

Learning aims

- Review the learning points of the topic summarised in the end of topic checklist.
- Test understanding of the topic content by answering the end of topic questions.

Resources

Student Book pages 376–377

Approach

Students may need practice at writing the chemical equations, particularly those students following the supplementary syllabus.

Supplement For these students there are also a number of ionic equations that can be used to describe some general reactions (that is, with the spectator ions removed).

Ask students to work with a partner to make a list of key words from this topic. They could then work together to produce a spider diagram showing how the different concepts are linked. They could compare their list with the list of key terms given in the Student Book. Discuss the checklist and ask questions to see how much of the content students are comfortable with.

Students could make flashcards of the key content and then use the flashcards to quiz each other on the information.

Ask students to work individually through the end of topic questions in the Student Book without looking at the text. As they work, walk around the classroom observing their answers and questioning them as necessary to find out which questions are causing difficulties.

The topic lends itself to a '20 questions' approach to revision or consolidation. Use questions such as:

- What is the test for hydrogen?
- What observation indicates a positive result in the identification of sulfate ions?

After a set period, ask students to stop working. Discuss any areas of difficulty you observed as you walked round the class.

Students should complete any unanswered questions for homework, but you should stress that they should answer the questions without looking at the text, so that they can see how much they have remembered.

Topic 12.2: Identification of ions and gases

End of topic questions mark scheme

The marks available for a question can indicate the level of detail you need to provide in your answer.

Question	Correct answer	Marks
1	C	1 mark
2	Completed table as shown below:	3 marks

Gas	Test	Observations
Chlorine	Damp universal indicator paper	Indicator paper bleached/goes white
Carbon dioxide	Bubble through limewater	White precipitate or suspension forms
Hydrogen	Apply a lighted splint	Burns with a 'pop'

Question	Correct answer	Marks
3	Add dilute hydrochloric acid and bubble any gas through limewater.	1 mark
	A carbonate will produce carbon dioxide that will turn the limewater cloudy.	1 mark
4 a)	Add dilute nitric acid.	1 mark
	Then barium nitrate solution.	1 mark
	A white precipitate indicates the presence of a sulfate ion.	1 mark
4 b)	Add dilute nitric acid.	1 mark
	Then silver nitrate solution.	1 mark
	A yellow precipitate indicates the presence of the iodide ion.	1 mark
4 c)	Add sodium hydroxide solution and warm.	1 mark
	Add aluminium powder.	1 mark
	An alkaline pH with universal indicator indicates the presence of the nitrate ion.	1 mark
Supplement 5 a)	$Cu^{2+}(aq) + 2OH^-(aq) \rightarrow Cu(OH)_2(s)$ (1 mark for ions; 1 mark for balancing)	2 marks
Supplement 5 b)	$CO_3^{2-}(s) + 2H^+(aq) \rightarrow CO_2(g) + H_2O(l)$ (1 mark for ions; 1 mark for balancing)	2 marks
	Total:	19 marks

Section 12: Exam-style questions mark scheme

Exam-style questions and sample answers have been written by the authors. In examinations, the way marks are awarded may be different. References to assessment and/or assessment preparation are the publisher's interpretation of the syllabus requirements and may not fully reflect the approach of Cambridge Assessment International Education.

The marks available for a question can indicate the level of detail you need to provide in your answer.

Question	Correct answer	Marks
2 a)	C	1 mark
2 b)	i) Test 2 result is anomalous.	1 mark
	ii) 0.14 g (1 mark for the units)	2 marks
2 c)	i) liquid to gas	1 mark
	ii) gas to liquid	1 mark
	iii) the water in the test-tube will not contain dissolved solids	1 mark
	iv) the cost of the energy required is too high	1 mark
2 d)	i) The water is filtered through gravel to remove solid particles.	2 marks
	ii) Chlorine is used to sterilise the water. It kills bacteria.	2 marks
Supplement 3 a)	i) draw a pencil line on the piece of filter paper as shown in the diagram.	1 mark
	ii) Carefully spot the two inks on the line.	1 mark
	iii) Suspend the filter paper in the beaker of water, with the water level below the pencil line and allow the water to soak up the filter paper until the line of water is near to the top of the filter paper. Marks from text or the diagram	1 mark
Supplement 3 b)	Correct positions of A and B in terms of the R_f factors. 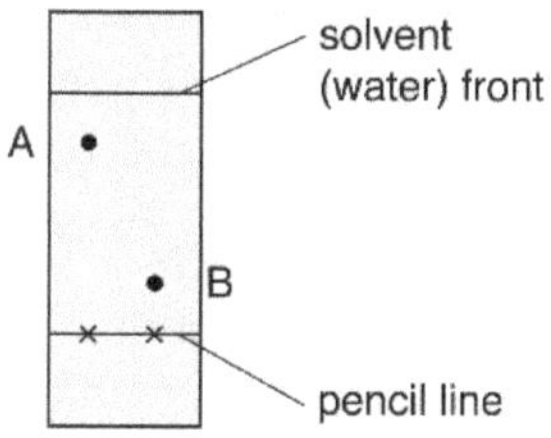	2 marks
Supplement 3 c)	If A and B were insoluble in water the spots would remain on the pencil line.	1 mark
4	Wash the 25 cm³ volumetric pipette with distilled water and then a small amount of sodium hydroxide solution. Wash the burette with distilled water and a small amount of the hydrochloric acid.	1 mark
	Pipette 25 cm³ of sodium hydroxide into a conical flask and add 3 drops of methyl orange indicator.	1 mark
	Fill the burette with hydrochloric acid so the acid level is near the top of the	1 mark

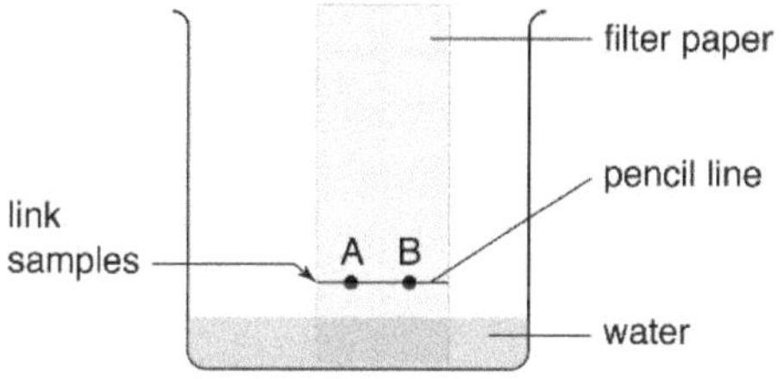

Section 12: Exam-style questions mark scheme

Question	Correct answer				Marks
	burette – take the initial reading of the burette.				1 mark
	Add the acid carefully to the conical flask until the methyl orange changes colour (yellow to pink). Take the second burette reading and work out the volume of acid added. This is the 'trial' reading.				2 marks
	Repeat the experiment on at least 2 further occasions, adding the acid dropwise close to the end point. Continue taking 'accurate' readings until two of the readings agree within 0.1 cm^3				
5	Gas	Formula	Test	Result of test	
	Oxygen	O_2	Put in a glowing splint	Splint relights, producing a flame	2 marks
	Chlorine	Cl_2	Damp indicator paper	The indicator paper is bleached	2 marks
	Ammonia	NH_3	Put in a piece of damp red litmus or universal indicator paper	The indicator paper turns blue	2 marks
	Sulfur dioxide	SO_2	Put in a piece of filter paper soaked in potassium manganate(VII) solution	Filter paper changes from purple to colourless	2 marks
6	Name of ion	Formula	Test	Observation	
	Chloride	$Cl^-(aq)$	Add dilute nitric acid and silver nitrate solution	White precipitate	2 marks
	Iodide	$I^-(aq)$	Add dilute nitric acid and silver nitrate solution	Yellow precipitate	2 marks
	Sulfate	$SO_4^{2-}(aq)$	Add dilute nitric acid and barium nitrate solution	White precipitate	2 marks
	Nitrate	$NO_3^-(aq)$	1. Add sodium hydroxide solution and warm 2. Add aluminium foil or powder 3. Test any gas produced with damp red litmus paper	Red litmus paper goes blue (ammonia gas is produced)	2 marks
	Total:				40 marks